MW01596463

Creating Visions for
University-School Partnerships

A Volume in:
Research in Professional Development Schools
Series Editors:
JoAnne Ferrara
Janice L. Nath
Irma N. Guadarrama

Research in Professional Development Schools

Series Editors:
JoAnne Ferrara
Manhattanville College

Janice L. Nath
University of Houston

Irma N. Guadarrama
University of Texas—Pan Am

University and School Connections:
Research Studies in Professional Development Schools (2008)
Edited by Irma N. Guadarrama, John Ramsey, and Janice L. Nath

Advances in Community Thought and Research (2005)
Edited by Irma N. Guadarrama, University of Texas - Pan Am; John Ramsey,
University of Houston and Janice L. Nath, University of Houston

Forging Alliances in Community and Thought (2002)
Edited by Irma N. Guadarrama

This book is sponsored by

The mission of NAPDS is to advocate for and support
a professional development school model that is committed to:
student learning; clinical educator preparation;
reciprocal professional development; and shared inquiry.

Creating Visions for University-School Partnerships

Edited by

JoAnne Ferrara
Janice L. Nath
Irma N. Guadarrama

INFORMATION AGE PUBLISHING, INC.
Charlotte, NC • www.infoagepub.com

Library of Congress Cataloging-in-Publication Data

The CIP data for this book can be found on the Library of Congress website (loc.gov).

Paperback: 978-1-62396-771-0
Hardcover: 978-1-62396-772-7
eBook: 978-1-62396-773-4

Copyright © 2014 Information Age Publishing Inc.

All rights reserved. No part of this publication may be reproduced, stored in a
retrieval system, or transmitted, in any form or by any means, electronic, mechanical, photo-
copying, microfilming, recording or otherwise, without written permission
from the publisher.

Printed in the United States of America

CONTENTS

PART II

STAKEHOLDERS' PERSPECTIVE

PART III

ENRICHING CONTENT AREA INSTRUCTION

PART IV

FAMILY ENGAGEMENT

ACKNOWLEDGEMENTS

First and foremost, we express our gratitude to those individuals who work tirelessly in professional development schools (PDSs) to build a vision for transforming the profession while also creating settings where unlimited possibilities exist for all stakeholders—especially the children in the school settings. Without the efforts of these dedicated educators to push the PDS agenda forward, we could not share the outstanding practices happening in the field.

We are forever grateful to Renee Roff for volunteering her free time, her copy editing expertise, and, most importantly, her ongoing encouragement during the process.

We thank our publisher, George Johnson for giving us the venue to showcase the work of PDS authors across the nation.

Creating Visions for University-School Partnerships, page ix.
Copyright © 2014 by Information Age Publishing
All rights of reproduction in any form reserved.

INTRODUCTION

As with the other volumes in this series, Volume 5 highlights the ways in which professional development schools (PDSs) provide a rich context for practitioner inquiry. Series contributors describe various methods of engagement in practitioner inquiry to foster collaboration and reflection among stakeholders. Through a lens of collaboration grounded in inquiry, these PDS researchers generate possible solutions to the complex problems facing PreK–16 educators. The diversity of their work represents perspectives of classroom teachers, preservice teachers, school leaders, and university faculty who grapple with identifying "ways of knowing" and "ways of doing" that enhance educational outcomes for PreK–12 students while also serving to transform the profession. Authors describe the richness of PDSs' work to support continuous improvement, to provide innovation, and to discover powerful insights so that informed decision making that is based upon "what works" can take place. We are honored to showcase the efforts of these PDS scholars in Volume 5 and share with you the collective wisdom for improving schools and increasing the quality of teaching.

This volume is organized around four themes: (1) clinically rich practices, (2) stakeholders' perspectives, (3) enriching content area instruction, and (4) family engagement. For the most part, the themes launched new ways for researchers to think about student success through PDS engagement. Although the chapters

Creating Visions for University-School Partnerships, pages xi–xiv.
Copyright © 2014 by Information Age Publishing
All rights of reproduction in any form reserved.

share a common focus, each one illustrates the unique PDS features that ignited researchers to further investigate areas of interest.

Section I (Clinically Rich Practices) offers solutions to the recent criticism leveled at educator preparation programs' inability to respond to ever-changing needs of today's classrooms. The sentiment expressed by researchers in these chapters underscores how colleges of education redesigned programs, coursework, and fieldwork components so that opportunities are made available for teacher candidates to be deeply embedded in the life of a school. Section I makes the case for the role of PDSs as perfect sites for clinically rich practices, replete with possibilities for making critical connections between theory and practice for preservice teachers and simultaneously serving to further the growth of all PDS stakeholders. The chapters remind us that PDSs are settings where practice-based leaning is the norm and the classroom is a laboratory for inquiry and learning.

In the first chapter, Dahlman, Chapman, Hoffman, Zierdt, Rosendale, Kennedy, Page, Hoffman, and Preimesberger share four specific examples of clinically rich practices from PDS partnerships between a university and eight partner school districts that have been successful in preparing teacher candidates for effective teaching practices. The specific strategies, together with supporting data and reflections, created win–win opportunities for all stakeholders.

In keeping with strategies to enrich clinical practice, Catelli, Carlino, and Petraglia examined classroom teaching effectiveness through an action research study at a PDS. This chapter focuses on the use of video-based findings to make changes in the PDS partnership. The study is the third in a series of five linked action studies. The overall project goal was to change and improve PreK–12 classroom teaching and the clinical aspects of their college's teacher education programs in an integrative way.

Dresden, Kittleson, and Wenner examine the causes for a renewed interest in clinically rich practices. Their discussion briefly investigates the use of clinically rich practices in other professions, reviews the theory and research on clinically rich practices in teacher education today, considers the vital role of professional development schools in facilitating these approaches to teacher education, and introduces the suite of clinically rich practices used in their undergraduate teacher preparation courses.

Curlette, Hendrick, Olgetree, and Benson in this section discuss clinical teaching employed through anchor action research (AAR) studies to evaluate the teacher preparation efforts in PDSs through K–12 student achievement. As a part of the teacher–intern–professor (TIP) Group, the intern participated in the planning and delivering of a unit of instruction that used a pretest and posttest as assessments. This study contributes a summary of 10 PDS studies that overall have a statistically significant effect size for student achievement using meta-analysis. The study demonstrated a clinical approach to teaching combined with a statistical approach to overcome small sample sizes through meta-analysis to show student academic achievement gains in PDSs.

Yanke, Shroyer, and Morales described a vision to collaboratively examine and promote teacher quality and teacher effectiveness across the educational continuum while simultaneously improving K–12 education for all students and educators within a PDS partnership that led to the development of an evidence-based teacher quality supervision model and performance portfolio process to determine both teacher quality and teacher effectiveness. Their chapter provides evidence that teacher quality and teacher effectiveness can be achieved through careful examination and assessment of preservice candidates and the teacher preparation program by all PDS partners involved in the assessment process.

Finally, Section I concludes with del Prado Hill, Day, Chicola, and Shandomo's international PDS model. For 22 years, Buffalo State's award-winning PDS consortium has worked to extend its sphere of influence beyond the campus to support the development of new and experienced teachers through local partnerships. Their consortium now partners with more than 45 PDS sites locally, regionally, and internationally. Responding to demographic changes in the city and beyond, Buffalo State expanded its commitment to support the development of children, teachers, and faculty to be global citizens. This chapter details the story of Buffalo State's journey, with excerpts from teacher candidates, and offers suggestions for developing effective international PDS partnerships.

Stakeholders' perspectives as means to inform decision making within PDS sites are the overarching foci of Section II. Through the collection of diverse data sets, including case studies, surveys, focus groups, questionnaires, artifacts, program evaluation, and student metrics, authors offer methods for strengthening PDSs, which, in turn, create effective educator preparation programs. Authors discuss the value of PDS participants' ongoing engagement in self-study as one of many instruments to foster continual growth and renewal in the dynamic, ever-changing entities known as PDSs.

We begin this section with a study from Michell, Nath, and Cohen, which investigates a program that was forced to change from an established PDS model to a modified version and focuses upon perceptions of the differences before and after. Authors posit that although teacher educators hope that they can maintain many types of university/school partnerships, not all professional development school (PDS) programs have been sustainable—for a variety of reasons. By comparing pre- and post-PDS implementation in a teacher education program, researchers found elements that could allow for better decision making or modifications when it becomes impossible for a teacher education program to preserve its full-fledged PDS model. This could, in turn, allow the basic premises of many crucial elements of PDS work to continue, even when the entire model cannot be supported.

In this study, Rodger, Prater, and Blocher discuss the results of a survey of alumni who participated in professional development school (PDS) training at their institution. Their purpose was to determine whether the teacher candidates from three different school/university teacher training programs felt that the program's intensity was ultimately beneficial. The study obtained information from the alumni to gain insight on their self-perceived practices in the classroom that they had acquired during their PDS experience.

Savick and Eckert's chapter describes their efforts as PDS coordinators at one institute of higher education (university) in Maryland to revitalize a network of 21 individual PDS sites. Through providing a historical overview of PDS at the university and documenting the strategic steps taken, this chapter uses an institutional framework to outline one method for creating self-sustaining partnerships. The chapter relies on documentary data, interviews, and first-hand observations to understand the systemic changes necessary to build a self-sustaining network.

"Learning together" is the focus of the study conducted by Grebs, Kirkman, and Grunau as they examine an ever-evolving eight-year school–university partnership providing opportunities for elementary students, university students, and faculty to come together as partners in learning. Utilizing the expertise of faculty from multiple colleges within the university, the elementary school curriculum was enriched through hands-on experiences both in the elementary school and on the college campus. The cross-curricular experiences that focused on student learning in this sustained and committed partnership provided benefits at both the university and the elementary school.

Siry, Ferrara, and Lang address the benefits of learning together to support the integration of theory and practice in preservice teacher education. This chapter elaborates the ways in which a series of three one-semester field-based teacher education courses were redesigned and co-taught by university faculty and elementary school teachers to facilitate teacher candidates learning to teach through supported, shared experiences in a PDS. Models of the courses and data excerpts from preservice teachers are provided in order to provide a variety of insights into the use of field-based methods courses.

Section III (Enriching Content Area Instruction) takes a refreshing look at strategies to enrich content area instruction. Researchers identify a range of PDS initiatives designed to target learning outcomes for PreK–12 students, teacher candidates, inservice teachers, school leaders, and university faculty. The diversity of studies in this section serves to highlight the interdependent nature of PDS work and ways in which PDSs continue to respond to constituents' multifaceted needs. A commonality among the research studies presented here is to uncover innovative approaches to address literacy development and mathematics instruction through co-teaching, action research, peer coaching, or professional development sessions for inservice teachers.

Tunks and O'Brien described a PDS project whereby PDS preservice teachers learned to tutor elementary and middle school students in mathematics. Both the university and schools in the PDS collaborative adjusted instruction, space, time, and general support for preservice teachers to tutor students. One result was an effective change in preservice teachers' perceptions of themselves as teachers of mathematics. A second result was significant achievement differences at the p<.05 level across all six years.

The work of Guerra, De La Cruz, and Phillips yielded positive results for all parties involved in field experiences in PDSs, which are vital to their teacher preparation program. This chapter describes research conducted with teacher candidates who taught a mathematics lesson to third graders in front of the collaborating teacher and peers. The peers provided feedback on the lessons. Data revealed that preparing to teach and teaching children as a section of field experiences pushes candidates to critically consider three areas: (1) student thinking, (2) mathematics content, and (3) their own practice.

Leach, Johnson, Blumhardt, and Bush investigate engagement in collaborative research to improve learning for all students as a cornerstone of university–school partnerships. This chapter examines the impact of co-teaching on the academic achievement of middle school students in an inclusive general education classroom setting. Using a quasi-experimental design, statistical analyses of standardized test results indicated greater gains made by students with and without learning disabilities when compared to their non-co-taught peers.

Continuing in this section, Walker and Downey address the problem of inadequate student literacy skills by creating an action research-based professional development program to assist high school teachers in a PDS. Results indicated that teachers used their action research findings to inform their practice, theory, and/or research, based in literacy skills, to assist students, colleagues, and preservice educators. Concepts such as (1) modeling best practices, (2) using multiple methods of measurement for assessment, (3) the use of higher-order thinking skills and transition time to a new or revisited literacy-based task or theory, and (4) the pertinence of engagement have all emerged as important elements for inservice practice as well as enhancement of student learning.

This section concludes with Cunningham describing her role in a three-year research study on a professional development initiative focused on foundational literacy skills and the outcomes for teachers, student teachers, and students. She discusses how the teaching of foundational literacy skills remains one of the greatest needs for teachers at the K–2 levels, particularly for teachers who are working with high populations of English language learners from low-income households. In addition, she shares how the PDS liaison was instrumental in supporting teachers and administrators at their PDS to navigate the dilemmas that surfaced as teachers underwent training in methods with which they were unfamiliar and how that impacted curriculum and instruction as well as the teachers' beliefs about literacy learning.

Section IV (Family Engagement) underscores the important roles PDSs play in supporting family engagement in underserved communities. The chapters encourage readers to create a range of experiences for teacher candidates to learn the value of working with families to support students' academic success while simultaneously strengthening the notion of parents as key partners in their child's education. Included in this section is a fresh look at the role PDS liaisons play in a community school serving under-resourced students and families.

In "Supporting Mathematics Learning in a PDS Network," Tunks and Williams address a need to engage Latino parents and children in community mathematics learning events. From this need, Fiesta Math Night/Fiesta de Noche de Matematicas was formed through the collaborative efforts of teachers, PDS interns, and university personnel. The events, across six years, served approximately 7,000 parents and children. In the final year of the project, 2012, parents were observed at FMN, were asked to complete surveys, and were interviewed. Results of the data analysis indicated that parents' perspectives of the events were positive, primarily because the parents were engaged in a fun, inclusive, and culturally relevant mathematics learning environment with their children.

Rosenthal, Bonafe, and Lebron's chapter addresses the need to support literacy efforts through a collaboration between the university faculty, teacher candidates, and school–parent liaison. This chapter focuses on assistance that the school–parent liaison provided in a section of a literacy course to engage teacher candidates in working with families of children. The results of this collaborative effort are reported, which include the impact that candidates' attitudes have about family involvement at this large, urban PDS, as well as developing their strategy use and efficacy for engaging families.

Ferrara and Gómez describe the expanded roles of two PDS liaisons as they negotiated the new dimensions of working to facilitate collaboration among all the partners in a full-service community school while fostering a focus on whole-child education. Qualitative data sources from the classroom teachers, partners, and liaisons demonstrate how the NAPDS' essentials 1, 3, and 8 are fundamental to the success of all partners of the full service PDS community school.

This volume continues the journey of entities throughout the country in their quest to share their work on PDSs. Authors have investigated diverse areas of research—all of which give us a more vivid picture of the work that partnerships are doing in the effort to bridge the theory-to-practice gap. What becomes clear is that these partnerships are worthwhile and should be studied continuously due to their promise for improving teaching and learning at every level, but most importantly, for our students.

—JoAnne, Janice, and Irma

PART I

CLINICALLY RICH PRACTICES

CHAPTER 1

PARTNERING TO ACHIEVE AUTHENTIC AND MUTUALLY BENEFICIAL TEACHER PREPARATION THROUGH INNOVATIVE CLINICAL PRACTICES

Anne Dahlman, Carrie Chapman, Patricia Hoffman, Ginger Zierdt, April Rosendale, Pamely Kennedy, Scott Page, Allen Hoffman, and Paul Preimesberger

ABSTRACT

In this chapter, the authors share four specific examples of an array of clinically rich practices from our PDS partnership between a university and eight partner school districts that have been successful in preparing our teacher candidates for effective teaching practice. The specific strategies, together with supporting data and reflections, include: (1) the use of technology for early field experiences, (2) co-teaching

Creating Visions for University-School Partnerships, pages 3–19.
Copyright © 2014 by Information Age Publishing
All rights of reproduction in any form reserved.

as a best-practice methodology for student learning, (3) the role of teachers of special assignment (TOSAs) in providing support, and (4) use of AVID (advancement via individual determination) to create win–win opportunities for all stakeholders.

The 25-year history of this partnership, which consists of a university and eight K–12 school districts in southern Minnesota, is a testimony to the collaborative spirit that has worked to launch multiple shared ventures between P–12 and Minnesota State University, Mankato (for more see Zierdt, Dahlman, Rosendale, & Kennedy, 2012). The network has evolved from sharing field placements and faculty consultants to constructing multilayered systems that embed best practices through numerous facets of education. The established professional development school (PDS) collaboration has woven the history of its partners into an enduring framework of support and excellence. This emphasis on understanding each of the partners' context and history and its collaborative narrative is the cornerstone of this work (Dahlman, & Hoffman, 2012). Active learning communities have been developed and sustained within and among these entities. These provide practice coaching and intentional reflection with teacher candidates. The PDS pursues high-level trainings to equip faculty for changing professional climates. A variety of collaborative needs assessments are completed with PDS teachers, administrators, students, and university faculty. There is "sight" beyond what is the current reality, and construction of new possibilities occurs. It is this innovative spirit that inspires the best work and evokes great pride in this partnership (Zierdt et al., 2012). It is this innovative spirit that also captured the eye of the Archibald Bush Foundation in awarding a multimillion-dollar grant to transform teacher education. It is this innovative spirit that compels the partnership to ask critical questions and also seeks best solutions.

This PDS context is a large, eight-district PDS partnership. The school districts in the partnership vary widely in size, geography, and student profiles, with several of them having a high percentage of English learners (ELs) as well as students from poverty. Diversity and equity are part of the key components and a focus of the articulation agreement of this partnership. The results from ongoing exploration of data to address achievement gaps among diverse racial and linguistic groups and students from poverty have been a priority in developing field placements. The shared expectations for these experiences are that (1) the university teacher candidates are assigned to placements where there is a genuine need whenever possible, (2) these teacher candidates add value to the learning experiences of their students from the very beginning, and (3) teacher candidates become more culturally competent and practice their future role as advocates for students from all backgrounds.

This chapter focuses on several strategies that have been implemented and researched surrounding efforts to provide teacher candidates with clinically-based teacher preparation. These include: (1) technology use in early field experiences, (2) co-teaching practice for enhanced student learning, (3) the importance of the TOSA role, and (4) AVID implementation across teacher preparation programs. This clinically based approach supports the recommendations shared by the NCATE Blue Ribbon Panel on Clinical Preparation (2010), which have also been endorsed by the American Association of Colleges for Teacher Education (AACTE). This kind of clinically based approach to teacher preparation

> will create varied and extensive opportunities for candidates to connect what they learn with the challenge of using it, while under the expert tutelage of skilled clinical educators. Candidates will blend practitioner knowledge with academic knowledge as they learn by doing. They will refine their practice in the light of new knowledge acquired and data gathered about whether their students are learning. (p. ii)

Throughout these extended field experiences, the teacher candidates at Minnesota State Mankato engage in guided reflections about teacher effectiveness, varied student needs, teacher identity, and the connections between theory and practice. This occurs via the use of Professional Learning Communities (PLCs) in class as well as during their field experiences. Ultimately, data were collected on these experiences and will be used for further refinement of the clinical experiences as well as improving the teacher education programs, curriculum and instructional strategies (Hoffman, Dahlman, & Zierdt, 2009). All of these practices are focused on ensuring collaboration and mutually beneficial relationships and interactions among faculty and students in both the P–12 and university settings.

In the following sections, the authors share specific examples of an array of clinically rich practices that have been successful in preparing the teacher candidates for effective teaching, as well as those that have helped move the partnership to a deeper level. The authors will describe the various ways that the university and its partner school districts collaborate around field experiences to intently prepare preservice teachers to effectively address the achievement gap between P–12 students who are predominantly white and students of color. The specific strategies discussed include:

1. The use of TeachLivE™ lab for early field experiences;
2. Co-teaching as a methodology as best-practice teaching for student learning;
3. The role of teachers of special assignment (TOSAs) to infuse support and modeling to clinical experiences; and
4. The use of AVID (advancement via individual determination) programs to create win–win opportunities for all stakeholders participating in clinical field experiences.

In each section, the authors provide an introduction and a rationale for the use of a specific strategy, approach, or resource, followed by supporting data; analysis and reflection based on this evidence; and discussion of: needs, plans, and actions for continuous improvement.

TECHNOLOGY PROMOTING AUTHENTIC LEARNING DURING EARLY FIELD EXPERIENCES: TeachLivE™

Introduction and Rationale

Teacher effectiveness is one of the most critical challenges in K–12 schools. Almost half of the teachers quit during the first five years of teaching (e.g., Ingersoll, 2001). Successful teaching practice requires that teachers are prepared to work efficiently with *all* students of differing backgrounds, interests, and needs. Teacher candidates typically learn how to teach and manage a classroom while on the job:

> Today's educators are asked to meet the diverse needs of all students, including those with emotional or behavioral disorders (EBD). The movement towards the inclusion of students with disabilities in the general education classroom combined with recent mandates requiring all learners to meet or exceed established curricular guidelines, makes it increasingly challenging for educators to meet their moral and ethical responsibilities. (Baker, 2005, p. 51)

The only way to learn how to interact and manage a classroom effectively is through targeted practice (Baker, 2005). To eliminate the trial-by-fire approach to classroom-management training, Minnesota State Mankato entered into a collaborative partnership with the University of Central Florida to utilize a teaching simulation system called TeachLivE for clinical teaching practice during early field experiences. The goal is to replace the trial-by-fire approach with something more instructive and valuable for teacher candidates and their future students.

The NCATE Blue Ribbon Panel Report on clinical practice emphasizes the importance of utilizing educational technology for additional clinical practice by embedding "laboratory experiences…throughout the preparation program" (p. 10). They explain that "such experiences offer the opportunity to analyze a virtual student's pattern of behavior, or engage candidates in the life of a virtual school, calling upon the candidates to investigate and make decisions, and to see the consequences of those decisions" (p. 10).

Minnesota State University Mankato utilizes the TeachLivE classroom simulation system, which allows teacher candidates to practice teaching and classroom management without involving real students but rather avatars (or virtual students) that are programmed with distinctive personalities. During each lesson, the avatars make comments and distracting noises as well as interrupt the lesson— behaviors that can be either be reduced or increased depending on the reaction of the teacher candidate.

Supporting Data

During the 2012–2013 school year, each of the teacher candidates enrolled in a secondary methods course taught a 10-minute mini-lesson in the TeachLivE lab. Teacher candidates who completed a pre- and post-survey created a 10-minute lesson plan, which was observed by their instructors. Teacher candidates were later asked to reflect and comment on their experience. The survey asked teacher candidates to rate themselves in various aspects of teaching before and after the lesson. The pre-survey aimed to determine students' perceptions about themselves as teachers and their perceived practices about such areas as sharing classroom expectations, creating a classroom community conducive to learning, and so forth.

Using a scale of 1 to 4 (1 = disagree to 4 = agree), the teacher candidates self-reported on a pre- and post-survey. Teacher candidates rated themselves higher on the pre-survey than on the post-survey in involving all students, evaluation, clear expectations, and creating an effective learning environment. For example, teacher candidates indicated that they had the skills necessary to ensure that all voices within their class would be heard. However, after the TeachLivE™ experience, they realized they did not succeed in attending to the needs of all students, and, in fact, most had left one avatar (Maria) out of many of the discussions. One teacher candidate, Susan (pseudonyms have been used), stated that it was less about the actual lesson plan and more about the different types of students with whom they would encounter and how to interact and react with them accordingly. The TeachLivE lab was very situational, and how to respond depended on many factors, such as the specific personality characteristics of the avatars or the size of the group or the level of engagement of the students in a given topic.

Each teacher candidate developed his or her 10-minute mini-lesson with achievable criteria (indicated in grading rubrics) and performance standards to evaluate the students. Although these preservice teachers had formal assessments planned and tried to implement them, they found that the avatars did not always understand them. This might have partially been due to the fact that the students/avatars were not involved in the development of the mini-lesson assessment criteria and were unfamiliar with the expectations. Michael, a teacher candidate, added, "There are a lot of things I need to learn, know, and understand to be an effective teacher. A major thing I need to learn is how to properly formulate questions for a student once I know their personality."

Prior to teaching, the teacher candidates indicated that their lesson plans were clear and concise and that they could develop an environment in which all students could learn. However, after participating in the TeachLivE experience, more than 90% stated that they needed more planning and preparation and needed to be aware of students' skills, knowledge, language proficiency, interests, cultural heritage, and special needs. One of the teacher candidates, Cody, was five minutes into his lesson before he realized that it would be impossible for him to finish it. Cody describes this by stating, "The students were asking questions and taking more time on things that I thought was going to take less time." In addition, 97% of the teacher candidates indicated that through the use of the TeachLive lab, they are now more aware of the need to establish clear directions, procedures, expectations, and explanations of content. Amanda stated that she could not keep focused on all areas of the classroom, and her so-called "lesson" became nonexistent. Another teacher candidate added that she needed to come up with ideas and activities that would get all students involved—even when they do not want to be.

Reflections on Impact

At present, there has been one deviation (for as well as many surprises) with this initiative. The digression was related to the purchasing of recording equipment. After discussion with teacher candidates and faculty, it became apparent that another method to capture the teacher candidates' experiences and allow for reflection was needed. As a result, equipment was purchased that will allow observers to capture both the avatars and the teacher candidate on a split screen during videotaping of the teacher candidate's lesson.

During the review of the teacher candidates' experiences with TeachLivE, the preservice teachers were surprised at how the student avatars reacted to them, and, in the case of C.J., a particularly challenging virtual student, that he was rude to them. Some could not get through their complete lesson, and, as some stated, "the students got in the way" of their teaching. Aaron, a teacher candidate, quickly learned that this was not about how well he could teach but how well he could manage a classroom.

As this collaborative partnership began, the aim was to enhance the learning experiences for university students by providing a robust technology for authentic learning via technology. During their exit interviews at the end of the course, teacher candidates stated that they had had a student like C.J. or Sean, a student who is quick to please the teacher with an answer (which might not always be the right one) in their class during their field experiences in area schools. In their discussion with other peers, teacher candidates would refer to some students as Sean or C.J. types, while some pointed out that they had "Marias" (very smart and quiet students) in their class and were aware that they needed to reach out to them. In the end, the teacher candidates were able to transfer their TeachLivE experience from the virtual world to the real-world experience; this was especially effective as teacher candidates participated in a virtual classroom teaching experience before they went on to their 30-hour field experience in area schools, but both were experienced during the same semester.

The instructors of the course stated that they gained more insight and knowledge of their teacher candidates in ten minutes through TeachLivE than they had in two months of interacting with them in class. Some teacher candidates who appeared to have everything ready and prepared to teach could not control and create an active learning environment, while others had complete control and addressed the avatars' questions and comments by relating them back to their own experiences.

Continuous Improvement

Further opportunities have been pursued to share about the use of the lab for teaching within the university. For example, a university-wide open house was held, which provided opportunities for others to view the TeachLivE lab but also to help think about how to collaborate using the lab. Currently, there are ongoing conversations about working with UCF and other higher education institutions to use the university site for their classes. Some K–12 schools are also interested in using the lab to assist their first- and second-year teachers with developing classroom management techniques.

Another idea might be to work together with mentor teachers in the PDS sites to have them gain knowledge of the strengths and weaknesses of the preservice teacher candidates prior to the teacher candidates going into their field experience placements in school with real students. This would build common vocabulary for experiences and continuity in goal setting for both the teacher candidates and mentors.

LEARNING THROUGH STRATEGIC COLLABORATION AND REFLECTION: TRANSFORMATION THROUGH CO-TEACHING

Introduction and Rationale

Co-teaching between mentor teachers and the university teacher candidates was a major initiative spearheaded by Minnesota State Mankato and its PDS partner districts. The needs of schools to attend closely to K–12 student learning accountability and the university's need to have improved mentorship for teacher candidates during student teaching became the strong impetus to move to the co-teaching model within our PDS partnerships. Together, co-teaching was conventionalized using the Chapman and Hart Hyatt (2011) definition and framework, where "co-teaching is an effective, evidence-based instructional strategy in which two or more caring professionals share responsibility for a group of students and work collaboratively to add instructional value to enhance their efforts" (p. 8). By focusing on the key elements of co-teaching (the students, the co-teaching partners, and the professional practices of the mentor teacher and the teacher candidate), these co-teaching partnerships bring value to their students and to the student teaching support system (Chapman & Hart Hyatt, 2011).

Supporting Data

As the co-teaching model was initiated, increasing numbers of partners were trained intensely on the fundamentals of (1) co-teaching, (2) self-knowledge and knowledge of joint-practice, (3) co-teaching models and best practice, and (4) understanding quality mentorship. During the first three semesters of this co-teaching program, both qualitative and quantitative evidence was gathered from surveys, focus group interviews, and co-teaching planning logs. Results from surveys given at three points during the student teaching semester to the teacher candidates and mentor teachers indicated movement from neutral or slightly positive responses on knowledge and belief-related co-teaching questions to extremely positive responses (95% agree/strongly agree) by the end of the semester. Exemplar results were evident, especially around co-teaching as enhancing K–12 students' academic and social/emotional achievement and the increased ability to provide a differentiated classroom environment to meet the diverse needs of the students. Interview and focus group questions illustrated the importance of skill development for both mentor teachers and teacher candidates, with major focus areas of planning, communication, and reflective practice (Werhan & Chapman, 2011).

Reflections on Impact

Through this model, both teacher candidates and mentor teachers co-plan and co-teach together to achieve the following important outcomes advocated by the college of education, the P–12 school partners, and by the education profession: (1) improve the teacher-to-K–12- student ratio in classrooms, (2) increase instructional options available to enhance student achievement, (3) strengthen teacher professional development opportunities, (4) encourage quality mentoring for teacher candidates, and (5) enhance teacher candidate and mentor teacher reflection on teaching and results. Continued work has been done together (the college of education and the PDS) to adjust and improve all facets of the preparation from early semesters through student teaching in our teacher preparation.

To that end, specific changes/emphases have developed. These include details and procedural components, such as daily and/or continual co-planning by the teacher candidate and the mentor teacher. Additionally, co-teaching will be used as the model for 60–70% of the total time, with 30–40% of the time being allotted for solo planning and teaching by the teacher candidate. Best results with co-teaching occur when the co-teaching partners: (1) jointly decide how to best offer instruction—engage in substantive co-planning; (2) consider the adults, the students, and the curriculum content as they co-plan; (3) use a range of approaches/models in teaching their students; (4) collaborate for best results; (5) have strong administrative support at the K–12 school level and the university level; and (6) discuss logistical issues to improve teaching and learning (Werhan & Chapman, 2011).

Continuous Improvement

In moving forward with the co-teaching model, the continual data collection on co-teaching during student teaching is a large part of all teacher preparation programs within the college of education. National accreditation is greatly impacted by this focus for both the university and the PDS partners. Data are used to engage in the continuous improvement process that impacts curricula at all levels, field experiences, and increasing interactions around decisions that impact all components of these programs. Joint mapping of co-teaching knowledge and experience across all semesters in the teacher preparation programs remains a main focus of program improvement. Most importantly, the nature and implementation of this co-teaching model for teacher preparation exemplifies the positive symbiotic relationship that can occur between K–12 districts and university teacher preparation programs.

CONNECTING PRESERVICE AND INSERVICE TEACHING AND SUPPORT: TOSAS MODELING MASTERFUL MENTORING

Introduction and Rationale

The teacher-on-special-assignment (TOSA)/graduate teaching fellowship program aims to meet the needs of partner districts and the University by releasing P–12 master teachers as TOSAs from their classroom duties for a minimum of three years to work directly between the university and the partnering school district. In place of the master teacher, a newly licensed teacher (a graduate teaching fellow) assumes full classroom teaching responsibilities in the school district as well as receiving a premier fellowship at the university to pursue a graduate program. This program's 23 years of success is becoming known regionally and nationally as an exemplar in P–20 resource sharing, sustainability, and innovation.

Currently, there are 19 TOSAs working in this PDS system. They function in many roles. In addition to mentoring their replacement graduate teaching fellows, TOSAs assume a half-time university role by advancing the PDS model, teaching courses in the college of education, leading seminars in best practices alongside of university faculty, and/or supervising teacher candidates.

The TOSAs are seen as a key component in modeling and providing a critical source of support to preservice teacher candidates and new practicing teachers throughout the continuum of teacher education (from teacher candidates during their first semester in the teacher preparation program to new teachers during their several years of teaching practice). Teacher candidates' first years of teaching are seen as a critical part of the *continuum of clinical practice* by which both the university and the PDS partners collaborate. This works toward tearing down the gap between preservice and inservice teaching and is shifting the responsibility for support and mentoring exclusively by P–12 school partners to collaborating fully with the university in making this transition successfully.

Supporting Data

The central importance of the TOSAs in this PDS system is strikingly clear from the data maintained in the PDS system. A description of the impact of the TOSAs begins the discussion from the early point of the teacher education continuum—with the preservice teachers. One of the key tasks of the TOSAs is to work in partnership with the office of field and international experience to help coordinate preservice placements in P–12 schools. Each year over a thousand preservice students are placed in the university's partnering schools where theory becomes reality, and the beginning steps toward induction are taken. The TOSAs are involved in every aspect of this process. They recruit carefully selected co-operating teachers to serve as mentors for our preservice students. They also facilitate communication between the university instructors of the specific courses that are associated with the field experiences and the teacher candidates in those courses as well the cooperating teachers. TOSAs also troubleshoot any conflicts or challenges that arise during field experiences.

Additionally, each of the TOSAs is responsible for a group of teacher candidates during student teaching and for evaluating their practice and facilitating learning communities. TOSAs are immediately available to the candidates should questions arise, either from the students or the mentor teachers. Similarly, they are present to affirm and celebrate the investments of all parties in creating avenues of success. When a two-candidate team taught a science lesson one day, their mentor teacher came away with new confidence that hands-on learning was impressive. One candidate left a post-observation conference with her TOSA saying, "Thank you for doing this. I would never have thought of half the things we talked about if you had not taken the time to ask such thoughtful questions. Please keep doing this for me." Without this support from the TOSAs, the rich preservice clinical field experiences that are currently offered could not be provided.

In the quest to close the gap between the pre- and inservice support and learning, learning is sought from the effectiveness of the TOSA/graduate teaching fellowship program. Feedback from various stakeholders speaks to the promise of the practices utilized in this program for teacher effectiveness and retention. While these observations have not been documented formally in a research study format, at least one research project is currently ongoing, focusing exclusively on the effectiveness of the program. According to the informal feedback from PDS school district partners, the teaching fellows are some of the best new teachers in their schools, which is partially achieved through a careful selection of candidates for the role of a fellow and largely due to the high degree of wrap-around support and mentoring that they receive in their classrooms while teaching. School districts also report that these new teachers are more likely to stay in the profession and seem to assume leadership roles more frequently as they continue on in their careers.

The TOSAs, in whose classrooms the fellows are teaching, model a unique and individualized form of mentoring for these graduate fellows who replace them in the classrooms. The activities range from such pragmatic actions as helping carry boxes into classrooms in August and setting up and organizing new classrooms to some of them co-teaching together with their fellow throughout the year. In addition, regular meetings, observations, or collegial events become the norm for this mentoring relationship between TOSAs and fellows. TOSAs provide resources, feedback, and coaching support to the new teacher, resulting in the vast majority of fellows being retained in most districts beyond their fellowship year.

In addition to their work with preservice teachers and the graduate teaching fellows, the TOSAs work with their districts to lead the development of new teacher induction programs, support systems designed for all new teachers (in partnership with the Center for Mentoring & Induction at the university), and provide leadership for curriculum development, staff development, and/or assessment and research within their home district for the remainder of the appointment. The TOSAs are not only carefully selected based on their potential for serving as masterful mentors, but they are also continuously trained by the university in areas such as cognitive coaching, instructional mentoring, coaching and observation, and analyzing student work. They also participate in professional conferences and institutes related to mentoring, Danielson's framework (Danielson, 2011), leadership, and signature trends in education.

Reflections on Impact

The impact of the TOSAs has been transformational in this PDS system. The ongoing professional learning supports that they provide for the teaching fellows help to launch new teaching careers. They are able to elicit and build upon strengths in the new teacher while fostering collegial and connected relationships. The large numbers of fellows who are retained by districts, around 90%, is a testimony to the high quality of support provided by the TOSAs.

The initial placements of candidates that TOSAs make are strategically done by considering the strengths and needs of students and teachers. Because they know their districts so well, these placements (and the resulting interactions and growth) become an inherent part of the process. Several teachers have commented on how well matched these placements have been, both personally and professionally. Students from K–12 classrooms have made connections to these placements and see the teacher candidates as integral to their learning. The statement, "We like it when we have two teachers!" has become a familiar refrain. Veteran teachers who work with teacher candidates or who may be involved with new teachers in a mentoring program frequently note how much they have grown as a result of their interaction with those new to the field.

Governance council members (a cabinet of PDS superintendents) and university faculty have frequently asked for input from TOSAs before moving forward with proposals. In asking, "What do the TOSAs think?" they are demonstrating a high degree of belief in and validation of the TOSA perspective. They come to look for TOSA input and clarification and also for when they need a "reality check." They see the TOSA as a valuable connection to their staff and to the resources of the college.

Continuous Improvement

One of the key systemic elements that have enabled the success of the role of the TOSAs, and something which has enabled the partnership to be successful over a long period of time, is the mutually shared commitment to the partnership by the PDS K–12 partner schools and the university. A critical part of the sustained shared governance is resource sharing. For example, the costs associated with our TOSA program are shared between the university and the PDS K–12 school districts. Although the TOSAs remain on district contract for 1.0 FTE, they also receive a full complement of professional development experiences from the university.

In turn, the fellows receive advising and support services from the Center for School–University Partnerships and Academic Departments for their graduate school experience and are welcomed as full-fledged members with all the rights and responsibilities of the cooperating site's teaching staff and are included in the district's new teacher support/mentoring program.

This PDS system continuously focuses on improving the infrastructure, whether related to use of finances, having the right people doing the right tasks, assuring space for learning and innovation, and carefully selecting leaders to create momentum and forward-movement. It is this basis that enables excellence to happen for the benefit of teacher candidates in these programs to become the effective teachers that K–12 students desperately need and all deserve.

CONNECTING K–12 AND UNIVERSITY: WIN–WIN LEARNING OPPORTUNITIES THROUGH AVID

Introduction and Rationale

AVID (Achievement Via Individual Determination) has existed in the K–12 context for 32 years, and its positive effects on students' college preparedness have been widely documented (see latest data report at http://www.avid.org/med_pub_yearinreview.html). AVID's K–12 success begat a more recent expansion into higher education focusing on first- and second-year students and, more recently, extending into teacher preparation programs. The AVID teacher preparation initiative (TPI) delivers AVID professional learning opportunities to teacher education professors, who, in turn, model and teach these strategies in courses for preservice teachers. These teacher candidates then practice and demonstrate these highly effective classroom strategies during initial field experiences in PDS sites, all of which offer AVID elective classes and content area courses infused with AVID strategies. This experience enables the next generation of educators to "hit the ground running" during their first year of teaching, as they have learned and practiced AVID strategies throughout their preservice experience. This makes them more prepared to tackle the high expectations cast on new teachers to assure K–12 student learning from the first day.

Minnesota State Mankato and its PDS partner K–12 districts partnered with AVID in forming the MSU/PDS/AVID Alliance with the goal of implementing the AVID system in all of our partner school districts. Following a period of planning and training, implementation of the AVID system began in the fall of 2011. In April, 2011, the MSU/PDS/AVID Alliance was named a "promising practice" by the Minnesota State Colleges & Universities (MSCU) system as a newly developed intervention to address college preparedness and developmental education innovations.

Complementing this effort, MSU's College of Education, joining just four other campuses around the nation, launched the AVID Teacher Preparation Initiative in the fall of 2012. This solidified a commitment to a PDS spectrum of preparing preservice teachers steeped in AVID instructional strategies, both from learning AVID strategies in teacher preparation classrooms and practicing them in K–12 classrooms—all prior to their first teaching jobs. Both AVID initiatives, especially their clinical components, have significantly enhanced the teacher preparation for teacher candidates as well as further strengthened the PDS partnership.

Supporting Data

An important source of data demonstrating the positive impact of AVID for teacher candidates has been the addition of AVID tutoring as an option for an early field experience. One of the challenges that has long been faced in the secondary education program was preservice teachers' Level 1 field experiences (teacher candidates' first semester in the teacher preparation program during their sophomore/junior years). For the roughly 90 teacher candidates at this first level, field experiences typically consisted of mostly passive observation or single student interventions and were often scattered across multiple sites. While well-intentioned, these experiences frequently lacked authenticity and often did not supply the level of challenge and growth that our teacher candidates needed in order to be successful in later, more intensive field experiences.

Under the leadership of the assistant director of the Center for School–University Partnerships at Minnesota State–Mankato and in collaboration with the K–12 PDS partners, Level 1 candidates have been offered the opportunity to serve as AVID tutors at PDS partner schools. AVID tutorials are conducted during the AVID class and comprise roughly 40% of the AVID elective curriculum. Tutorials are a critical component in supporting AVID students in their most rigorous courses. The main objective of the AVID tutor is to guide the tutorial group—typically consisting of four to seven students—through the inquiry process, pushing the thinking of the student presenter, all while managing the dynamics of small group collaboration. Identifying a point of confusion, tapping into prior knowledge, asking key comprehension and critical thinking questions, checking for understanding, and reflecting on the learning are all steps in the tutorial process. Since these skills are not ones teacher candidates (or, even, occasionally, practicing teachers) immediately possess, all of the tutors attend a comprehensive, one-day training that delves into the 10-step tutorial process. This training provides an overview of the tutorial process and, more importantly, strategies relating to note-taking, collaboration, inquiry, reflection, feedback, and coaching.

Although this experience is not feasible for all teacher candidates, there are currently around 25 students per semester who opt to serve as AVID tutors (tutors come from across different levels of the teacher preparation programs, mostly from Level 1 for their field experience). This change has enabled our participating Level 1 teacher candidates to undergo a more robust, structured field experience, where they have an authentic role in advancing the achievement of underperforming students. In fact, participating students accrue more than twice the hours in an AVID tutor field placement than the students who opt for a more traditional field experience. Furthermore, many of the teacher candidates (around 40% during the past two semesters) continue to serve as AVID tutors beyond their Level 1 requirement, often doing so in concert with subsequent field experiences.

Another piece of evidence demonstrating the positive influence of the AVID initiatives is the impact on the recruitment and retention of diverse teacher candidates. Frequently, the college of education's teacher recruitment coordinator speaks to AVID classrooms during her recruiting visits to Minnesota middle and high schools. When these students hear that the university's college of education has implemented the AVID teacher preparation initiative and utilizes teacher candidates as AVID tutors, they recognize the commitment on part of the university to the strategies that have contributed to their success as K–12 students. This has a positive impact on recruitment and retention in that K–12 students feel more connected to a university where they implement strategies, such as AVID, that they are accustomed to in their K–12 context, and with which they have experienced success in their studies. This positive association is a great selling point for prospective students to choose that college.

In addition, our retention specialists, who provide academic support for diverse teacher candidates in our Teachers of Tomorrow (ToTs) program, utilize AVID strategies in their weekly seminars. Lastly, partner school principals have indicated that MSU teacher candidates begin with "a leg up" on other applicants for teaching positions because of their exposure to and experience with AVID strategies as preservice teachers.

Reflections on Impact

Although still early in their implementation, both the MSU/PDS/AVID Alliance and the AVID teacher preparation initiative at MSU have positively impacted the PDS partnerships and teacher preparation program. As part of a recent, ongoing strategic planning process with the PDS districts, the AVID Alliance was identified as one of the major shared program areas moving forward. The districts listed many reasons for this commitment, including that AVID has the potential to make a school-wide impact, deepen everyone's understanding of diversity, create strong linkages for school–college readiness, become a primary recruitment tool for teacher candidates of color, and equip teacher candidates with more strategies for engaging, effective teaching. Teacher candidates have expressed a very high degree of satisfaction pertaining to their experience as AVID tutors. They find the experience to be challenging, but very fulfilling, and that it provides direct application to subsequent field experiences. Many of them go on to utilize AVID strategies during their student teaching experience, as well.

Teacher education faculty participating in the AVID TPI initiative share that teacher candidates who are part of the AVID elective tutoring in PDS schools bring back useful questions, comments, and observations for discussion to teacher education courses for *all* teacher candidates on which they can reflect. In addition, these classmates who have served as AVID tutors play a critical role in modeling the AVID strategies that the teacher education faculty are teaching as part of their course content, whether it be Cornell Notes or Costa's levels of thinking.

Continuous Improvement

Currently, there are roughly 25 students who count AVID tutoring as their field experience. Although a lack of reliable transportation and/or scheduling conflicts frequently inhibit participation for many teacher candidates, it is hoped that this number will grow, both for the students' sake and the program's sake, as the number of AVID sections is expanding at all of the PDS sites.

Developing an AVID tutor "meet and mentor group" is also part of the continuous improvement plan. A pilot group last year proved to be very beneficial to the tutors and their instructors. So far, there has been little success in getting another group going due again to scheduling conflicts, but it is hoped that next year a consistent cadre can be established.

CONCLUSION

In conclusion, the PDS system described in this chapter has committed itself to a continuous improvement process in its focus on clinically based teacher preparation. One of the main goals has been to increase the number of opportunities for teacher candidates to practice teaching in the field while learning about teaching in coursework. This has been achieved by infusing practice opportunities through technology, as well as the AVID tutoring program with the PDS partner school sites, where teacher candidates can gain structured and well supported direct experience with working with students in the classroom.

In addition to increasing the number of opportunities for practice, a critical component of the continuous improvement process has been its focus on reflective practice and data-based decision making. Professionals across school boundaries within the PDS system come together to talk about data derived from the various aspects of clinical practice such as co-teaching to gauge their effect in generating the best possible teachers.

A third component of this focused quest for continually improving the quality of teacher learning opportunities offered to the teacher candidates has been the focus on supporting the teacher candidates throughout their teacher preparation journey. This is achieved through the use of the teachers on special assignment (TOSA) model for mentoring and supervision as well as the co-teaching model in field experiences.

Through reflection on a variety of perceptual and achievement data, this PDS system continues to revisit collaboratively revisit each element in the portfolio of experiences. Feedback from teacher candidates, cooperating teachers, university faculty, and supervisors contributes to this improvement process. The main guiding goal is to provide the teacher candidates with meaningful and engaging fieldwork to better prepare them for the complex classrooms and the interconnected, global society that they will inherit by virtue of our changing student populations. This remains a moving target. Each field experience must be continuously evaluated for its impact and effect on P–12 student learning. As students' learning needs change, so too must teacher preparation.

REFERENCES

Baker, P. H. (2005). Managing student behavior: How ready are teachers to meet the challenge? *American Secondary Education, 33*(3), 51–64.

Chapman, C., & Hart Hyatt, C. (2011). *Critical conversations in co-teaching: A problem-solving approach.* Bloomington, IN: Solution Tree Press.

Dahlman, A., & Hoffman, P. (2012). Fixing the implementation gap: Creating sustainable learning spaces for successful co-teaching and collaboration. In A. Honigsfeld & M. Dove (Eds.), *Co-teaching and other collaborative practices in the EFL/ ESL classroom: Rationale, research, reflections, and recommendations* (pp. 37–47). Charlotte, NC: Information Age Publishing.

Danielson, C. (2011). *The framework for teaching evaluation instrument.* Princeton, NJ: The Danielson Group.

Hoffman, P., Dahlman, A., & Zierdt, Z. (2009). Professional learning communities in partnership: A 3-year journey of action and advocacy to bridge the achievement gap. *School–University Partnerships: The Journal of the National Association of Professional Development Schools, 3*(1), 28–42.

Ingersoll, R. (2001). Teacher turnover and teacher shortages: An organizational analysis. *American Educational Research Journal, 38*(3), 499–534.

NCATE Blue Ribbon Panel on Clinical Preparation and Partnerships for Improved Student Learning. (2010). *Transforming teacher education through clinical practice: A na-*

tional strategy to prepare effective teachers. Retrieved from *http://www.ncate.org/ LinkClick.aspx?fileticket=zzeiB1OoqPk%3D&tabid=715*

Werhan, C., & Chapman, C. (2011). *Co-responsibility for all learners: Co-teaching as a methodology to increase capacity for K–12 students, cooperating teachers and teacher candidates.* Unpublished manuscript. College of Education, Minnesota State University, Mankato.

Zierdt, Z., Dahlman, A., Rosendale, A., & Kennedy, P. (2012). Minnesota State–Mankato P–20 professional development school partnership: The cornerstones of 25 years of success. *School-University Partnerships, 5*(2), 19–23.

CHAPTER 2

MEASURING CLASSROOM TEACHING EFFECTIVENESS AND USING FINDINGS TO MAKE CHANGES

A PDS Video-Based Action Research Study

Linda A. Catelli, Joan Carlino, and Gina Marie Petraglia

ABSTRACT

This chapter focuses on a video-based action research study and the use of the find-ings to make changes in the PDS Partnership. The study is the third in a series of five linked action studies that are part of Phase II of the partnership's research project. The overall project goal is to change and improve PreK–12 classroom teaching and the clinical aspects of the college's teacher education programs in an integrative way. The study seeks to (1) measure classroom teaching effectiveness with differ-ent rubrics, observational tools, and scorers and (2) identify the plausible causes of the students' successful achievement of the learning outcomes of selected units of instruction.

Creating Visions for University-School Partnerships, pages 21–41.
Copyright © 2014 by Information Age Publishing
All rights of reproduction in any form reserved.

ABOUT THE STUDY AND RESEARCH PROJECT

The authors present the third study in a series of three linked, video-based PDS action research studies that were conducted during the years of 2009 to 2012. The purpose of this chapter is to present selected findings of the entire third study and the use of its data to make changes in the professional development school (PDS) partnership. This study is part of Phase II of Dowling College's PDS partnership research project. The overall goal of the project is to change and improve K–12 classroom teaching and the clinical aspects of the college's teacher education programs in its PDS and partnership settings. Phase I of the project focused on the PDS teacher candidates' teaching performances of lessons and the changes that took place over time in their classroom teaching and in the partnership structure. The research and video-based studies of Phase II were aimed at investigating teaching effectiveness and the linkages between observable classroom teaching actions and student achievement.[2] The studies included in Phase II of the project have taken place within the context of Race to the Top (RttT) reforms. The study that is presented in this chapter was directed at (1) measuring classroom teaching effectiveness with different rubrics, observational tools, and scorers, and (2) identifying the plausible causes of the students' successful achievement of the learning outcomes of selected units of instruction. The study advances *PDS action research*[3] and, in an integrative way, the four-pronged PDS mission: preparation of preservice educators, enhanced professional development for in-service educators, improvement of learning and achievement at both the school and university levels, and the design of collaborative and innovative research on learning and educational practice. It is distinguished from other studies in that it furthers *PDS action research* by assessing teaching effectiveness in PDS settings and by linking observable classroom teaching actions to student achievement in the context of the new teacher performance assessment (TPA) systems for certifying and evaluating teachers.

Participants and collaborators of the study include PDS teacher candidates in elementary education, an experienced high school teacher, three PDS supervising teachers, two education course instructors, and two professors who are teacher education specialists at the college (see Table 2.1). Also, a team of 11 graduate students who make up the eighth cohort of Dowling College's PDS action researchers served as the researchers and trained scorers of the teaching performances for this study. The cohort of researchers engaged in a year-long graduate course that prepared them to conduct an action research study. The course was taught by the professor-director of the PDS partnership who currently serves as the principal investigator of the project. The cohort of researchers included teacher candidates who were in a year-long student teaching experience at the Belmont Elementary PDS of the North Babylon School District on Long Island in New York State.

TABLE 2.1.   Listing of Participants and Their Role in the Study. (T# represents the number assigned to the teacher or teacher candidate.)

Participants and Collaborators	Role
2 Elementary Teacher Candidates	Designed and taught units in mathematics
T21 (Second-grade mathematics unit)	
T22 (Third-grade mathematics unit)	
1 High School Teacher (T24) of physics	Designed and taught a unit in physics
3 PDS Teachers	Served as the supervising-cooperating teachers of the Teacher Candidates
11 Graduate Students – 8th Cohort of PDS Researchers	Served as the action researchers and trained scorers of the study
2 Teacher Educators/Professors at the College	Served as specialists and untrained scorers of the study
Early Childhood Specialist	
Secondary Education Specialist	
1 PDS Lead Teacher	Served as the student-teacher seminar leader, supervisor, and action researcher of the study
1 PDS Teacher-Course Instructor	Served as the instructor for the clinical education course and an action researcher of the study
1 Director of the PDS Partnership	Served as the instructor of the action research course and principal investigator for the project

General Research and Inquiry Questions of the Study

The general questions that guided the researchers of the entire study of the project were:

1. How well did the PDS teacher candidates and teacher of the study perform the selected instructional actions that are identified in the literature as effective in promoting student learning?
2. Do the ratings of the same teaching performances by different scorers differ? That is, do the ratings of trained scorers versus teacher education specialists differ? Also, do the ratings of classroom teaching obtained with different rubrics and observational tools differ in important ways (e.g., rubrics from *Danielson's Framework for Teaching Evaluation Instrument*, [Danielson, 2011] versus rubrics from Performance Assessment for California Teachers—PACT [Performance Assessment for California Teachers, 2010])?
3. Which of the instructional teaching actions cited in the literature as effective in facilitating learning are identified in this study as the plausible causes of the students' successful achievement of the learning outcomes

of the selected units of instruction in elementary mathematics and high school physics?

4.   Which of the performance indicators of the New York State Teaching Standards (Frey, 2010) appear to correlate in this study with student learning in the selected units of instruction?

For purposes of this chapter, the authors focus on the second and third questions of the study. Selected findings that are relevant to answering the two questions are reported and discussed. In the final section of the chapter, the authors briefly describe how the data and findings were used to make integrative changes in the clinical aspects of the partnership's elementary teacher education program. For example, based on the resulting data, reading assignments that focused on the teacher's efficient use of time during a lesson and strategies for increasing student involvement were emphasized during an introductory teacher education course. The course was co-taught by the director of the partnership and a PDS teacher of the program. This was followed by having the PDS supervisor(s) highlight practical strategies for involving students during their interactions with student teachers and then emphasized in the student teacher seminar taught by the PDS lead teacher. The changes that took place prompted an increase in student engagement during the candidates' teaching of lessons. In addition, revisions were made to a course that is used to train PDS supervisors and develop their observational skills. Also, in a graduate course offered to pre- and inservice teachers, the topic of types of teacher feedback and an observational tool for capturing feedback comments were added to the course content and assignments as a result of the findings. All of the revisions were based on relevant findings from the study.

Although this action study is small in scale, and in the number of cases examined, it provided valuable information to make important revisions in the partnership's pre- and inservice programs in integrative ways to impact student and candidate learning. In addition, the information obtained from the series of Phase I and Phase II PDS studies were used (1) in the assessment process for accrediting the college's elementary teacher education program, (2) to provide evidence to support the unit's effectiveness in implementing its conceptual framework and (3) to support the partnership's conceptualization and perspective on effective teaching.

Conceptualization and Theoretical Perspective

A conceptualization of teaching that describes the teacher's role as an effective facilitator of student learning and achievement was developed and used in this study, as well as in other studies of the project. The conceptualization guided the selection and adaptation of rubrics and observational tools. Simply put, teaching effectiveness is represented by those teachers who can demonstrate good practice and instructional actions in a consistent manner to facilitate and effect learning regularly. Effective facilitators intentionally perform instructional interactions that are directed at learning and supported by evidence of student achievement. Effectiveness involves consistency of performance and a relatively high degree of goal attainment under varied conditions and in different situations (see Catelli, 1981, 2002, 2005; Catelli, Likon, Vonta, & Pisot, 2009; and Gentile, 1972 for an explanation of the conceptualization of teaching). More particularly, this study embraced a theoretical description of an effective teaching performance as a critical thinking performance that is grounded in epistemology and placed in the study of performative knowledge (Catelli, 1981, 2005, 2010; Ryle, 1949; Scheffler, 1965). This view of teaching and the teacher's role as an effective facilitator also draws from Linda Darling-Hammond and Joan Baratz-Snowden's (2005) *A Good Teacher in Every Classroom,* as well as from summaries of research on teacher effectiveness (e.g., Campell, Kyriakides, Muijs, & Robinson, 2004; Chance, 2008; Danielson, 2007; Muijs & Reynolds, 2005). The instructional actions that were measured in this study are reflective of the role of the teacher as an effective facilitator of student learning.

Action Research Methodology

As mentioned previously, the overall goal of the research project is to change and improve classroom teaching and learning in PDS settings and in the pre- and inservice teacher education programs. Therefore, action research and collaborative inquiry was chosen as the research method to conduct the study. As a research methodology, action research has long been established as a viable vehicle for instituting change, reform, and improvement in education and professional education (Hollingsworth, 1997; Lieberman, 1986; Somekh & Zeichner, 2009). Rock and Levin (2002) have also used action research to enhance professional development in PDS settings. Recently, action research has been identified as an important research method in the world of PDS research (see Catelli, 2011; Tunks, 2011). The steps and cycles of action research lend to making change and continuous improvements in a PDS partnership a reality—thus, the coined term *PDS action research.*

Sources of Data

Three units of instruction were selected by the researchers for examination. The units were in second- and third-grade mathematics and one in high school physics. The mathematics units were part of the first study in the series of three, and the physics unit was part of the second study in the series. The units in mathematics included 9 to 12 lessons taught by two elementary PDS teacher candidates, and the unit in physics had 9 lessons taught by an experienced teacher. All individuals had volunteered for the study and the research project. It should be mentioned that each of the units was considered "successful" in that more than 75% of the students in the class had either achieved an acceptable level of performance for the unit's learning outcomes on summative tests and/or they had demonstrated growth in one or more of the unit's learning outcomes on a formal assessment test (e.g., Thinklink Learning Tests, 2005).

There were 15 high school students who participated in the physics unit, 21 elementary students in the second-grade mathematics unit, and 24 elementary students in the third-grade mathematics unit for a total of 60 students in the PDS partnership study. Permission slips were obtained from parents, teacher candidates and the teacher of the study. Students who participated in the study were members of two school districts that were assessed as having at least 25% of their student population from low-income families or families in poverty.

A minimum of five video-recorded lessons for each unit (15 total) were viewed, assessed, and analyzed by trained scorers of the study. The trained scorers were the 11 graduate students who were also the action researchers of the study. They are referred to in the chapter as researcher-scorers. The untrained scorers were professors and teacher educators at the college. They were selected because of their expertise. Using a set protocol, the trained researcher-scorers observed and then rated the teaching performances for each of the video-recorded lessons. A total of 15 video-recorded lessons were observed, assessed, and analyzed by the trained researcher-scorers. Arranged in five pairs, the trained researcher-scorers applied established and adapted rubrics and performance assessment criteria to rate the teaching performances on 18 key instructional teaching actions or rubrics (see Tables 2.2 and 2.3).

TABLE 2.2.   Adjusted Assessment Tool of Instructional Actions (rubrics) for Scoring Effective Classroom Teaching (Catelli, Likon, Vonta & Pisot, 2009)

Educational Testing Service's (ETS)—Pathwise Program (ETS, 1995)	
[1]C1a.	Making learning goals clear to students
[2]C1b.	Making instructional procedures clear to students
[3]C2.	Making content comprehensible
[4]C3.	Encouraging students to extend their thinking
[5]C4a.	Monitoring students' understanding of the content via questioning and providing feedback
[6]C4b.	Adjusting learning activities as the situation demands
[7]C5.	Using time efficiently and effectively
National Board for Professional Teaching Standards (NBPTS) Middle Childhood/Generalist Scoring Guide (NBPTS, 1998)	
[8]C6.	Building classroom community
[9]C7.	Building an understanding
Performance Assessment for California Teachers (PACT, 2010)	
[10]C8.	Engaging students
[11]C9.	Monitor student learning

TABLE 2.3. Selected Instructional Actions (Rubrics) from Danielson's Revised Framework for Teaching Evaluation Instrument (The Danielson Group, 2011).

Domain: The Classroom Environment	
[12]2c.	Managing classroom procedures
[13]2d.	Managing student behavior
Domain 3: Instruction	
[14]3a.	Communicating with students
[15]3b.	Using questioning and discussion techniques
[16]3c.	Engaging students
[17]3d.	Using assessment in instruction
[18]3e.	Demonstrating flexibility and responsiveness

Such teaching actions as "making content comprehensible," "monitoring student understanding of the content," and "engaging students" were three of the 18 actions the scorers observed and rated. A scale ranging from 1.0 and 1.5 (low) to 3.5 to 4.0 (high) with points in between was used to rate the teaching performances of each of the 18 instructional teaching actions seen in Tables 2.2 and 2.3. A criterion performance level of 2.5 was set for a "competent" performance for each instructional teaching action. The high school teacher, who was also trained in the use of the rubrics during the second study, rated her performance on the instructional actions for all nine of her video-recorded lessons included in the physics unit. She justified her ratings in a daily journal, providing evidence to support her ratings. It should be noted that the instructional teaching actions listed in Tables 2.2 and 2.3 were not only drawn from established teaching rubrics in the field but also from the literature on teaching effectiveness. The selected instructional acts are known to facilitate student learning (see Bransford, Brown, & Cocking, 2000; Danielson, 2007; Muijs & Reynolds, 2005). Also, they are reflective of the conceptualization of the teacher's roles as a facilitator of learning (see Catelli, 1981, 2002; Catelli, Likon, Vonta, & Pisot, 2009; Chance, 2008; Darling-Hammond & Bransford, 2005; Gentile, 1972). Further, it should be noted that in this study, the instructional actions appear as rubrics on observational tools and systems that were used to rate classroom teaching.

Observational Tools, Rubrics and Procedures

The rubrics and performance assessment criteria that were used by the trained researcher-scorers to rate the teaching performances were drawn and adapted from four different observational tools or rubric systems: Danielson's *Framework for Teaching Evaluation Instrument* (2011), National Board for Professional Teaching Standards (NBPTS) *Middle Childhood/Generalist Scoring Guide* (1998),

Educational Testing Services' *Pathwise Program* (ETS, 1995) and *Performance Assessment for California's Teachers* (PACT, 2010). The rubrics selected from these tools were then placed in 18 categories. The 18 categories of instructional teaching actions along with their associated performance criteria (or rubric descriptions) were arranged in two major observational tools for the study seen in Tables 2.2 and 2.3: (a) *The Adjusted Assessment Tool of Rubrics for Scoring Effective Classroom Teaching* (Catelli et al., 2009) and (2) *Danielson's Revised Framework for Teaching Evaluation Instrument* (Danielson, 2011).

Each of the 11 researcher-scorers had achieved a minimum of 80% inter-judge reliability during a two-month training period. The training period was conducted by the principal investigator of the study who is also a systems developer of an observational instrument (see Catelli, 1981). After achieving 80% inter-judge reliability or better, the researcher-scorers in five teams comprised of two scorers each began rating the teaching performances using their assigned observational tool and rubric system. The researcher-scorers employed a protocol that required them to rate the teacher's performance on each of the 18 instructional actions for each nine-minute segment of the video-recorded lesson. They then computed a mean score for the lesson for each instructional action. The mean score was converted to a rating (e.g., 2.0, 2.5, 3.0, etc.). Each pair of researcher-scorers repeated this procedure with their assigned observational system for each of the five video-recorded lessons of the unit; thus, all 15 video-recorded lessons were rated with two different observational tools.

During the period of time that the 11 researcher-scorers were involved in rating the teaching performances of the lessons, they did not know that the units of instruction had already been assessed as "successful" by another cohort of researchers in a previous study; that is, they did not know that more than 75% of the students in each of the units had either demonstrated growth and/or achievement of the unit's learning outcomes. This was done to minimize rater bias, as part of the research design for the study. It was only after the researcher-scorers had computed their mean scores and final ratings for each of the 18 instructional actions for each lesson were they then made aware of the fact that the units were assessed as successful.

Also, as part of the design and procedures for this study, three of the video-recorded lessons in the second-grade mathematics unit and three in the high school physics unit were observed and rated by professors who are teacher education specialists at the college. One of the teacher educators is a specialist in secondary teacher education and the other is a specialist in early childhood teacher education. Each specialist had not been trained in the use of the rubrics and tools prior to their observations of the video-recorded lessons. However, each was given a listing and brief rubric description of the 18 instructional teaching actions to use in their observations of the video-recorded lessons. Also, a survey-questionnaire containing a list of the 18 instructional actions was administered to the each of the specialists after they had observed the video-recorded lessons. In addition,

TABLE 2.4. Sample Questions from the Study's Survey-Questionnaire

1. What specific classroom teaching actions would you say "effected" student learning in the video-recorded lessons you have observed?

2. Which of the 18 categories of instructional actions listed do you think were most responsible for the students' successful achievement of the objectives in the video-recorded lessons you have observed?

3. Which three instructional actions listed do you think were the plausible causes of the students' achievement of the lesson objectives and learning outcomes of the unit of instruction?

4. Which of the "performance indicators" of the New York State Teaching Standards (Frey, 2010) listed would you say were the most probable correlates of students' learning in the video lessons you observed?

an abbreviated version of the survey-questionnaire was administered to the all of the 11 trained researcher-scorers after they had applied the rubrics and computed their final ratings. A sample of the questions that were answered by both groups is found in Table 2.4.

The trained researcher-scorers were encouraged to answer the questions based on a review of their ratings and additional data they had obtained about each lesson from the previous studies (e.g., the percentage of time students were engaged during a lesson; the percentage of time the teacher and each teacher candidate spent observing students and giving students corrective feedback, etc.). The two teacher education specialists (untrained scorers) were asked to answer the same questions based on their observations and expertise. All responses from the researcher-scorers and the teacher education specialists, along with their ratings of performances were compared, analyzed, and linked to (1) measures of the students' successful achievement of the learning outcomes of the units and (2) the performance indicators of the New York State Teaching Standards (Frey, 2010). The teacher's self-ratings were also included in the analyses that were conducted by the researcher-scorers and principal investigator. A working organizational schema was employed to align all teacher and student performance data (e.g., video profiles of teaching, ratings, and student outcome data—formative and summative). This was done in an effort to answer research questions 2 and 3. Also, other information and performance data (e.g., percentage of time devoted to an instructional act, student scores on quizzes and work samples, etc.) were triangulated by the researchers and principal investigator of the study. The data were triangulated in an effort to (1) make comparisons, (2) support and strengthen the findings of the study, (3) arrive at conclusions, and (4) make recommendations for action plans in the next action-research cycle and study.

REPORT AND DISCUSSION OF
SELECTED FINDINGS OF THE STUDY

In this section of the chapter the authors report on data and findings to answer the second and third research questions of the study. The section is arranged in two subsections, followed by a final section that describes how the findings were used to make changes in aspects of the PDS Partnership.

Findings: Research Question 2

Do the ratings of the teaching performances by the different scorers of the study differ; and do the ratings of classroom teaching obtained with different rubrics and observational tools differ in important ways?

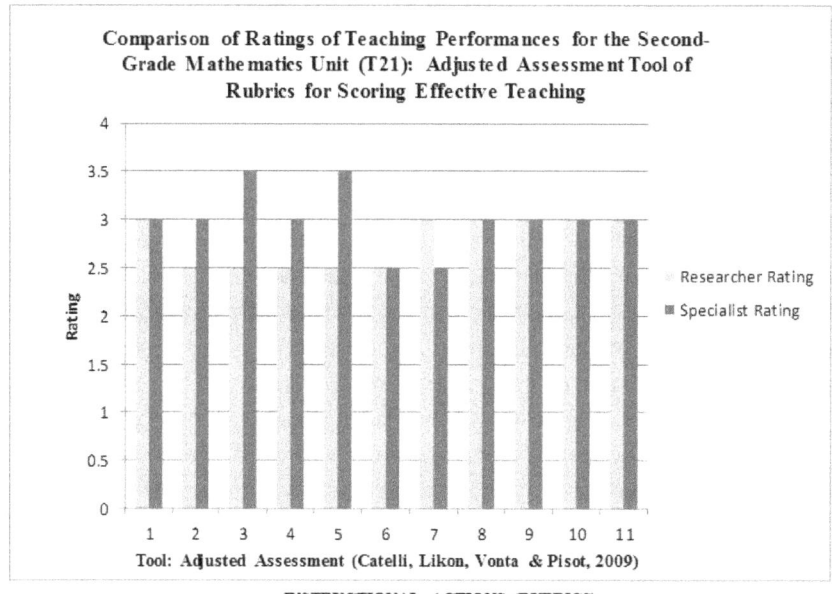

INSTRUCTIONAL ACTIONS (RUBRICS)

ETS- PATHWISE
(1) C1a. Making Learning Goals Clear to Students
(2) C1b. Making Instructional Procedures Clear to Students
(3) C2. Making Content Comprehensible to Students
(4) C3. Encouraging Students to Extend Their Thinking
(5) C4a. Monitoring Students' Understanding of Content During Instruction
(6) C4b. Adjusting Learning Activities as the Situation Demands
(7) C5. Using Instructional Time Efficiently and Effectively

National Board - NBPTS
(8) C6. Building a Classroom Community
(9) C7. Building an Understanding
PACT
(10) C8. Engaging Students
(11) C9. Monitoring Student Learning

FIGURE 2.1. A comparison of ratings given by the trained researcher-scorers versus the untrained scorer (early childhood specialist) using the *Adjusted Assessment Tool* (Catelli et al., 2009) for the unit of instruction in second-grade mathematics taught by a PDS teacher candidate (T21).

For the second research question of the study, the researchers found that the ratings given by the trained researcher-scorers and those assigned by the specialist in early childhood education to the teaching performances (T21) for the second-grade mathematics unit were the same or "in agreement" for 6 of the 11 instructional actions when using the *Adjusted Assessment Tool of Rubrics for Scoring Effective Classroom Teaching* (Catelli et al., 2009) (see Figure 2.1). The six actions (or rubrics) that were assigned the same ratings were:

[1]C1a. Making learning goals clear to students—3.0
[6]C4b. Adjusting learning activities as the situation demands—2.5
[8]C6. Building a classroom community—3.0
[9]C7. Building an understanding—3.0
[10]C8. Engaging students—3.0
[11]C9. Monitoring student learning—3.0

Whether one has been trained in the rubrics or had expertise in the area of childhood education, it appeared that the trained researcher-scorers and the early childhood specialist agreed on the same level of performance for each of the above six (6) instructional teaching actions.

The five (5) teaching or instructional actions from the *Adjusted Assessment Tool of Rubrics for Scoring Effective Classroom Teaching* (Catelli, et al., 2009) that did not receive the same ratings by the different scorers were:

[2]C1b. Making instructional procedures clear to students (2.5/3.0)
[3]C2. Making content comprehensible (2.5/3.5)
[4]C3. Encouraging students to extend their thinking (2.5/3.0)
[5]C4a. Monitoring students' understanding of the content via questioning and
        providing feedback (2.5/3.5)
[7]C7. Using time efficiently and effectively (3.0/2.5)

With the exception of C7, "using time efficiently and effectively," the trained researcher-scorers' ratings were consistently lower (2.5) than the ratings given by the early childhood education specialist (3.0 and 3.5) (see Figure 2.1). For the instructional teaching action C7, the reverse was true. The early childhood specialist rated the teacher candidate's level of performance as 2.5, whereas the researcher-scorers' rated the candidate's performance of the action as 3.0.

Why was there agreement of ratings (whether high or low) on six of the instructional actions and no agreement on five of the actions? Was it a function of the rubric's narrative description and assessment criteria? That is, were the six instructional actions already well defined in their titles and brief descriptions, and, therefore, the untrained rater-specialist did not need to be trained in applying the performance criteria of the rubric; were the six teaching actions easier to observe or more evident in the teaching performances; or were the six actions more frequently occurring than the other five actions? Based on the analyses of the quantitative data (e.g., the percentages of time devoted to an action) and the qualitative data (e.g., ratings that indicated how well the individual performed an action), as well as an examination of the observational tools, the researchers concluded that the rubric descriptions and criteria for each of the six teaching actions were well defined and adequately represented in just their titles. Further, these instructional actions (rubrics) were of low inference and more frequently occurring during the lessons. Thus, such attributes and features left little room for subjectivity or a misinterpretation on the part of a rater. This was true whether the rater was trained or untrained in the use of the rubrics.

In contrast, the five teaching actions that were not given the same ratings required a rater to study and be trained in the performance criteria and levels of the rubric. Comments made by the trained researcher-scorers also revealed a preference for the rubrics that were extracted from National Board (1998) and PACT (2010). The researchers commented that the narrative- descriptions of those rubrics allowed them to easily assess instructional teaching actions.

With regard to the use of *Danielson's* (2011) set of rubrics, there was "no agreement" found between the researchers-scorers' ratings and those ratings given by the early childhood education specialist for any of the seven (7) instructional actions extracted from *Danielson's Domains* (Figure 2.2):

Domain: The Classroom Environment
[12]2c. Managing classroom procedures
[13]2d. Managing student behavior

Domain 3: Instruction
[14]3a. Communicating with students
[15]3b. Using questioning and discussion techniques
[16]3c. Engaging students
[17]3d. Using assessment in instruction
[18]3e. Demonstrating flexibility and responsiveness

Further examination of the data revealed that the early childhood specialist's ratings on each of the above seven instructional actions of Danielson's (2011) set of rubrics were consistently higher than those ratings given by the trained researcher-scorers (Figure 2.2).

The researcher-scorers concluded that having been formally trained in a specific protocol for rating teaching performances with rubrics that have well-defined levels of performance may have greatly influenced their assignment of lower ratings than those of the specialist, or perhaps it may be that the early childhood specialist brought to the situation a better understanding of the complexities of a teaching situation and, thus, leaned more toward assigning higher ratings to the

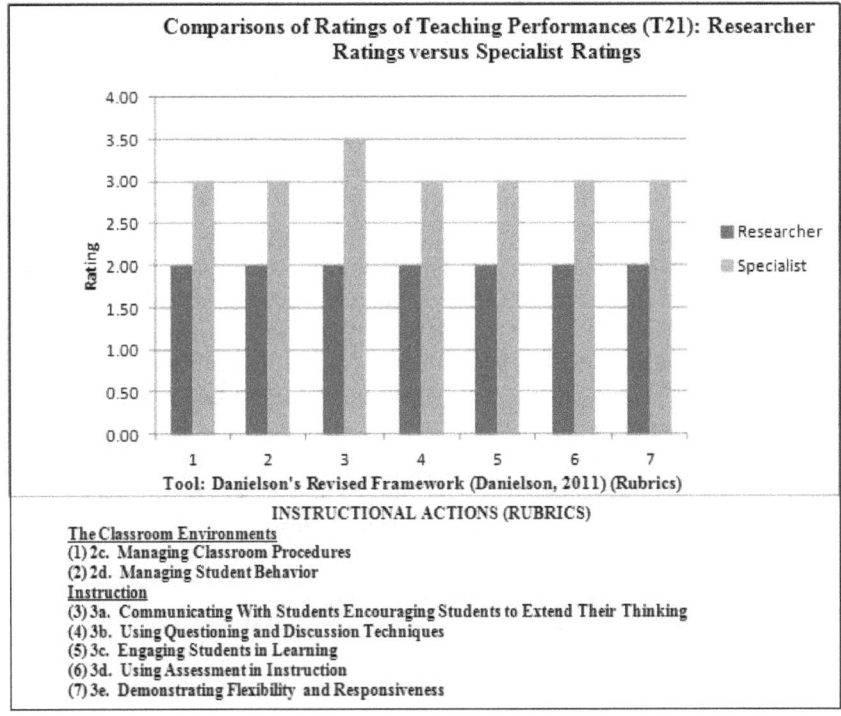

FIGURE 2.2.   A comparison of ratings given by different scorers for the unit of instruction in second-rade mathematics for the PDS teacher candidate: *Danielson's Revised Framework* (Danielson, 2011).

candidate's performance. Which of the two sets of ratings, the researcher-scorers' ratings or the early childhood specialist's ratings, provides a truer representation of the teaching performances? This is a question that is still being pursued along with conducting analyses of the additional data collected in subsequent studies of Phase II.

It should be noted that teacher candidate (T21), who conducted all of the lessons of the second-grade unit, was successful in having more than 75% of the class achieve the unit's objectives and demonstrate growth in mathematics while having received a 2.5 rating (basic) and a 3.0 rating (proficient) for many of the instructional actions (Figures 2.1 and 2.2). Teacher (T24) was successful in having more than 80% of her students reach mastery level (see Figures 2.3 and 2.4 for the teacher's performance ratings). This resulting situation begs for further investigation. For example, does it mean that such ratings may be sufficient for producing a 75% or 80% success percentage-rate for student growth or achievement in a class, or were there other variables related to the rubrics or the scorers that operated in this situation to produce such results? Does a teacher need only to be basic or satisfactory (2.0, 2.5) in their ratings to have an acceptable level or impact on student growth and achievement? Further investigation of the observational instruments and rubrics in the next cycle of studies will be needed to adequately answer question 2. However, the authors recognize the need to have the partnership's PDS cooperating teachers, mentors, supervisors, and professors involved in a type of inter-rater training that will adequately represent a candidate's level of classroom teaching performance on those key instructional actions that promote learning. Also, the PDS personnel will need to be made aware of the problems that exist with the use of different observational instruments or rubrics and with different scorers. This is especially so if the instruments are to be used for developing and evaluating teachers and teacher candidates, as well as for improving classroom teaching.

Data for the unit in physics taught by the high school teacher (T24) are seen in Figures 2.3 and 2.4. There was only one agreement in ratings between the trained researcher-scorers and the specialist in secondary teacher education (see Figure 2.3):

[11]C9. Monitoring student learning during instruction—3.0

Also, there were only "two agreements" in ratings between the teacher's self-assessment ratings and the ratings given by the secondary education specialist:

[5]C4a. Monitoring student understanding of the content—3.0
[7]C5. Using time efficiently and effectively—3.0

There was no agreement found among the three different scorers: (1) the trained researcher-scorers, (2) the specialist in secondary education, and (3) the high school teacher of physics (Figure 2.3). Further, there was no agreement in ratings found between the researcher-scorers and the high school teacher. In general, the trained researcher-scorers' ratings were lower than the secondary education specialist and teacher's ratings.

It is important to remember that the teacher (T24) was asked to provide evidence in a daily journal to support and justify her self-ratings after each of her nine lessons of the unit. The principal investigator of the study reviewed, confirmed, and approved her ratings. The researcher-scorers who rated the teacher's performance were in pairs and had achieved an acceptable measure of inter-judge reliability in the use of their assigned observational tool.

Also, when asked to provide an overall performance rating of the actions for the unit, it was interesting to note that the teacher gave herself an overall rating of 3.0, and the four trained researcher-scorers assigned the teacher a 2.5, 3.0, 3.0, and 3.0 rating, respectively. The specialist in secondary education gave the

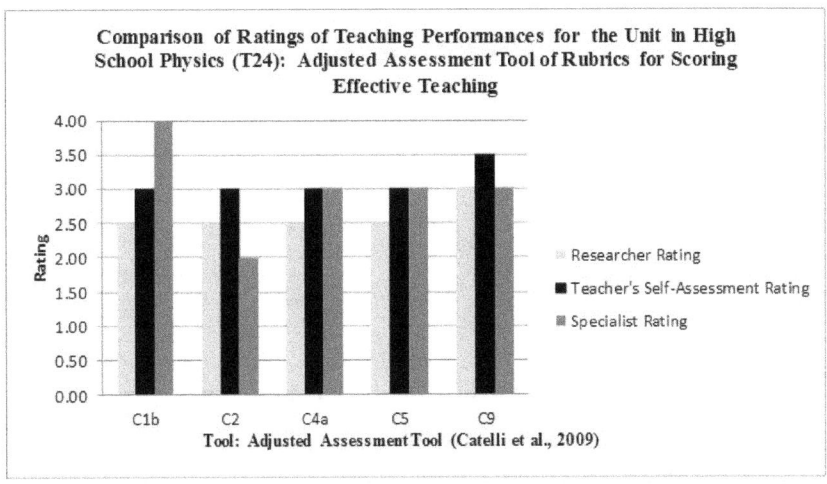

INSTRUCTIONAL ACTIONS (RUBRICS)
C1b. Making Instructional Procedures Clear to Students
C2   Making Content Comprehensible to Students
C4a. Monitoring Students' Understanding of Content (e.g., Questions and Feedback)
C5. Using Instructional Time Efficiently and Effectively (Pacing)
C9. Monitoring Student Learning During Instruction

FIGURE 2.3.   A comparison of ratings given by the different scorers—the trained researcher-scorers versus teacher (T24) versus the untrained scorer (secondary education specialist)—for the unit of instruction in high school physics using the *Adjusted Assessment Tool* (Catelli et al., 2009).

teacher two overall performance ratings (2.5 and 4.0) for the teacher's (T24) performance. The specialist commented that if one is a teacher who is implementing traditional, direct-style methods or didactic teaching, then the observed teaching performance of the lessons merited a rating of 4.0. However if you are a teacher enacting a constructivist approach then the teacher's performance may merit a 2.5; thus, it appears that if one employs direct methods of instruction the chances are that he or she will score low (receive low ratings) on a few of the rubrics of the Danielson's instrument (2011). For example, one may score low on "using questioning and discussion techniques" and on "communicating with students." Danielson's set of rubrics leans more toward a constructivist viewpoint. Many of the established observational instruments appear to "smuggle in" a particular teaching concept, perspective, or method of instruction. It is extremely important for PDS teachers, principals, teacher candidates, mentors, supervisors, and professors to be aware that an observational system may be slanted toward a particular concept of teaching and learning.

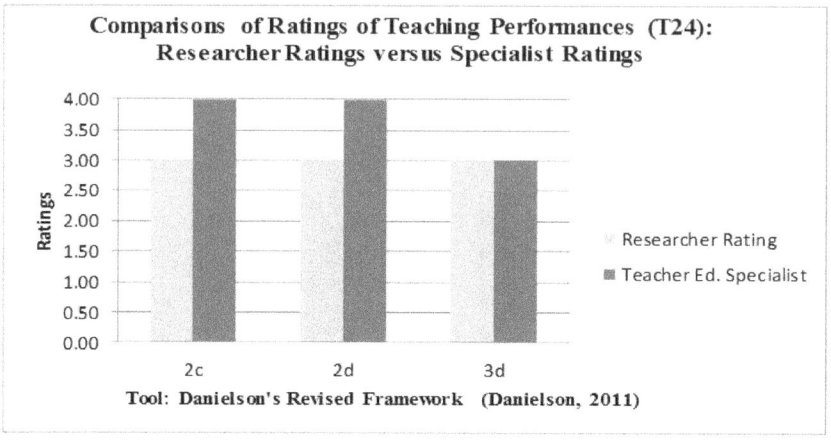

INSTRUCTIONAL ACTIONS (Rubrics)
2c. Managing Classroom Procedures
2d. Managing Student Behavior
3d. Using Assessment in Instruction

FIGURE 2.4.   A comparison of ratings given by different scorers—the trained researcher-scorers versus the untrained scorer (secondary education specialist)—for the unit of instruction in high school physics using Danielson's Revised Framework (Danielson, 2011).

Findings: Research Question 3

Which of the instructional teaching actions (rubrics) cited in the literature as effective in facilitating learning were identified in this study as the plausible causes of the students' successful achievement of the learning outcomes of the units of instruction?

For the third research question, the researchers compiled and analyzed responses from the survey-questionnaire of the study (see Table 2.3).

The survey-questionnaire was administered by the principal investigator of the study to the researcher-scorers and to both teacher education specialists. The researcher-scorers then aligned the resulting frequencies of the responses with all of the performance ratings and quantitative measures of teaching (e.g., the percentage of time the teacher spent engaging students; the percentage of time the teacher spent asking questions, giving feedback, etc.) Based on the researchers' analyses and an alignment of the data, the effective instructional actions that were identified as the plausible causes of the students' successful achievement of the learning outcomes for each unit of this study were:

For the Unit of Instruction in High School Physics

- Monitoring students' understanding of the content through a variety of means (e.g., questioning) and providing feedback to students to assist learning
- Using time efficiently and effectively
- Engaging students in learning

For the Unit of Instruction in Second-Grade Mathematics

- Monitoring students' understanding of the content through a variety of means (e.g., questioning) and providing feedback to students to assist learning
- Communicating with students
- Making content comprehensible to students

For the Unit of Instruction in Third-Grade Mathematics

- Engaging students in learning
- Managing student behavior
- Using assessment in instruction

Based on the analyses of the findings and data collected from all sources, the four instructional actions that emerged as the plausible causes of the students' successful achievement of the units' objectives and learning outcomes were:

- Engaging students
- Using time efficiently and effectively
- Monitoring students understanding of the content
- Providing feedback

USE OF FINDINGS TO MAKE CHANGES AND CONTINUOUS IMPROVEMENTS

The findings of the study sent a signal to the PDS personnel that emphasis must be placed, in a more intentional way, on the above instructional actions in our integrated pre- and inservice teacher education programs of the PDS Partnership; that is, course and field assignments, readings, and so on, along with supervisory practices and professional development courses, must be designed to promote a better understanding and an enactment of these teaching actions. Also, there should be better training in the use of the observational rating systems. Well-structured training of PDS mentors, supervisors, and professors in helping candidates and teachers develop these instructional acts and training for assessing them is crucial. The findings confirmed our suspicion about the relative importance of the four instructional actions as the probable causes of student learning and achievement.

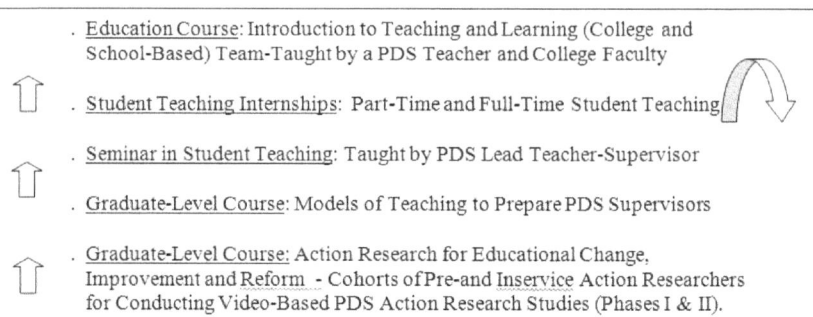

. Education Course: Introduction to Teaching and Learning (College and School-Based) Team-Taught by a PDS Teacher and College Faculty

. Student Teaching Internships: Part-Time and Full-Time Student Teaching

. Seminar in Student Teaching: Taught by PDS Lead Teacher-Supervisor

. Graduate-Level Course: Models of Teaching to Prepare PDS Supervisors

. Graduate-Level Course: Action Research for Educational Change, Improvement and Reform - Cohorts of Pre-and Inservice Action Researchers for Conducting Video-Based PDS Action Research Studies (Phases I & II).

FIGURE 2.5. Strategic and integrative use of findings for continuous change and improvement in the clinical aspects of the PDS Partnership's pre-and inservice teacher education programs.

With little time available to practice teach in a program, it becomes important to highlight and develop high-level performances of these actions that appear to hold promise for facilitating student achievement in a more efficient and effective way.

More particularly, the findings of the study were strategically used to make integrative changes in the component parts of the PDS mission and in specific aspects of the PDS partnership (see Figure 2.5).

Over the years, much of the resulting data and findings generated by the PDS video-based action research studies have changed classroom teaching in desirable directions, and they have made positive changes to the clinical courses of the PDS Partnership seen in Figure 2.5: Introduction to Teaching and Learning; Seminar in Student Teaching; Action Research for Educational Change, Improvement, and Reform; and Models of Teaching and Learning. Such changes have resulted in revised (1) course content, (2) PDS supervisory practices, and (3) classroom teaching procedures, actions, and so on. As part of the action research cycle, the changes were monitored and assessed in terms of their impacts on the PDS candidate's classroom teaching and, in turn, on student learning and engagement. The PDS lead teacher and a PDS course instructor along with the director of the partnership have collaborated to use the findings from the partnership's video studies for continuous and integrative improvement as depicted in Figure 2.5. As a PDS group of researchers, we clearly recognize that the small number of cases examined in the study prevent us from making sweeping generalizations. We encourage further investigation and the creative design of *PDS action studies* to answer the research and inquiry questions. Recently, the new accrediting body entitled the Council for the Accreditation of Educator Preparation (CAEP, 2013) has sanctioned action research measures as feasible measures for institutions to provide evidence of improvement of their educator programs. Also, CAEP has identified in their Standard 2 (Clinical Partnerships and Practice) a PDS partnership as an example of a partnership agreement that will be accepted as a school–university arrangement for meeting the standard.

Finally, this study has merit for advancing *PDS action research*, the notion of continuous improvement, and the use of data in integrative ways for four-pronged PDS mission. The ultimate goals of this line of research are to:

- Identify PDS classroom instructional actions and performance indicators that correlate with and eventually predict student growth and achievement
- Change and continually improve classroom teaching and learning in partnership settings
- Change and improve the PDS partnership's pre- and inservice teacher education programs in integrative ways to favorably impact learning

The study is distinguished from other studies in that it measures PDS teaching effectiveness by linking observable classroom teaching actions to student learning within the context of RttT reforms and the new teacher performance assessment (TPA) systems for certifying and evaluating teachers.

NOTES

1. The chapter is an expanded version of a paper presented at the 2013 Annual Meeting of the American Educational Research Association (AERA). The authors received the 2013 *Claudia A. Balach Teacher Researcher Award* from the PDS Research SIG of the AERA for their collaborative PDS action research.

2. The authors of the linked, video-based action studies of Phase II were members of the sixth, seventh and eighth cohorts of Dowling College's PDS Researchers:

6th Cohort	*7th Cohort*	*8th Cohort*	
Sabrina Beecher	Joseph Battelli	Shari Coghill	Alexine Parpa
David Denton	Cristina Brazzelli	Dennis Donovan	Christina Ricca
Aubrey Gray	Dorothy Burns	Jennifer Downey	Erin Skidmore
Silvia Maldonado	Melissa Farrell	Christina Hayes	Breanne Kempton
Jennifer Messier	Jonathon Porter	Athena Iliou	James Mullaney
Erin O'Boyle	Patricia Langer		
Nancy Pancella			
Stephanie Alkes			

3. See Tunks (2011) and Catelli (2011) for an explanation of *PDS action research.*

REFERENCES

Bransford, J., Brown, A., & Cocking, R. (Eds.) (2000). *How people learn: Brain, mind, experience, and school.* Washington, DC: National Academy Press.

Campell, J., Kyriakides, L., Muijs, D., & Robinson, W. (2004). *Assessing teacher effectiveness.* New York, NY: Routledge Falmer.

Catelli, L. A. (1981). *Verbal and non-verbal moves in teaching: A descriptive system for analyzing teaching.* Eugene, Oregon: Micro publications, CHPER, University of Oregon.

Catelli, L. A. (2002). *A conceptual framework for a new era in education at Dowling College: The process and the outcome.* Unpublished document. Oakdale, NY: X College.

Catelli, L. A. (2005). Performative knowledge and skillful performances. In S. J. Farenga & D. Ness (Eds.), *Encyclopedia on education and human development* (pp. 676–683). Armonk, NY: M.E. Sharpe.

Catelli, L. A. (2010). Action research video studies for improving classroom teaching-learning performances. In R. Pelton (Ed.), *Making classroom inquiry work* (pp. 83–114). Lanham, MD: Rowman & Littlefield.

Catelli, L. A. (2011). Response to section III: What's needed now in PDS action research and program evaluation. In J. Neapolitan (Ed.), *Taking stock of professional development schools: What's needed now.* 110th Yearbook of the *National Society for the Study of Education (NSSE)* (Vol. 2, pp. 486–510). New York, NY: Teachers College Press.

Catelli, L. A., Likon, B., Vonta, T., & Pisot, R. (2009). *Analyzing effective teaching performances.* Koper, Slovenia: Zalozba Annales.

Chance, P. (2008). *The teacher's craft: The ten essential skills of effective teaching.* Lake Grove, IL: Waveland Press.

Council for the Accreditation of Educator Preparation (CAEP). (2013, June 11). *CAEP accreditation standards and evidence: Aspirations for educator preparation.* Recommendations from the CAEP commission on standards and performance reporting to the CAEP Board of Directors. Retrieved from *http://www.caepnet.org/*

Danielson, C. (2007). *Enhancing professional practice: A framework for teaching* (2nd ed.). Alexandria, VA: Association of Supervision and Curriculum Development.

Danielson, C. (2011). *The framework for teaching evaluation instrument.* Princeton, NJ: The Danielson Group.

Darling-Hammond, L., & Baratz-Snowden, J. (Eds.). (2005). *A good teacher in every classroom: Preparing the highly qualified teachers our children deserve.* San Francisco, CA: Jossey-Bass.

Darling-Hammond, L., & Bransford, J. (2005). *Preparing teachers for a changing world: What teachers should learn and be able to do.* San Francisco, CA: Jossey-Bass.

Educational Testing Service (ETS). (1995). *Pathwise: Orientation guide.* Princeton, NJ: Author.

Frey, J. P. (2010). New *York State Standards Development* [Letter to the State Education Department Committee on Higher Education]. Albany, NY: New York State Department of Education.

Gentile, A. M. (1972). A working model of skill acquisition and application to teaching. *Quest, 17,* 3–23.

Hollingsworth, S. (1997). *International action research: A casebook for educational reform*. London, UK: Falmer Press.

Lieberman, A. (1986). Collaborative research: Working with, not working on. *Educational Leadership, 43*(45), 28–32.

Muijs, D., & Reynolds, D. (2005). *Effective teaching: Evidence and practice*. Thousand Oaks, CA: Sage.

National Board for Professional Teaching Standards [NBPTS]. (1998). *Middle childhood/ generalist scoring guide.* San Antonio, TX: Author.

Performance Assessment for California Teachers [PACT]. (2010). *Rubrics: PACT teacher performance assessment.* Retrieved from *http://www.pacttpa.org/rubrics/*

Rock, T., & Levin, B. (2002). Collaborative action research projects: Enhancing pre-service teacher development in professional development schools. *Teacher Education Quarterly, 29*, 7–21.

Ryle, G. (1949). *The concept of mind*. Chicago, IL: Charles C. Thomas.

Scheffler, I. (1965). *Conditions of knowledge*. Glenville, IL: Scott Foresman.

Somekh, B., & Zeichner, K. (2009). Action research for education reform: Remodeling action research theories and practices in local contexts. *Educational Action Research, 17*(1), 5–21.

ThinkLink Learning. (2005). *ThinkLink predictive assessment series*. Retrieved from *http://www.thinklinklearning.com*

Tunks, J. (2011). Action research as primary vehicle for inquiry in the Professional Development School. In J. Neapolitan (Ed.), *Taking stock of Professional Development School: What's needed now*. 110th Yearbook of the *National Society for the Study of Education (NSSE)* (Vol. 2, pp. 463-485). New York, NY: Teachers College Press.

CHAPTER 3

CLINICALLY RICH PRACTICES IN TEACHER EDUCATION

Review and Recommendations

Janna Dresden, Julie Kittleson, and Julianne Wenner

ABSTRACT

In response to growing criticism of teacher preparation programs, there is interest in the specific pedagogical strategies used in teacher education (National Council for Accreditation of Teacher Education, 2010). In this chapter, the authors describe practice-based pedagogy in teacher education and present a set of clinically rich practices they use in their undergraduate teacher preparation courses. These clinically rich practices include look and learn, teaching rounds, talks with teachers, scavenger hunts, and the supported collaborative teaching model. Such clinically rich practices are intended to help teacher candidates make connections between theory and practice. The authors also describe the vital role of professional development schools (PDSs) in implementing clinically rich practices in teacher education.

Recognizing the value of clinically rich practices in teacher education is certainly not a new idea. The "belief that all genuine education comes about through expe-

Creating Visions for University-School Partnerships, pages 43–60.
Copyright © 2014 by Information Age Publishing
All rights of reproduction in any form reserved.

rience" (Dewey, 1938, p. 25) has its contemporary roots in much of the work of John Dewey and a much longer history in the apprenticeship model used to train new trades- and craft-people for centuries. Nonetheless, there is currently a renaissance of appreciation for approaches that engage college students in the work and life of P–12 classrooms throughout their programs of study. In this chapter, the authors (1) examine the causes for this renewed interest in clinically rich practices, (2) briefly investigate the use of clinically rich practices in other professions, (3) review the theory and research on clinically rich practices in teacher education today, (4) consider the vital role of professional development schools (PDSs) in facilitating these approaches to teacher education, and (5) introduce the set of clinically rich practices now used in the university's undergraduate teacher preparation courses. The authors conclude by showing the connections between the theory and practice of teacher education and making recommendations for future practice and research.

THE NEED FOR CLINICALLY RICH PRACTICES IN TEACHER EDUCATION

Teacher education has been subject to harsh critique in recent years (Darling-Hammond, 2000). This general dissatisfaction with teacher preparation, combined with a focus on the importance of connecting theory and practice, has led to a renewed interest in programs and practices that provide preservice teachers with clinically rich experiences. In addition, it is apparent that the field of teacher education must consider reform at all levels in order to refute the charges that the field has become out of touch with the realities of American schools, or worse, superfluous to the cause of improving educational access and attainment.

There have been strongly worded criticisms of education in general and of teacher preparation in particular for nearly three decades. Most scholars view the 1983 publication of *A Nation at Risk: The Imperative for Educational Reform* (National Commission of Excellence in Education, 1983), as the beginning of a critical and politicized perspective on American education (Rutter, 2011). Since this time, there have been many calls for the improvement of teacher preparation (Darling-Hammond, 2000), but often the focus has been on suggested changes to the assessment and evaluation of teachers and their effectiveness (e.g., American Association of Colleges for Teacher Education [AACTE], 2011) rather than on recommended changes to programs of teacher preparation. When critiques of teacher preparation have included suggestions for specific reforms, they have generally highlighted the need for additional classroom experience for teacher candidates, and both scholars and policymakers have stressed the need for more field work in programs of teacher preparation (Darling-Hammond, Hammerness, Grossman, Rust, & Shulman, 2005; Feiman-Nemser, 2001; Zeichner, 2010).

Participation in clinical experiences during teacher preparation has been shown to have an impact on the success of beginning teachers, as described by Boyd, Grossman, Lankford, Loeb, and Wyckoff (2008). According to these authors, "Teachers who have had the opportunity in their preparation to engage in the actual practices involved in teaching...show greater student gains during their first year of teaching" (pp. 26–27). Reports from teachers also indicate that they believe extensive clinical preparation is essential to their work as teachers (Levine, 2010). Finally, teachers report that their preparation programs generally did not provide them with sufficient clinical experiences. Levine (2010) report, "New and experienced teachers repeatedly cite the opportunities to practice as being the most critical element of their preparation...[and typically] their preparation did not provide adequate opportunity for them to learn how to use what they knew" (p. 3). Given teachers' assessment of the power of clinical experiences, the data about the impact of clinical experience on the ability of teachers to support the learning of their students, along with a strong theoretical rationale, scholars of teacher education have concluded that "practice must be at the core of teachers' preparation" (Ball & Forzani, 2009, p. 497).

Despite the enormous importance of clinical experience for teacher preparation, just spending time in a classroom is not sufficient for the development of expertise (Levine, 2010). "Classroom experiences alone...cannot justify what teachers do, nor teach teachers to think about their work" (Feiman-Nemser, 2012, p. 176). Instead teacher candidates must learn to connect theoretical principles to their daily interactions with students in classrooms.

> Professional preparation requires opportunities to master a solid knowledge base along with opportunities to learn when and how to use knowledge in practice. The relationship and interplay between these two necessary knowledge bases and ways of learning is at the heart of the design of a teacher education program for preparing professional practitioners. (Levine, 2010, p. 4)

The ability to integrate theory and practice is the hallmark of a competent professional, but gaining this ability is not easy to accomplish. The difficulty inherent in connecting theoretical principles taught on university campuses with the exigencies of daily classroom life is both the cause and consequence of the frequently noted disconnect between campus and school-based components of programs (Zeichner, 2010). This disconnect is often seen as a major culprit in our troubled system of education (NCATE, 2010). Perhaps most unfortunate of all, the difficulty of creating a seamless blend of theory and action is often underestimated or ignored. As Feiman-Nemser (2012) points out, there is an all too frequent and "false assumption that making connections between these two worlds is straightforward and can be left to the novice" (p. 177). Whether or not teacher educators recognize the arduous challenge that making these connections present to teacher candidates, it remains a task that teacher candidates themselves are typically expected to accomplish on their own (Zeichner, 2010).

Instead of expecting teacher candidates to independently construct an understanding of the relationship between theory and practice, teacher educators should provide an environment in which habits of inquiry into practice can be cultivated

(Feiman-Nemser, 2012). This should be the primary goal of teacher preparation because the "capacity to connect classroom experience with formal knowledge and to learn from further experience by thinking about it…[are both] central to teaching, but they must be learned" (Feiman-Nemser, 2012, p. 170). Similarly, Darling-Hammond (2006) stated that in order to reform teacher education we need to "incorporate newly emerging pedagogies…that link theory and practice in ways that theorize practice and make formal learning practical" (p. 307).

Clinically rich practices that foreground the ways in which theory and practice interact can serve as exemplars of these new pedagogies. The authors view clinically rich practices as a subset of the larger group of practice-based approaches to teacher education. In this view, clinically rich practices are a specific type of practice-based education and are qualitatively different from the pedagogies employed in on-campus classes and also qualitatively different from traditional field experiences. Clinically rich practices are pedagogical strategies that place teacher candidates in real-world contexts with the expectation that they will engage with P–12 students, while they are also provided with direct and specific support and guidance from both mentors and teacher educators. In these situations, teacher candidates may be asked to do targeted observations of students and master teachers or implement specific teaching routines that have been carefully planned and rehearsed. In addition to thoughtful planning, structured review and reflection are essential elements of all clinically rich practices in teacher education. Through planning, action, and reflection, clinically rich practices both support new learning and make explicit the relationship between what is known and what is done. Thus, clinically rich practices enable teacher candidates to learn from their experiences and to develop the ability to act with intention and professional judgment in both routine and ambiguous situations.

In their pursuit of high-quality education and teacher preparation, some scholars have focused less on specific practices and pedagogies and have instead called for the creation of new systems or structures, such as John Goodlad's "center for pedagogy" (Goodlad, 1994). A center of pedagogy was envisioned as a new organizational structure that would include faculty members from colleges of education, colleges of arts and sciences, and P–12 school districts.

The purpose of this setting was to strengthen the connections among these three groups and thus improve teacher preparation and facilitate the renewal of education more broadly. As another example of the emphasis on large-scale infrastructure, Howey has recommended that professional development schools should receive additional federal support in the same manner as teaching hospitals (Howey, 2011). While such visionary approaches would be exciting and might support, extend, and institutionalize specific forms of practice, it is not clear how feasible or realistic such a goal might be. On the other hand, important changes can be made more immediately by reshaping teacher education pedagogy at the level of direct practice. Clinically rich practices offer an alternative route to reform that is more pragmatic and more responsive to the needs of specific schools and programs. It is possible that, in the quest to reinvigorate teacher preparation, what happens *within* programs and courses is more important than external structures.

In summary, clinically rich practices are essential for improving teacher education. Programs of teacher education have been criticized for not providing sufficient amounts of clinical practice and for not maintaining a clear focus on the connections between field experiences and the theories that can both explain and provide direction for practice. Clinically rich practices can fill a void in the field by creating opportunities for practice and, more importantly, by creating spaces in which the intersection of theory and practice is both evident and tangible. Finally, clinically rich practices provide an approach to the improvement of teacher education, which, because it is conducted locally, can be within the reach of all teacher educators.

CROSS-PROFESSIONAL PERSPECTIVES ON CLINICALLY RICH PRACTICES

A concern with helping teacher candidates make the transition from the world of tests used to measure factual knowledge and conceptual understanding to the world of complex professional practice is not unique to the field of teacher education. Teaching is one of many practice-based professions such as medicine, law, and social work that aim to develop in their students "the ability to use specific tools and skills of the field, and the capacity to make complex decisions based on informed judgments" (Levine, 2010, p. 5). These professions share an interest in clinical experiences designed to facilitate the growth of individuals from knowledgeable novices to competent professionals able to use their knowledge to solve complex problems of practice. "Underlying the assertion that teacher preparation be redesigned to include more clinical experiences embedded in school–university partnerships is the concept that teaching is a practice-based profession, akin to medicine, nursing, or clinical psychology" (Levine, 2010, pp. 3–4).

A review of the literature on other practice-based professions revealed that some professions have made more progress than teacher education towards the effective use of clinically rich experiences for their students; other professions are struggling to move beyond the textbook-driven and "practice-free" curricula so common on university campuses. Medical training is the gold standard for appropriate training of practitioners, and, in many cases, professions are urged to emulate medicine's approach to practice-based education and use the teaching hospital as a model for the context within which to provide clinically rich training for novices. For example, a recent article in the *Chronicle of Higher Education* (Mangan, 2012) reported on a letter to university presidents written by the leaders of several major newspaper publishing companies and journalism foundations. In this letter, they critique the outdated approaches of most journalism schools and suggest a greater emphasis on clinical practice. "Journalism should take a page from medical schools by immersing students in hands-on, real life experience using teaching hospitals as models" (Mangan, 2012, p. 1). Law schools, too, are generally considered to be bastions of tradition and far removed from the actual work of practicing lawyers. Recent articles in the *Wall Street Journal* (Lee, 2011) and *New York Times* (Segal, 2011) have commented on how the legal profession suffers from a disconnect between the theoretical training proffered on campus and the practical and personal skills lawyers need for successful careers. Lee described how a number of law schools are attempting to rectify this situation through changes to programs and course syllabi. What is perhaps most notable about this discussion is that the inclusion of courses with "actual case work" is seen as new, if not revolutionary.

Seen from this perspective, the field of teacher education would seem to be "ahead of the game" as regular clinical experiences are a part of all programs of teacher education. However, when compared with certain other professions, teacher education appears to be sorely lacking in the quality of clinical experiences included as part of professional training. This is especially true when teacher preparation is compared to the preparation for other "relational practices" such as clinical psychology and the clergy (Grossman, Compton, Igra, Ronfeldt, Shahan, & Williamson, 2009). Grossman and colleagues examined not the amount of time spent in clinical experiences but rather the specific pedagogies used to help students make sense of complex practices and the experiences designed to help students develop the specific skills needed to engage in practice themselves. Through extensive research with three professions, they found that novices in the clergy and clinical psychology had more opportunities to engage in tightly "scaffolded" clinical experiences (e.g., supported approximations of practice that occur in authentic contexts) than did novice teachers (Grossman et al., 2009). Thus, there is clearly a need for programs of teacher preparation to carefully consider the construction of clinical experiences that successfully support the development of teachers. The following section will review the current landscape of teacher education with specific attention to the role of clinically rich practices.

THEORY AND RESEARCH ON CLINICALLY RICH PRACTICES IN TEACHER EDUCATION

There are strong indications that practice-based approaches, and clinically rich practices more specifically, have the potential to significantly improve the preparation of teachers. If the field of teacher education is to make sustained and systemic changes in the direction of practice-based pedagogies it will be important to base our course of action on a theoretical understanding of the value of these approaches and the mechanisms by which they operate. To provide an operational definition of these approaches to teacher education, the authors rely on the work of Ball and Forzani (2009), who stated that a practice-based approach "means unpacking and specifying practice in detail and designing professional education that will offer novices multiple opportunities to practice the work and to fine tune their skills" (p. 498). The characteristics of "clinical based programs," as explained by Levine (2010), include "opportunities for novice teachers to apply all the knowledge they are acquiring…and a focus on students' needs" (pp. 9–10). Levine also discussed various types of clinical experiences and distinguished between laboratory experiences (simulations, observations, journaling, virtual professional learning communities, etc.), and school-embedded clinical experiences such as grand rounds, co-teaching, and study groups that utilize protocols for analyzing student work.

One proposal for a theoretical understanding of practice-based approach is found in the work of Hollins (2011) who described a "holistic practice-based approach [which] integrates academic knowledge of theory, pedagogy, and curriculum across experiences in authentic contexts" (p. 395). To help novices focus on salient aspects of teaching practice, Hollins described a model that encompasses (1) essential knowledge, skills, and understandings believed to support quality teaching, and (2) epistemic practices intended to support learning to teach. Hollins (2011) argued that essential knowledge should include a focus on the topics of learners, the learning process, subject matter, pedagogy, and accountability and assessment. Hollins went on to explain that the epistemic practices that support teacher development are focused inquiry, directed observation, and guided practice. Taken together, the elements articulated by Hollins highlight aspects of practice that should be used in the creation of a practice-based pedagogy.

Similarly, Grossman et al. (2009) used the concept of *decomposition* as a key for understanding the pedagogies of practice in teacher education: "Decomposition makes visible the grammar of practice to novices…. By decomposing complex practices, professional educators can help students learn first to attend to, and to enact, the essential elements of a practice" (p. 2069). Specifically, Grossman and colleagues have described three essential aspects associated with pedagogies of practice: representations, decomposition, and approximations of practice. Representations "provide novices with opportunities to develop ways of seeing and understanding professional practice" (p. 2065). However, simply witnessing a representation does not guarantee that significant elements of practice are made apparent to novices. One way to make elements visible is to name the parts of practice, which is what Grossman and colleagues called decomposition. By decomposing complex practice, teacher educators can turn novices' attention toward fundamental elements of practice. Further, these researchers note that decomposition allows novices to "practice a relatively narrow skill in a safe space" (p. 2072). While isolating fundamental elements of practice is useful for learning particular skills, translating these skills into authentic practice requires that novices be provided with opportunities to approximate practice, which is the third element of Grossman et al.'s framework. Approximation, they note, "allows for the errors that novices inevitably make when enacting complex practice" (p. 2077). In addition, "approximations are designed to focus students' attention on key aspects of the practice that may be difficult for novices but almost second nature to more experienced practitioners" (p. 2078). Taken as a whole, this framework provides a theoretical foundation and guide for designing practice-based approaches to teacher education.

Yet another set of theoretical constructs is found in the work of Ball and colleagues (Ball & Cohen, 1999; Ball & Forzani, 2009). In recognition of the complexity of teaching, these scholars have postulated a continuum of practice settings that range from "virtual" settings to "designed" settings to "actual" settings (Lampert, 2006, cited in Ball & Forzani, 2009). This perspective extends the view that authentic contexts are necessary for learning to teach and highlights the reality that all contexts for practice are not the same, nor are they all equally productive for helping teachers learn the skills that are important for teaching (Ball & Forzani, 2009). Specifically, some contexts may be "too authentic" and present an overload of information (Ball & Cohen, 1999). The development of designed settings makes it possible for teacher educators to reduce the interference of extraneous information and makes it easier for novice teachers to focus on a few important skills or strategies at a time. "Novices need opportunities to try out and experiment, with support, aspects of complex practice, gradually increasing their complexity and reducing the scaffolding" (Ball & Forzani, 2009, p. 504). By conceptualizing practice as existing on a continuum from limited and defined to completely authentic, it is possible to create a context in which teacher candidates can be gradually introduced to the complexity of teaching.

Making the transition from what is known to what is done is perhaps the greatest challenge of teacher education; therefore, mapping the application of theory to practice is central to a practice-based pedagogy. In the work of Hollins (2001), Grossman and colleagues (2009), and Ball and colleagues (Ball & Cohen, 1999; Ball & Forzani, 2009), we find an emphasis on constructing specific learning environments that give teacher candidates an opportunity to try out defined elements of practice. The assumption underlying all three proposals is that it is easier to enact some elements of practice when one is not trying to implement all possible elements. Thus, teacher educators should create a scaffold that enables teacher candidates to experience success in the application of new ideas, methods, or strategies. Hollins (2011) calls this "guided practice" and describes it as "experimenting with planning and enacting a short sequence of learning experiences for a small group of students under the careful supervision of university faculty or an experienced teacher" (p. 404). Ball and Forzani (2009) used the term "designed setting" to explain a space which would "eliminate or reduce the need for students to engage with some aspects of the work of teaching while focusing attention on particular parts of the work" (p. 504). Grossman and colleagues (2009) claimed that structured experiences such as these can provide teacher candidates the opportunity to "experiment, falter, regroup, and reflect…through the use of approximations of practice" (p. 2077). The work of all these scholars emphasizes the importance of providing a clearly delineated pathway from theory to practice to support the development of novice teachers.

Finally, reflection as an act of inquiry into one's own practice is seen as a critical element of a practice-based approach to teacher education as well as in the practice of excellent teachers (Feiman-Nemser, 2001; Hollins, 2011). While independent reflection is often beneficial, reflection supported by instructors or peers is more likely to be both meaningful and powerful (Ball & Cohen, 1999; Feiman-Nemser, 2001; Hollins, 2011). It is thus through experiences deliberately constructed by the teacher educator to encourage thoughtful conversations that teacher candidates can become more skilled in the "critical colleagueship" and act of inquiry into practice that is so vital to becoming a reflective practitioner (Schön, 1983, 1987).

THE ROLE OF PDSS IN SUPPORTING CLINICALLY RICH EXPERIENCES

By definition, clinically rich teacher education practices cannot be fully enacted in universities, isolated from schools and P–12 classrooms. While it may be possible to produce some types of practice-based strategies in university classrooms (e.g., micro-teaching and simulations), most practice-based pedagogies, especially that subset the authors have labeled clinically rich practices, require ready and consistent access to students. The kinds of experiences and activities discussed in the previous section will not simply occur randomly or "out of the blue"—they must be carefully planned and thoughtfully implemented, and they can only occur in the context of ongoing relationships between personnel from schools and universities. As several authors have noted, this will require a change in the relationship between schools and universities.

Levine (2010) noted that "the transformation of clinical preparation of teachers cannot be achieved by preparation programs acting alone. Intensive clinical preparation, especially when it is school embedded, requires the collaboration of preparation provider and schools, and the support of all the stakeholders in its success" (p. 12). Darling-Hammond (2006) concurred and stated that, in order to improve teacher education, "schools of education must design programs that transform the kinds of settings in which novices learn to teach...the enterprise of teacher education must venture further and further from the university and engage ever more closely with schools" (p. 302).

Close engagement with schools demands that colleges of education recognize school district personnel as their partners rather than viewing schools as locations for field experience and personnel as potential subjects for research studies. Darling-Hammond (2006) notes that pedagogical "strategies for connecting theory and practice cannot succeed without a major overhaul of the relationships between universities and schools" (p. 308). It is unreasonable to expect that it would be possible to integrate theory and practice for teacher candidates unless the institutions of theory (the university) and of practice (schools) have a strong relationship that allows for and encourages a dynamic exchange of resources and ideas.

The need for strong, collaborative relationships between colleges of education and P–12 schools has rekindled an interest in the teaching hospital model as a context for clinically rich practices. Howey (2011) suggested that the field of teacher preparation is moving toward an emphasis on partnerships between universities and schools, "in a parallel manner to other professions and especially the clinical type of preparation that occurs in teaching hospitals" (p. 327). The best developed and most well-known model of such partnerships in teacher preparation is that of the PDS, first proposed and described by the Holmes Group in the early 1980s (Rutter, 2011). This group advanced the idea that a PDS

> would be a teacher education version of medical school's university teaching hospital, which embraces a broad group of stakeholders, including the partnering school sites. A PDS would be built on a mutuality of purpose and vision rather than imposed from above. They would be schools in which pre-service teachers could benefit from authentic settings, and in-service teachers would be treated as professionals undergoing simultaneous renewal, becoming collaborative field-based teacher educators partnering with the university faculty in their inquiry of teaching and learning. (Rutter, 2011, p. 298)

A PDS, like a teaching hospital, is a professional institution that takes on an additional responsibility and serves as a location for the preparation of the next generation of practitioners. These types of settings have been shown to be very successful. "The extensive experience of PDSs has taught us that a clinical preparation program that is grounded in collaboration, professional community, high standards of practice and is dedicated to student success can change an entire school, and can have a positive impact on the achievement of students in that school" (Levine, 2010, pp. 10–11). Because clinically rich practices require a clinical setting, a PDS, or other similar partnership, is a necessary factor in the reform of teacher education.

THE CHALLENGES INHERENT IN USING CLINICALLY RICH PRACTICES IN TEACHER EDUCATION

The purpose of clinically rich practices in teacher education is to provide a clear, meaningful and useful connection between theory and practice. Through the use of clinically rich practices, teacher educators delineate a well-marked pathway between theory and practice rather than leaving teacher candidates to blaze this trail on their own. Clinically rich practices enable teacher educators to support teacher candidates and show them how to use and apply theoretical principles as they encounter decision points throughout their day. However, the development and use of clinically rich practices is not without risk or difficulty.

The development of specific pedagogical strategies designed to integrate theory and practice should begin by recognizing that they are different. It is important to acknowledge "that the worlds of thought and action are legitimately different… and each has a potential for making a contribution to learning to teach…one does not overcome this duality by eliminating it. The goal of professional education is acting with understanding" (Feiman-Nemser, 2012, p. 178). The challenge for teacher educators then is to create specific experiences that assure that the lessons learned from clinical interactions will be truly educational. This is indeed a challenge, because despite the enormous benefits of experience in real-world settings discussed earlier in this chapter, there are also pitfalls associated with field experiences. Feiman-Nemser has explicated the specific pitfalls that may render various types of field experiences less beneficial than expected. For example, when teacher candidates are told simply to spend time observing in classrooms, as sometimes happens in early field experiences, they are subject to the "familiarity pitfall." In these situations, teacher candidates may have a tendency to assimilate new observations into their existing schema of schooling and teaching. Teacher candidates may assume that they know what is happening and may continue to focus on those elements of classroom activity that were most salient to them when they were themselves students in K–12 classrooms.

> People generally do not recognize that their experience is limited and biased, and future teachers are no exception. The 'familiarity pitfall' stems from the tendency to trust what is most memorable in personal experience.... Classroom experience in itself cannot be trusted to deliver lessons that shape dispositions to inquire and to be serious about pupil learning. On the contrary, it may block the flow of speculation and reflection by which we form new habits of thought and action. (Feiman-Nemser, 2012, p. 170)

Teacher educators also need to be wary of the "two-worlds pitfall" that can occur in many types of field experiences and is the result of the differing goals and methods of classroom teaching and university coursework. For example, teacher candidates (TCs) are often asked by their university instructors to observe or engage in other activities that are related to, but very different from, the actions of the classroom teacher.

> Classrooms are busy places, and Tom [a TC] sees that the teacher must attend to many things. The observational skills that he is developing are related to helping children learn. Without training in how to look and what to notice, it is easy to miss important clues about pupil response to instructional activities. Tom can afford to concentrate on mastering this way of looking precisely because he is not responsible for what goes on. But there is a pitfall. If Tom does well on this assignment, he will have the gratification of a good grade. The immediate reward, however, is indigenous to the university culture, not to the culture of schools and teaching. The very structure of Tom's assignment shows that university learning and classroom teaching are worlds apart. (Feiman-Nemser, 2012, p. 173)

Not only are the goals of classroom teaching and university coursework different, but they may, at times, even be contradictory. Classrooms are complex places, and asking teacher candidates to focus on one aspect may make it difficult or impossible for them to attend to other issues or carry out other responsibilities. Thus, teacher educators may inadvertently put their teacher candidates in the position of feeling caught in the middle between their mentor teacher and their university instructor.

Finally, there is the "cross purposes pitfall," which emphasizes the fact that the purpose of a classroom is to educate the children in that classroom rather than to serve as a training ground for new teachers (Feiman-Nemser, 2012). Therefore, the structure and routines that are best for the pupils in the classroom may not always give teacher candidates the necessary opportunities to try out new forms of practice, and the exploratory approach best suited to an emerging professional may have negative consequences for pupils.

There is no easy solution or quick fix to the challenges inherent in attempts to foster clinical approaches to teacher preparation. However, several scholars of teacher education provide direction as they have pointed out that there are a variety of types of clinically rich practice—each with different benefits and potential pitfalls. Grossman and colleagues (2009) recommended that we study approaches such as "microteaching, model lessons, unit planning, simulations, role-plays, and student teaching…and investigate the affordances and constraints of these different approximations in preparing novices for different aspects of practice" (p. 18). The work of Lampert (cited in Ball & Forzani, 2009) postulates a continuum of "designed settings" for teacher education and further explicates the need for a range of clinical experiences in programs of teacher preparation. Not all designed settings, practice-based pedagogies, or clinically rich practices need have the same educational goal. No one strategy will meet all the goals that are necessary for the development of competent teachers—it would be unreasonable to expect that any one strategy could fulfill so large a mission. Therefore, the authors would suggest that in order to have successful practice-based programs of teacher preparation, it will be necessary to employ an intentionally designed array of clinically rich strategies within courses and programs. By using an assortment of approaches, it is possible to maximize the benefits and counterbalance the negative consequences or pitfalls of some clinical experiences. The following section describes the set of clinically rich practices the authors use in courses for teacher candidates.

EXAMPLES OF CLINICALLY RICH PRACTICES IN ELEMENTARY TEACHER EDUCATION

The first and second authors teach, respectively, Integrated Curricular Practices in Early Childhood Education and Elementary Science Methods to the same cohort of students in their third semester of a four-semester undergraduate teacher education program. After completing the program, the teacher candidates will be certified to teach in grades P–5. The science methods course was taught on campus, and the early childhood course was taught on-site at an elementary PDS. However, the authors collaborated to prepare and carry out a number of clinically rich practices designed to help teacher candidates develop both competence and confidence. The authors used some widely known strategies and created several new ones in order to take advantage of the opportunities made available through the partner school. The authors' use of clinically rich practices evolved over four years and currently includes five distinct pedagogical strategies—each with a clear purpose and benefit.

Look and Learn

This brief activity is essentially observation training and was precipitated by two occurrences. First, it was found that when teacher candidates were asked for their thoughts or observations after time spent in a classroom, they would typically comment on the "bad" behavior of one or more students. They seemed unable to look beyond, or underneath, these "acting out episodes" to see what other students were doing or how the classroom was organized and how student activity was orchestrated. In addition, some teacher candidates commented that they were often asked to observe but didn't really know what or how to do so—a common problem for beginning teacher candidates (Feiman-Nemser, 2012).

"Look and learn," an example of the directed observation recommended by Hollins (2011), was designed to show teacher candidates two methods for observation and to require them to look beyond the dramatic behaviors of a few students. Early in the semester, pairs of teacher candidates are sent into classrooms for about 20 minutes with clipboards and observation forms (based on protocols for research in *The Subject Matters* by Stodolsky, 1988). One teacher candidate is asked to focus on the activity structure of the classroom (How many children? How are they grouped? What materials are being used? Where is/are the teacher(s) located? What is the topic/goal of the lesson?). The other teacher candidate is told to pick three students in the classroom and to observe them in rotation for about 20 seconds at a time, recording on their form exactly what the student is doing, saying, and so on. When the teacher candidates return to the university's area, they debrief with one another, talking about what struck them as important and examining the relationship between activity structure and student behavior. Teacher candidates and course instructors then debrief as a whole group. The following week the exercise is repeated, except that the teacher candidates change roles for the observation period.

Anecdotally, the authors have found this activity to be quite successful. Teacher candidates quickly realize that they are seeing student behaviors that they might otherwise have ignored—for example, the quiet child who is more off-task than his noisy peer. They also begin to be aware of the impact of activity structure on student behavior. Significantly, this pedagogical strategy helps to interrupt teacher candidates' typical ways of viewing classrooms, thus avoiding the familiarity pitfall, and does not alter the activity of the classroom, thus minimizing the negative consequences found in the cross purposes pitfall. Finally, this activity provides an experience that helps teacher candidates learn to observe with more intention and purpose with the aim to "foster [their] capacity to learn from future experience" (Feiman-Nemser, 2012, p. 168).

Teaching (Grand) Rounds

Grand rounds, a pedagogical strategy borrowed from the practice of medical training, is now a common occurrence in many professional development schools (PDSs). In this strategy, the entire class of teacher candidates files into a classroom to watch a volunteer master teacher conduct a 20-minute lesson. Following the lesson, the teacher returns with the course instructor to the classroom assigned to the university and responds to questions from the teacher candidates. Because the teacher candidates have been instructed to be thinking of questions to ask following the observation, this strategy also helps to disrupt the sense of familiarity, and, because there is minimal change to the daily routine for the elementary students, there is only a small risk of the cross purposes pitfall. In contrast, there are notable benefits to this strategy. As Thompson and Cooner (2001) explain, "Grand Rounds provides pre-service teachers first-hand experience in observing, questioning, and reflecting upon the 'best practice' strategies of master teachers in a collaborative and supportive environment" (p. 87).

Scavenger Hunts

Scavenger hunts are another brief and nonintrusive pedagogical strategy that nonetheless guides teacher candidates to make direct links between course discussion and what is going on in the classrooms all around them. For example, if the course discussion focuses on the value of graphic organizers with the requisite examples as slides or hand-outs, it is still critical for teacher candidates to see this strategy in action. Therefore, during a break in class, the teacher candidates are asked to go around the school, looking for examples of various types of graphic organizers. The authors or course instructor then compiles this information and looks for differences by grade level or subject matter. Though quite simple, this is a clear example of a clinically rich practice as it connects the theory and research about why graphic organizers are useful with the plentiful examples found around the school at any given point in time. Further, this strategy is an example of the decomposition noted by Grossman and colleagues (2009), as the attention of teacher candidates is directed to one specific element of practice.

Talks with Teachers

Another simple strategy, "talks with teachers," offers teacher candidates an avenue for determining a portion of the course content. At the beginning of the semester, the course instructor asks the teacher candidates what they are interested in or would like to learn more about and then arrange with teachers from the partner school to come to class to make very brief presentations or just come in to answer questions. Although the teacher candidates are not present in the school's classrooms for this strategy, they are interacting as novice professionals with their more experienced colleagues. The teacher candidates are able to have professional conversations with practicing teachers and are thus engaged in a critically important clinical practice. In this way, talks with teachers are a concrete manifestation of one aspect of the focused inquiry advocated by Hollins (2011). Importantly, this strategy also recognizes the expertise and professionalism of the practicing teachers and supports their growth and development.

Supported Collaborative Teaching Model

The "supported collaborative teaching model" (SCTM), known colloquially as "science centers," is the most complex of the clinically rich practices used by the authors. Science centers are held three times each semester with one grade level at a time so that each grade level in the school (K–5) participates once each year. During science centers, small groups of teacher candidates teach activity-based science lessons to small groups of elementary students. The teacher candidates are in groups of three and take on the roles of lead instructor, supporting instructor, and observer. The elementary students rotate to three different centers (for about 15 minutes per center), and, as the elementary students rotate to new centers, the teacher candidates rotate roles. This entire rotation is then repeated with new elementary students so that each pre-service teacher typically has a chance to take on each role twice. Between rotations the authors have deliberately built in time for group reflection—a crucial element of the SCTM. (For a more thorough description of the SCTM see Kittleson, Dresden, & Wenner, 2013). The SCTM exemplifies the designed setting discussed by Lampert (2006, cited in Ball & Forzani, 2009) and was developed to offer the guided practice discussed by Hollins (2011), as well as to give teacher candidates the space to engage in the approximations of practice suggested by the work of Grossman et al. (2009).

CONCLUSIONS AND RECOMMENDATIONS

The review of the literature on clinically rich practices in teacher education, along with personal experiences, has led the authors to conclude that no one strategy, no matter how well-designed or how deeply rooted in the practice of the profession, can fully prepare teacher candidates for their future careers. Instead, it is necessary to investigate the range of possible practice-based approaches and clinically rich practices, and then assemble a group of strategies that meets the needs of a particular group of teacher candidates. This must also be feasible within the context at hand. Teacher educators should consider not only the benefits and possible pitfalls of each strategy but should pay careful attention to the way in which these strategies work together. There are a number of pedagogies of teacher education that "are intended to support teachers' abilities to learn *in* and *from* practice.... However, the interrelationship of these pedagogies to one another is also important. It is possible that these pedagogies may work more powerfully in relationship to one another" (Darling-Hammond, et al., 2005, p. 441).

It is also evident from the literature that clinically rich practices demand a clinical setting. While this may seem obvious, it is far from trivial. Clinically rich practices that engage teacher candidates in direct experiences with P–12 students while under the watchful eye and with the supporting hand of teacher educators cannot occur on a university campus, nor can they occur in a traditional field placement setting. Clinically rich practices require settings that combine the best of "real-life" teaching and a theoretical perspective.

While there are many individuals who possess these dual qualities, institutions must be intentional about attending to both theory and practice—at times, they do not automatically do so. It is this intention that distinguishes PDSs from other schools, no matter how excellent they may be, and it is this focus on the connection of theory and practice that makes PDSs not only an ideal site for the implementation of clinically rich practices but the fertile ground in which these practices can be created and nurtured.

The authors' experiences have clearly shown that it would not be possible to engage teacher candidates in the pedagogical strategies described in this chapter if they were not fortunate enough to have a close working relationship with their partner school, a PDS. For example, it is difficult to imagine schools that were not proud PDSs, allowing 25 teacher candidates to roam their halls with clipboards on a regular basis. Nor is it likely that teachers would volunteer to be observed during teaching rounds if they did not see themselves as integral members of an institution that was profoundly connected to the reform of both P–12 education and teacher education. Thus, the reform of teacher education cannot be achieved in isolation; it is dependent upon close, mutually supportive, and mutually beneficial relationships between schools and universities.

Finally, there is cause for optimism: The current review of the literature has shown that the implementation of well-known clinically rich practices and efforts to create new examples of these pedagogical strategies provide a compelling lesson for teacher educators. It is possible to improve teacher education without dramatic changes to the structure or funding of teacher preparation programs. Through the use of specific clinically rich practices embedded in collaborative contexts, the development of teaching expertise can be facilitated and teacher educators can make a meaningful contribution to the improvement of our nation's educational system.

REFERENCES

American Association of Colleges for Teacher Education. (2011). *Transformations in educator preparation: Effectiveness and accountability*. Washington, DC: Author.

Ball, D. L., & Cohen, D. K. (1999). Developing practice, developing practitioners: Towards a practice-based theory of professional education. In G. Sykes & L. Darling-

Hammond (Eds.), *Teaching as the learning profession: Handbook of policy and practice* (pp. 3–32). San Francisco, CA: Jossey-Bass.

Ball, D. L., & Forzani, F. M. (2009). The work of teaching and the challenge for teacher education. *Journal of Teacher Education, 60*(5), 497–511.

Boyd, D., Grossman, P., Lankford, H., Loeb, S., & Wyckoff, J. (2008). *Teacher preparation and student achievement.* National Center for Analysis of Longitudinal Data in Education Research, Working Paper 20. Washington DC: Urban Institute

Darling-Hammond, L. (2000). How teacher education matters. *Journal of Teacher Education, 51*(3), 166–173.

Darling-Hammond, L. (2006). Constructing 21st century teacher education. *Journal of Teacher Education, 57*(3), 300–314.

Darling-Hammond, L., Hammerness, K., Grossman, P., Rust, F., & Shulman, L. (2005). The design of teacher education programs. In L. Darling-Hammond, J. Bransford, P. LePage, K. Hammerness, & H. Duffy (Eds.), *Preparing teachers for a changing world: What teachers should learn and be able to do* (pp. 390–441). San Francisco, CA: Jossey-Bass.

Dewey, J. (1938). *Experience and education.* New York, NY: Simon and Schuster.

Feiman-Nemser, S. (2001). From preparation to practice: Designing a continuum to strengthen and sustain teaching. *Teachers College Record, 103*(6), 1013–1055.

Feiman-Nemser, S. (2012). *Teachers as learners.* Cambridge, MA: Harvard Education Press.

Goodlad, J. (1994). *Educational renewal: Better teachers, better schools.* San Francisco, CA: Jossey-Bass.

Grossman, P., Compton, C., Igra, D., Ronfeldt, M., Shahan, E., & Williamson, P. W. (2009). Teaching practice: A cross-professional perspective. *Teachers College Record, 111*(9), 2055–2100.

Hollins, E. (2011). Teacher preparation for quality teaching. *Journal of Teacher Education, 62*(4), 395–407.

Howey, K. R. (2011). Response to Section I: What's needed now. In J. E. Neopolitan (Ed.), *Taking stock of professional development schools: What's needed now* (pp. 325–336). Yearbook of the National Society for the Study of Education, Vol. 110. New York, NY: Teachers College.

Kittleson, J., Dresden, J., & Wenner, J. (2013). Describing the 'supported collaborative teaching model': A designed setting to enhance teacher education. *School-University Partnership, 6*(2), 20–31.

Lampert, M. (2006, October). *Designing and developing a program for teaching and learning teaching practice.* Paper presented to the secondary teacher education program faculty. University of Michigan, Ann Arbor.

Lee, P. (2011, July 11). Law schools get practical. *The Wall Street Journal.* Retrieved from http://online.wsj.com

Levine, M. (2010). *Developing principles for clinically based teacher education.* Washington, DC: National Council for the Accreditation of Teacher Education.

Mangan, K. (2012, August 3). Journalism schools are urged to adopt teaching hospitals' approach to hands-on education. *The Chronicle of Higher Education.* Retrieved from http://chronicle.com

National Commission of Excellence in Education. (1983). *A nation at risk: The imperative for educational reform.* Washington, DC: U.S. Government Printing Office.

National Council for Accreditation of Teacher Education (NCATE). (2010). *Transforming teacher education through clinical practice: A national strategy to prepare effective teachers*. Washington DC: Author.

Rutter, A. (2011). Purpose and vision of professional development schools. In J. E. Neopolitan (Ed.), *Taking stock of professional development schools: What's needed now* (pp. 289–305). Yearbook of the National Society for the Study of Education, Vol. 110. New York, NY: Teachers College.

Schön, D. A. (1983). *The reflective practitioner: How professionals think in action.* New York, NY: Basic Books.

Schön, D. A. (1987). *Educating the reflective practitioner*. San Francisco, CA: Jossey-Bass.

Segal, D. (2011, November 19). What they don't teach law students: Lawyering. *The New York Times*. Retrieved from http://www.nytimes.com

Stodolsky, S. (1988). *The subject matters: Classroom activity in math and social studies*. Chicago, IL: The University of Chicago Press.

Thompson, S., & Cooner, D. D. (2001). Grand rounds—not just for doctors. *Action in Teacher Education, 23*(3), 84–88.

Zeichner, K. (2010). Rethinking the connections between campus courses and field experiences in college- and university-based teacher education. *Journal of Teacher Education, 61*(1-2), 89–99.

CHAPTER 4

STUDENT ACHIEVEMENT FROM ANCHOR ACTION RESEARCH STUDIES IN HIGH-NEEDS, URBAN PROFESSIONAL DEVELOPMENT SCHOOLS: A META-ANALYSIS

William Curlette, Robert Hendrick, Susan Ogletree, and Gwendolyn Benson

ABSTRACT

Clinical teaching employed through anchor action research (AAR) studies helps to evaluate teacher preparation efforts in professional development schools (PDSs) through K–12 student achievement. As a part of the teacher–intern–professor (TIP) group, the intern participates in the planning and delivery of a unit of instruction that uses a pretest and posttest as assessments. This study contributes a summary of 10 AAR studies in PDSs which overall have a statistically significant effect size for student achievement using meta-analysis. The results show that Cohen's *d* effect size

Creating Visions for University-School Partnerships, pages 61–72.
Copyright © 2014 by Information Age Publishing
All rights of reproduction in any form reserved.

between groups is .387 in favor of the PDS TIP Groups, which is typical of effect sizes of meta-syntheses of educational interventions. Thus, this study demonstrates a clinical approach to teaching combined with a statistical approach to overcome small sample sizes through meta-analysis to show student academic achievement gains in PDSs.

Although support for professional development schools (PDSs) is found in many quarters, there tends to be a lack of quantitative evidence for increasing student academic achievement in K–12 classrooms. To address this need, a clinical teaching approach was investigated, consisting of intern(s), a mentor teacher, and a professor working with a unit of instruction in a K–12 classroom. This was combined with a method for summarizing the studies—meta-analysis. The research was conducted in the Network for Enhancing Teacher Quality (NET-Q), a PDS partnership, which prepares beginning teachers in urban high-needs partnership schools.

Developed over the past six years, the approach used to evaluate K–12 student learning during NET-Q teaching internships at this university is called teacher–intern–professor (TIP) groups with anchor action research (AAR) (Curlette & Ogletree, 2011). The anchor action research study is a quasi-experimental study using an intern's class with TIP compared to another class in the same school without the TIP Group approach. Though other interns or student teachers who are not affiliated with the NET-Q partnership may be active within the schools, this evaluation measures student achievement within NET-Q PDS classrooms. For each TIP with AAR study, the same teacher-made pretest and posttest are employed in both classes, and all comparison classroom teachers are fully certified. More specifically, the purposes of this chapter are the following: (1) to describe the TIP (teacher–intern–professor) approach with AAR (anchor action research), and (2) to provide a summary of TIP with AAR studies using meta-analysis.

As will be seen, this approach to clinical teaching in PDSs results in an overall summary of 10 studies in K–12 classrooms showing statistically significant gains in student achievement using teacher-made achievement pretests and posttests even though the sample sizes for each study tend to be small. As far as can be determined, this is the first publication that shows the use of meta-analysis to summarize the overall effectiveness of TIP with AAR. This study, therefore, addresses the gap in the literature related to evaluating this approach for obtaining student achievement in PDSs and their classrooms.

PERSPECTIVE

A discussion of the benefits of clinical teaching can be found in Bohan and Many's (2011) book titled *Clinical Teacher Education: Reflections from an Urban Professional Development School Network*. Another perspective for TIP groups with AAR is support for the action research approach, which values participants conducting research to improve their teaching practices (Hendricks, 2009). The TIP

Group approach is consistent with Darling-Hammond and Richardson's (2009) position that asserts the importance of professional development in communities of practice. A further description of the TIP with AAR can be found in a chapter by Curlette and Ogletree (2011) in an edited book by Bohan and Many.

Although scarce, some empirical results supporting achievement in PDSs have been cited by Teitel (1999a, 1999b) in the Benedum collaborative study. One finding in the Benedum collaborative study was that student achievement in mathematics as assessed by effect size was larger for students who had attended a PDS compared to students who had not attended a PDS. Another study that provided some limited support for achievement in PDSs was reported by Houston, Hollis, Clay, Ligons, and Roff (1999). Among their findings was that in the year after becoming a PDS, 14 of the 16 now PDSs showed an increase in reading means, and all 16 PDSs had an increase in means for mathematics. In general, qualitative studies have indicated the positive effects of PDS on student achievement; however, limited evidence of positive effects using quantitative methods within PDS has been published (Vescio, Ross, & Adams, 2008).

TIP (Teacher–Intern–Professor) Groups with AAR (Anchor Action Research)

TIP groups are designed to help engage mentor teachers with university professors to enhance instructional design and planning by the teacher candidate or intern for a unit of instruction (typically two weeks to six weeks). The AAR study is a quasi-experimental study using an intern's class (with a TIP group) compared to another class in the same school using the same teacher-made pretest and posttest which are constructed by the TIP group for both classes following the prescribed curriculum. The teacher in the comparison class concurs with the appropriateness of both the pretest and posttest. More specifically, a comparison of the teaching effectiveness in terms of student achievement is obtained by comparing the change from the pretest to posttest achievement means of the students in the TIP classroom(s) with the mean change of students in the comparison classroom(s). TIP groups may also help improve teachers' abilities to collect, analyze, and use data for instruction and decision making in addition to providing an opportunity for the intern to demonstrate student achievement related to her or his teaching.

The TIP group unites the leadership and instructional experience of the mentor teacher and professor with the abilities of the intern to help to prepare instruction and facilitate student achievement and meets the five essential characteristics of a professional learning community defined by Vescio et al. (2008). These five essential characteristics are (1) developing shared values, (2) focusing on student learning, (3) engaging in reflective dialogue, (4) making teaching public, and (5) focusing on collaboration. AAR is a form of action research that is anchored in three aspects:

(1) Through commonalities among the studies in methodology, primarily quasi-experimental designs, and (2) through the use of a general construct underlying the outcome measures (which for education is typically defined as student academic achievement outcome variables). There is a third anchor (3) which is that the projects attend to participants' inquiry skills and data interpretation abilities. (Curlette & Ogletree, 2011, p. 120)

This innovative approach to instruction within the PDS can take many forms and is dependent on the expert guidance of the mentor teacher and professor and the delivery by the intern. The expectation is that the intern-delivered instruction will be as effective as (or even more effective than) the comparison class instruction for influencing a gain in mean student achievement.

USING META-ANALYSIS TO SUMMARIZE
TIP WITH AAR STUDIES

In order to summarize quantitatively the 10 TIP with AAR studies across different outcome measures, a summary statistic that measures the results of the studies on a common scale is needed. In meta-analysis, the summary statistic is an effect size which for the TIP with AAR studies is the difference of two means divided by a standard deviation. For example, if the effect size were 1, this would imply that the average TIP group student scored one standard deviation higher than the average comparison group student. In this research, the two means are the mean of the gain scores for the TIP group and the mean of the gain scores for the comparison group. The standard deviation in the effect size measure is obtained from the pooled variance of the gain scores. The particular effect size employed in this research is Cohen's *d*.

By summarizing AAR studies using meta-analysis, three of the challenges that are present in AAR studies are overcome. First, action research studies conducted in classrooms typically suffer from small sample sizes; consequently, there is a tendency to have lower statistical power than desired given the other quantities typically employed in power calculations in student achievement research. Meta-analysis essentially takes into account the sample sizes in each action research study during the process of weighing each study in the summary across studies, which is reported as an overall effect size. Thus, the small sample sizes in particular action research studies and resulting lower statistical power become less critical because the summary statistic in meta-analysis, an overall effect size, is based on all the studies.

Second, another challenge when drawing conclusions from one particular anchor action research study is generalizing the results across classroom settings, different achievement tests, teachers, community contexts, and student populations. By summarizing across different studies that are similar, meta-analysis increases the generalizability of the findings. Although the following quote is from a text on meta-analysis methodology in medical research, the idea that meta-analysis enhances the generalizability of findings is inherent in meta-analyses across content areas. "Meta-analysis, by including studies carried out in different places, possibly with different entry criteria, may also produce more generalizable results which average over a range of settings and contexts" (Sutton, Abrams, Jones, Sheldon, & Song, 2000, p. 11). It should be noted that in this NET-Q PDS research, the similarity of the studies is addressed to some extent by the nature of the TIP with AAR structure.

Third, in anchor action research as well as other types of research, the impact of study characteristics that are unique to a particular study, and thus constant for that study, cannot be statistically evaluated using only the data within that study. However, meta-analysis allows these study characteristics to be investigated as long as they vary across studies with the possibility that some may become moderator variables.

EXAMPLE OF TIP WITH AAR STUDY

To explain further the TIP with AAR studies and the type of study summarized in the meta-analysis, one study from the meta-analysis, AAR_8, was selected to provide an example of a TIP group and the type of research study employed in an AAR. The TIP classroom was a tenth-grade mathematics class at an urban high school with a predominately Hispanic population (53%). The unit of instruction in the TIP class had a duration of two weeks. The intern, in consultation with the mentor teacher and a professor, selected a unit that addressed completing the square, using the quadratic formula, interpreting solutions to the quadratic equation from the result of the discriminant, and graphing quadratic inequalities. The TIP group addressed the fact that many of the students had English as a second language and were currently in ELL classes. This characteristic of the class caused the intern to provide the students with guided notes, to use color coding and highlighting during note taking activities, and to require that students create graphic organizers for step-by-step directions. The intervention in this class also included the interactive use of a Smartboard at which students, arranged in dyads, would utilize the quadratic formula to find solutions and to explain the steps they took to solve the equation.

In the comparison class, the teacher taught as she typically did using lecture and note taking, but did not use color coding, highlighting, or step-by-step directions. In other words, in the comparison class the teacher taught the way she normally did. Furthermore, students in the comparison class assumed a rather passive role in the teaching and learning process, with the teacher making most of the presentations about subject matter.

The teacher in the comparison classroom was between 41 and 45 years old, held a specialist degree, had more than 10 years teaching experience, and was a highly qualified teacher. Similarly, the teacher in the TIP classroom was 41 to 45 years of age, held a master's degree, had more than 10 years teaching experience, and was a highly qualified teacher. The content taught in both classes was prescribed by the Georgia Performance Standards for this specific tenth-grade mathematics subject.

The pretest and posttest assessment that consisted of 13 items was administered to the students in the TIP and the comparison classrooms. For the TIP class there were 21 students who took both the pretest and posttest assessments. The students' mean on the pretest was 29.95 (SD = 14.78), and the students' mean on the posttest was 68.9 (SD = 23.34). The TIP class mean gain between the pretest and posttest assessments was 38.95 (SD = 29.43). For the comparison class there were 19 students who took both the pretest and posttest assessments. The students' mean on the pretest was 44.58 (SD = 19.68), and their mean for the posttest was 60.79 (SD = 16.33). The comparison class mean gain between the pretest and posttest assessments was 16.21 (SD = 20.60).

The formula for the calculation of Cohen's d is

$$d = \frac{\bar{x}_1 - \bar{x}_2}{\sqrt{\dfrac{(n_1 - 1)s_1^2 + (n_2 - 1)s_2^2}{n_1 + n_2 - 2}}}$$

TABLE 4.1. Statistics for Each of the Ten Studies in the Meta-Analysis

		TIP Classes			Comparison Classes		Effect Size	SE	95% Confidence Interval		
Study Name	N	Mean	SD	N	Mean	SD			Lower	Upper	Weight
AAR_1 (2012)	26	36.31	15.13	19	32.89	22.06	0.186	0.302	– 0.407	0.779	0.117
AAR_2 (2012)	15	27.67	14.62	15	35.13	12.05	– 0.557	0.373	– 1.287	0.174	0.077
AAR_3 (2012)	10	24.00	19.12	12	17.08	9.40	0.474	0.435	– 0.378	1.326	0.057
AAR_4 (2012)	27	28.89	17.61	25	21.60	14.05	0.456	0.281	– 0.096	1.007	0.136
AAR_5 (2012)	23	32.17	17.41	21	19.10	19.29	0.713	0.312	0.102	1.324	0.111
AAR_6 (2012)	22	46.14	18.77	20	37.25	18.53	0.477	0.314	– 0.138	1.091	0.109
AAR_7 (2012)	16	26.88	14.93	13	20.77	17.06	0.384	0.377	– 0.355	1.123	0.076
AAR_8 (2011)	21	38.95	29.43	19	16.21	20.60	0.887	0.333	0.235	1.539	0.097
AAR_9 (2011)	15	35.20	19.19	21	26.71	17.41	0.467	0.343	– 0.204	1.139	0.091
AAR_10 (2011)	22	33.00	17.80	27	28.33	19.11	0.252	0.288	– 0.313	0.817	0.129

	Effect Size	95% Confidence Interval		T^2	H	I^2	Q	DF	P-Value
Pooled	0.387	0.165	0.609	0.020	1.089	0.156	10.667	9.000	0.299

where $\bar{x}_1$ is the mean gain score of the n_1 students in the TIP Group classroom and $\bar{x}_2$ is the mean gain score of the n_2 students in the comparison group classroom. The variances of the gain scores for the TIP and comparison classrooms are denoted as s_1^2 and s_2^2, respectively. Substituting the values for the TIP and comparison classes from Table 4.1 we get,

$$d = \frac{38.95 - 16.21}{\sqrt{\dfrac{(21-1)(29.43)^2 + (19-1)(20.6)^2}{21+19-2}}} = 0.887$$

As can be seen in Figure 4.1, the effect size for AAR_8 is reported as .887. This implies that the typical TIP student in AAR_8 scored .887 of a standard deviation on the gain scores for the student achievement measure higher than the typical student in the comparison class.

There was a significant difference between the pretest means for the TIP and comparison classes ($t = 2.674$, $p = 0.011$, $\alpha = 0.05$), according to an independent

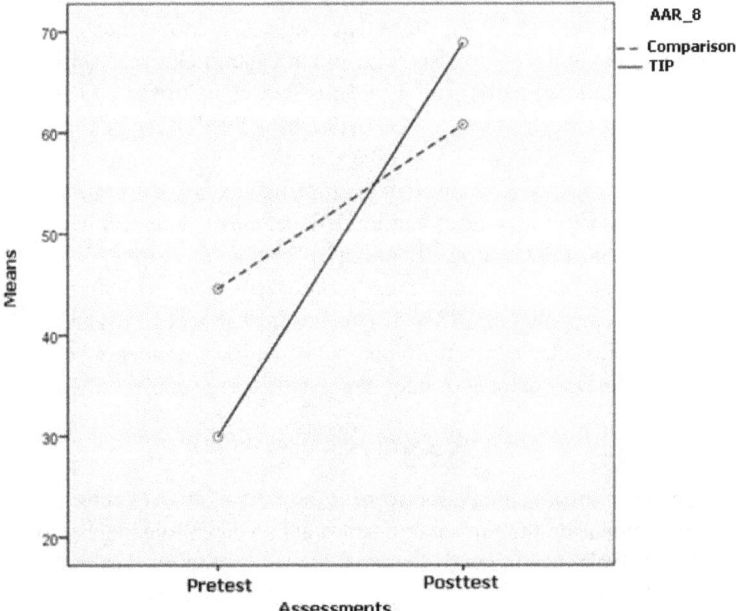

FIGURE 4.1.   Pretest and posttest assessments of the AAR_8 TIP and comparison classes

t-test. This possibly indicates that the groups were slightly different due to the selection process or the students' histories regarding previous instruction. There was no significant difference between the posttest means for both groups. A repeated measures ANOVA indicated that a statistically significant interaction between the groups was found ($F = 7.854$, $p = 0.008$, $\alpha = 0.05$). The interaction is shown on the graph in Figure 4.1 by the crossing of the pretest and posttest assessment lines. Incidentally, according to Shadish, Cook, and Campbell (2002, p. 143), an interaction outcome in this type of quasi-experimental research design is "particularly amenable to causal interpretation," implying more likelihood of attribution of the change to the TIP group. The mean gain for the TIP group between pretest and posttest was 38.95, and the mean gain for the comparison class between pretest and posttest scores was 16.21. Due to the significant interaction using the repeated measures ANOVA, two dependent *t*-tests, one for each class, were conducted on the pretest to posttest gain scores to see the main effects. Both the TIP and comparison class gains were shown to be statistically significant ($t = 6.065$, $df = 20$, $p < 0.001$ and $t = 3.431$, $df = 18$, $p = 0.003$). This analysis supports reporting an effect size in favor of the TIP class; this is .887 in AAR_8.

DATA SOURCES

The meta-analysis data were collected over a two-year period from 2010 to 2012 and comprised 10 NET-Q AAR studies that met the inclusion criteria of having a pretest and posttest and a comparison classroom. Other inclusion criteria were that there were more than 20 participating students in each pair of treatment and comparison classes, the intervention or treatment was defined, the grade level was between fourth and eleventh grade, the subject area was science or mathematics, and the pretest and posttest were equivalent instruments. Each pretest and posttest was deemed to be based upon subject and grade-level curriculum and have construct validity based upon the Georgia Performance Standards. In total, 389 individual students' pretest and posttest assessment scores were included within the 10 TIP with AAR studies ranging from 22 to 52 students in each set of TIP and comparison classrooms. Studies selected for the report have met the aforementioned criteria as confirmed by LiveText, records of interviews, and other documentation.

META-ANALYSIS RESULTS

An assessment of the teaching effectiveness in terms of student achievement was obtained by comparing the pretest to posttest achievement mean gains of the students in the TIP classrooms with the mean gains of students in the comparison classrooms. The method to analyze the data was random effects meta-analysis (Borenstein, Hedges, Higgins, & Rothstein, 2009; Morris, 2008). In Table 4.1, the means and standard deviations (*SD*) on the teacher-made achievement tests are given for each of the 10 studies in the meta-analysis. In the last row of Table 4.1, the estimated total Cohen's *d* effect size is 0.387. The tau-squared (τ^2) statistic indicates the variance between studies, which is low; H and I^2 statistics are measures of the heterogeneity within a meta-analysis. H values near 1 indicate low heterogeneity and I^2 indicates the amount of variability due to heterogeneity and not sampling error, which is low for this meta-analysis. Finally, the Q statistic tests for heterogeneity ($Q = 10.667$, $df = 9$, $p = 0.299$), which is not statistically significant, indicating that one may consider using fixed effects; however, due to the varying treatment and increased generalizability, random effects meta-analysis was employed.

The overall mean difference effect size for the random effects meta-analysis is .387 with a confidence interval from .165 to .609 (see bottom of Table 4.1), which is a substantial and statistically significant effect size in favor of the TIP group. In other words, the typical student in a TIP group classroom gained .387 of a standard deviation, based on the achievement measures in the meta-analysis, more than the typical student in a comparison classroom. This finding supports the qualitative research that PDSs have a positive influence on student achievement and is consistent with previous meta-syntheses examining student achievement. These findings show that the PDS teacher preparation using the TIP with AAR within these 10 studies produces beginning teachers who are as effective as or slightly more effective in facilitating student achievement than teachers in comparison classrooms in a unit of instruction.

A forest plot (Figure 4.2) is used to illustrate the weight and mean gain comparison of the 10 studies within the random effects meta-analysis. As shown within the forest plot, there was a negative gain in only one (AAR_2) of the 10 TIP and comparison class studies, which indicates that in AAR_2 the comparison class had a higher mean gain than the TIP class. In the AAR_2 study, a repeated measures ANOVA indicated that although there was a significant increase from pretest mean to posttest mean in both groups ($F = 158.054$, $p < 0.001$, $\alpha = 0.05$), no statistically significant interaction between the groups and time of testing was found. The mean gain for the TIP group in the AAR_2 study between pretest mean and posttest mean was 27.667, and the mean gain for the comparison class between pretest and posttest means was 35.133. The difference in the mean gain in favor of the comparison class resulted in a moderate negative effect size for AAR_2. The results indicate that the intern, although successful in the student gain between pretest and posttest means, did not influence a student gain in the AAR_2 study between the TIP AAR_2 class greater than the student gain influenced by the teacher in the AAR_2 comparison class. A negative mean difference effect size of –0.557 was found using Cohen's d in AAR_2 and recorded in the meta-analysis.

The random effects meta-analysis assumes that the observed estimates of the TIP AAR effects can vary across studies because of different teaching strategies used within each study, as well as some variability within each class. Such heterogeneity in treatment effects is caused by uncontrolled differences in the target classes, interventions received (teaching strategies), lengths of the unit, and other factors (Riley, Higgins, & Deeks, 2011).

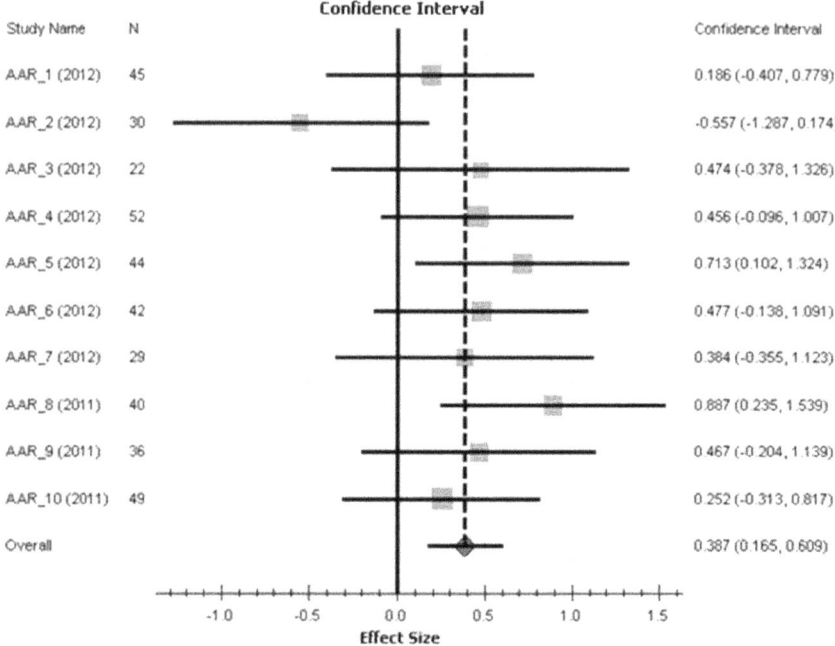

FIGURE 4.2.   Forest plot of ten anchor action research studies.

In the forest plot, the 95% confidence intervals for each study's effect size are reported both with a line and with numerical values. If the confidence interval covers zero, then the reported effect size is not significantly different from zero. Only two studies (i.e., AAR_5 and AAR_8) are statistically significant as stand-alone studies. Nevertheless, when all studies are considered, the overall effect is .387 with a confidence interval from .165 to .609, which does not cover zero.

This statistically significant .387 overall effect size produced by the random ef-fects meta-analysis results of these 10 AAR studies closely relates to the effect sizes (.375 and .40) referenced by large meta-syntheses conducted during the last couple of decades related to educational interventions and student achievement (Hattie, 1992; Sipe & Curlette, 1996). This is noteworthy because the intern using the TIP with AAR approach does not simply equal the comparison group teacher in student achievement but outperforms the comparison group teacher in the unit of instruc-tion evaluated. The findings of the PDS NET-Q partnership, using clinical teaching through TIP with AAR, compared to other overall effect sizes for educational inter-ventions show an effect size (.387) typical in the published literature, thus providing evidence for a PDS approach for improving student achievement.

CONCLUSIONS

The goal of TIP with AAR is to inform the PDS process of preparing beginning teachers who are as effective as or more effective at facilitating student achievement as the comparison teachers. In this research, we have shown that the TIP with AAR approach produced student academic achievement gains for a unit of instruction that exceeded the gains of students taught by comparison group teachers. Thus, for the data in this study, this clinical teaching approach for interns in PDSs has been shown to work. One indicator of the success of the interns' educational programs that included the TIP with AAR studies reported here is that all interns were hired by the NET-Q PDS partnership school districts during a time when employment opportunities for new teachers tended to be scarce.

Finally, the lessons learned over the past six years have refined the TIP with AAR approach for clinical teaching in urban settings. These lessons include revising the steps for data collection, focusing on effect sizes from a meta-analysis perspective, looking at study characteristics for moderator variables, and increasing TIP group members' exposure to action research. Given the success of the TIP with AAR meta-analysis, additional comparisons with only interns and mentor teachers providing instruction in traditional classrooms could help clarify the influence of the PDS approach. Furthermore, we are also investigating the possible increase in research knowledge from belonging to a TIP with AAR group through qualitative interviews. Future efforts may involve conducting more TIP with AAR studies and perhaps implementing a cumulative meta-analysis approach.

NOTE

This meta-analysis was made available through the Network for Enhancing Teacher Quality (NET-Q) Partnership, which is a federal Teacher Quality Partnership (TQP) Grant awarded by the U. S. Department of Education. The contents do not necessarily represent the policy of the Department of Education, and you should not assume endorsement by the Federal Government.

REFERENCES

Bohan, C., & Many, J. (2011). *Clinical teacher education: Reflections from an urban professional development school network.* Charlotte, NC: Information Age Publishing.

Borenstein, M., Hedges, L., Higgins, J., & Rothstein, H. (2009). *Introduction to meta-analysis.* Chichester, UK: John Wiley & Sons, Ltd.

Curlette, W., & Ogletree, A. (2011). An approach to increasing student achievement: Teacher-intern-professor groups with anchor action research. In C. Haeussler Bohan & J. Many (Eds.), *Clinical teacher education: Reflections from an urban professional development school network* (pp. 117–127). Charlotte, NC: Information Age Publishing.

Darling-Hammond, L., & Richardson, N. (2009). Teacher learning: What matters? *Educational Leadership, 66,* 46–53.

Hattie, J. (1992). Measuring the effects of schooling. *Australian Journal of Education, 36,* 5–13.

Hendricks, C. (2009). *Improving schools through action research: A comprehensive guide for educators* (2ⁿᵈ ed.). Upper Saddle River, NJ: Pearson.

Houston, W. R., Hollis, L. Y., Clay, D., Ligons, C. M., & Roff, I. (1999). Effects of collaboration on urban teacher education programs and professional development schools. In D. M. Byrd & J. McIntyre (Eds.), *Research on Professional development schools: Teacher Education Yearbook VII* (pp. 6–28). Thousand Oaks, CA: Corwin.

Morris, S. B. (2008). Estimating effect sizes from pretest-posttest-control group designs. *Organizational Research Methods,* 364–386. doi: 10.1177/1094428106291059.

Riley, R. D., Higgins, J. P. T., & Deeks, J. J. (2011). Interpretation of random effects meta-analyses. *BMJ, 342(7804), 964.* Retrieved from http://www.bmj.com/content/342/bmj.d549. doi: http:dx/doi.org/101136/bmj.d549

Sipe, T. A., & Curlette, W. L. (1996). A meta-synthesis of factors related to educational achievement: A methodological approach to summarizing and synthesizing meta-analyses. *International Journal of Educational Research, 25*(7) 583–660.

Shadish, W., Cook, T., & Campbell, D. (2002). *Experimental and quasi-experimental designs for generalized causal inference.* Boston, MA: Houghton Mifflin Company.

Sutton, A., Abrams, K., Jones, D., Sheldon, T., & Song, F. (2000). *Methods for meta-analysis in medical research.* Chichester, UK: Wiley.

Teitel, I. (1999a). *How professional development schools make a difference: A review of research.* Washington, DC: National Council for the Accreditation of Teacher Education.

Teitel, I. (1999b). An assessment framework for professional development schools. *Journal of Teacher Education, 52*(1), 57–71.

Vescio, V., Ross, D., & Adams, A. (2008). A review of research on the impact of professional learning communities on teaching practice and student learning. *Teaching and Teacher Education, 24*(1), 80–91.

CHAPTER 5

ASSESSING TEACHER QUALITY AND TEACHER EFFECTIVENESS THROUGH PROFESSIONAL DEVELOPMENT SCHOOL PARTNERSHIPS

Sally Yahnke, M. Gail Shroyer, and Amanda Morales

ABSTRACT

This chapter provides one example of a professional development school (PDS) partnership and the process used to design and restructure the way preservice teachers are prepared to ensure that all students can have the effective teachers they deserve. More specifically, the focus is the story of change within a PDS partnership to respond to local, state, and national challenges to more authentically define and assess what effective teachers should know and be able to do.

Since the 1980s, the United States government has been increasingly focused on accountability in public education. While initial focus was aimed at K–12 school systems, the institutions of higher education that prepare teachers working in the

Creating Visions for University-School Partnerships, pages 73–86.
Copyright © 2014 by Information Age Publishing
All rights of reproduction in any form reserved.

schools have come under scrutiny more and more over the past 20 years. Many point to the lack of accountability in teacher-education programs that continue to provide traditional, primarily coursework-based models, "despite decades of research concluding that hands-on experience focused on student achievement and guided by expert educators is the key to producing high-quality teachers" (Wasburn-Moses, 2013, para. 4). Barnett (1992) indicates that now "with greater expectations being placed on it, higher education is being obliged to examine itself or be examined by others" (p. 16). This requirement has led colleges of education to be more responsive, redesigning the structure of their programs to provide increased quality, field-based experiences and to assess more effectively the impact on and outcomes of students' performance (Alexander, 2000; Barnett, 1999).

This chapter provides one example of a professional development school (PDS) partnership designed to restructure the way we prepare teachers to ensure that all students can have the effective teachers they deserve. More specifically, we will focus on the story of change within the PDS partnership to respond to local, state, and national challenges to more authentically define and assess what effective teachers should know and be able to do.

DEVELOPMENT OF THE PROFESSIONAL DEVELOPMENT SCHOOL PARTNERSHIP

The Kansas State University (KSU) professional development school (PDS) partnership began in 1989. Before the formalization of this partnership, KSU had engaged in numerous other partnerships with local school districts. These partnerships had revolved around providing professional development opportunities for practicing teachers and administrators. The initial preparation of preservice teachers had not surfaced as a common need for both university and school faculty members. But a professional development project in 1988, designed to enhance the way practicing teachers were teaching science, mathematics, and technology, led to challenging conversations about needed changes in the initial preparation of preservice teachers in science, mathematics, and technology. The practicing teachers believed their current practices would have been stronger if their initial preparation had been stronger. School district and university faculty began to recognize the continuous flow of preservice into inservice teacher preparation and this led to further conversations regarding the inseparable link between K–12 school education and 13–16 college education. Educational partners across the K–16 continuum ultimately agreed that improvement in one part of the system was not possible without improvements across the entire system. Through these initial conversations between school district and university faculty, the concept of K–16 simultaneous improvement become the cornerstone of the PDS partnership that was to emerge the following year.

The early concept of K–16 simultaneous improvement resulted in a proposal and funding from the National Science Foundation to improve the mathematics, science, and technology (MST) teacher preparation program at KSU while also enhancing the MST instruction of practicing elementary teachers from the partner school district. This grant provided the opportunity for university faculty from both the college of education and the college of arts and sciences to work with teachers and administrators from three Manhattan-Ogden 383 elementary schools to conceptualize ideal MST teaching and learning at the elementary level and, consequently, to rethink the MST teaching and learning required in content courses, methods courses, and field experience at the university level to better prepare elementary teachers for enhanced MST teaching. By 1990, three elementary PDSs had been established, three clinical instructors had been selected to coordinate work within each PDS, a PDS coordinator and cooperating teachers had been identified, and university and school partners had formed planning teams to support their collaborations.

ASSESSMENT CHALLENGES

One of the first challenges faced by the initial PDS planning teams was how to assess teaching and learning of preservice teacher candidates. PDS partners were creating a collaborative vision for teaching at the elementary school level, but struggled to articulate what elementary teachers should know and be able to do to reach this vision. Existing assessment practices for preservice teacher candidates included formative classroom observations during student teaching and the completion of a generic checklist *final evaluation* at the end of student teaching. The observational process was not standardized, and formal observations were completed only by university supervisors. Notes and suggestions were recorded on triplicate paper with a copy left for the cooperating teacher and the student teacher. The cooperating teacher was encouraged to provide regular feedback to the student teacher, but this process was not formalized. The university supervisor and the cooperating teacher both completed final evaluations, but they were completed separately, based on their own unique perspectives of good teaching.

As the partnership continued to grow and new elementary, middle, and high schools and districts were added to the partnership, a consistent and fair system of authentic assessment was needed. All those responsible for assessing preservice teacher candidates at the university as well as within the PDS needed to collaboratively decide what new teachers should know and be able to do and how this would be assessed. In addition, the preservice teacher candidates themselves needed to know, upon entry into the teacher education program, expectations for the knowledge and skills they needed to demonstrate by the end of the program.

MEETING THE CHALLENGE THROUGH AN AUTHENTIC ASSESSMENT SYSTEM

Change within a PDS teacher education partnership is dependent upon the multiple stakeholders that make up this complex system. But change with any teacher education program also is dependent upon state and national issues and trends. The following example of designing an authentic assessment system for our teacher education program demonstrates the complex process of managing state and national standards, policies, and recommendations while also meeting the unique needs of PDS partners. A performance-based portfolio model and an evidence-based observation process allowed us to meet our local challenge for authentic assessment while addressing growing national concerns for improvements and accountability in teacher education.

A PERFORMANCE-BASED PORTFOLIO MODEL

Several elementary teachers practicing in the first three PDSs had been early adopters of authentic assessments in their own classrooms. Based on the concept of simultaneous improvement, they suggested that a portfolio assessment system was needed for the preservice teacher candidates practicing within their schools. These teachers designed the original portfolio requirements for elementary preservice teacher candidates, based on their own experiences using portfolio assessments. This initial portfolio was a compilation of teaching artifacts based on the teachers' definitions of good teaching. Secondary education did not have a formalized portfolio at all. If the secondary preservice teacher candidates completed a portfolio, it was based on expectations of individual content faculty and not shared across the program.

In recognizing a need for change, clinical instructors, university faculty, and cooperating teachers began to explore the use of performance-based portfolios for assessing teaching practices. Over a period of several years, portfolio assessment systems were being developed across the nation and KSU. PDS partners examined many of these systems, including the Teacher Assessment Project (TAP) at Stanford University, the portfolio entries from National Board for Professional Teaching Standards (NBPTS), the work of the Interstate New Teacher Assessment and Support Consortium (INTASC), and the performance-based portfolio system for preservice teachers developed at Ball State University. This was not an easy process, as not all stakeholders agreed on the use of portfolios as an effective way to assess teaching.

After over a year of study and discussions between the college and PDS faculty and administrators and multiple variations of the model, a performance-based portfolio was officially implemented in 2003 and required of all KSU elementary and secondary preservice teacher candidates. The portfolio was designed around the characteristics of effective teaching outlined in *Enhancing Professional Practice—A Framework for Teaching* (FFT) by Charlotte Danielson (1996). The portfolio consisted of four entries based on the FFT: (1) Planning and Preparation, (2) Classroom Environment, (3) Instruction, and (4) Professionalism. Preservice teacher candidates completed the portfolio during their 16-week student teaching semester. It included several inquiries designed to provide examples of both student and teacher work that illustrated key features of a teacher's practice.

In 2005, a statewide teacher work sample, the Kansas Performance Assessment (KPA), was developed for beginning teachers based on the newly adopted state professional teaching standards (slightly modified INTASC standards). Teachers were required to complete the KPA during the first two years of their practice to be fully licensed to teach. The KSU portfolio was examined and aligned with the statewide teacher assessment system to ensure the KSU preservice teachers would be prepared to successfully complete the KPA once they began teaching. Many components of the KSU portfolio were retained in the revision, including the four entries based on Danielson's FFT. However, these entries and the rubrics to assess each entry were revised to more thoroughly align with the new state professional teaching standards. From 2005 to 2010, the KSU portfolio was continually refined and revised as the PDS coordinators worked with faculty and clinical instructors to establish validity and reliability of the portfolio assessment system.

In 2010, the state revised their new teacher work sample to become the Kansas Performance Teaching Portfolio (KPTP). The KPTP was designed with assistance from Educational Testing Services (ETS) to align with the revised InTASC standards. In addition, based on suggestions from district superintendents, the KPTP was designed to be completed as part of preservice teacher preparation programs rather than completed during the first two years of teaching. Once again, the KSU portfolio was revised and aligned with the state KPTP. The portfolio KSU that preservice teacher candidates complete today still maintains many of the original entries from the initial portfolio. The final portfolio consists of six different entries and must be completed by the end of the 16-week student internship.

The first entry in the portfolio, Professional and Philosophical Platform, allows the preservice teacher candidate the opportunity to provide evidence of his or her understanding of educational foundations and essential dispositions. The preservice teacher candidates are asked to synthesize their educational perspectives, as well as their knowledge and beliefs about teaching and learning, in order to create a personal rationale for their approach to teaching.

In the second entry, Contextual Information and Implications for Student Learning, preservice teacher candidates are asked to provide evidence of their understanding of students and to identify contextual information (race/ethnicity, exceptionality, gender, cultural and linguistic diversity, and socioeconomic factors), as well as the possible impact these factors have on teaching and learning in their classroom. Preservice teacher candidates then describe adaptations and/or equitable teaching strategies designed to address each contextual factor identified. In addition, each preservice teacher candidate identifies two focus students with unique needs related to exceptionalities, cultural and linguistic diversity, and/or socioeconomic background. The preservice teacher candidate then must track these focus students closely throughout their internship and identify specific plans to meet their unique needs. They also must identify environmental factors within the school and community—such as rural or urban environments and the presence of military connected families—and develop strategies for differentiating their instruction to fit each unique environmental factor identified.

The third entry in the portfolio, the Instructional Unit Plan, is the heart of the portfolio, and it includes the design, implementation, assessment of and reflection on a multiweek instructional unit plan. The information documented under contextual information must be applied to the preservice teacher candidate's curricular, instructional, and assessment practices. After each lesson and unit is taught, the candidate is asked to disaggregate assessment data to look for achievement gaps based on the contextual factors identified for her or his class. Assessment data also are analyzed for both of the focus students, and the preservice teacher candidate then identifies future steps to help each student achieve the desired educational outcomes.

The final component of the third entry is a self-evaluation of the instructional unit. In this reflection, the preservice teacher candidate is asked to assess his or her teaching during the unit and its impact on student learning and to indicate how he or she will use this information to plan future learning opportunities. Candidates also identify their strengths and weaknesses, particularly in terms of helping each student succeed. Preservice teacher candidates are asked to identify professional development needed to improve their practice and to describe the next steps they will take to enhance their own teaching.

Portfolio entry four, Analysis of Classroom Learning Environments, asks the preservice candidate to provide evidence that indicates that they have created a learning environment that encourages positive social interactions, interactive engagement in learning, and student self-motivation and responsibility. The preservice teacher candidate provides evidence of what actions they have taken during their student internship semester to build and maintain a positive learning environment.

The fifth entry in the portfolio, Formal Observations, provides the opportunity for the preservice teacher candidate to demonstrate their competence in instruction. Using Danielson's Framework for Teaching as the supervision model, student interns are observed at least five times throughout the semester and all five observations are included in the final portfolio; including one observation from the multiweek unit.

The final and sixth entry in the portfolio, Professional Logs, requires the preservice teacher candidate to document the contributions they made to the school, district, and profession as a whole, including communication with families and the larger community. For each one of these categories, the preservice teacher candidate is asked to identify professional strengths and weaknesses, to establish personal goals to continue to grow professionally, and to provide a plan for achieving each goal.

The final student intern portfolio is assessed using a checklist and rubric. The preservice teacher candidate must achieve at least 80% of the total points possible on their completed portfolio. Two years ago, in 2011, the PDS partners decided to set higher expectations for all teacher candidates related to specific components within entry three, the Instructional Unit Plan. Candidates now must earn all total points available to demonstrate proficiency in writing learning goals and objectives, developing an instructional design, and analyzing their assessment data, and self-evaluation within the instructional unit. This was done to ensure that candidates are prepared to meet the challenges they will face during their first year of teaching.

As we continued to improve and refine our performance-based portfolio process, we applied the concepts of backward design (Wiggins & McTighe, 2005) and developed a portfolio for each of the three semester-long field experiences that precede the final internship experience. These field experience portfolios prepare the preservice candidates by having them complete various components of the final portfolio before the student internship semester. In addition, the partnership leaders work annually with clinical instructors from partner districts and faculty to maintain the validity and reliability of the entire assessment process (to be described under "The Critical Role of the Clinical Instructors").

AN EVIDENCE-BASED OBSERVATION PROCESS

As previously mentioned, the KSU PDS Partnership began in 1989 with an informal observation process that included formative observations and a checklist-style final evaluation. This process was not standardized, and each assessor used his or her own unique definition of good teaching to complete formative observations and the final evaluation. In addition, there was no training for the university supervisors or the cooperating teachers, and clear expectations were not available for the preservice teacher candidates. Since there was no training, supervisors observed using their own process, most likely the same process they had experienced when they were preparing to be teachers. Observations most often consisted of scripting what was said or done in the classroom and then making suggestions for improvement on the triplicate sheet that was completed and left with the preservice teacher candidate and cooperating teacher.

Obviously, this early system of assessment would not have met current standards for validity and reliability. Most significantly, this early system was not fair. Preservice candidates were not assessed using a standard set of criteria. Consequently, the criteria used to assess one preservice candidate could have been completely different than the criteria used to assess another candidate. Most often, the supervisor focused the observation on the first event that caught their attention. This event might have related to classroom management for one student, the objective of the lesson for a second, and the use of the overhead projector for a third. Once the supervisor identified *the problem,* this often became the focus of the observation, with few other issues addressed. In addition, supervisors tended to make recommendations for improvement based on the opinion of the supervisor rather than evidence collected during the teaching episode. Similarly, preservice candidates were not routinely asked to provide evidence of student learning. The preservice candidates focused their own self-assessments on the popularity of the activity and the *fun* students appeared to be having. On a positive note, most preservice teacher candidates had excellent rapport with their students!

The impetus for revising the KSU observation system was, once again, the PDS simultaneous improvement model. University faculty, clinical instructors, and cooperating teachers were expressing growing dissatisfaction with the preservice teacher observation process at the same time that teachers and administrators in the PDS were expressing dissatisfaction with their in-service teacher assessments. In addition, all partners were exploring strategies to mentor and support beginning teachers. PDS and university faculty and administrators regularly attended National Education Association (NEA) conferences together in the early 2000s as part of the NEA Learning Laboratory.

Two of these partners, the PDS coordinator and a district director of professional development, attended a presentation on the *framework observation process* (FOP) sponsored by ETS. The FOP utilized Danielson's Framework for Teaching (2007) as the foundation for an evidence-based teacher observation process. It was soon clear to all PDS partners that this process could be used across the PDS partnership as a self-assessment and supervision model for new and experienced inservice PDS teachers and for preservice candidates in the teacher education program. In 2001, the college of education and two PDS districts agreed to adopt the FOP for use in preservice teacher preparation, new teacher mentoring, and inservice teacher evaluations.

Once the adoption decision was made, ETS provided a week-long Trainer of Trainers program for university and PDS faculty and administrators. In utilizing the standardized descriptions, indicators, and rubrics of teaching effectiveness identified in the *Framework for Teaching,* all new and experienced inservice teachers and preservice teacher candidates were soon assessed using the same domains of perspectives and preparation, learning environment, instruction, and professionalism (Danielson, 2007).

Since the first adoption, the FOP has been modified to meet changing state and national standards and PDS partner needs. But the foundational, evidence-based observation process using Danielson's FFT is still in use across the PDS. All new partners involved in the supervision and mentoring of teachers and teacher candidates continue to receive professional development routinely to effectively use the evidence-based observation process. These partners include faculty from the college of education, K–12 clinical instructors, cooperating teachers, college of education and partner school administrators, and graduate teaching assistants. All supervisors also are provided with ongoing professional development to ensure their methods of supervision are current, valid, and reliable (to be described under "The Critical Role of the Clinical Instructors").

During the first of four semester-long field experiences, preservice teacher candidates are introduced to the four domains of the evidence-based observation process: (1) planning and preparation, (2) classroom environment, (3) instruction, and (4) professionalism. In subsequent field experiences, students learn about each domain in greater detail—building their understanding of the components and elements within each domain and the indicators and rubrics used to assess that domain. Then, during their final student internship semester, they are assessed using the complete evidence-based observation process. This process requires the preservice teacher candidate to: (1) answer preplanning questions, (2) develop a lesson plan, (3) participate in a preobservation conference and a classroom observation based on the lesson planned, and (4) complete a postobservation conference and a self-assessment of his or her teaching. This process is based on evidence, as identified by the teacher candidate and the observer, and the process provides specific feedback to the teacher candidate based on this evidence. Through this collaborative process, candidates have the opportunity to develop their understanding of the framework over the course of their field experiences.

THE CRITICAL ROLE OF THE CLINICAL INSTRUCTORS

As of 2013, the PDS Partnership at KSU includes six school districts and 22 elementary, middle, and high schools. In addition, the PDS coordinators work with 17 clinical instructors to carry out the work of the partnership. From the creation of the PDS partnership in 1989, clinical instructors have played an integral role in the development of the partnership and, in particular, the development of the performance-based portfolio model and evidence-based observation process. Clinical instructors have helped to design, pilot, evaluate, and revise each version of the portfolio. They identify items to be clarified or modified within entry descriptions or rubric criteria on an annual basis. The clinical instructors also mentor the preservice teacher candidates during the student internship semester and through the development of their portfolios. They introduce the portfolio to the student interns, conduct seminars during the semester to ensure the success of each intern, and assess the final portfolio. If needed, they work with the interns to make improvements to their portfolio.

The role of clinical instructors in the use of the evidence-based observation process is also invaluable. They served on the original *FFT* trainer of trainers team, providing professional development and assistance to cooperating teachers and university faculty preparing to be supervisors. The clinical instructors also developed intermediary steps to assist cooperating teachers in the use of the observation forms. This included developing *short forms* that the cooperating teachers could use as they adjusted to an evidence-based observation process. These short forms consisted of breaking the larger observation forms into smaller components and making the forms user-friendly. Clinical instructors also serve as *university supervisors* and use the evidence-based observation process to make two or three formal observations of each intern in their building.

Clinical instructors meet with the PDS coordinators every two weeks to engage in professional development activities, share experiences, assess and enhance the effectiveness of the PDS partnership, and to maintain the validity and reliability of the teacher preparation assessment system. At least once a year the clinical instructors and other university supervisors independently score sample portfolio entries. Portfolio scores are then compared and discussed until an agreement is reached regarding the most appropriate rubric or checklist score, based on the evidence provided. In a similar fashion, clinical instructors and other university supervisors watch videos of teaching episodes and independently score the teaching episodes using the evidence-based observation process. Individual scores are compared and differences in scoring are discussed until agreement is reached on the most appropriate rubric score, based on the evidence gathered. This process also has led to revisions in both the performance-based portfolio and the evidence-based observation process. The rubrics used to score both assessments are revised annually to enhance clarity and improve inter-rater reliability.

ASSESSMENT OUTCOMES

The ultimate goal of the authentic assessment system was to enhance the preparation of preservice teacher candidates by more clearly articulating what effective future teachers should know and be able to do. To determine the success in reaching this goal, assessment data are gathered every semester. Portfolio scores and final intern assessment forms are maintained. Surveys are completed by preservice teacher candidates, university faculty, clinical instructors, PDS cooperating teachers and administrators, and the employers (principals) of first-year teachers. These data indicate the success of the performance-based assessment system in helping preservice teachers become more effective educators. Effective teaching has been defined by various researchers to be (1) knowledge of learners and their development and assisting them in advancing in their learning, (2) knowledge of subject matter, (3) knowledge of teaching, (4) knowledge of and use of assessments to monitor student progress and engage students in learning, and (5) knowledge of their communities (Darling- Hammond, 2006; Darling-Hammond & Baratz-Snowden, 2005; NCATE, 2010).

At the completion of their 16-week student internship experience, each preservice teacher candidate is assessed by his or her cooperating teacher, clinical instructor, and university supervisor. The final internship assessment form is based on a 7-point scale. The preservice teacher candidates are considered to be unsatisfactory with a score of 1, basic with a score of 2–4 and proficient with a score of 5–7. Similar to the evidence-based observation process, the final intern assessment form is aligned with the four domains of *The Framework for Teaching* (Danielson, 2007): perspectives and preparation, learning environment, instruction, and professionalism. The KSU target rating for preservice candidates is *basic* with scores of 2–4. Scores in the proficient category, 5–7, are designated for use with inservice teachers. Data from the final assessment of all preservice teachers in 2011–2012 indicate that the preservice candidates score above the target rating of *basic* in all areas assessed: perspectives and preparation (μ=5.03), learning environment (μ=5.48), instruction (μ=5.3), and professionalism (μ=5.60).

The evidence-based portfolio is designed to authentically assess each preservice teacher's performance in designing and teaching lessons and units to meet the needs of all students in their classrooms. The final portfolio is assessed using a checklist and rubric to determine proficiency. Each preservice candidate must achieve a pass rate of 80% for successful completion of the evidence-based portfolio. In Entry 1 (biographical data) the pass rate for preservice teacher candidates was 97%. In Entry 2 (contextual information and implications for student learning), the pass rate was 97.7%. In Entry 3 (the instructional unit plan, which includes learning goals and objectives, instructional design, analysis of assessment procedures, and self-evaluation of the instructional unit), the pass rate was 99.2%. For Entry 4 (analysis of the classroom learning environment), the preservice teacher candidates achieved a pass rate of 92.2%; in Entry 5 (formal observations) the pass rate was 95.8%, and in Entry 6 (professional logs) the pass rate was 85.4%.

Preservice teacher candidate exit surveys in 2011–2012 (247 of 315 surveys were returned with a response rate of 78.4%) indicated that they are confident in the areas of general education, foundations of education, students and learning, content and pedagogy, planning, learning environment, instructional strategies, and professionalism. On a scale of one to six, median responses range from five to six in all 39 areas assessed.

An analysis of 170 PDS surveys, last collected in 2009, indicated that PDS administrators, cooperating teachers, student interns, and university faculty all agree that they have "confidence that candidates are developing skills and knowledge needed for success as beginning teachers as a result of their involvement in the PDS partnership."

The employers (principals) of KSU graduates are asked to rate the first-year teachers on a scale from *grossly inept* to *extraordinarily distinguished* in the categories of (1) planning, (2) instruction, (3) learning environment, (4) professionalism, (5) technology, (6) diversity, (7) foundations, and (8) students and learning. Across all eight categories, the first-year teachers were determined to be "competent" or higher at a rate of 93% with individual categorical rankings of 97.6% in planning, 91.6% in instruction, 86% in learning environment, 93% in professionalism, 94% in technology, 91.7% in diversity, 97.7% in foundations, and 93% in students and learning. A sample of written remarks from these employers include: "a person would be hard-pressed to know that this beginning teacher is not a veteran teacher"; "this individual has done a commendable job as a first-year teacher"; "highly capable and done an excellent job"; and "this graduate is a highly effective teacher".

Data from preservice teacher candidates, PDS cooperating teachers, clinical instructors, and administrators, university supervisors, and first-year employers demonstrate the KSU preservice candidates are exhibiting indicators of effective teaching as defined by NCATE (2010), Darling-Hammond (2006), and Darling-Hammond and Baratz-Snowden (2005). We believe this success has been positively influenced by the design and implementation of our authentic assessment system. The development of a performance-based portfolio and an evidence-based observation process allows all stakeholders to clearly articulate and assess effective teaching for preservice teacher candidates and to mentor and guide each candidate toward this vision of teaching. This is one of many benefits of the authentic assessment system.

ADDITIONAL BENEFITS OF AUTHENTIC ASSESSMENT

The KSU assessment system has provided all members of the PDS partnership the opportunity to self-assess their practice using the same language and to discuss their progress in becoming effective teachers. It provides a shared understanding among educational partners of the key components of professional practice. The *Framework for Teaching* serves as the foundation for this professional practice that provides "well-established definitions of expertise and procedures to certify novice and advanced practitioners" (Danielson, 2007, p. 2). The framework has the "power to elevate professional conversations that characterize the interaction of exemplary teachers everywhere" (Danielson, 2007, p. 13). Furthermore, it serves as a roadmap for navigating through the complexities of teaching throughout one's career. Ultimately, the framework "conveys that educators, like other professionals, are members of a professional community" (Danielson, 2007, p. 2).

The performance-based portfolio and the evidence-based observation process are used to identify and enhance effective teaching and to create productive, exemplary teachers and preservice teacher candidates. By continually assessing and revising the shared assessment process and working with clinical instructors, university supervisors, and cooperating teachers to enhance reliability and validity, we have reduced the gap in portfolio and final student teaching assessment scores based on supervisor roles. Perhaps most importantly, we have a fair and accountable system in which preservice teacher candidates are aware of what they should know and be able to do to demonstrate effective teaching through each step of their preparation process.

CONTINUING CHALLENGES

As with any change, time and patience are needed for continuous improvement. In working with multiple partners it is important to remember that everyone brings his or her own context, and depending upon what context that may be, we must provide the time and opportunity for those partners to figure out where they fit in the partnership. We also learned that we must be patient with new people as they adapt to the work involved in both the performance-based portfolio and the evidence-based observation system.

When these new assessments were first introduced, we had cooperating teachers who decided not to be involved because the observation system was too much work and they didn't have the time to devote to the preservice teacher candidates.

With time, patience, mentoring from clinical instructors, and the development of the short forms, reluctant cooperating teachers are now very involved in the partnership. Additionally, a deeper understanding of the assessment of preservice teacher candidates has increased the inservice teacher's understanding and appreciation of their own assessment process.

Growth in the PDS partnership also has resulted in continuing challenges. The partnership began with three elementary schools and clinical instructors in one school district. Gradually, additional elementary schools were added, and then secondary schools and additional districts joined the partnership. Turnover in teachers, administrators, and faculty added to these growing pains. New partners, at any level, must learn to find their place in the partnership and develop a sense of ownership for policies and decisions. So practices such as those within the authentic assessment system must remain flexible to meet differing needs and the partnership must be open to continuous examination and revisions. The *old guard* needs to welcome the *newcomers* and respect their insights, rather than assuming *the way we have always done it* is the way it should always be done.

CONCLUSIONS

The goals of the earliest collaborations were to form relationships, identify the various roles needed to make the PDS partnership work, establish responsibilities for each of the roles, and to share resources needed to sustain collaboration. This is similar to what is described as the "Time Before the Beginning" in *Standards for Professional Development Schools* (National Council for Accreditation of Teacher Education, 2001):

> This foundation is often laid by individuals from both schools and universities working together over some period of time. Partners either need to have this pre-existing relationship or spend time in their initial stages building it, before they can enter into the very difficult and high stakes work of a PDS partnership. (p. 4)

After 25 years we can look back on our challenges and realize with each year, each challenge, and each additional PDS partner, we must go back to this time before the beginning and identify our roles, reexamine our responsibilities, and form new relationships. And most importantly, the complex PDS system needs to continually respond to the changing and diverse needs of all the partners and the state and local context within which they exist. Part of this changing context for the KSU PDS partnership has been the renewed national emphasis on accountability. As stated, many point to the lack of accountability in teacher education programs that continue to provide traditional, primarily coursework-based models (Wasburn-Moses, 2013). Barnett (1992) indicates that now "with greater expectations being placed on it, higher education is being obliged to examine itself or be examined by others" (p. 16). This requirement has led colleges of education to be more responsive, redesigning the structure of their programs to provide increased quality, field-based experiences and to assess more effectively the impact on and outcomes of students' performance (Alexander, 2000).

The PDS partnership has enabled KSU to remain responsive to local, state, and national recommendations to continuously assess, revise, and enhance the effectiveness of the future teachers it prepares. Through the use of a performance-based portfolio and an evidence-based observation process, KSU has addressed the national emphasis on accountability; creating a fair system to help preservice teacher candidates as well as practicing inservice teachers enhance teacher quality and teacher effectiveness across the educational continuum.

REFERENCES

Alexander, F. K. (2000). The changing face of accountability: Monitoring and assessing institutional performance in higher education. *The Journal of Higher Education, 71*(4), 411–431.

Barnett, R. (1992). *Improving higher education: Total quality care.* London, UK: The Society for Research into Higher Education and The Open University.

Danielson, C. (2007). *Enhancing professional practice: A framework for teaching* (2nd ed.) Alexandria, VA: Association for Supervision and Curriculum Development.

Danielson, C. (1996). *Enhancing professional practice: A framework for teaching.* Alexandria, VA: Association for Supervision and Curriculum Development.

Darling-Hammond, L. (2006). Constructing 21st- century teacher education. *Journal of Teacher Education, 57*(3), 300–314.

Darling-Hammond, L., & Baratz-Snowden, J. (Eds.). (2005). *A good teacher in every classroom.* San Francisco, CA: Jossey-Bass.

National Council for Accreditation of Teacher Education (NCATE). (2001). *Standards for professional development schools.* Washington DC: Author.

National Council for the Accreditation of Teacher Education (NCATE). (2010). *Transforming teacher education through clinical practice: A national strategy to prepare effective teachers.* Washington, DC: Author.

Wasburn-Moses, L. (2013, July 23). A fix for teacher education: A three-year degree. *The Chronicle of Higher Education.* Retrieved from *http://chronicle.com/article/A-Fix-for-Teacher-Education-/140565/?cid=at&utm_source=at&utm_medium=en*

Wiggins, G., & McTighe, J. (2005). *Understanding by design.* Alexandria, VA: Association for Supervision and Curriculum Development.

CHAPTER 6

PDS AS PASSPORT TO THE WORLD

Preparing the Next Generation of Educators for a Global Community

Prixita del Prado Hill, Leslie Day,
Nancy A. Chicola, and Hibajene Shandomo

ABSTRACT

SUNY Buffalo State's award-winning Professional Development Schools (PDS) Consortium has extended its sphere of influence for 22 years. Starting with one partner school in 1991 with a mission to support the development of new and experienced teachers through local partnerships, this consortium now partners with more than 45 PDS sites locally, regionally, and internationally. Responding to demographic changes in our city and beyond, the consortium expanded its commitment to support the development of children, teachers, and faculty to be global citizens. This chapter narrates the journey of this unique and growing network of global PDS partnerships with excerpts from teacher candidates and offers suggestions for developing effective international partnerships.

Creating Visions for University-School Partnerships, pages 87–102.
Copyright © 2014 by Information Age Publishing
All rights of reproduction in any form reserved.

The world is a book, and those who do not travel read only a page.
—*St. Augustine*

As of Fall 2013, SUNY Buffalo State's Professional Development Schools (PDS) Consortium has more than 45 PDS partnership sites at all levels of early childhood and elementary programs, including introductory and methods courses as well as student teaching cohorts. Three of these sites are international with locations in Lusaka, Zambia; Santiago, Chile; and Cabrete, Dominican Republic. Plans are underway to establish partnerships in Sienna, Italy, and Beijing, China, while also ensuring that every one of our 650 undergraduate candidates develops a global framework for teaching and has multiple global experiences throughout the program. Designing a program that serves as "a passport to the world" for teacher candidates and faculty has taken over 20 years but was made possible by the flexible yet structured framework of the PDS model. This chapter details the story of the progression of this PDS (in narrative fashion) by providing the theoretical framework for this direction and explaining how this theory has been actualized through our coursework, field experiences, and partnerships by means of various projects and programs. Excerpts regarding impact as well as suggestions for developing effective international partnerships will be included.

THE JOURNEY BEGINS

In line with a constructivist view and the belief that teaching skills and strategies are best learned and honed through mentored immersion in the classroom experience, the Department of Elementary Education and Reading (EER) at SUNY Buffalo State established its PDS program in 1991. Previously a member of the Holmes Partnership (Holmes Group, 1986) that promoted clinically rich experiences for teacher candidates, the PDS grew from one school partner to its current network encompassing a consortium of more than 45 PDS sites, four for introductory level courses, 20 for methods course, and additional school sites for student teaching cohorts. For a complete list of PDS schools, see http://www.buffalostate.edu/pds/.

SUNY Buffalo State's PDS Consortium dedicated itself to a better way of educating future teachers, supporting young learners, and participating in continual renewal and professional development for all partners; thus, the mission statement became clear. When the National Council for Accreditation of Teacher Education PDS Standards were published (NCATE, 2001), the mission statement took written form:

> The Professional Development Schools (PDS) Partnership between the School of Education at SUNY Buffalo State and participating schools is a collaborative effort. The partnership is dedicated to college faculty, school administrators, practicing teachers, teacher candidates, and PreK–6th grade learners as we explore effective practices to:

1. Cooperatively supervise teacher candidates and provide closer connections to authentic classroom practice;
2. Promote professional development for in-service teachers, college faculty and administrators;
3. Improve young student learning; and
4. Research best practices for the education of all partners (*http://www.buffalo-state.edu/pds/x796.xml*).

The PDS partnership between SUNY Buffalo State and the participating schools is a collaborative effort currently based on three main PDS frameworks: (1) the NCATE Standards for Professional Development Schools (2001), (2) the National Association for Professional Development Schools Nine Essentials (Brindley, Field, & Lessen, 2008), and (3) the NCATE Blue Ribbon Panel Report (2010). In addition, the consortium's mission and vision are closely coupled to the college and its school of education's (SOE) mission, which explicitly expresses a commitment to equity and diversity.

> The community of faculty and staff within the SOE at State are committed to the intellectual, personal and professional growth of future and practicing professionals in the field of education. Transformative educational experiences frame our programs, engaging faculty, candidates and the learners they serve, schools, and industry and community partners to improve the quality of life for all. We work collaboratively to ensure that graduates become inspired, reflective practitioners who possess the knowledge, skills, and dispositions to model and promote a lifelong passion for learning; recognize the value of diversity; learn to implement inclusive pedagogies that celebrate the abilities of all individuals; and embrace the rich cultural heritages of the communities they serve. (http://www.buffalostate.edu/schoolofeducation/x784.xml)

The conceptual framework for teacher preparation at SUNY Buffalo State articulates the department's vision and ensures coherence across teacher candidates' programs and the PDS (Figure 6.1). This reflects a commitment to prepare teacher candidates to work effectively with children from all backgrounds and learning needs. An evolutionary process based on program evaluation has resulted in the present model that conceptualizes teaching as facilitating student learning.

It was important for the consortium to acknowledge that all learning occurs within an ever-changing context: the school environment, the local community, the broader society, and a global community. By integrating the college's strategic vision, the conceptual framework, the NCATE standards (NCATE, 2001), the needs and mission statements of the PDS schools, the NAPDS Nine Essentials (Brindley et al., 2008), and Blue Ribbon Report (NCATE, 2010), this consortium has achieved a comprehensive mission that is broader in its outreach and scope than the mission of any individual partner. This consortium has a strong commitment to furthering the education profession and advancing equity within schools throughout the local partnerships and into the global community.

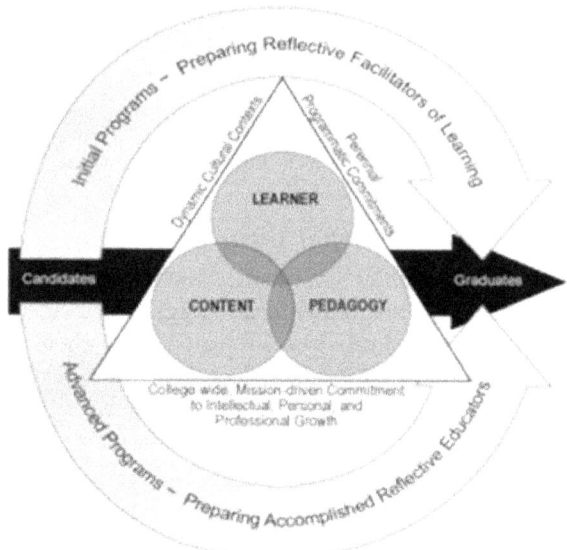

FIGURE 6.1.   SUNY Buffalo State teacher education conceptual framework

How the PDS Consortium Works

All teacher candidates in the program have opportunities for observations and service learning at the introductory course level and sustained participation in at least four different PDS situations over a two- to three-year period before they graduate. One of the most important goals is to develop effective teachers for high needs settings and to create educators who can use theory and reflection to improve their practice to the benefit of all learners. Across their courses teacher candidates learn about multicultural education (e.g., Banks, 2007), culturally relevant pedagogy (e.g., Ladson-Billings, 1995), and culturally responsive teaching (e.g., Gay, 2010; Nieto, 1999). They utilize and reflect on these theoretical frameworks in the context of their clinically rich practices.

Teacher candidates generally begin their field experiences in partner schools with observation and shadowing. By their third year, they are teaching in one-on-one, small group, and whole classroom settings. Their final year includes two student teaching placements, but depending on their certification, teacher candidates will have taught for 125–175 hours prior to their student teaching experience. Two-thirds of these pre-student-teaching hours will take place in schools with culturally diverse student populations. Since these courses are taught in real school settings with faculty on the premises, close supervision is provided; the college and school personnel are able to efficiently and effectively share their expertise and insights about working with all groups of students. Children also benefit due to the additional caring adults in each classroom.

Student teaching cohorts guide the culminating experience. These cohorts consist of four to six candidates, each of whom is assigned to a PDS classroom and mentored by a SUNY Buffalo State supervisor who stays on site for two full days each week throughout the 7–8-week placement. This group of student teachers moves, as a cohort with the same supervisor, to a second PDS school in a different milieu for experience at a new grade level. Upon completion, teacher candidates log approximately 450 hours during this student teaching experience. It is central to the mission that teacher candidates have opportunities for diverse classroom experiences which this PDS Consortium has enabled. Each student teacher will complete at least one of his/her placements in an urban school; some student teachers choose two different urban placements. The cohesive and vertical alignment of these clinically rich practices is guided by the course-level faculty convener groups who meet regularly to conduct programmatic assessment and adjustments. The department uses TaskStream (*www.taskstream.com*) as a data collection tool to analyze common assignments for each course, identifying strengths and needs in the teacher education program. A critical thread that runs through all of these assignments and course work is the essential and underlying belief that teacher candidates understand and embrace equity and diversity in their classrooms.

This PDS seeks to benefit all members of the consortium. A primary goal is that children benefit through a co-teaching model that brings dedicated and skilled new teachers into the classroom under the supervision of experienced mentor teachers. Teacher candidates are served by the rich clinical experience discussed above. Through multiple professional development opportunities, school-based leaders, mentor teachers, and university faculty also benefit from the PDS structure. This goal is achieved through a variety of rich professional activities. An annual retreat for all members of the consortium is held every fall. During this day-long free professional development experience, teaching is celebrated, networking is accomplished, and knowledge and skills are built through presentations of research. Other meetings are held four times throughout the year at various partner schools to continue working together as professionals.

Each university faculty member is connected to a school where he or she develops a long-lasting relationship. This faculty member establishes a liaison committee with the principal and a representative mentor teacher to build and strengthen the partnership. In addition to ensuring that the clinically rich experience runs smoothly, this group troubleshoots, plans for partnership activities, and serves as the central communication body between the school and the university. This group may also identify an action research project and submit a proposal to receive a PDS Consortium mini-grant to support this work. (For details, see http://www.buffalostate.edu/pds/x503.xml.) The faculty member provides requested expertise to the school while also remaining current in the field through continued work at the school and classroom level. Many faculty also conduct research at the site to support their scholarship agenda.

Moving Beyond Local Borders

From 1991 to 2008, the focus was at the local and regional levels where university faculty worked with schools in surrounding areas for the development of teachers. The PDS Consortium committed itself to the preparation and support of high quality teachers for all classroom settings, and the program was recognized in numerous ways for work in this area. Awards have included (1) the 2003 NYSATE/NYACCTE Distinguished Teacher Education Program, (2) the 2005 ATE Distinguished Teacher Education Program finalist, (3) the 2005 Bronze Community Award, (4) the 2011 NAPDS Exemplary PDS Award, and (5) the 2013 NAPDS National Conference Spirit of Partnership Award. In recent years, however, important changes were occurring in local and national classrooms which have led the college to utilize the consortium to meet these new needs.

The city in which SUNY Buffalo State is located has consistently been one of the poorest cities in the United States with approximately 40% of children living in poverty, and, as noted, PDS activities have been committed to the preparation of candidates who could potentially work effectively in all classroom settings. In recent years, however, many immigrants have arrived in Buffalo due to the city's designation as a refugee resettlement area by the State Department. As a Rust Belt city, Buffalo has lost more than half of its population since the 1950s. The State Department's designation was initiated to stop population loss in Rust Belt cities like Buffalo by subsidizing refugee resettlement there. For example, about 1,500 refugees came to Buffalo in 2010. Due to abundant and low-cost housing and easy access to public transportation, the majority of the refugees that come each year reside in West Side neighborhoods where the campus happens to be located. This has transformed classrooms culturally, ethnically, and linguistically. Approximately 75 languages are spoken in the Buffalo public schools, and children represent nations from across the globe. The consortium began to explore ways to adapt the PDS framework to prepare the teacher candidates for this changing world.

Because SUNY Buffalo State's 2008 strategic goals included the objective of developing global citizens among our student body, the mission has expanded to include a systematic approach to integrating global experiences into this program to build awareness in teacher candidates so that they, in turn, will help their future students become citizens of a global world. (See SUNY Buffalo State's Strategic Direction #1 at http://www.buffalostate.edu/strategicplanning/x668.xml.) In 2009, the PDS began to explore ways to move beyond our local borders by establishing the Elementary Education and Reading Global Taskforce (whose purpose was to suggest ways to meet these new goals). This group consisted of members of the faculty and the chair. Essential questions were developed first to explore global issues in education, and these were included in a poster that was displayed throughout the education building and discussed in college classrooms. This gave global issues a visual and conceptual presence, and faculty began utilizing the questions in their curriculum and instruction. The questions were:

- What does a global society look like? How do teachers become citizens of a global society? How do teachers help their students become citizens of a global society?
- Who are today's students in a diverse society? What differences matter in the classroom? How can those differences to be honored to develop a community of learners?
- What are the characteristics of the United States early childhood and childhood educational system? How does this system compare to the educational systems of other countries? What can we learn from exploring educational systems outside the U.S.?

Meanwhile, a faculty study group was established to read and discuss together the following books to learn more about the lives and experiences of refugees and explore the educational implications of global education: *From Every End of the Earth: 13 Families and the Lives They Made in America* (Roberts, 2009), *The Flat World of Education: How America's Commitment to Equity Will Determine Our Future* (Darling-Hammond, 2010), and *What Every Teacher Should Know About Multicultural and Global Education* (Brown & Kysilka, 2009).

The next step was to identify global issues as the PDS Consortium Theme for the 2009–2010 academic year (*see http://www.buffalostate.edu/pds/x965.xml*). During that time, each consortium meeting was devoted to exploration of global concerns at theoretical and practical levels. For example, the chair made a presentation on integrating high-quality global literature into our courses. As a result, many assignments began to include exploration and analysis of children's global literature, and a number of service learning projects grew out of this interest. One of these projects was the Global Book Project, which promotes family literacy and global understanding through a weekly interactive read-aloud. Located at two sites (a local grocery store and a laundromat), the project provides a rich opportunity for teacher candidates to design and deliver an integrated literacy experience to children who have recently immigrated to this city from all over the world. Its mission states, "The Global Book Project seeks to use high quality literature, global awareness and nutritious eating for the growth of children and development of new teachers" (*http://globalbookproject.buffalostate.edu/*). Reflecting on her experience with the project, a teacher candidate wrote, "Through participating, I got to meet a series of new people, learn an abundant amount of information, plan and create lesson ideas, put into practice what I've learned in class, receive constructive feedback, reflect on my teaching, and address many community needs" (spring 2013). Since its inception in spring 2010, the Global Book Project has distributed hundreds of books to dozens of families, many of whom return each week, and has introduced teacher candidates to the larger world through children's literature and the weekly read-aloud.

Another example of how faculty began globalizing their courses is the Cross-Cultural Pen Pal Project that connects children in the Buffalo public schools with children in Lusaka, Zambia. Three urban elementary classrooms in the city became pen pals with children in three urban elementary classrooms in Lusaka to provide children in both settings with a broader view of the world, develop social and cultural awareness, and expand content knowledge about each other's homes. In addition, the project served as a preparatory activity for SUNY Buffalo State teacher candidates to develop cross-cultural professional relationships with Zambian teachers and was the first step to a much deeper and more complex international partnership that will be discussed below.

These early projects led to other global service learning activities such as tutoring within our city's growing refugee community as faculty began collaborating with local agencies such as Journey's End Refugee Services (http://jersbuffalo. org/). This type of "boundary spanning" as described in the NCATE PDS Standards (2001, p. 4) marked a significant step toward globalizing the PDS. At this point, all global activities were happening at the local level, drawing on the many international resources and opportunities provided within our own city. The next logical step was to build on the global experiences and connections of department faculty to develop international school partners to extend the PDS Consortium family.

One faculty member is from Zambia with many connections to teacher education leaders and schools in the capital of Lusaka. She traveled to Zambia in 2011 to secure a partnership with the University of Zambia (UNZA) teacher education program and the Libala Basic School. Meanwhile, another faculty member with roots in Latin America received a Fulbright award to work and study in Santiago, Chile, where she established partnerships with Universidad Mayor and a local public school. A year later, a third partnership was established with a Montessori school in Cabrete, Dominican Republic. Building on a personal relationship with this school, a faculty member in early childhood education traveled to establish this partnership.

Although the partnerships began from these personal and professional connections, the NCATE PDS Standards (2001) and the NAPDS Nine Essentials frameworks (Brindley et al., 2008) were utilized to ensure that the international school partnerships developed into meaningful professional development opportunities. As beginning stage partnership sites (NCATE, 2001), the schools signed formal PDS agreements with SUNY Buffalo State. These agreements (NAPDS Nine Essentials, #6) provided a small honorarium for the school along with the understanding that SUNY Buffalo State's teacher candidates would be welcome in these international classrooms. Working across institutional settings (NAPDS Nine Essentials, #8) was an essential component of the collaboration, but this sometimes proved challenging, such as finding ways to transport resources like children's books and laptop computers to partner schools. Also significant were opportunities to communicate with colleagues in related institutions of higher education and other PDS directors. For example, the opportunity to Skype with the PDS director in Chile was extremely valuable for both institutions. The traveling professors were also able to communicate directly to share innovative practices and current research (NAPDS Nine Essentials, #4). Teaching in these international schools provided rich research and presentation opportunities for both faculty and teacher candidates (NAPDS Nine Essentials, #3) (Brindley et al., 2008).

Back on SUNY Buffalo State's campus, informational sessions were offered to encourage teacher candidates to apply for one of the international PDS programs. Interested teacher candidates wrote essays discussing the reasons to participate, requested letters of recommendation, and participated in individual interviews. Teacher candidates accepted into the program took part in orientation and team building activities and also learned about scholarship and funding opportunities to help pay for the trip. For participants in the most recent round of applications, a weekly module has been developed to learn about the targeted country through book discussions and guest speakers.

By June 2012, the chair, the Zambian faculty member, and 12 teacher candidates traveled to Lusaka, Zambia, where they worked in the classrooms of our new partner school and gathered research data to analyze education in Zambia. Teacher candidates had the opportunity to observe and practice teaching methods within the large class sizes common to Zambian schools (50–60 children in one classroom, for example) where direct instruction and choral response were often used. At the university level, SUNY Buffalo State teacher candidates observed teaching at UNZA and participated in the class led by the UNZA coordinator. One of the candidates in the summer semester, who seemed to represent the views of many other candidates noted, "I found [the cultural differences] difficult for me to process, but I kept an open mind and focused on the positive in the educational system and culture in general. This enabled me to really experience Zambia instead of being turned off by differences" (summer 2012). All teacher candidates reported that Zambian elementary students were eager to learn, despite the large class sizes and lack of textbooks for every child. Eleven of the twelve (92%) teacher candidates reported that the visit to Zambia increased their cultural awareness, and the experience was invaluable and will help them become well-rounded teachers.

Upon return, this group of faculty and students presented their experiences and research in a variety of venues to disseminate information about the project and recruit another group to travel in June 2013. Following one of these informational sessions, one student commented, "When [Dr. Shandomo] came to speak to my class about the opportunity to study in Zambia, I slumped into my seat, ready to look at beautiful pictures and hear amazing stories, none of which I would get to experience in person, when she suddenly said the magic words: three weeks. Three weeks?! I could do three weeks, maybe!" (fall 2012). Creating a study abroad program that candidates believe is accessible was crucial. Therefore, the programs are connected to a semester-long methods course with a three-week extension for the travel and teaching abroad component. In the case of the Zambian and Chilean trips, candidates participate in a spring methods course and travel for three weeks in June. With the Dominican Republic trip, candidates enroll in a fall course with travel experiences for two and a half weeks in January. SUNY Buffalo State is a comprehensive four-year liberal arts institution serving many first-generation college students. The programs are purposefully structured so that they are financially feasible for our teacher candidates who have many work and family responsibilities.

The Zambia project continued in June 2013 with 15 new candidates, the original faculty member, and a new faculty member. Participating candidates from both semesters have been posting reflections and photographs to a blog dedicated to documenting the experience (http://zambiapdsatbsedu.wordpress.com/). The public sharing of ideas as participants prepare to travel, while they travel, and once they return enhances and sustains the PDS experience (NAPDS Nine Essentials, # 5) (Brindley et al., 2008). For example, one posting noted, "I think this experience will change me in all the right ways. I look forward to learning about the people of Zambia and their culture. I also look forward to observing and teaching in ways that may be different from the way we teach here. I'm slightly nervous about the flight, since we will be traveling for a full day. I also feel like I don't know quite what to expect when we get there, but I'm looking forward to every second of it!" (summer 2013). Readers of the blog then have the opportunity to follow this teacher candidate's growth and development as more postings are added.

Meanwhile, another faculty member developed a similar partnership with an elementary school in Santiago, Chile. In preparation, participating teacher candidates completed their nine-credit literacy and social studies methods block at a bilingual school (Spanish and English) at a PDS site to consider issues related to English language learning. Then in June 2012, seven teacher candidates traveled to Santiago, where they were immersed in Spanish language learning through a daily Spanish intensive program, home stays with Chilean families, and daily living in Santiago. Through the collaboration established in the previous year, the SUNY Buffalo State teacher candidates also spent time shadowing Chilean candidates at Universidad Mayor who are preparing to become teachers of English to explore teaching and learning outside the U.S. The third component of the program included teaching children in a public school of Santiago through a satellite Global Book Project established at the school. During the three weeks, the teacher candidates maintained a blog site with special emphasis given to changes in thinking when elementary teachers of literacy become language learners themselves (http://chilepdsatbsedu.wordpress.com/). One candidate reflected, "Being totally immersed has deepened my understanding of what it means to be a language learner and what I plan to do as a teacher to make sure that the language learners in my own classroom will benefit.... I have acquired patience and empathy for non-English speakers and a curiosity and appreciation for cultures unfamiliar to my own" (summer 2012). One year later, this same candidate noted,

> Because of the wonderful experience I had in Chile, I've learned the importance of communication. I was able to successfully teach multiple lessons with my co-teacher by my side even with a language barrier involved. We were able to work as a team sharing teaching experiences by actively listening to one another and trying our hardest to fully understand what the other was saying. From my experience in Chile, it has even inspired me to get a master's degree in ESL. I made such a connection with the children in Chile that I hope to do the same for my own students here in the U.S. (summer 2013)

The mutual benefits and the sharing of resources (NAPDS Nine Essentials, #9) (Brindley et al., 2008) encourage the continuation of the PDS relationship.

To promote the language learning of teacher candidates here on campus (and to support those who have traveled or are planning to travel to a Spanish-speaking country), Club HoLA (Hour of Latino Awareness) was established, which utilizes bilingual children's literature in developing Spanish language skills and building knowledge of Latino culture. This club meets once a week for 10 weeks each semester and is open to all interested teacher candidates and teacher education faculty. A teacher candidate who participated in the club during the spring of 2013 and traveled to Chile in June posted on her blog site, "This afternoon, we went to Pablo Neruda's house. It was so cool because in the book club this semester, we studied him and one of his books.... His work is absolutely beautiful and his words are full of imagination. It was really great to make a connection between the author we studied to where he lived and worked in Chile, of which his writings are about" (summer 2013).

In the spirit of full exchange and collaborating across institutional settings, SUNY Buffalo State welcomed a faculty member and two teacher candidates from Santiago's Universidad Mayor in February of 2013 for three weeks. The two teacher candidates developed their professional English language skills by attending our methods classes, increased their pedagogical tools by participating in the bilingual PDS partner school mentioned above, participated in the Global Book Project and Club HoLA (also explained previously), and experienced U.S. campus life by taking part in campus activities. At the completion of the trip, one of the visiting Chilean candidates wrote, "I want to thank you for everything you did for me during my stay in Buffalo. It was the best experience I ever had and I hope I can come back next year if things keep going well" (spring 2013).

Similar to the Zambian experience, the Chilean group has made multiple presentations to extend the reach of the project and recruit new students for a second trip. The chair and a group of eight students traveled in June of 2013 to Santiago (along with a group of 11 SUNY Buffalo State sociology students and their respective chair). A candidate recently posted about her experience this year,

It just makes me appreciate and respect in a new light all of those people that come to our country. I hear so often that immigrants need to "just learn English" as if it is a simple task, or people expressing frustration that signs are often in English AND Spanish, but let me tell you, when things are in English here or there are pictures to go along with signs, it's the most helpful thing in the world! It is tiring constantly not understanding things and people around you. The simplest tasks become daunting and intimidating when you are not fluent or comfortable with a language—and my three-week experience in Chile is so tame in comparison to what millions of others around the world face every single day. (Summer, 2013)

THE JOURNEY CONTINUES

In January of 2014, a new group will travel to the Dominican Republic for the first time, where they will share and learn teaching techniques through service learning activities. Teacher candidates will observe and teach at an early childhood Montessori school, engage in intensive Spanish language experiences, and develop an understanding and appreciation of Dominican culture through daily mealtime with families from the school. Another faculty member with ties to a Reggio Emilia school in Italy will complete her sabbatical developing a second early childhood partnership in Sienna that will integrate the arts and expose teacher candidates to the Reggio Emilia philosophy. A faculty member with ties to Beijing, China, has interest in developing an early childhood mathematics partnership in the future.

It is believed that the PDS Consortium has achieved many successes in its attempt to globalize the experiences of faculty, teacher candidates, and school partners; however, the need to reflect, evaluate, and readjust is recognized. Several projects are in place to work toward these goals. For example, the faculty member with ties to Zambia has been approved for a sabbatical to further her research and write a book about this project. The objective of her sabbatical is to write the first draft of a manuscript, *From XXX to Lusaka, Zambia: Exploring Ways to Increase Cultural Awareness and Appreciation in U. S. Pre-service Teachers.* She will use the data collected during her three visits to Zambia, the first an exploratory visit to Lusaka, where she met with faculty and administrators at UNZA, Ministry of Education officials, and teachers to establish a collaborative relationship and begin planning. The second and third visits involved teacher candidates. In the book, she will explore changes in her own thinking as a teacher educator as well as changes in the thinking of participating candidates.

In addition to scholarship associated with the global activities, the program seeks to ensure that all teacher candidates have multiple global experiences during their program. Therefore, the chair has been approved for a sabbatical that will map the department's curriculum to infuse global issues into common readings, assignments, and field experiences. This will lead to more effective and systematic advisement so candidates can plan service learning and travel experiences from the moment they begin the program. An important goal for these travel and international teaching experiences is the development of a group of well-organized

PDS sites with systematic governance policies, thus strengthening collaboration, reflection, and research opportunities (NAPDS Nine Essentials, #7) (Brindley et al., 2008). In addition, other options are being sought for those candidates who may not be able to travel due to particular circumstances or responsibilities. These options might include service and undergraduate research opportunities that utilize the local community with global ties or the use of technology to connect virtually with international partners. The ultimate goal is to ensure that all teacher candidates engage in global experiences throughout their program. Additionally, during this sabbatical, the chair will explore systems of evaluation to measure impact for both program evaluation and dissemination purposes. Upon acceptance into the elementary education program, teacher candidates will be evaluated on their global awareness using a global knowledge assessment tool that currently exists or will be designed. This assessment will again be utilized as an exit tool upon graduation to assess student global awareness as well as program effectiveness.

SUNY Buffalo State faculty and administration are also interested in finding ways for students to build on undergraduate international experiences such as those described above. A committee was formed in early 2013 to begin planning for a peace studies graduate program in collaboration with the Peace Corps. This program would be open to students across the campus, including new teachers.

With the support of the PDS Consortium and SUNY Buffalo State's School of Education, new goals include ways to increase candidates' ability to work with English language learners. Teacher education faculty are being trained in the SIOP (Sheltered Instruction Observation Protocol of the Center for Applied Linguistics) model so they, in turn, can support the development of teacher candidates in this area. In addition, the school of education has submitted a proposal to the New York State Education Department to develop an English as a Second Language certificate for graduate students with corresponding field experiences to prepare teachers to work with the growing global community in Buffalo and beyond.

SUGGESTIONS FOR OTHERS INTERESTED IN MAKING THE JOURNEY

This journey has taken 22 years, and there is more to accomplish in the road ahead to build and develop this PDS Consortium so that it continues to serve as a passport to the world for teacher candidates. Other teacher education programs are encouraged to develop their international possibilities, and the following suggestions are respectfully made with consideration to the discussion above:

- Align with the institution's strategic goals as they relate to global education to increase the likelihood of leadership support and funding opportunities.
- Begin with an inquiry approach by developing program-wide questions for faculty, teacher candidates, and school partners to explore. Form book

clubs in which faculty, teacher candidates, and school partners read a professional text and/or global children's literature together.

- Build on the strengths and interest of the faculty by encouraging faculty with university and school-based partners in other countries to develop connections. However, it is also important to encourage other faculty to participate so that a program moves beyond a personal project of one individual to an integrated experience within a PDS.
- Utilize PDS partnerships to build opportunities for global experiences by working with local schools, agencies, and businesses serving culturally and linguistically diverse populations in your community.
- Work with local schools to identify the needs of culturally and linguistically diverse groups of students and muster the human, financial, and knowledge resources of the institution to help meet those needs.
- Work across the campus to collaborate, share resources, and support common goals. These groups can include other education programs, the arts and sciences faculties, the international education office, and so on.
- Seek to develop partnerships that include both a university and a P–12 school. For a variety of reasons, it is often difficult to work directly with the public schools in the target country. A university partner can often help navigate the complex bureaucracies of public schools. Moreover, the university partnership provides people with whom faculty and teacher candidates can collaborate and develop exchange opportunities.
- When establishing partnerships internationally, find out what each institution hopes to gain from the collaboration and work continually to build open communication, trust, and ongoing support. Formalize a partnership through PDS structures.
- Clearly articulate the incentives for candidates so they understand the intrinsic and extrinsic rewards of participating in global experiences locally and internationally.
- Find ways to support candidates financially so that everyone can participate in international travel experiences. For example, we drew on the resources of the college through our undergraduate research office, graduate office, and international education office. In addition, the school of education dean, in collaboration with our college foundation, actively seeks donors who will support scholarships that contribute to the cost of travel. Finally, we recommend planning for travel through advisement as students enter the program so teacher candidates can begin saving for a study abroad experience.
- Experiment, evaluate, and readjust—it is truly worth the effort!

REFERENCES

Banks, J. A. (2007). *Educating citizens in a multicultural society*. New York, NY: Teachers College Press.

Brindley, R., Field, B. E., & Lessen, E. (2008). *What it means to be a professional development school*. Columbia, SC: National Association for Professional Development Schools (NAPDS).

Brown, S. C., & Kysilka, M. L. (2009). *What every teacher should know about multicultural and global education*. Boston, MA: Pearson Education.

Darling-Hammond, L. (2010). *The flat world of education: How America's commitment to equity will determine our future*. New York, NY: Teachers College Press.

Gay, G. (2010). *Culturally responsive teaching: Theory, research, and practice*. New York, NY: Teachers College Press.

Holmes Group. (1986). *Tomorrow's leaders*. East Lansing, MI: Author.

Ladson-Billings, G. (1995). Toward a theory of culturally relevant pedagogy. *American Educational Research Journal, 32*(3), 465–491.

National Council for Accreditation of Teacher Education (NCATE). (2001). *Standards for professional development schools*. Washington, DC: Author.

National Council for Accreditation of Teacher Education (NCATE). (2010). *Transforming teacher education through clinical practice: A national strategy to prepare effective teachers*. Report of the Blue Ribbon Panel on Clinical Preparation and Partnerships. Washington, DC: Author.

Nieto, S. (1999). *The light in their eyes: Creating multicultural learning communities. Multicultural Education Series*. New York, NY: Teachers College Press.

Roberts, S. V. (2009). *From every end of the Earth: 13 families and the lives they made in America*. New York, NY: Harper Collins.

WEBSITES

Chile PDS Blog: http://chilepdsatbsedu.wordpress.com

Global Book Project: *http://globalbookproject.buffalostate.edu/*

Journey's End Refugee Services: from *http://jersbuffalo.org/*

Professional Development Schools, Consortium: http://www.buffalostate.edu/pds/

Professional Development Schools, Globalization Themes and Initiatives: *http://www.buffalostate.edu/pds/x965.xml*

Professional Development Schools, Mini Grant/Action Research: *http://www.buffalostate.edu/pds/x503.xml*

Professional Development Schools, PDS Mission Statement: *http://www.buffalostate.edu/pds/x796.xml*

School of Education, Office of the Dean, SOE Mission and Core Values: http://www.buffalostate.edu/schoolofeducation/x784.xml

SUNY Buffalo State, Strategic Planning, Strategic Direction #1: http://www.buffalostate.edu/strategicplanning/x668.xml

Zambia PDS Blog: http://zambiapdsatbsedu.wordpress.com

PART II

STAKEHOLDERS' PERSPECTIVE

CHAPTER 7

WHEN A PROFESSIONAL DEVELOPMENT SCHOOL PROGRAM BECOMES UNSUSTAINABLE

Trying to Keep the Best of Both Worlds

Laura A. Mitchell, Janice L. Nath, and Myrna D. Cohen

ABSTRACT

Although teacher educators hope that they can maintain many types of university/school partnerships, not all professional development school (PDS) programs have been sustainable—for a variety of reasons. By comparing pre- and post-PDS implementation in a teacher education program, researchers found elements that could allow for informed decision making or modifications when it becomes impossible for a teacher education program to preserve its full-fledged PDS model. This investigation could, in turn, allow the basic premises of many crucial elements of PDS work to continue, even if the entire model cannot be supported. It may also aid in

Creating Visions for University-School Partnerships, pages 105–128.
Copyright © 2014 by Information Age Publishing
All rights of reproduction in any form reserved.

smoothing the transition period between models. This study investigates a program
that was forced to change from an established PDS program to a modified version
and focuses upon perceptions of the differences before and after.

The professional development school (PDS) model has been lauded since its conception nearly two decades ago as to its positive influence on participants (Gill
& Hove, 2000; Houston, Hollis, Clay, Ligons, & Roff, 1999; National Council
for Accreditation of Teacher Education [NCATE], 2010–2014; Neubert & Binko,
1998; Teitel, 2004; and also see studies in Nath, Guadarrama, & Ramsey, 2011;
Guadarrama, Nath, & Ramsey, 2002, 2005, 2008). In terms of its exceptional
contribution to teacher preparation, the PDS movement began to show its strength
as a teacher education model in the late 1990s by providing an answer to calls
for a change in pedagogy that would closely link theory and practice (Ball, 2000;
Korthagen & Kessels, 1999). Wise and Levine (2007), for example, stated, "The
PDS is to teacher preparation as the teaching hospital is to physician preparation"
in that it "provides high-quality service to students while preparing new genera-
tions of teachers." Teacher candidates in PDSs are well supported throughout
their teacher education program by both university faculty and mentors in schools
as they learn about teaching with children in the actual arena in which they will
someday work in a classroom of their own.

The constructive effects of PDSs on teacher candidates, mentors, and university
professionals have been well documented (Basile, 2011). The academic achievement of the K–12 students in PDSs has been studied less frequently (Breault &
Breault, 2012), although there has been some such work (NCATE, 2002; Maryland Higher Education Commission and Maryland Partnership for Teaching and
Learning, 2007). However, both formal and informal evidence reported by those
who work in PDS schools is prevalent to support its use as a model for training future teachers and for improving schools in numerous ways (Basile, 2011;
Darling-Hammond, 2006).

PDS sustainability has recently become an important question, as many PDSs
began with time-limited grant funds and other support that may be coming (or
has already come) to an end. In some instances, state and/or university mandatory
requirements for field-based models spurred the establishment of numerous PDSs
throughout the country. When funds and other support were depleted or mandates/
accreditation pressures lifted, some teacher education programs reverted to more
traditional models out of choice, need, or directive. In some instances, there was a
combination of factors that forced teacher education programs to reconfigure their
structures and to move away from their original PDS framework. There are, however, few studies that investigate what happens when a department or college can
no longer support its PDS model or when interest wanes and universities move
on to other models. This study gives the context and history of the change in one
department from a full teacher preparation PDS model to a modified model when
state and institutional support for the PDS model collapsed.

The university itself is a noted Hispanic-serving institution with the most diverse student body west of the Mississippi River. University students are not only diverse ethnically but are also nontraditional in age and income—with many being first-time graduates in their families. Even so, a number of education majors are young white females who have not worked with diverse school children, or, if they are students of color themselves, they are sometimes ethnically and/or economically different from students in schools where they are likely to be employed in this large urban area. For this reason, the teacher education program from its conception recognized the importance of placing teacher candidates in metropolitan area schools as often as possible; thus, the initial PDS model involved resident field hours for two semesters, followed by a 14-week student teaching semester in urban or suburban schools that were designated as being low-income and diverse campuses.

The teacher preparation program in question was created in 1999 as a PDS program and was sustained by grants and by state funding that generously supported field-based hours. Teacher candidates were placed in cohorts for their two field-based semesters (Block I and Block II) prior to their traditional student teaching capstone semester (Block III). Three courses (educational psychology and/or various methods) blocked future teachers together in their professional development coursework and in their school experience on site. Each cohort was placed in a PDS site (or, if the cohort was too large, two neighboring schools) within a choice of 10 partnering school districts in the vicinity of the university. Teacher candidates were closely supported by a team of three full-time faculty members (one of whom was designated as the block coordinator), a university supervisor, a school mentor, and others in the schools. The block coordinator collaborated with the school principal to designate and train mentor teachers for the teacher candidates, locate a classroom on the school campus for the cohort's university courses, plan teacher workshops, and determine service activities for the teacher candidates at the school. The block coordinator also served as a problem solver for the cohort throughout the semester, took care of a variety of accreditation- and university-related paperwork, coordinated the block syllabus and calendar, scheduled meetings with the cohort faculty, arranged for final portfolio presentations, set up mentor appreciation events, and so forth. Each teacher candidate was required to spend at least 60 hours in Block I and 60 hours in Block II in an assigned mentor's classroom. The university faculty taught their classes at the diverse schools sites and enhanced their courses with elements from the field. For example, literacy students worked with young children at the schools to tutor and to assess reading skills, and the science methods teacher candidates often arranged for a special Earth Day for children. Content area specialists and administrators at the schools often shared their expertise with the teacher candidates within the framework of the university classes. Moreover, each teacher candidate was required to teach at least two observed lessons in Block I (preferably reading and math, if specializing in Early Childhood–6, or content area if specializing in 7–12) and two lessons in Block II (preferably science and social studies for EC–6 and content area for 7–12) and to have constructive feedback provided to the teacher candidates based upon the state appraisal instrument.

This field-based PDS model proved to be very effective in terms of teacher preparation. Principals often vocalized their appreciation of the skills of these teacher candidates, as well as their acculturation and comfort levels in the urban settings. Because of this, many teacher candidates were offered teaching positions even before they completed the program, and almost all graduates were rapidly employed throughout the city upon graduation. Five-year retention rates of the graduates of this program were the highest of the of the 40 teacher preparation programs associated with the five largest university systems in Texas (Center for Research, Evaluation, and Advancement of Teacher Education [CREATE], 2012). Overall, the field-based schools positively reported their satisfaction with the involvement of the teacher candidates and were stable partners with the university program. Although many of the issues and concerns that typically plague many PDSs were also experienced by this program, it nonetheless expanded and flourished over the years. For example, in 2004, there were five Block I cohorts and five Block II cohorts, while in 2011 there were 11 Block I cohorts and 9 Block II cohorts, and the number of partner schools sites and districts increased accordingly.

However, the program was costly. Expenses beyond those collected through the student credit hours included: (1) a half-time course release for each of the block coordinators (15–20 coordinators per semester on average, resulting in 8–10 course releases per semester); (2) mileage for field-based faculty members (some faculty members drove over 120 miles day); (3) payment and travel expenses for the block supervisors, which amounted to over $120,000 per semester; and (4) a minimum of three professors who were required to maintain each established site for at least two semesters (even if the student enrollment changed significantly in the second semester). In addition, it was imperative to grant a course release each semester to a faculty member who directed the overall program. This program director met monthly together with all of the block coordinators, negotiated with the school districts, conducted partnership meetings, oversaw the paperwork and program policies, conducted semester orientations and special sessions, met with teacher candidates who needed growth plans, and so forth. Another two course releases were assigned to a coordinator who managed the supervisors. Responsibilities for the latter position included supervisor training; constant updating of a modified state observation instrument that was used for field observation; and organizing paperwork for the observations, student evaluations, and supervisors' pay. An additional financial strain on the program was that of stringent course caps. Because seating space was often constrained in designated public school rooms, university classes had to be capped at low numbers, limiting the number of student credit hours to be earned per course. In the early years of the program, generous state funding for field-based courses and modest student fees helped fray the expenses of the model. However, over the years, state funding for field-based courses was gradually eliminated due to the decrease in state monetary support for universities (and schools) and the decrease in state support for field-based student credit hours. Faced with these financial restraints, the institution mandated that the education department "do something differently" because of the expense involved in the PDS model. Therefore, after administering the full PDS program for eleven years, the department was charged with changing the costly model to a financially self-sufficient one.

Thus began over a year and a half of faculty/administration discussion, brainstorming, and planning for program revision for the department. When embarking on this endeavor, it was kept in mind that the new program would need to (1) be true to the philosophy of the department, particularly with regard to early field experiences; (2) be collaboratively developed; (3) be supported by the whole faculty; (4) be beneficial to teacher candidates; (5) be held to the state-mandated hours; and (6) satisfy to requests of the institutional administration.

The simplest solution to the problem would have been to change the block semesters to a traditional model with classes at the university, dissolve the idea of a cohort, and require the field experiences only for the student teaching semester. Yet, when the strengths of the current program were examined, the faculty agreed that the extended field experiences and the cohort model were values that should not be sacrificed. In order to validate this view, a survey was administered to teacher candidates in which they were asked to evaluate various aspects of the program. Their responses, at that time, confirmed the importance of both the extended fieldwork and the cohort model.

The department engaged in 18 months of intensive work in order to find a way to maintain the extensive fieldwork and cohort model in a program that could be financially self- sufficient. The faculty met as a whole and in numerous committees and subcommittees throughout three long semesters with optional meetings during the summer months—all of which were well attended. The key to the plan was to count the hours of fieldwork in what was Block I (60 hours) and Block II (60 hours) each as a three-hour course that would earn tuition for the institution. The previous model of independently paid supervisors would then change to that of university adjuncts who would be paid for a course. However, simply adding hours to the program was not an option due to state mandates that limit the number of hours permitted for an undergraduate degree. It was therefore necessary to develop a revision that kept to the same number of program hours and that included six hours of fieldwork courses. The department was forced to consolidate, synthesize, and eliminate course hours to make room for a total of six new credit hours of fieldwork in the program. Although the faculty felt that this was a difficult sacrifice, the commitment to maintaining the extensive field experiences motivated them to find innovative adjustments. Courses were combined, streamlined, and compacted. Another major hurdle was administering the program without the model of block coordinators, as this was another major financial drain on the institution. These responsibilities were shifted to university adjuncts teaching/ supervising in the new fieldwork courses. It was also determined that although the teacher candidates would do their fieldwork in public schools, university classes would no longer be taught in the schools. This eliminated mileage for the faculty and allowed for larger classes (bringing in more revenue per course). The elimination of the block coordinators and their related course releases, the allowance for larger classes, and the addition of paid student credit hours for the fieldwork helped defray the costs of the former format.

A crucial step in this process was discussing these changes with partner schools and districts and obtaining their feedback. Throughout the lifetime of this PDS, school partners did not *financially* support the program. Mentor teachers were not paid by the district; their work was voluntary as was the time and effort of the staff and administrators at the campuses. The schools also provided space for the program to hold its classes. Professional development, research, and teacher candidate projects were voluntarily provided by the university and were not paid for by the district. The university rewarded the mentor teachers with certificates documenting professional development hours and with small tokens of appreciation when the department budget could manage the cost, but the districts did not compensate the work of the mentor teachers. The argument could be made that in order to sustain the PDS program, the school districts could have offered some monetary support. It would have been financially beneficial for the partner districts to invest in this program because the new teacher hires graduating from the program saved the district money. The excellent preparation and the high retention rate of the graduates helped districts minimize costs for new teacher mentoring and for recruitment and teacher turn-over expenses. However, the university revision directive for the PDS came at a time when the school districts themselves were faced with severe budget cuts causing them to lay off teachers, increase class sizes, use all possible spaces/classrooms, do away with enrichment programs, and other measures. Therefore, conversations about financial district support for the PDS never took place as the department was sensitive to these factors. The major impacts for the schools in the revision plan were: (1) there would no longer be classes held on their campuses, (2) the schools would not be communicating through an on-site block coordinator, (3) mentor training might move to be online rather than face to face, (4) the teacher candidates would not all have the same schedule at the school for their fieldwork and so would not all be at the school at the same time, (5) university faculty would not be on the campus, (6) service projects (including teacher candidates' volunteer projects) might not take place, and so forth. As the new program was implemented, most of the partner schools remained in place as fieldwork sites and transitioned into the new model along with the department. The partners were understanding and supportive of the department's challenges and needs.

One positive ramification of the revised program for the teacher candidates was increased financial aid. Previously, the block fieldwork was embedded in their courses, and, in order to be enrolled as a full-time student, taking an additional three-hour course during the nine hours of Block I and Block II was necessary. In the revised program, Blocks I and II included the three-hour fieldwork course, so what was previously nine hours became a full-time twelve hours for the students, better serving those who apply for financial aid. Another positive impact for the students was more flexibility in their scheduling and in their choice of field experience locations.

During the transition process into this new model, the department continues to revise and perfect this program as much as possible, especially in terms of efficient administration and curriculum. To assess how the transition to a new structure was developing, researchers sought information from a number of sources. At this point in the transition period, there is no cohort of teacher candidates who are completers of the entire revised program. However, valuable information was available from in-depth interviews with faculty and staff who participated in both models. In particular, those who were former block coordinators and who are current instructors in the new structure contributed important insights. In addition, interviewing individuals who held organizational positions and administrative offices throughout the years of the former program provided valuable data.

METHODS

In this qualitative research study, ten professors completed open-ended interviews to compare the implementation between the pre- and post-PDS systems. The participants were invited to participate in the study so that they could add their perspectives to the changes that were made between the two systems and the transitions to a new PDS program. The 30–45-minute open-ended interviews were analyzed through the qualitative data software program, ATLAS.ti 7.0. This program allowed the authors to code the interviews both inductively and then deductively (Lewins & Silver, 2007). The themes that emerged were identified through Glaser's (1965) constant comparative data analysis.

Each participant must have been a former block coordinator and, at the time of the interview, must have been an instructor in a professional development course. Each had held the position of organizing a PDS site (often with up to three schools each) and had served as the liaison between these schools and the university. Each participant would still be teaching the same course to teacher candidates as he/she did previously—but would be relocated to a university campus (either at the main campus or a distance campus). Nine faculty members were interviewed in depth—all having served in a PDS school(s), with two participants doubling as the program director (overall organizer) and two also serving as chair during this time period. The average years of service in the role of block coordinator were about eight years for participants. One participant served three years as overall program director in the former PDS framework and was a coordinator prior to that for a number of years in this (and another) university. The other program director interviewed had served one year in the modified program and a number of years as a block coordinator prior to that. One chair interviewed served four years in the administrative position concurrent with being a block coordinator, while the other chair interviewed served as block coordinator for a number of years prior to her term as chair.

All of the participants who were interviewed were first asked to confirm their status as having taught both in a PDS situation and, currently, in the modified version. The open-ended interview protocol also included the following:

Can you explain any differences in your roles then and now?
What would you say were the three most important things you did for students then—and now?
Have you noticed some things that may have been *more difficult* then (when working with a PDS)? (with organization, mentors, teacher candidates)
Have you noticed some things that were *easier/better* then (when working in a PDS)? (with organization, mentors, teacher candidates)
Have you noticed some things that may have been *more difficult* now (with just field placements)? (with organization, mentors, teacher candidates)
Have you noticed some things that were *easier/better* now (with just field placements)? (with organization, mentors, teacher candidates)
Can you compare any differences that you have noticed in teacher candidates between then and now? (skills, confidence, relationships with mentors, ease in going into school setting, communication, paperwork, peer connections, teacher candidate time spent in schools, other)
If you could choose either system, which would you prefer and why?

By using the open-ended interviewing process, the participants were asked questions that would help them reflect about their past experiences in order to gain a deeper understanding of their participation in the pre- and post-PDS systems.

RESULTS

Emerging Themes

The themes that emerged from the data analysis showed that the participants had deep beliefs in the professional development system. They described their dedication and commitment to the program and wanted to express their concerns for the changes in the programs. The participants also described ways that the post-PDS is evolving into a program that they could support. They found that there were elements of both programs that were important to the PDS system and that they would want to keep in the present system. The themes that emerged helped the authors understand the differences in the two programs that were important to the participants. The participants identified elements that they would want to keep, change, and eliminate from the present program. The themes that will be discussed are: (1) maintaining theory to practice, (2) faculty cohesiveness, (3) having a central voice for clear communication, (4) time and energy, (5) the stress of maintaining relationships, (6) connections with mentors and administrators, (7) the loss of the added value of a PDS, (8) the effect on university students, and (9) keeping the best of both worlds.

Theory to Practice

This seems to have been a major concern for many of the participants. One professor remarked:

> I am an instructor now in a university classroom, but I maintain a strong link in my course assignments to the fieldwork still required of students. For example, we always have some "group shares" about what they [teacher candidates] have seen in relationship to management, motivation, development theory, etc. and written assignments dealing with case studies or other assignments where they must bring in theory into what they have observed. There are observation instruments regarding lesson plan formats they must use. They have to go through our state teacher assessment instrument item by item (which their supervisors use with them when they teach their lessons), so it is still tightly connected in terms of that. We don't have a classroom any more at the school and there isn't the opportunity for them to go from my class to their mentor's class, but that link of good theory to real life is still a solid part of my instruction that carries over. It is not so different from the former program in that [my course] is not a methods class, so teacher candidates never did try out various methods for me. Because they still are in schools every week, they still are doing much of the same type of work for me. There are lots of "ahas" in the theory to practice area still.

A professor who teaches methods, however, noted, "All I've ever been in is a field-based program, so I had to revamp my whole instructional style." He continued to talk about the trust that he has to place in others at the school sites to "carry their end of things [instructionally]. I come in now about 45 minutes before class and stay [late] until I am kicked out just to listen to hear what my students are talking about," and that often directs the flow of what will happen in class the following week. He noted that the PDS used to provide him with constant contexts and scaffolding, but he now has to be sure to proactively approach information in multiple ways without having the shared information immediately at hand. Another concurred, noting that she now has students carefully document through technology, whenever possible, to make those common contexts visible to those who were "not there." On the other hand, it was also noted by one methods instructor that there is a new instructional freedom without the PDS structure and mindset.

A literacy teacher told of her lessons in reading:

So many of the assignments that our students did helped in understanding the levels and assessment of the children.... Class was in school with model lessons; children came in eight different times (during the semester).... To understand the instruction and assessments of the student, you had to practice with the students.... [This semester] I added lots of video clips.

Faculty Cohesiveness

The former program created a natural process for faculty cohesiveness. The professors reported that they depended on each other to create a block syllabus, block grade, and portfolio presentations. They shared resources and worked together to develop positive experiences for the students. Because of the structure of the PDS, the faculty found that they communicated closely together. They shared information about students, mentor teachers, and school experiences. They depended on each other's skill sets and expertise to integrate the various subjects that they taught in the blocks. The block coordinator was the person who worked directly with the students and the mentor teachers. The block coordinator and PDS faculty were problem solvers because they knew the mentor teachers and the teacher candidates well. The faculty found that they developed connections together that built interdependence among the full faculty. Now, one noted, "We don't seek out other faculty to build, and don't build on each other's assignments in other content. I don't want to overwhelm students, but I don't necessarily know what other [professors] are giving [now]." Another pointed out that she had students from three different professors in just one of her courses, so multiplying that by all the former PDS courses she taught would be overwhelming to continue to try to coordinate with hers.

Several former coordinators remarked that the team approach was strong in identifying those teacher candidates who, for various reasons, became at risk. The block coordinator was in charge of overseeing all students at a PDS site, so methods professors who were also assigned to his or her site, along with mentors, supervisors, and/or administrators, would always contact the block coordinator if there were any signs of academic difficulty, professionalism issues in the school, excess absences in courses or in fieldwork, or other any other difficulties a teacher candidate might be experiencing. This group would often have suggestions to help in turning the situation around in various ways. If the teacher candidate needed to change but did not move in a positive direction, the entire university team (usually consisting of the coordinator, methods professor(s), program director, and the supervisor with input from the field site) would meet with the candidate to discuss and problem solve for redirection with a better chance of success. Very occasionally, if the problem seemed insurmountable, the team would encourage the candidate to examine an alternative career and graduate without certification. This team approach was seen by participants as highly effective, even when the block coordinator alone was dealing with the teacher candidate because information had come from a number of sources. These types of "extra connections" were also seen as opportunities to quickly identify issues that might work against future success in the classroom for the teacher candidate and/or his/her students. One former coordinator noted, "I can't really 'get on someone' [now] because it might not be a person from my class." She continued to say that she had been more forceful with students when there was a red flag early on. "I used to address a red flag. The role of coordinator is to make the student successful. One of my students last semester failed two other classes. Those [red flag] conversations need to happen but are not." This was echoed by another former coordinator who stated:

> [I] really didn't know one of the other methods professors this semester, whereas in the past, we would have all met. If I have a student who is in jeopardy, I have to go to the director of the program to see what other classes she is taking and who is teaching them. They could be in anybody's class, even an adjunct who I may have never met.... On the flipside of that, students used to occasionally come to me about "professor problems" as well (too much work for the site, due dates for big projects that were right together, and many others), and, if the situation seemed warranted, I could ask the professor in question to help me work with it.

Yet another coordinator confirmed that, "We don't seek out other faculty to build together and don't build on each other's assignments in other content. I don't want to overwhelm students, but I don't necessarily know what others are giving [now]."

Course/content integration was also mentioned as more difficult now. "Because courses aren't formally blocked, I might not have the same group of students as another methods professor," mentioned one professor. Another of the professors pointed out that now in the new program there tends to be a disconnect within the faculty. Because the faculty members are currently not on a school campus, they do not interact with each other as much. They communicate less and feel that a lack of these relationships affect their interactions with teacher candidates.

A Central Voice

Another theme that closely ties into the faculty cohesiveness, yet is a bit different, is having one person (a block coordinator) for students to see as the "authority figure" and as the voice of the university on site. At times, as mentioned above, the block coordinator might have directly and immediately contacted the teacher candidate who was at risk about his or her difficulties to "deal with it" (but with the force of a group behind the directive). A central voice also becomes important in having students obtain information that makes their entry into fieldwork smoother and answers to their questions about the program easier to obtain—and often more correct. "I don't feel there is a connection between the department and students now, and supervisors can't always give a 'united front' because sometimes they give the wrong information because they don't stay current," one former coordinator said. "There is no central person to get everything in line—there is an info gap," this coordinator exclaimed. "Coordinators," one stated, "were used to having such tight reins on everything.... It was difficult to let that go." Yet another had mixed feelings, stating:

> Before, there was always some information "coming down" to give to students. I took up half my course [which was a very important one for state testing] giving out information. Now it is given by supervisors and the director. I can have all my time back to prepare students, and, although there are still a few things I have to do, it is much better.

Another coordinator restated that she felt that the information gap had been a little shaky at first in the new configuration but that certain roles for information giving had become designated and that information was flowing correctly now. A methods professor said, "because I was a coordinator [before], I continue doing much of the same." However, as time goes on, the knowledge of the various roles the block coordinator played may be lost—as instructors simply "teach their courses."

All of the participants felt that the role of the block coordinator affected the transition to the new program. They found that the block coordinator was the person who took care of the administrative duties such as teacher candidate placements. This person also was the "trouble shooter" or the problem solver for the student complaints or mentor teacher situations. The block coordinator not only made the administrative contacts and the mentor teacher placements, but this person knew the teachers well at their campuses. The block coordinator could make changes quickly and easily at the campus. All of the participants reported that the job of the block coordinator was time intensive. Instruction time had to be sacrificed in the methods courses to complete the administrative tasks. One participant reported that it was frustrating to give up so much time and not be able to cover all of the material in the class.

However, the professors recognized that the role of the block coordinator was important because they all valued the field-based experiences. They also noted that the supervisors and adjunct professors took over many of the jobs of the block coordinators in the new system. The participants discovered that they were spending less time on the school campuses and regretted not knowing the mentor teachers as well. They worried that the teacher candidates would not get the attention that they used to get because the block coordinator was such a strong advocate for them.

Time and Energy

The time spent in various tasks and building relationships at a PDS is a notorious concern for those professors on sites. Breault and Breault (2012) noted, "This phenomenon represents a critical issue in PDS work" (p. 136), with a large portion of articles reviewed in their study showing considerable stress placed on professors (particularly nontenured professors) who experience the ambiguity of expectations versus rewards from their universities. As noted earlier, one-half semester course load (which often became an overload for this person) was granted to one of the three field faculty members per site to be the PDS site coordinator, but this role became difficult to fill due to the amount of work and problem solving involved commensurate with the amount of compensation. These issues were all able to be overcome for many years due to the faculty "buy in" of the concept of PDS work, but the time and effort were always seen as a "difficult but necessary" part of PDS maintenance.

One former block coordinator in this study shared:

> It became so much work and time spent that the extra money for being a coordinator just plain wasn't worth it—almost at any price—even though it was "the best" for all of the stakeholders! It often had to become an overload, but I didn't necessarily want an overload—even if paid—every semester. Without that position, I feel like I have time for the other university commitments I am supposed to do now.

Another who has kept up with her PDS because of a small grant noted that she still serves her PDS

> ...constantly (8–10 hours week). The grant paid for some helpers to get materials, etc. for science with cross-department soft money, but my time is really going.... I probably won't get recognized for the service, so it might have to go soon. Even though I love what I'm doing, I don't know how long it can be done.

Only one of the 15–20 PDS coordinators per semester has remained teaching in her school. Another maintains close ties with a school due to a science/math grant. "These classes [associated with staying in the schools and with the role of the block coordinator] should be a 1.5 load," one professor noted, while continuing to say that the course load is "more time consuming than a masters course." "In a city this size," yet another noted, "I used to spend so much time on the roads and in traffic. I must have gained 5 working hours a week just in travel time alone [with the modified version]," while still another said, "I found the time before the semester very time consuming.... We needed a block syllabus and a calendar with the three professors.... I enjoyed doing it, but it was very time consuming."

Other professors spoke about how much energy it took to teach in the PDS.

> The trunk of my car was always full of my course materials the whole semester, and it would always take me two or three trips to and from the school parking lot to bring everything in—and all of us are fairly middle aged—or over! I had more than one PDS, at times, so it wasn't a matter of leaving it at the site, although we rarely had storage. It was draining! Sometimes they needed our room for testing, so we'd have to find a corner somewhere. I had two PDSs on the same day sometimes, and I always had to get there early to carry heavy materials back and forth, so it was really a long hard day—physically.

Another interviewee added to the differences of teaching in the university classroom versus teaching in the field—schools that were not always well equipped:

> We were in this little conference room…. We had to bring our own screen, computer, and projector. We had to set it all up ourselves. We never had Internet…we had to talk over [lots of noise]…. The actual teaching situation was not good. Sometimes all of my attention would go to setting up.

Yet another block coordinator spoke to the fact of never teaching on the university campus during the full PDS model, so she felt that there was a loss of energy that comes from continued collegial interactions. "I was teaching methods in four sites. I felt really isolated from my content area colleagues, and I didn't have the interactions we have when your peers are down the hall or next door."

Although the comments were overwhelmingly disparaging about the time and effort of this work, most also commented that the role of the coordinator was indispensable and that it should be "reinstituted somehow." There was a concern that the current program director did not have to assume the role of all block coordinators in terms of problem solving with teacher candidate difficulties. "That would be overwhelming," one former coordinator noted.

The Stress of Maintaining Relationships.

This seemed to be a theme that was widely felt in various ways.

> I loved being in the schools with children of all ages while I was there, but there is a lot of stress with PDSs. There are many kinds of stressors! As a coordinator, I often felt like I had to beg a principal to place our students. Sometimes I didn't get placement far into the semester, and then our teacher candidates were upset at me because there was required fieldwork and they couldn't get started. I would be "written up" in my course evaluations [for the course taught for the block], even though I couldn't do anything about it, and it wasn't about an instructional issue. I really resented that this role flowed over into evaluations sometimes in that way, and I stressed over it considerably. Sometimes the principal at a PDS would change over the summer, and all the plans and relationships you had made were gone. Sometimes you knew the school didn't want you, but the principal wanted "the name" of the PDS on his/her resume. Sometimes we didn't want to be at a particular school because the environment wasn't what we wanted for our teacher candidates, but it was "politically incorrect" to pull out. There was the stress of being the go-between with a teacher candidate and a mismatched mentor. There was always the pressure of being the "face of the university" in every single sentence one would say in that setting, and, being aware of the power issues in a PDS, I was always careful to try to balance my actions and my words to that effect. If any type of accrediting agency was coming, you couldn't have a teacher, a principal, or a teacher candidate who wasn't happy about everything. It was also hard to maintain lack of stress when a teacher candidate was not doing well or when another instructor was causing irritation at the school for some reason. Those are the stresses that I don't miss at all…but I do miss the children and "my kids" being there, and I feel to some extent like I am back in the Ivory Tower…but I don't miss the stress.

One of the interviewees who was in an organizational position spoke further to this aspect:

From district to district, it was like apples, oranges, and alligators. They were so radically different in paperwork…it ruined four years of semesters for me. It took me about a month to wrap up a semester with problems that were pending. By the time I ramped up for field placements, then the semester started…. There were so many degrees of freedom that were out of your control that you were literally riding the tiger all the time.

Another ex-coordinator mentioned the lack of suitable mentors at a site where many students were placed.

I would know, for example, that some of my students wouldn't have the best of classrooms, and it would bother me quite a bit. Sometimes you could change it, and sometimes you couldn't…but it was stressful. That still occurs in the new program, but I don't have any control at all over it now.

Yet another stressor that is still part of the program occurs during state testing when mentors themselves often became stressed, and teacher candidates are trying to fulfill their university requirements. "That just comes with the territory in this state," one noted, "but there is currently less worry because the supervisory role (scheduling lesson observation) is not as tied to the block coordinator position."

Connections with Mentors and Administrators

The loss of connections with the mentors seems to be an important area that cannot be replicated by a modified version of a PDS model. In the past, a university PDS coordinator (1) communicated with the school administrators about placing teacher candidates, (2) met with mentors at the beginning of the semester, (3) conducted mentor training, (4) hosted an appreciation event, (5) organized teacher candidates' oral portfolio events for mentors and administrators, and (6) a number of other activities. The coordinator was often there in schools to teach and touch base with the school personnel on a weekly basis. When asked if it was difficult in the former PDS model to establish and keep up with these relationships, one ex-coordinator said, "No, I liked meeting with teachers; there were thank yous, I emailed teachers to see if all was okay; there was a nice relationship with the administration." Another reminisced about when the teacher candidates "threw thank you parties for the mentors and others who helped their schools. I think it really made them [the school-based partners] feel that they made a difference in teacher education." Another coordinator's comment noted that "we used to assist mentor teachers, but now there is no direct contact. You don't put a face with an email. They are stakeholders, too," and a fourth said, "As time is going by and I will know the teachers less and less, I will have to trust them more and more [to work with their teacher candidates] in using current (content) techniques." In a PDS, professors often have *carte blanche* to have their teacher candidates try activities or lessons that methods instructors want them to experience, but, without that relationship, the professors found that, many times, the teacher candidates are locked into what the teacher/school is doing and will not let the teacher candidate deviate from that.

Loss of Added Value

One interviewee mentioned the loss in some PDSs of special activities for school students by methods faculty (such as on Earth Day, math nights, etc.), professional development for teachers, co-authorship in grants, student tutoring programs, and other school-based activities that have decreased. Some professors maintained their former relationships with schools with which they had worked for a number of years, but others do not. These are value-added issues that are felt as being a great loss. One professor told that this was the greatest difference he felt—that is "making an impact based at the campus. That seems to impact me the most. Dr. ___ goes into the school at [one former PDS]. I thought about doing that but I didn't want to subvert the new program." Another told of her effect on schools: "A school got exemplary [ratings] because of [a] tutoring project when we were there…it gives students message 'I do it, I truly do it.' I am a better teacher because of it." Keeping current with teaching skills based on being in the classrooms with children was mentioned more than once by professors as an aid to their credibility with teacher candidates and constantly updating their skill sets.

Another issue is loss of ready researchers who may want to help easily investigate issues in the school and want to investigate related issues. "It was certainly easier to gain access to schools in the past," said one participant. "It will be hard to think about research with children now. I don't have those connections to get started."

A huge loss noted by one professor is considering knowledge and how it is being used.

> I have learned so much over the last 10 years working with teacher candidates [in the field]…what are their flaws are in their thinking, what do we need to address. That in itself is a professional development [for me]. I probably have gained more from that than any formal professional development.

The PDS required mentor training was discussed as a highly valued-added loss across the board. When teachers receive information on how to interact effectively with colleagues and novices, all benefit. Zadeh (2011) noted that in his medical training,

> The ideal mentor will help you take what you've learned in the books and apply them to the real world….The beauty of mentoring is that there are just as many rewards in the relationship for the mentor as there are for the protégé….both indi-

viduals are investing a part of their lives into the relationship. The result is a feeling of commitment value, appreciation, and the development of a loyal future colleague for life.

A study by Badiali, Nolan, Zembal-Saul, and Manno (2011) confirmed that 81% of their PDS mentors (n=60) responding to a survey reported that the PDS positively changed their teaching in general, which, of course, is added value for their students, too. Seen as a reason for change included the mentors seeing themselves as valuable in contributing to molding the university's curriculum as "co-experts." Mentors were also affected by seeing excitement in interns and having content knowledge university faculty there constantly. Many engaged in inquiry, and some mentors, in fact, took on action research either alone or in partnerships with interns. Participating in a "community of learners" was also a key in change for the researchers mentioned above, where most everyone became highly supportive in the mutual learning process and transparency for improvement. Adult learning seems to flourish in a climate (such as a PDS) when there is a "continuous cycle of collaborative activity and reflection on that activity" (Badiali et al., 2011, p. 339). Change may also take place in mentors as many teacher candidates observed them (which make mentors more metacognitively aware of their instruction and other work as teachers), but teacher candidates also shared new teaching strategies and knowledge in nonthreatening ways, which, in turn, can renew a mentor's practice.

How It Has Affected University Students

"There was a 'team approach,' so if there were issues, there would be extra connections. For example, if a student was removed or held back, the team would 'work together' to place her again; one was transformed," began one faculty member.

"I was forceful with students when there was a red flag early on. I used to address a red flag. The role of coordinator is to make student successful. Students this semester failed two other classes [and I didn't know it]. Those conversations need to happen but are not now," another participant pointed out. Having immediate attention is one area of concern for teacher candidates in the new program.

As noted, teacher candidates were, perhaps, helped earlier. "I do see a difference that is profound," yet another verbalized in referencing an expectation of a higher degree of professional dress and behavior for teacher candidates. "Now," he stated, "because they still have a history of being university students and bringing that into the classrooms...I am having to stress the importance of professionalism in the classroom. In the schools, that was just part of the culture, but here they are not making the transition from student to teacher candidate as easily." Yet another wrote that she saw that students did not care as much—that they "just want a course grade," and she also added that because in the PDS the faculty discussed the semester as a team but that, "now students compare profs and get mad when one is 'harder.'" She attributed it to less teamwork and to seeing the university faculty working with the teachers and the school administrators. "I see them [teacher candidates] as less prepared."

Another issue is the extension of work because, in the PDS setting, students would interact with each other in a three-day cycle. It has been observed that the teacher candidates don't get together formally or after class and that there is a breakdown in group projects because it requires more effort on their part. "They tweet each other and Facebook each other and have discussions on Blackboard" because they are not together; "they are communicating in more unusual ways."

On the positive side for many students, they are able to have more flexibility in taking their required professional development courses. Several participants commented that many of their students work, so they are more likely to be able to arrange their employment issues without the constraint that a formal PDS often requires. Many PDSs had, for example, parking issues that required teacher candidates to be there only certain days. In addition, there is more flexibility for sites. In the past, there were only a few sites per district, so many teacher candidates were forced to drive considerable distances (as were professors). This could also affect their work schedules along with possible childcare issues.

The Best of Both Worlds

Interestingly, the discussions in the interview process seemed to move former block coordinators into an analysis of taking the best from each program and to problem solve in order to resolve the issues that were seen as problematic in the new program. For example, most interviewees felt that the role of the block coordinator should be a part of the program in some manner; the former "cohort" structure had morphed into a new format that should be supported by faculty in different ways; the flexibility of the new program offered more to university students; and so forth. This type of program evaluation has not yet been completely formalized as a department, but it has been a part of various committee discussions. One reason for the lack of formal evaluation for the new program is that it would have been the group of "now dissolved block coordinators" who would have initiated that analysis. Another reason for this is that a full cohort of teacher candidates has not yet completed the entire program. Studies such as this one serve in the interim.

The instructors in the PDS found that they had less control over what they did in the PDS and that made them uncomfortable. Instead of giving up and saying that it "just couldn't be done," the faculty looked for ways to make it work. They have found ways to make the present PDS work for the benefit of their students.

The instructors found that they had more flexibility in teaching their classes at the university versus the school campus. They had to revamp or change their classes and, at first, that was frustrating. Then they looked for ways to integrate technology into their classes to create real contexts. They were able to make their classes hybrid or blended so they could give assignments for the students to relate to and watch for during their observations. The instructors also found that they could facilitate discussions in their classes differently. One professor found that the discussions changed in her class from looking at one school perspective to several school perspectives. Another professor used the discussion board from Black Board Learn (BBL) to facilitate discussions about what the students were seeing in the schools.

Now former faculty members find that teaching in the PDS was quite different from the current modified program. They are learning to utilize their expertise to overcome some of the differences. They have found different ways to communicate with the faculty at the partner schools. One group of professors sends out a letter of introduction to the mentor teachers explaining their courses and the assignments that need to be completed in their classes. Then the professors have the cooperation of the mentor teachers—even though they are no longer talking to them face to face. The PDS faculty found that the connections were different for the teacher candidates. The teacher candidates did not have the formal cohort connections anymore, so now the instructors are looking for more informal ways to set up the cohort experience among the teacher candidates.

DISCUSSION

A number of organizations and authors have held that to be a "true PDS," certain standards and structures must exist (National Association for Professional Development Schools [NAPDS], 2008). NCATE (2010–2014) standards require that their accredited programs be totally integrated with schools (see 3a. Collaboration between Unit and School Partner) and their *Standards for Professional Development Schools* (NCATE, 2001) are exact in guidelines that establish solid university/school partnerships. The new Council for the Accreditation of Educator Preparation (CAEP) standards (2013b), recently available (and in their 2013 annual report [2013a] to the public), integrate many of the former NCATE standards, noting the importance of "effective partnerships and high-quality clinical practices." Inclusive of many types of partnerships, they stop short of the term PDS, but the terms used clearly describe the PDS framework. However, not all teacher education programs can sustain many of these levels/standards due, for example, to diminished financial support and other issues. It is evident that these types of standards listed by various organizations make a powerful program for all partnership members. However, the aim of preparation programs that cannot retain all of these elements should be to strengthen those areas they *can* retain and to modify other elements to produce future teachers who still have exceptional clinical experiences and training.

One such element seen as critical in this study is early and ongoing high-quality clinical experiences (CAEP, 2103c). Evidence from the historical course of change in this program indicates that this area of preparation should not be given away at any cost. Although the department was forced to move out of teaching in schools, the faculty found a way to retain the semesters of fieldwork with university supervision. A key issue, though, is that professors still continue to integrate assignments that closely link their courses with fieldwork. However, one may wonder if this is because the PDS model is still fresh in the minds of this faculty, and the value of the theory–practice link is unquestioned. It may turn out that as time passes and as the experience of the PDS fades more into the past, the commitment to including real school contexts into curriculum may dissipate. If this is predicted, ways to ensure integration of field experiences into the coursework when the faculty members are not engaged in the field need to be investigated.

Team building was another issue that the respondents discussed. Although the formal blocking of teacher candidates in a cohort for several semesters was given up with much regret, some natural, informal cohort group developments were mentioned by the faculty. It was noted that although the students are not blocked together in classes and although they are not physically at the schools on the same schedule to debrief and share real-time experiences, they do communicate using social media. Using technology to achieve the cohort bonding that was integral in the PDS model could be a way of the future. In addition, in light of the program change, the professors who teach the professional development courses have tried to keep "learning-community building" as much as possible in their courses. One professor noted that the teacher candidates seem to bond through cooperative learning stressed in coursework and that when one student must move to another course section, many others in their group may move as well to keep the group together. In the new format it is still possible to schedule courses so that teacher candidates share many of the same courses. The leaders and schedulers of the department see this as a priority because of their understanding of the former model. This informal cohort format is seen as optimum for support for the teacher candidates as they work on group projects, form study groups for their state examinations, begin to see each other as resources, and so forth. Moreover, a number of teacher candidates are still placed in the same school to facilitate supervision. There may be bonding in these groups of which the interviewed faculty members are unaware because they are no longer instructing these students in the field. If team building and cohort support are valued by program leaders, there are ways to encourage their development, although this is not assured to occur as in the PDS model.

Cohesiveness among faculty was another theme that emerged from the interviews. It was mostly discussed in relation to helping students who were having difficulties, but the team development of curriculum and assignments was also noted. Although it may seem that this kind of faculty team work could take place without a PDS model, in reality it seems that when the faculty share experiences at a school and when they share the same cohort of teacher candidates, teamwork is a natural by-product as well as a necessity. Without those shared elements the faculty collaboration *can* take place, but it requires more initiative. Some faculty could easily slip into isolation whereas this was not a prerogative in the PDS format. Department leaders who value faculty collaboration might consider instituting ways to ensure more faculty teamwork as this was perceived as such positive factor by the interviewees.

Those involved in modifying "total PDSs" should also consider value-added losses far ahead of transitioning. Many faculty members in PDSs often count on much of their service as coming from PDS opportunities. Once school–university partnerships are no longer taken for granted, faculty will have to plan ahead to make connections on their own to serve public schools. Moreover, accepting "service in schools" as a criterion in tenure portfolios should be openly discussed and hopefully valued by rank and tenure committees so that education faculty who continue their public school service receive credit for doing so.

The loss of the role of the block coordinator was noted as being detrimental by all. The question remains, should the adjunct/supervising professor be the one responsible for acting as the block coordinator? The "information highway" is an important one to consider ahead of a transition—should a PDS need to go to a modified version, provision must be made for how important program information will be transferred and for when teacher candidates may become at risk. "When a student would have trouble (in academics, attendance, professionalism, etc.)," noted one interviewee, "we cannot wait for the [former] block coordinator to recognize it (and act on it together with the block faculty)." Provision must be made ahead of time "where all faculty have to step up." One modification made by this department has been to form a new committee—the student success committee. The main work of this committee has been to examine all areas where teacher candidates may not attain graduation and certification. This committee informally acts as a central place to address these issues because key individuals serve on it. In addition, the role of the program coordinator still exists, and this has become a "clearing house role" for teacher candidates who may be experiencing difficulties. However, it may become too much work for one individual (in addition to assigned duties). In the prior PDS model, however, all professors and mentors would immediately go to the block coordinator if the least question occurred concerning a teacher candidate, and this alert would trigger early intervention (especially if everyone at the site was seeing the same behaviors or problems). Communication chains that address these needs can be structured into modified programs.

From interviewee responses it appears that there is a perceived tradeoff regarding work load and public school relationships. On the one hand, many faculty members welcomed the teaching of classes at the university rather than at the school sites because of the savings of time for travel, not having to manage heavy equipment and materials, the ease of technology use, and so forth. On the other hand, by teaching at the schools the positive development of personal relationships with the mentor teachers, principals, and other staff members in the school community was often assured. This involvement often served as a natural resource for applied research. With the new model, as noted by the faculty, developing and retaining these relationships will be considerably more difficult.

Therefore, although the faculty may have more time for research and service in the schools, the field is no longer part of their everyday context and may not be automatically open to their endeavors.

A positive move away from a very structured PDS was noted in the flexibility of class scheduling in the new modified program. Teacher candidates were previously required to "block" their last three semesters for these courses, which could often be difficult for them because of work and/or other obligations. Future teachers, at times, were required to drive considerable distances once assigned a PDS (for at least two semesters) and often had to attend other university classes far from their PDS. In the modified structure, teacher candidates can take courses in a variety of time slots or take courses at various campuses, according to their needs, and can request a variety of placement schools in different areas of the city. This is believed to have an eventual impact on increased enrollment, as it was felt that in the past that one reason students may have chosen a different university or program for their teacher education was the rigidity of the placements and blocked courses.

As funds for PDS work remain tight at universities, as politics continue to lean towards alternative certification rather than colleges of education, and as many public schools continue to focus more on their testing results (rather than accepting teacher candidates, particularly during testing semesters), the feasibility of maintaining a "perfect" PDS becomes more and more difficult. The purpose of this study was to investigate a program that lost much of its PDS funding and support and to learn from the transition process that ensued. Even if a complete PDS model is not viable, recognizing its positive elements and trying to infuse them into a modified teacher preparation version is a struggle that might be well worth the effort.

REFERENCES

Badiali, B., Nolan, J., Zembal-Saul, C., & Manno, J. (2011). Affirmation and change: Assessing the impact of the professional development school on mentors' classroom practice. In J. L. Nath, I. Guadarrama, & J. Ramsey (Eds.), *Investigating university–school partnerships: A volume in research in professional development schools* (pp. 321–346). Charlotte, NC: Information Age Publishing.

Ball, D. L. (2000). Bridging practice: Intertwining content and pedagogy in teaching and learning to teach. *Journal of Teacher Education, 51*(3), 241–247.

Basile, C. G. (2011). Assessing university partnership impact on school climate and culture. In J. Nath, I. Guadarrama, & J. Ramsey (Eds.), *Investigating university-school partnerships: A volume in research in professional development schools* (pp. 3–28). Charlotte, NC: Information Age Publishing.

Breault, R., & Breault, D. (2012). *Professional development schools: Researching lessons from the field.* Lanham, MD: Rowman & Littlefield.

Council for the Accreditation of Educator Preparation. (2013a). *Annual report to the public, the states, policy makers, and the education profession.* Retrieved from caepnet. files.wordpress.com/2013/05/annualreport_final.pdf

Council for the Accreditation of Educator Preparation. (2013b). *Standard 2: Clinical partnerships and practice*. Retrieved from www.caepnet.org/accreditation/standards/standard2/

Council for the Accreditation of Educator Preparation. (2013c). *Standard 2: Rationale.* Retrieved from *www.caepnet.org/accreditation/standards/standard-2-rationale/*

Creative Center for Research Evaluation and Advancement of Teacher Education. (2012). PACE (Performance Analysis for Colleges of Education) 2012. Retrieved from *www.createtx.org*

Darling-Hammond, L. (2006). Constructing 21st century teacher education. *Journal of Teacher Education, 57*(3), 300–314.

Glaser, B. G. (1965). The constant comparative method of qualitative analysis. *Social Problems, 12*(4), 436–445.

Gill, B., & Hove, A. (2000). *The Benedum Collaborative Model of Teacher Education: A preliminary evaluation*. Retrieved from *www.rand.org/content* /dam/rand/publs/documented_briefings/2005/RAND_DB303/pdf

Guadarrama, I., Nath, J., & Ramsey, J. (Eds.). (2002). *Forging alliances in community and thought*. Charlotte, NC: Information Age Publishing.

Guadarrama, I., Nath, J., & Ramsey, J. (Eds.). (2005). *Advances in community thought and research*. Charlotte, NC: Information Age Publishing.

Guadarrama, I., Nath, J., & Ramsey, J. (Eds.). (2008). *University and schools connections: Research studies in professional development schools*. Charlotte, NC: Information Age Publishing.

Houston, W. R., Hollis, L., Clay, D., Ligons, C., & Roff, L. (1999). Effects of collaboration on urban teacher education programs and professional development schools. In D. Byrd & J. McIntyre (Eds.), *Research on professional development schools. Teacher education yearbook VII* (pp. 6–29). Thousand Oaks, CA: Corwin.

Korthagen, F., & Kessels, J. (1999). Linking theory and practice: Changing the pedagogy of teacher education. *Educational Researcher, 28*(4), 4–17.

Lewins, A., & Silver, C. (2007). *Using software in qualitative research: A step-by-step guide*. London, UK: Sage Publications.

Maryland Higher Education Commission and Maryland Partnership for Teaching and Learning. (2007). Professional Development Schools (PDS) Report. Retrieved from www.mhec.state.md.us/publications/jcr_2007_mhec_pds.rpttag.pdf

Nath, J., Guadarrama, I., & Ramsey, J. (Eds.). (2011). *Investigating university-school partnerships: A volume in research in professional development schools*. Charlotte, NC: Information Age Publishing.

National Association for Professional Development Schools (NAPDS). (2008). *NAPDS releases policy statement on professional development school*. Retrieved from www.napds.org/nice_essen.html

National Council for Accreditation of Teacher Education (NCATE). (2001). *Standards for professional development schools*. Retrieved from www.ncate.org/LinkClick.aspx?fileticket=P2KEH2wR4Xs%3d&tabid=107

National Council for Accreditation of Teacher Education (NCATE). (2010–2013).*What makes a teacher effective?* Retrieved from Public/ResesrchReports/TeacherPreparationResearch/WhatMakesaTeacherEffective/tabid/361/Default.aspx

Neubert, G., & Binko, J. (1998). Professional development schools: The proof is in the performance. *Educational Leadership, 55*(5), 44–46.

Teitel, L. (2004). *How professional development schools make a difference: A review of research* (2nd ed.). Washington, DC: National Council for Accreditation of Teacher Education.

Wise, A., & Levine, M. (2002). *The 10-step solution: Here are 10 steps to help urban districts boost achievement in low-performing schools.* Retrieved from www.ed-week.org/ew/articles/2002/02/27/24wise.h21html?querystring=The%2010%20 Step%20S

Zadeh, M. (2011). The value of a mentor during medical training. Retrieved from www.kevinmd.com/blog/2011/09/mentor-medical-training.html

CHAPTER 8

ALUMNI PERCEPTIONS OF THEIR SCHOOL—UNIVERSITY PARTNERSHIP PROGRAMS

Emilie Rodger, Greg Prater, and Michael Blocher

ABSTRACT

This study discusses the results of a survey of alumni who participated in professional development site (PDS) preparation in their teacher education program to determine whether the former teacher candidates felt that their program's intensity was ultimately beneficial.

In 2008, the National Association for Professional Development Schools (NAPDS) (2008a) released a policy statement, "What It Means to Be a Professional Development School." In this statement, NAPDS President Dr. Elliott Lessen shared the following:

The purpose of the statement is to share with the educational community the NAPDS' articulation of the term, "Professional Development School." This statement is not intended to be either an evaluation or a critique of the phenomenal work that has punctuated PDS over the past 20 years but, rather, the association's recognition that there is a tendency for the term "PDS" to be used as a catch-all for various models of

Creating Visions for University-School Partnerships, pages 129–139.
Copyright © 2014 by Information Age Publishing
All rights of reproduction in any form reserved.
129

school–university partnership work that may or may not be best described as PDS. (NAPDS, 2008a, para. 2)

Prior to the statement above, the association (in August of 2007) gathered at a summit of "educators from across the P–20 continuum, along with leaders from national education organizations, to hammer out Nine Essentials which define the PDS mission" (NAPDS, 2008b, para. 2)

Furthermore, the NAPDS encourages all those working in school–university relationships to embrace the Nine Essentials of PDS work communicated in this statement. The essentials are written in tangible, rather than abstract, language and represent practical goals toward which PDS work should be directed (NAPDS, 2008b).

They are listed as follows as applies to the research in this study:

1. A comprehensive mission that is broader in its outreach and scope than the mission of any partner and that furthers the education profession and its responsibility to advance equity within schools and, by potential extension, the broader community
2. A school–university culture committed to the preparation of future educators that embraces their active engagement in the school community
3. Ongoing and reciprocal professional development for all participants guided by need
4. A shared commitment to innovative and reflective practice by all participants
5. Engagement in and public sharing of the results of deliberate investigations of practice by respective participants
6. An articulation agreement developed by the respective participants delineating the roles and responsibilities of all involved
7. A structure that allows all participants a forum for ongoing governance, reflection, and collaboration
8. Work by college/university faculty and P–12 faculty in formal roles across institutional settings
9. Dedicated and shared resources and formal rewards and recognition structures.(NAPDS, 2008b, para. 3)

Although each of the programs mentioned in this study began in the late 1980s or early 1990s, six of the principles delineated in 2008 are addressed in the survey designed for this study either directly or indirectly. In addition, it is worthy of note that although each of the three programs were initially started with a different emphasis, once again, the principles were all incorporated as the programs changed and developed over the ensuing years.

THE MISSION

The mission of the college of education states in part that we "prepare competent and committed professionals who will make positive differences for children, young adults, and others in schools" (College of Education, Northern Arizona University, Office of the Dean, n.d., para 2). In the body of the mission statement, it continues, "We recognize that preparing such professionals requires us to build programs that offer the broad range of learning experiences necessary for the complexities of practice."

From this university's inception, one of the authors' primary professional foci has been the creation, development, and support of successful teacher education programs. A main concentration over the last two decades has been the school/university programs that prepare knowledgeable, reflective, and committed elementary education teachers, as well as the implementation and support for multiage education. Even though the college had numerous partnerships over the years, this study includes participants from only three of the programs, as one of the authors was directly involved in three programs: the professional development school program, the Sedona partnership program, and the Flagstaff partnership program.

Linda Darling-Hammond (2006) makes a compelling argument for the continuation of field-based experiences in teacher training:

> Schools of education must design programs that help prospective teachers to understand deeply a wide array of things about learning, social and cultural contexts, and teaching and to be able to enact these understandings in complex classrooms serving increasingly diverse students; in addition, if prospective teachers are to succeed at this task, schools of education must design programs that transform the kinds of settings in which novices learn to teach and later become teachers. This means that the enterprise of teacher education must venture out further and further from the university and engage ever more closely with schools in a mutual transformation agenda, with all the struggle and messiness it implies. (p. 3)

Additionally, Sirotnik and Goodlad (1988) state that there are two essentials for partnerships:

- "First, the workers—at all levels—must have optimal opportunity to infuse their efforts with the expertise of others engaged in similar work" (p. 10).
- "Second, there must be continuous infusion of both relevant knowledge and alternative (indeed, countervailing) ideas for practice stemming from inquiry into the enterprise" (p. 10).

In reality, the college has had school/university partnerships since the late 1980s, which predates the NAPDS statements mentioned earlier in this paper, yet complies in many ways with the preceding statements. The programs prepared and continue to prepare future educators and to encourage professional development for all involved. According to Goodlad (1991), a school–university partnership represents a planned effort to establish a formal, mutually beneficial interinstitutional relationship characterized by the following:

- Sufficient dissimilarity among institutions to warrant the effort of seeking complementarily in the fulfillment of some functions
- Sufficient overlap in some functions to make clearly apparent the potential benefits of collaboration
- Sufficient commitment to the effective fulfillment of these overlapping functions to warrant the inevitable loss of some present control and authority on the part of the institution currently claiming dominant interest

Although each of the current school–university programs has differing foci, the programmatic intent of each has been to establish the formal, mutually beneficial interinstitutional relationship suggested by Goodlad. To that end, the preservice teachers are in classrooms daily where they prepare and implement lesson plans while also learning the pedagogy of instruction in their coursework. This is all prior to their required semester of student teaching in order to obtain their teaching certificate.

The following is a brief history of the programs from which surveyed alumni graduated. In each of the programs, the preservice teachers (known as interns) are in the unique position of having many of the responsibilities of a teacher while simultaneously taking university coursework. Mentor teachers and university supervisors in each program provided constant support and guidance throughout the two-semester programs.

HISTORICAL PERSPECTIVE OF THE PARTNERSHIPS

The first partnership started by the university was a site-based teacher education program in 1985. The emphasis of this program was basically to give the preservice teachers "real-life" experiences while taking integrated coursework from the university on an elementary campus. The program in this study started at one elementary school campus and is currently being run at a local elementary and a middle school campus. Mentor teachers from both schools are involved in the direction and implementation of the program.

The next program was planned in 1992. The planning for this program was coordinated by the dean of the college and the school district's superintendent with input from the elementary teachers and many college of education professors. This program was then implemented from 1993 to 2003. The emphases of this teacher preparation program were curriculum integration, reflective practice, creative arts integration, and praxis experiences. With the ever-shifting administrative personnel (at both the university and the school district), the program was not continued in 2004—even though the teachers in the district supported the program.

In response to the 1983 National Commission for Excellence in Education convened by President Reagan, educators from 96 major research universities began to look at how colleges of education could improve education, both in the school system as well as in the teacher preparation programs at universities (NAPDS, 2007). A consortium was formed called the Holmes Group. This group made a number of suggestions on how to reform education in America. One of those was the formation of PDSs, in which university teacher candidates could inform practicing teachers of cutting-edge research and methods; in return, school teachers could mentor the university students in practical application. A professional development school program was established in 1995. This program had an emphasis in multiage education with interns placed in (and currently working in) a local elementary school (K–6) and an elementary charter school (K–5). The school district has approximately 9,738 students enrolled. Of these students, 45% are White, 50% are Hispanic or American Indian, and the rest are multiple races.

In each of these three programs, university students were consistently encouraged to be thoughtful about their own and others' work, and multiple opportunities for metacognition (e.g., response journals, critical analyses of lessons delivered) were provided. Reflection is cyclical in nature; that is, students reflect on their understanding of theory plus their experiences in elementary education classrooms and how/why their experiences and reflection affirm or are dissonant with their educational philosophies. The value of reflection stems from its role in aiding professionals, something that has been emphasized so that they could progress in their practices (Schön, 1983). Also, the emphasis of its value in developing a deep understanding of complex issues is based on rational thought analyzing available evidence (Dewey, 1933). In this study, the authors wanted to know if the teacher candidates continued to use reflection as a means of analyzing their practice, the practice of their colleagues, and the demands placed upon them within their different states and districts after they had graduated.

The project investigated alumni from three different school/university teacher training programs. During the alumni's partnership year, the faculty and classroom mentor-teachers model theory balanced with "best practice" and/or legislated practice, which often provide cognitive dissonance. During their intensive year-long program, the interns completed anywhere from 34–36 hours of university coursework, and, depending on the program, were placed in two different grade levels (one per semester in the PDS program) or three to four different grade levels in the other two programs. The purpose of numerous grade-level experiences during this year prior to student teaching was to encourage preservice teachers to learn about the expectations of each grade level. During this time, in collaboration with their mentor teachers, teacher candidates planned and implemented lessons in elementary and middle school classrooms for over 300 field hours during the course of the year.

Having spent the majority of the authors' tenure involved in partnership programs and having reviewed much of the literature regarding teacher attitudes, the authors wanted to survey partnership alumni to obtain a better picture of their perceptions regarding their teacher training. The purpose of this study, therefore, was to obtain information from the alumni to gain insight on their self-perceived practices in the classroom that they had acquired from their PDS program. Two of the three partnerships were based on Goodlad's (1991) notion of a "symbiotic relationship" (p. 8). Basically, the elementary school's first priority is the student in the classroom and, secondarily, is the university student; conversely, the university's first priority is the intern experience and, secondarily, the elementary student.

It is also important to have critical thinkers as education professionals. To that end, the survey asks questions (based on educational philosophy) about how the program may have changed over the years and about their field experiences in the schools. The survey continues to ask whether these alumni are student advocates and/or teacher leaders, and if these graduates continued in a graduate program and/or have taught in public schools, charter schools, and/or private schools. Finally, the survey questions if the graduates have remained in teaching and if their ideals/beliefs about education, student learning, and school culture have changed (and, if so, how and why).

Collecting data involved a survey using Google Docs. The survey was not designed to be a comprehensive evaluation of the partnership programs, but, instead, to provide anecdotal information from the graduates concerning their personal perspectives regarding their preparation with respect to their roles within school communities. The alumni were asked to respond to a four-point Likert-type instrument concerning their experiences, as well as narrative responses. The specific questions on the Likert-type scale were:

1. My partnership experience prepared me for teaching.
2. I was more marketable as a result of my partnership experience.
3. I felt well prepared to teach lessons/themes.
4. I felt well prepared to teach the state standards.
5. I felt well prepared to assess and evaluate students.
6. I would describe myself as a reflective practitioner.
7. I believe I am a teacher leader in our school community.
8. I would be described by my administrator and colleagues as a leader.
9. My experience in a partnership program encouraged me to adapt for individual learning styles.
10. I felt well prepared to work with students from diverse backgrounds.
11. I felt prepared for the AEPA (or any other equivalent teacher examination).

The narrative questions included:

1. Are you teaching? Why or why not?

2. Has your philosophy of education changed as you have remained in teaching? Has your philosophy been validated or have there been conflicts?
3. Have your professional ideals (e.g., pedagogy, belief systems, philosophy) changed over time? Why? How?
4. How would you define your role as a student advocate?
5. Do you see yourself as a change agent?
6. Do you have any recommendations for our school/university programs?

Using a university database, we were able to contact 90 alumni. Twenty-eight, or approximately 30%, of those individuals responded. The university had a 20-year history of graduates from various programs, but, interestingly, through the data system, only e-mail addresses from 2003 to the present were available—and only if those students had pursued their graduate degrees through the college. The sample is less than ideal. A request was given to all alumni responding asking them to forward the survey to any of their colleagues. Because of the nature of Google Docs, all responses were anonymous; therefore, other than the survey responses, no data were collected on who actually answered. There were some alumni who chose to personally contact the authors to offer further responses or clarification of responses if needed.

RESULTS

Based on the responses received, the majority of the alumni taught in the public school system, although a very small percentage taught in private or charter schools or a combination of each. An even smaller percentage of respondents have chosen to home school their children.

When reviewing the responses regarding grade levels/curriculum areas taught, it would seem that the partnership graduates felt confident in a diversity of grade levels and programs, since their responses indicated experiences from kindergarten through twelfth grade, multiage, gifted and talented, special education, middle school, and administrative positions.

The mean (M) results of the Likert questions are as follows, with 4 being "most strongly agree" to 1 indicating "strong disagreement":

1. My partnership experience prepared me for teaching: ($M = 3.31$)
2. I was more marketable as a result of my partnership experience: ($M = 3.25$)
3. I felt well prepared to teach lessons: ($M = 3.31$)
4. I felt well prepared to assess and evaluate students: ($M = 3.21$)
5. I would describe myself as a reflective practitioner: ($M = 3.34$)
6. I believe I am a teacher leader in our school community: ($M = 3.0$)
7. I would be described by my administrator and colleagues as a leader: ($M = 2.96$)

8. My experience in a partnership program encouraged me to adapt for individual learning styles: ($M = 3.31$)
9. I felt well prepared to work with students from diverse backgrounds: ($M = 3.31$)
10. I felt well prepared for the AEPA (or any other equivalent teacher examination): ($M = 3.25$)
11. I felt well prepared to teach the state standards: ($M = 3.06$)

The responses to the narrative questions proved enlightening:

1. Are you teaching? Why or why not?
    The majority of the alumni had taught in the public school system, although a very small percentage of respondents had taught in private or charter schools, or a combination of each. An even smaller percentage had chosen to home school their children. A number of the alumni responding are currently in administrative positions including a principal, two instructional coaches, and two assistant principals. Six had chosen to stay at home and raise their families.
2. Has your philosophy of education changed as they've remained in teaching? Has your philosophy been validated or have there been conflicts?
    Over 90% of the responses indicated that their philosophy of education had remained similar (if not the same) in terms of their beliefs that all children can succeed, that the environment has to be one of acceptance and nurturing (a healthy environment), and that teacher collaboration is very important.
3. Have your professional ideals changed over time? Why? How?
    Again, over 90% responded that their professional ideals had changed over time; that is, most of those with experience have added to their original ideals.
4. How would you define your role as a student advocate?
    Slightly more than half of the respondents indicated that their role as advocates was to ensure student success. They felt that teacher behaviors and communication were also important.
5. Do you see yourself as a change agent?
    Interestingly, 50% indicated *yes* and 50% indicated *no*.
6. Do you have any recommendations for our school/university programs?
    The overwhelming response was to stay the same in intensity, practice, and workload, with two respondents recommended adding more information about classroom management.

SUMMARY OF RESULTS

The alumni who had participated in PDSs indicated through their responses and narratives that they were enthusiastic about choosing their partnership programs because they felt the program had offered them a balance of theory and practice. They felt well prepared to enter their chosen profession and continued, for the most part, to be enthusiastic about education.

Out of four possible points, 4 indicating "strong agreement" and 1 indicating "strong disagreement," 90% of the alumni felt confident in their teaching practices, citing that they were teacher leaders and were often consulted for ideas and lessons from their colleagues. Of course, these are self-reported data. Interestingly though, the only answer with a mean minimally below 3 was, "I would be described by my administrator as a leader." When further perusing the responses regarding being change agents, many stated that they see themselves as "someone who is willing to fight for teachers and students" (Student survey response, 2012). One respondent, whose current job title includes instructional coach, provides support to teachers in numerous ways.

In terms of their philosophy of education, over 50% of the alumni stated that they believed and still believe that all students can succeed, that a healthy environment is essential to learning, and that they must teach to the whole child by differentiating their instruction. Many indicated the importance of constructivism in their teaching practices. Of the 28 respondents, only four indicated that their professional ideals had not changed. Most indicated that they had changed, and five indicated that they are constantly reevaluating and changing. One respondent clarified by stating: "I have come to realize that I have to pick my battles, and that in today's education I have to find a balance of what I believe and what I have to do and make it work for my students." Most all felt that their validations come from their students and parents.

When asked about student advocacy, most addressed the importance of offering learning opportunities that would engage students in meaningful and relevant activities, individualizing to meet the needs of their students, and, ultimately, treating all of their students with respect. All indicated that student success and constant communication with their colleagues meant that they were truly student advocates.

The question regarding being a change agent produced some interesting results and was, perhaps, the most important and constant theme in this response. Fifty percent responded yes, that they saw themselves as being change agents to better complement student achievement. This group stated that their willingness to fight for teachers and students, or being an instructional coach, provided the vehicle for helping change instructional practices, student interaction, and educational philosophies.

When asked about the programs themselves, most indicated that everyone should go through this type of an intensive program because (1) they felt very prepared; (2) they had been complimented on their organization, understanding of curriculum, and planning; and (3) they felt that their marketability was high. Again, several alumni recommended a course in classroom management. A few of the respondents cited the realization of how "tough education really is," as well as the value of being in classrooms many hours where they actually taught prior to student teaching.

Ultimately, the survey sought recommendations for future teacher preparation/partnership programs. Using actual quotes adds to the authenticity of the responses:

- "Education is changing and if we want it to change for the better, we need to get rid of the old way of training teachers. Partnerships are one of the biggest ways we will save education. Well prepared, passionate, and competent individuals changing the way education is viewed."
- "Keep the programs. It is amazing to have the opportunity to be in a classroom teaching before it's yours. I feel like I am paying it forward for all the great people and teachers that I met who helped me be the teacher I am today!"

CONCLUSIONS

As indicated before, the results of this survey helped solidify the beliefs of the authors that the collaboration necessary in school–university partnerships truly helps strengthen teacher preparation programs in that the preservice teachers must engage in professional discourse on a daily basis in order to provide school students with relevant, engaging, and meaningful lessons. The results also indicate that continued communication and collaboration is important in their current teaching practices. By encouraging preservice teachers to be reflective about their pedagogy, it is imperative that they also adhere to the expectations of the schools in which they are placed as well as the university's expectations. As stated in the article, preservice teachers study "best practice" and also often teach in classrooms that are being highly regulated in terms of the curriculum taught.

A number of themes emerged from the survey respondents. Professional self-confidence, the positive belief that all students can learn, and the value of building a learning community for students while providing safe environments were some very positive and consistent replies in terms of alumni perceptions. Most felt well prepared to teach utilizing the state standards, and many also stated that their different experiences helped them accommodate individual learning styles. Graduates' experiences also prepared them for working with students from diverse backgrounds. Overall, as a result of their year-long participation in the school–university partnership, they felt highly prepared to teach in terms of being organized, confident teachers. Many also indicated that they continue to be reflective practitioners, and that this continues to guide their practice.

One area of note is that teacher educators believe that their candidates should be able to analyze a required curriculum and make some definitive judgments as to the strategies necessary to reach all students in positive ways. However, many student teachers may find that entering a school's culture can be very challenging, and this might require a shift in their professional philosophy. In the survey, only 50% of the respondents indicated that they were "change agents," suggesting that the rest were not. The questions remains: Are we truly preparing students to critically assess and voice their thoughts, beliefs, and concerns regarding some of the dictates in this current educational system?

This study brings to light several areas for future research. Gathering data from a much larger, perhaps national pool may provide a clearer picture of several areas: the notion and impact of diverse backgrounds, a preservice teacher's perspective of "change agent," and perhaps detailing the challenges of changing a school's educational paradigm. School–university partnerships seem ripe for this kind of educational investigation because, although the sample was small, the authors believe that the survey responses serve to reinforce the importance and value of school–university partnerships as a means of weaving theory and practice together in pragmatic ways to reinforce the learning of all involved: students, preservice teachers, mentor teachers, and university professors.

REFERENCES

College of Education at Northern Arizona University, Office of the Dean. (n.d.). *Greetings from the Dean.* Retrieved from *http://www.nau.edu/COE/Message-from-the-Dean/*

Darling-Hammond, L. (2006). Constructing 21st-Century Teacher Education *Journal of Teacher Education, 57*(3), 300–314.

Dewey, J. (1933). *How we think: A restatement of the relation of reflective thinking to the educative process.* Boston: D.C. Heath.

Goodlad, J. (1991). School-university partnerships. *Education Digest, 56,* 8.

National Association of Professional Development Schools. (2008a). *What it means to be a professional development school.* Retrieved from the National Association of Professional Development Schools at *www.napds.org/9%20Essentials/statement.pdf*

National Association of Professional Development Schools. *(2008b). NAU releases policy statement on professional development school.* Retrieved from the National Association of Professional Development Schools at http://www.napds.org/nine_essen.html

National Association of Professional Development Schools. (2007). What it means to be a professional development school. NAPDS, 3(2). Retrieved from www.napds.org/9%20Essentials/statement.pdf

Schön, D. A. (1983). The reflective practitioner: How professionals think in action. New York, NY: Basic Books.

Sirotnik, K. A., & Goodlad, J. (Eds.). (1988). *School–university partnerships in action: Concepts, cases, and concerns.* New York, NY: Teachers College Press.

CHAPTER 9

LESSONS LEARNED IN STRENGTHENING AND SUSTAINING SCHOOL– UNIVERSITY PARTNERSHIP NETWORKS

Stephanie L. Savick and Sarah Anne Eckert

ABSTRACT

This chapter documents the efforts of two PDS coordinators at one institute of higher education in Maryland to revitalize a network of 21 individual PDS sites. Through providing an historical overview of PDSs at the university and documenting the strategic steps taken, this chapter uses an institutional framework to outline one method for creating self-sustaining partnerships. The concept of self-sustaining partnerships is especially important, as maintaining a consistent "critical mass" of invested stakeholders is highly unlikely in wide PDS networks. The chapter relies on documentary data, interviews, and first-hand observations to analyze the systemic changes necessary to build a self-sustaining network. Findings reveal that two factors are critical to producing this type of self-sustaining system: communication and accountability.

Creating Visions for University-School Partnerships, pages 141–166.
Copyright © 2014 by Information Age Publishing
All rights of reproduction in any form reserved.

141

The building and sustaining of professional development school (PDS) partnerships is an evolutionary process, a process that focuses on the continual evaluation and reevaluation of the networks and resources required to sustain PDS infrastructures over time. A number of variables can affect the growth and/or stagnation of PDS partnerships during the cyclical process involved in sustainability. This chapter documents an attempt to harness these variables. Successful implementation of any system requires both stakeholder buy-in (Desimone, 2013) and fidelity to the system (O'Donnell, 2008). Specifically within the PDS, some of the variables that can threaten these two necessary elements involved in sustainability include a change in leadership, personnel shifts at various levels within the structure, fluctuating resources, differences in stakeholder buy-in and support, and vacillating levels of accountability (Berkeley, 2006; Edens, Shirley, & Toner, 2001; Teitel, 2001; Thornton, 2005). Even more specifically, Teitel, Reed, and O'Connor (1998) explain that without a critical mass of invested participants, it is difficult to sustain even an individual PDS. The intuitive leap, therefore, is that an even bigger critical mass is necessary to sustain an entire system. However, due to the nature of both higher education and the public school system, maintaining this mass is often difficult as teachers transfer, retire, or leave teaching for various reasons and university personnel battle competing demands for their time.

The life of PDS networks runs in cycles, with rebirth and regeneration acting as part of that cycle (Berkeley, 2006). Using data collected through interviews, document analysis, and first-hand observations, this chapter explains the steps taken by new leadership at one university to strengthen and sustain the system-wide PDS infrastructure and the partnerships that the university holds with 21 local public schools. This chapter begins by providing an historical overview of the PDS infrastructure at the institution. Using two case studies, the authors then explain in detail some of the improvements initiated in two individual PDS sites. Relying on lessons learned from individual schools, the authors document all of the systemic changes that have been implemented for the entire PDS network of 21 schools over the past two years. Lastly, a summary is provided of the efforts that have begun to further increase the sustainability of this PDS network.

HISTORICAL CONTEXT: THE SCHOOL–UNIVERSITY PARTNERSHIP NETWORK

Era One—The Birth of the PDS Model in Maryland Supported by Grant Money

In the mid 1990s, Maryland's Redesign for Teacher Education (1995) mandated that higher education institutions in Maryland adopt the PDS model. According to the redesign, still in place today, all teacher education candidates must be placed in cohorts of five students in formal PDS partnerships with local universities. In exchange, local universities are called upon to support the school improvement efforts of local schools by making human and capital resources available to the schools to which they are connected. The first PDS coordinator at this university, who has since retired, served on the initial taskforce that developed the standards and components of professional development schools in Maryland. She also served as part of the team in Maryland's first formal PDS partnership between a local university and public school. Her knowledge base and personal commitment to the model were critical in building the existing framework under which the described PDS system now works.

During the first decade, grant money from the Maryland State Department of Education (MSDE), and the Maryland Higher Education Council (MHEC) allowed this university to build PDS partnerships with local schools that not only placed interns with well-qualified mentors, but also supported professional development opportunities for teachers in partner schools and ongoing training for all PDS stakeholders. Likewise, it allowed the university to host orientations for interns, dinners for action research participants, and strategic planning sessions focused on school improvement efforts. In addition, the grants assisted in developing teacher mentors through graduate-level coursework, paying for substitutes when teachers were pulled from their classrooms to address PDS responsibilities, and securing web-based data resources for teachers in partner schools. Most importantly, the grant money helped to pay the stipends of school-based site coordinators (individuals at the schools—teachers or administrators—who work with the university liaison to coordinate PDS activities in that school), university liaisons (representatives from the university who serve as the university's presence in individual schools), and mentor teachers working directly with interns in each of the PDSs. In summary, the grant money gave the university the fundamental need and required accountability to get the PDS structures up and running so that collaborative PDS partnerships could begin to take form.

Era Two: Learning How to Sustain PDS Partnership Networks without the Support of Grant Money

By 2007, PDS grant money had been exhausted and new leadership was brought in to guide the Institute of Higher Education PDS network into a new era. Maryland's redesign was now an unfunded mandate under which local universities were held to the same standards for maintaining PDS partnerships and supporting interns, but without the financial support of the state department of education or the state higher education council. The new PDS university coordinator's experience with leading PDS networks related exclusively to what he had learned while working as the placement coordinator at the university. Under his administration, many of the original systems, such as staffing a site coordinator and liaison in each partner school, remained in place, although increased turnover in key stakeholder positions made it difficult to maintain an understanding of individual responsibilities without the additional monies for professional development.

Many of the newly hired university liaisons and school-based site coordinators participated in an "on-the-job" training that would carry them through the next era. For example, newly hired stakeholders learned how to place interns, code artifacts, and organize professional development sessions when faced with the immediate responsibility to do so. While the new PDS coordinator from the university sought to visit as many partner schools as possible over the course of any given year to provide meaningful feedback and to maintain a consistent system for accountability, the task proved to be overwhelming while maintaining his other role as the university's intern placement officer. Also presenting a challenge was his lack of having had any formal training from the state (MSDE) related to the key roles and responsibilities of liaisons and site coordinators, and on building and sustaining individual PDS partnerships within the university network. To address this challenge, the PDS coordinator was able to depend on the assistance of a few seasoned university liaisons and school-based site coordinators to the extent possible by embracing an informal "train-the-trainer" model. For example, when a new university liaison began a position, the PDS coordinator shared with her/him the contact information of a more experienced liaison who would be able to answer the questions of the new liaison as they arose.

Despite the challenges related to a lack of formal training for newly hired PDS stakeholders, limited time to provide meaningful feedback, and the absence of a solid system for accountability, the PDS coordinator was able to implement a governance structure to document yearly progress across the schools in the university network. This was an important piece in sustainability as the state required formal documentation of individual and network progress each year. In addition, the PDS coordinator during this era was able to institutionalize annual stipends for university liaisons, school-based site coordinators, and university supervisors, while maintaining a small working budget to provide to the PDS sites when needed. Likewise, he was able to continue to hold bimonthly university liaison meetings to promote communication and collaboration among and between school partnerships, one of the most important systems put into place by the original university PDS coordinator. While he experienced challenges at many levels, the PDS coordinator was able to keep the PDS network afloat and maintain fidelity to the PDS model during the second era of PDS sustainability at this university.

Era Three: Strengthening and Sustaining PDS Partnership Networks Strategically by Addressing Communication and Accountability across the Board

In 2011, the authors were called upon to share the role of university PDS coordinators alongside the current coordinator/placement officer. Even though the authors were newly hired, had limited knowledge about the PDS network structure, and had teaching responsibilities, they were nevertheless invited to take on additional roles as university liaisons to two local PDS partner schools and teacher candidate supervisors across other partner schools. These additional roles allowed a greater understanding of the entire university PDS process and accompanying expectations. Having an insider view across stakeholders provided the authors with the first-hand experiences needed to complete a quick and thorough study of all aspects of this university PDS infrastructure. Within in the first few months on the job, it was also learned that active roles would be required in drafting two sections of an institutional report for the NCATE (National Council for Accreditation of Teacher Education) review that would take place the following year. The focus of these reports dealt specifically with field experiences and clinical practices, both of which had a direct connection to the roles of PDS co-coordinators. This additional responsibility prompted quick learning about how the present infrastructure influenced and supported university certification programs within the institution and further complimented the perceived near vertical learning curves.

Phase 1: Collecting Data

As initial preparation in familiarizing themselves with the new roles as PDS Co-Coordinators and the upholding of the standards associated with the PDS in Maryland, the authors completed an accelerated study of the PDS resources available to them through the state department. These resources included the PDS Implementation Manual (2003) and the Maryland PDS Assessment Framework (2007). These two documents in particular helped frame the direction that would be taken in participating in a year-long, in-house self-study of the current PDS program model.

The first step in the journey focused on evaluating the current status of the university PDS program that had been inherited. A two-pronged self-study was initiated to begin the data collection process. One of those prongs focused specifically on an evaluation of the university PDS structure itself. The second prong focused on gaining an understanding of the building-level structures in each of the university's 21 local partner schools. In order to conduct the self-study, the authors relied on a modified case study approach in which the case or cases existed at multiple levels and the researchers were participants in the research. The system of 21 PDS sites constituted one bounded system, but two individual PDS sites represented smaller bounded systems, allowing the researchers to focus on building-level efforts. The two individual sites were chosen using purposive sampling as one site was a brand new PDS and the other was in the process of restarting.

The major data source for this project consisted of document analysis; however, in order to triangulate data, the authors utilized questionnaires, focus groups, and individual interviews. Two types of documents constituted the main data source in this process: (1) partnership teams (usually one representative from the university and one or two people from the school) each generated a 4–5 page document highlighting the history, strengths, and weaknesses of their partnership; and (2) partnership teams collected artifacts that each PDS felt best described their partnership (Appendix 9.B contains an example one artifact box table of contents). Questionnaires mostly took the form of needs assessments both from the PDS coordinators regarding the system as a whole and also within each PDS site focusing on building-level needs. Focus groups were conducted with university liaisons five times during the year, while focus groups with school-based site coordinators occurred only once. During these focus groups, participants were asked to discuss their successes and challenges about the renewal process. The researchers examined documents and notes from the focus groups in order to find major themes and areas of impact to enhance and understand the implementation process.

In addressing the evaluation of the university PDS structure, a historical understanding was sought to make clear how the current PDS network functioned. The authors benefitted by working alongside a third co-coordinator who provided them with the background knowledge necessary to conduct the self-study. Furthermore, the very fabric of sustaining the PDS program was already in place: The roles of critical stakeholders (such as university liaisons and supervisors) and school-based site coordinators and mentors had been defined and were currently funded through the university. Bimonthly liaison meetings had also been institutionalized and were well attended by each of the university liaisons. In addition, there was an amicable working relationship between members of the state department of education and the university. Each of these pieces played a critical role in allowing the new university PDS coordinators to build on existing structures rather than starting from scratch. The key to making the PDS network more effective was greater communication and accountability within the existing network. This took the form of developing a two-year strategic plan based on present needs—increasing the effectiveness of the university PDS committee and developing accountability tools to measure progress as a university network.

After collecting enough information about the context in which the current university PDS structure functioned, the researchers deepened their understanding of the present levels of performance in each of the 21 partner schools. Liaison focus groups indicated that some school partnerships were strong; others were stagnant; and still others were barely holding on to partnership status. Over the course of the first year as co-coordinators, they visited each of the 21 partner schools at least once, examined and discussed documentary data (artifacts) from each of the schools with their respective university liaisons and school-based site coordinators, and provided feedback using a modified version of the state's assessment framework (Professional Development School Assessment Framework for Maryland, 2007) in an attempt to learn about their individual stories and support their ongoing efforts. Again, the authors discovered that greater communication and accountability were necessary to strengthen individual partnerships with existing schools. As a result, they set about developing resources to assist stakeholders in carrying out their assigned responsibilities, offering follow-up training sessions to all stakeholders groups, and developing accountability tools to measure progress and promote sustainability in individual partner schools.

A final component of the new coordinators' self-study encompassed participation in local, state, and national networking meetings and conferences. Interacting with others who had gone through the process of building, evaluating, and sustaining PDS partnerships proved to be an invaluable experience as they sought creative solutions to the challenges they were experiencing. This also allowed them to gain a greater understanding of the bigger picture related to PDS work as it supports teacher education across all levels and programs. Before they could fully understand the bigger picture of PDS, it was important that they understood how individual PDS sites operated and evolved.

Phase 2: Instituting Structures with Two PDS Sites

A benefit each author experienced in evaluating how the individual school partnerships were operating followed from their additional roles as acting university liaisons in their assigned local schools. One of the authors was tasked with building a brand new PDS partnership with a local school, while the other was tasked with revitalizing a stagnant partnership. The front-line work that went into developing these two schools allowed them to experience the triumphs and challenges that the university liaisons were experiencing.

Maryland's PDS Implementation Manual (2003) provided the most practical overview of how to establish an effective school–university partnership. Using this manual as a guide, the co-coordinators began to define roles, establish trust, build relationships, acquire materials, and establish school-based governance teams. In addition, they attended school improvement team meetings and conducted needs assessments for each of their schools in an attempt to connect PDS goals to local school improvement goals. Building the partnerships and understanding the status of their partnerships using the implementation manual coupled with a participatory action-research approach proved to provide them with the firsthand knowledge needed to lead a team of liaisons and site coordinators attempting to do the same. The background the authors gathered from working with each of these schools to strengthen the partnership efforts afforded them the knowledge to begin implementing system-wide changes. One school, an elementary school in a low-income area, had been a PDS for several years but was under new leadership. The other school, an academically competitive citywide girl's high school, had just become a PDS. The sections below provide an overview of what was learned and what the authors did as they started and restarted individual PDS sites.

County Elementary. County Elementary serves over 600 students in PreK through fifth grade. The school hosts two self-contained communication and language support (CALS) classrooms for students with autism spectrum disorders. The majority of the students in the school (75%) are eligible for free and reduced priced meals, and the school has a growing limited English proficient (LEP) population, especially in the lower grades. Seventy percent of the students are Black or African American, 15% are Hispanic, 7% are Asian American, 5% are White, and 3% identify as two or more races. The partnership began in 2009; however, the 2011–2012 school year welcomed a new site coordinator, a new liaison, and a new principal. While the conditions were perfect to restart a PDS that had become inactive during the previous year, this PDS coordinator/university liaison encountered several challenges along the way.

County Elementary may have been ready for a new beginning, but there were several obstacles that prevented a smooth transition. Events that had unfolded two years prior to the transition had generated a great deal of baggage of which members of the new leadership team were intimately aware. In order to focus the work of partners at this school and promote a new spirit of collaboration, it was necessary to begin by focusing on a single PDS standard: collaboration. Because the PDS team at County Elementary needed to work together to define and carry out the mission of the PDS, a steering committee was organized to govern the work. The team conducted a needs assessment to generate buy-in and sought to find a place where university partners could be the most useful.

While the purpose of the steering committee at County Elementary was to collaboratively develop and carry out the mission of the PDS, the important unintended side effect was to build a productive working relationship between the administration, the university liaison, and the school-based site-coordinator for the benefit of interns, teachers, and students. The steering committee worked together to define roles with which each member felt comfortable. In this manner, dividing responsibilities equally was incredibly important, as it was clear that the school-based site coordinator had contributed more than any other member of the team in previous years. It was important that the university liaison share in the various duties such as running meetings, communicating with mentors, managing the artifact collection, and completing paperwork.

As communication and collaboration between various partners strengthened, the presence of the university liaison in this school grew. Although she began by participating in the school improvement team, as the year progressed, she also joined the academic action committee. As a part of this smaller, more focused committee, she was able to increase her participation level and make a more meaningful impact on specific programs. For example, she was able to contribute to the school's annual math and reading night by planning activities and recruiting interns to participate.

After the group worked to build a collaborative relationship, a needs assessment was created and distributed to the school-based faculty. The goal of the needs assessment was to identify what types of professional development would be most useful for teachers and interns at the school. Based on the results of the needs assessment, the County Elementary steering committee decided to hold a three-credit graduate technology course for the teachers on the school's campus. This course, which was funded jointly by the local school system and the university, ran in the fall of 2012 and was a complete success. Evaluations revealed that teachers appreciated the practical information that they learned in the course. Furthermore, the steering committee was able to use local school system funds to pay course participants to lead technology workshops for interns and other teachers who had not taken the course. The discussion will now move to implementing the PDS framework in a new PDS site through the second case study school, City High for Girls.

City High For Girls. City High for Girls serves over 900 students in 9th–12th grade. It is a city-wide, National Blue Ribbon School with admissions criteria. The school hosts four academic programs: college preparatory, accelerated college preparatory, a teacher academy, and a specialized program in biomedical sciences. The attendance rate for City High is 94.1%; the graduation rate is 94.09%; and 82.73% of the teachers at the school are considered highly qualified. The school consistently meets adequate yearly progress according to the state (MSDE). The majority of the students at the school are African American (85.6%); 10.9% are White; 1.2% are Hispanic; 1.9% are Asian/Pacific Islander; and .4% are Native American Indian. Just over half of the students are eligible for free and reduced lunch (57.8%), and 6% of the student population qualifies for special education services.

The partnership was established in December 2010 with a formal signing of a memorandum of understanding. By early spring of 2011, a school-based site coordinator and university liaison were identified, a governance structure was formed, and the first two interns were placed on site. The first strategic planning meeting took place by the end of that spring. In the fall of 2011, a faculty needs assessment was conducted and the first full cohort of interns was placed at the school. By the spring of 2012, the university was able to begin offering faculty development opportunities to teachers and interns at the school. Within the first year of its birth, the City High for Girls PDS was running as a full-blown partnership with documentation that could support this claim—but not without meticulous attention paid to best practices outlined in the literature on effective PDS implementation.

The PDS coordinator/university liaison at City High for Girls identified three focus areas in setting up the partnership: identifying stakeholder roles, establishing trust, and developing the infrastructure. Using Maryland's Implementation Manual for PDSs (2003) as a guide, she set about acquiring materials to help her become more knowledgeable about the process and the school. She began by reading as much as she could find on PDS implementation and assessment literature from online and print sources. She also contacted various central office school system personnel to gain information about system-wide policies and practices related to PDS. In addition, she acquired an updated list of professional development services that could potentially be offered through the university to faculty members and interns at City High for Girls.

This PDS coordinator/university liaison's next priority was to get to know the school itself. Again, she accessed information about the school from online, print, and human resources. She read about its rich history in addition to its present-day strengths and challenges. She downloaded the school improvement plan to understand and anticipate student needs and studied all academic program offerings and extracurricular opportunities. It was her hope that having knowledge of the school itself would allow for a smoother transition into the role and lead to a stronger foundation for building relationships within the building.

Gaining access to the school and building relationships across faculty members became this liaison's next responsibility. She knew that she would not get very far in building a partnership if no one knew or trusted her, so she set about becoming a presence in the building. She established an immediate professional relationship with the site coordinator, joined the school improvement team, presented at faculty meetings when asked to promote the program, offered to supervise the first two interns placed in the building, asked to be part of supervisor observation conferences when possible, and attended school events on site when practical. Being connected to school leaders, supervising teachers, faculty members from all departments, and students in general allowed her the opportunity to form the relationships necessary to promote partnership efforts. Recognizing that trust and relationships are not developed overnight, this liaison continues to be a presence in the school building and at the school functions when possible.

The nuts and bolts of building the partnership began when the infrastructure was put into place. The school-based site coordinator and university liaison established a governance structure referred to as the coordinating council, whose job it was to oversee future partnership planning efforts. Acting as co-chairs, they shared responsibility for planning and leading all meetings. The site coordinator identified and invited several key members of the faculty to become part of the council. With representation extending beyond the co-chairs, greater buy-in from the faculty took place. The coordinating council became a team of seven who used the school improvement plan and faculty needs assessment to drive planning ideas. In addition, the team brainstormed ideas to assist interns in becoming immersed in the school community, an expectation outlined in Maryland's PDS Assessment Framework. Likewise, the team conducted strategic planning as a group, which allowed them to identify long- and short-term goals for future planning efforts.

In evaluating the successes of this first-year partnership using Maryland's PDS standards, the team was able to show growth in each of the five standards (learning community; collaboration; accountability; organization, roles and resources; and diversity and equity) outlined in the framework (see Appendix 9.A). The accomplishments included the following: identifying and conducting needs-based professional development for faculty, establishing best practices in mentor training, providing complimentary intern/mentor matches, participating in strategic planning emphasizing short- and long-term goals, sharing partnership efforts with the entire faculty in the form of monthly newsletters, hosting mentor appreciation receptions, hosting university speakers at the school's campus, and soliciting of mentor and intern feedback to inform future practices. In terms of future planning, it is the goal of the City High for Girls PDS team to address the following in their strategic planning efforts next year: (1) more intentional induction of interns into the school building, (2) more participation from faculty in collaborative professional development opportunities, and (3) more connections to partnership efforts related to student achievement.

Lessons learned from case studies. The case study of County Elementary underscored the importance of establishing clearly defined roles, sharing responsibilities, and conducting a yearly needs assessment to drive PDS activities. In addition to clearly defining roles, the City High for Girls case study emphasized the value of establishing trust, building the infrastructure, and connecting PDS work to the defined needs of the school. Several of the structures that were put in place in these two PDS case studies were incorporated into the university network system as a whole. Phase 3 turns to this discussion subsequently.

Phase 3: Strengthening the Network Through Systematic Changes to the Process

Based on the data collected from the case studies of individual schools, the authors engaged in an intensive self-study of the entire PDS network at this university. Through communicating with representatives from each of the schools and reviewing artifacts collected by school-based site coordinators, they were able to create a more holistic picture of the entire network. They utilized information from this data analysis to incorporate systematic changes into the operating procedures of the entire network. They began by formulating a strategic plan that laid out PDS network goals for the next few years. Among these goals were the following: (1) reformulating a governing structure PDS committee, (2) developing informative handbooks for each stakeholder groups and holding workshops to review the handbooks, (3) systematizing the building-level strategic plans, and (4) maintaining accountability through quarterly reports and continuous review of the artifacts collected. Many of these structures, notably, allow the governing body to maintain a presence in each school and ensure a level of consistency across the network. Consistent implementation is an important indicator of positive reform outcomes; therefore, the authors put significant emphasis on these consistent and concerted efforts (Desimone, 2002; McLaughlin, 1990; O'Donnell, 2008; Sherer & Spillane, 2011).

Strategic plan. To ensure that the structures that were planned to be put in place would be implemented in a way that was both thorough and interconnected, the authors developed a two-year strategic plan that prioritized identified goals and articulated the steps that would need to be followed in order to achieve those goals. The goals included the following: (1) increase the effectiveness of PDS coordinator position, (2) increase the efficacy of the liaison's meetings, (3) increase accountability and efficacy of the university liaisons, (4) increase accountability and efficacy of school-based site coordinators, (5) increase the effectiveness of mentor teachers, (6) increase the sustainability of individual PDS sites, and (7) make recommendations regarding the value of intern assignments and coursework. The authors began by drafting the strategic plan and then solicited feedback from liaisons and others in order to refine it. The details involved in several of these goals are summarized below, but the strategic plan itself served as an organizational element that brought focus and direction to their work.

Transitioning the PDS committee. One of the major goals articulated in the strategic plan was to increase the effectiveness of the PDS committee. During their first year as a committee, the authors were joined by the field placement coordinator, the former university PDS coordinator, and a seasoned university liaison. During year two, the goal was to streamline leadership and gain more feedback from various university liaisons working in network schools. As the work of the PDS leadership was streamlined, it became important to seek additional feedback from the university liaison committee. In this way, decisions were not made in a top-down fashion, but collaboratively, a type of authority that generates greater buy-in from stakeholders (Daly & Finnigan, 2010; Desimone, 2002, 2013). With a smaller PDS committee, it was easier to make decisions and develop programming, but it was extremely important to ensure that various stakeholder groups were empowered to make decisions and share ideas (Bubb & Earley, 2008; Darling-Hammond & McLaughlin, 1995; McLaughlin, 1990; Priestley, Miller, Barrett, & Wallace, 2011). One example of this collaborative effort concerns the handbooks that were created for each of the stakeholder groups. Before writing each handbook, the authors developed a table of contents and solicited input from university liaisons and program coordinators to develop, modify, or refine it. Using this feedback, the authors drafted each of the handbooks and then sought additional feedback from stakeholders before going to print. The authors turn to these handbooks now.

Handbooks. During the first year as co-coordinators of the PDS system, the co-coordinators spent a good deal of time both learning about various standing procedures and identifying where gaps existed in communication within the PDS system itself. To fill those gaps and create a more cohesive set of processes, a series of handbooks were developed for each stakeholder group. When this process first began, the interns were the only stakeholders provided with a handbook. It was this handbook that was intended to be used as a resource for interns, mentors, supervisors, university liaisons, school-based site coordinators, and administrators as a whole. While the intern handbook provided some important information related to programming, it was not particularly helpful for the various roles that all others were expected to play. To eliminate role confusion across stakeholders, the authors created three additional handbooks: one for mentors, one for supervisors, and one combined volume for school-based site coordinators and university liaisons.

Because each of these stakeholders plays a completely different role in the PDS process, each required a different guide with a distinct set of resources. Mentors required information about each of the university programs, tools for observing interns, and resources related to differentiation instruction. Mentor handbooks, notably, contained schedules for the internships and information on co-teaching, delivering feedback, and building relationships with interns. Supervisors, on the other hand, needed information about the specific procedures to be followed in evaluating interns and the grading of intern assignments. Therefore, supervisor handbooks included hard copies of all required intern assignments and accompanying scoring tools. Lastly, school-based site coordinators and university liaisons were most likely to benefit from information about how to run a PDS and collect data on their progress. Likewise, their handbook contained information about the history of PDSs in Maryland. In addition, it offered practical resources related to mentor training, the collection of artifacts, running coordinating council meetings, conducting needs assessments and participating in state and national PDS conferences. These distinct handbooks would help the PDS sites run as independent entities, with site-based autonomy (Desimone, 2002; Priestley et al., 2011), while ensuring that all actors were meeting the needs of teachers, mentors, interns and students alike.

Training workshops. The information and resources contained in the aforementioned handbooks became even more useful when they were introduced in workshop settings and accompanied by explanations about how to use the handbooks most effectively. School-based site coordinators and liaisons, for example, gathered before school began for a half-day workshop meant to bring everyone up to speed on PDS changes and updates. The workshop was interactive, allowing participants to practice the work of analyzing artifacts and to plan for the year ahead. This workshop also allowed for a type of strategic collaboration between site coordinators and liaisons and provided an excellent setting to discuss and plan for building-level mentor training.

As part of their job responsibilities, university liaisons were required to carry out mentor training in each school in which they worked. These mentor trainings allowed the liaison to review the new mentor handbook with mentors and identify certain sections that they might find to be most useful. Mentor training was individualized and varied across buildings depending upon the number and experience levels of the mentors. Many of the mentor trainings, however, focused specifically on implementing co-teaching strategies and providing effective feedback to interns, two areas that mentors have identified as needing the most support.

Lastly, supervisor handbooks were distributed during the annual internship orientation. During this orientation, the authors gathered all supervisors together for a 45-minute discussion focused on information provided in the handbooks. Only two supervisors were new, and the vast majority had been supervising intern teachers for several years; therefore, it was important for the authors both to discuss this handbook and to get important feedback from these tenured supervisors. Each of these workshops/training sessions/discussions helped to ensure that these handbooks were actually utilized as intended. It was not the co-coordinators' intent to create handbooks for the sake of creating handbooks; their goal was to be sure that they would act as useful tools and resources.

Accountability tools. One of the most important components of the school-based site coordinator/liaison handbooks was the accountability measures that were put into place. These accountability measures were not communicated as a way to "check up on" individual partnerships, but rather to "check in with" each. The difference between "checking up" and "checking in" is subtle but important. Checking up on someone implies a level of mistrust, while checking in simply helps all stakeholders better understand what is happening in each PDS. Checking in allowed the co-coordinators to stay informed and offer assistance when needed. While this may seem insignificant, research documents that perception of an issue is related to the level of buy-in (Sherer & Spillane, 2011; Spillane, Reiser & Reimer, 2002). Three important structures allowed the checking-in process to occur smoothly within each school: (1) building-level strategic plans with accompanying budgets, (2) quarterly reports, and (3) yearly artifact box reviews.

The drafting of a building-level strategic plan gave each PDS the opportunity to articulate their overall partnership goals for the year and provide a proposed budget for achieving those goals. It was required that the strategic plan connect to both the Maryland PDS standards and to the individual school improvement plan and/or needs assessment. Each PDS was also asked to submit an accompanying budget (also connected to school improvement efforts) that allowed partnerships to request small sums of money from the university to assist with their school-based efforts. University liaisons were asked to submit short, quarterly reports outlining the activities in each of their PDS sites linked to both budgets and strategic plans. Finally, the co-coordinators conducted yearly artifact box reviews wherein they studied the contents of each school's artifact box and made recommendations for additional documentary data that could be connected to partnership efforts. The artifact box contains documentation related to meeting each of the five PDS standards (Appendix 9.A) including, but not limited to: photographs, meeting agendas, intern assignments, intern lesson plans, student work, and intern reflections (see Appendix 9.B for an example table of contents for one of these artifact boxes). This yearly artifact box check allowed the PDS co-coordinators to engage in a conversation with various stakeholders in each PDS site about where they were as a partnership and where they wanted to be.

While the co-coordinators implemented the systematic changes, they were cognizant of the fact that in order to strengthen the entire PDS network, it was important to be strategic in every message that was sent and in every decision that was made. Through consistent communication and implementation, quality professional development and accountability tools based on checking in rather than checking up, they were able to implement reform in a manner that generated stakeholder buy-in.

Phase 4: Sustaining the Network Through Increasing Participation/ Extending the Reach

Developing routines and structures that increase consistency and ensure accountability are important in sustaining partnership efforts (Desimone, 2002; O'Donnell, 2008; Sherer & Spillane, 2011). There is, however, an equally important element in the process: ensuring that various stakeholders buy in to the entire process (Darling-Hammond & McLaughlin, 1995; Desimone, 2013; McLaughlin, 1990). During the past year, a major goal of the authors was to help all stakeholders understand the importance of the planning and accountability pieces of the system. Although the network has been through a drastic change in the past two years, several individual stakeholders have remained the same. Therefore, one major challenge has been to increase the level at which all individuals believe in the mission and purpose of these changes. Research demonstrates that when stakeholders do not "buy in" to the systems put in place from the top, they are less likely to put in effort to carry out the task at hand (McLaughlin, 1990).

The main method used by the co-coordinators to achieve buy-in from all stakeholders was to provide a balance between top-down changes and community-developed strategies. The main conduit for encouraging community input has been to increase both the level and quality of communication between stakeholders. The authors have begun by refocusing liaison's meetings around sustainability topics to engage in more structured feedback. They have also developed a Wikispace to share information and encourage collaboration between groups and across schools in the network and have increased the level at which they share meeting minutes, reviews, and other information with various groups. The following sections outline these efforts.

Refocusing liaison's meetings. To ensure that the authors gathered more meaningful and structured feedback from liaisons and site coordinators, they chose to focus monthly meetings on specific sustainability topics. Based on their initial artifact box reviews, the authors decided to focus on the "continuing professional development" component of the Maryland PDS standards (PDS Assessment Framework for Maryland, 2007). At the heart of this component is working collaboratively to provide professional learning time for teachers and interns that both increase student learning and strengthen partnership efforts. In the 2012–2013 school year, professional development took many different forms: thematic book studies, graduate-level courses, workshops, and guest speakers. Liaisons shared their ideas during monthly meetings and used university resources to deliver professional development opportunities. Lee Teitel's (2003) *Professional Development Schools Handbook* provided a framework to focus monthly university liaison meetings. As a group of coordinators and liaisons, engaged conversations related to what each stakeholder was doing and what they could be doing in order to increase the sharing of ideas and stimulate unique opportunities for school-based stakeholders related to the professional development component. These brainstorming sessions led to the development and implementation of a handful of unique strategies across schools.

Wikispace. In effort to extend these discussions beyond the monthly liaison's meetings, the authors developed a Wikispace that was made available to all stakeholders. This Wikispace initially served as a digital storehouse for electronic access to handbooks and various documents. The authors placed links to templates for strategic planning and quarterly reports and announcements pertaining to state conferences. However, as the project evolved, it has become a space to share ideas and increase communication. PDS partnerships are welcome to share success studies and crowd-source various ideas related to their work in partner schools. This effort has led to a sharing of ideas that has increased buy-in across the board (Wenger, 2000).

Additional efforts. The co-coordinators also increased communication and participation in a number of small, yet significant ways. For example, they now share the minutes from each liaison meeting with school-based site coordinators. This effort, while just a small change, increases the level of openness and trust among various partners, sending a message to site coordinators that they are an important part of the process. Additionally, the co-coordinators were also able to find a small amount of grant money to bring one site coordinator to the national PDS conference. Through allowing this site coordinator to see the bigger picture of PDS development and implementation, she was able to evaluate her current efforts in light of the larger purpose.

Furthermore, the authors have worked to increase the communication between university supervisors, university liaisons, and school-based site coordinators. Supervisors are now asked to inform liaisons and site coordinators when they hold introductory meetings and when they conduct observations with interns. In increasing communication among the three individuals who have the most direct contact with interns in school buildings, the authors have eliminated the feeling and appearance of being disconnected. The aforementioned efforts have instigated a great deal of buy-in among various partners. Each effort described previously works to systematize the processes essential for building a self-sustaining PDS network.

Phase 5: Looking to the Future to Build a Self-Sustaining System

As these authors reflect on the strides that their PDS network has made over a two-year period, it is important to maintain momentum and encourage growth. To build a system that is self-sustaining, it is not enough to simply develop routines and accountability systems. A self-sustaining PDS network requires a systematic method for soliciting and incorporating feedback at each level of the system (Wenger, 2000). This year the authors plan to continue implementing these systems. They will hold "brown bag" forums with mentors, interns, supervisors, school-based site coordinators, and administrators to gain feedback on current systems and experiences. That feedback will then be incorporated into operating procedures and handbooks and, when appropriate, communicated with university curriculum committees.

The artifact box check described previously demonstrates one method for soliciting feedback that is presently in place. This particular process will continue to allow the reviewers to understand on which particular components and tasks schools need to focus. Based on a thorough review of the artifacts available, the authors have determined that the PDS network will focus on the idea of increasing opportunities to engage in research and inquiry. These structures will not only increase communication between various stakeholder groups, but will also help to generate the type of buy-in that is necessary for building sustaining systems. One thing that is unique to this PDS system is the understanding that the cycle of building a PDS system (Berkeley, 2006) is never complete. In order to sustain the PDS network, it is necessary to follow the cycle by focusing on different elements each year in an effort to continue the process of reinvention. Research has documented that a critical mass of invested participants is necessary to sustain a PDS system (Teitel et al., 1998), but the research presented herein outlines systems that can alleviate any burdens that arise when a substantial number of these people leave the system for various reasons. This knowledge, therefore, is easily passed on from generation to generation.

A great deal of research has been done on building PDS systems (Berkeley, 2006; Neubert, Binko, & McNelis, 2004; Teitel, 2001, 2003), but little has been done to document specific strategies involved in restarting an entire PDS network. Not only does this chapter offer a theoretical perspective on restarting a PDS network, but it also provides specific tools that can be utilized to generate buy-in and provide accountability. While a great deal has been learned in their two years as PDS co-coordinators, the work of building strategic and sustainable PDS sites is an ongoing process. They have implemented structures that will encourage continuous growth, but we will need to reevaluate each structure yearly in the continued process of institutionalization. Through ongoing professional development, clear communication, and consistent accountability practices, the authors hope to build a self-sustaining PDS network for their institute of higher education.

REFERENCES

Berkeley, T. R. (2006). Interweaving, interwoven: Perspective on PDS leadership from the university with the school. In J. E. Neapolitan & T. R. Berkeley (Eds.), *Where do we go from here? Issues in the sustainability of professional development school partnerships* (pp. 149–164). New York, NY: Peter Lang.

Bubb, S., & Earley, P. (2008) *From self-evaluation to school improvement: The importance of effective staff development.* Reading, PA: CfBT Research Report. Retrieved from http://www.cfbt.com/evidenceforeducation/pdf/Self-evaluationReport_v4 (W).pdf

Daly, A. J., & Finnigan, K. S. (2010). A bridge between worlds: Understanding network structure to understand change strategy. *Journal of Educational Change, 11,* 111–138.

Darling-Hammond, L., & McLaughlin, M. W. (1995) Policies that support professional development in an era of reform. *Phi Delta Kappan, 76*(8), 597–604.

Desimone, L. (2002). How can comprehensive school reform models be successfully implemented? *Review of Educational Research, 72*(3), 433–479.

Desimone, L. (2013). Reform before NCLB. *Phi Delta Kappan. 94*(8), 59–61.

Edens, K., Shirley, J., & Toner, T. (2001). Sustaining a professional development school partnership: Hearing the voices, heeding the voices. *Action in Teacher Education, 23*(3), 27–32.

Maryland Higher Education Commission. (1995). *Teacher education task force report: Redesign of teacher education.* Annapolis, MD.

Maryland State Department of Education. (2003). *Professional development schools: An implementation manual.* Annapolis, MD: Maryland Partnership for Teaching and Learning K–16, Superintendents and Deans Committee.

Maryland State Department of Education. (2007). *Professional development schools assessment framework for Maryland.* Annapolis, MD: Author, Program Approval and Assessment Branch.

McLaughlin, M. W. (1990). The Rand change agent study revisited: Macro perspectives and micro realities. *Educational Researcher, 19*(9), 11–16.

Neubert, G. A., Binko, J. B., & McNelis, S. J. (2004). "You want us to do what?" The story of the conversion of a secondary education faculty to the professional development school movement. In J. E. Neapolitan, T. D. Profit, C. L. Wittmann, & T. R. Berkeley (Eds.), *Traditions, standards & transformations: a model for professional development school networks* (pp. 71–80). New York, NY: Peter Lang.

O'Donnell, C. L. (2008). Defining, conceptualizing, and measuring fidelity to implementation and its relationship to outcomes in K–12 curriculum intervention research. *Review of Education Research, 78*(1), 33–84.

Priestley, M., Miller, K., Barrett, L., & Wallace, C. (2011). Teacher learning communities and educational change in Scotland: The Highland experience. *British Educational Research Journal, 37*(2), 265–284.

Sherer, J. S., & Spillane, J. P. (2011). Constancy and change in work practice in schools: The role of organizational routines. *Teachers College Record, 13*(3), 611–657.

Spillane, J. P., Reiser, B. J., & Reimer, T. (2002). Policy implementation and cognition: Reframing and refocusing implementation research. *Review of Educational Research, 72*(3), 387–431.

Teitel, L. (2001). An assessment framework for professional development schools: Going beyond a leap of faith. *Journal of Teacher Education, 52*(1), 57–69.

Teitel, L. (2003). *The professional development schools handbook.* Thousand Oaks, CA: Corwin Press.

Teitel, L., Reed, C., & O'Connor, K. (1998). Institutionalizing professional development schools: Successes, challenges, and continuing tensions. *Professional development schools: Confronting realities,* 1-63.

Thornton, H. (2005). Examining how school-based partners bring PDS to Life: NCATE standards in their own words. In I. Guadarrama, J. Ramsey, & J. Nath (Eds.), *Professional development schools: Advances in community thought and research* (pp. 3–8). Greenwich, CT: Information Age.

Wenger, E. (2000). Communities of practice and social learning systems. *Organization, 7*(2), 225–246.

APPENDIX 9.A. MARYLAND STANDARDS FOR PROFESSIONAL DEVELOPMENT SCHOOLS (FROM PROFESSIONAL DEVELOPMENT SCHOOLS IN MARYLAND: AN IMPLEMENTATION MANUAL)

PDS Standards

Learning Community

As a learning community, the PDS recognizes and supports the distinct learning needs of all stakeholders by integrating the development of students and adults. Interns complete extensive internships as a part of the learning community and share responsibility with school faculty for the academic performance of PreK–12 students. In turn, school-based preservice mentors share responsibility with the teacher preparation program for the academic and clinical performance of interns. Throughout the process, PDS partners model reflective practice and self-initiated learning and assessment. Instruction and professional development at all levels is data-driven and focused on increasing student capabilities.

Collaboration

The mission of the PDS is jointly defined and mutually supported by the university and the school(s). Roles and structures are collaboratively designed to support the PDS work and to improve outcomes for PreK–12 students and interns. Arts and sciences, school-based, teacher education, and clinical faculty plan and implement intern curriculum and professional development initiatives centered on student achievement. The partners set standards for participation and learning outcomes together. Respect for the needs and goals of all stakeholders is central to the PDS.

Accountability

The PDS accepts the responsibility of and is held accountable for upholding professional standards for preparing and renewing teachers in accordance with the redesign. Consequently, PDS partners jointly identify standards for interns and participate in evaluating intern performance. Accomplished PreK–16 faculty are engaged in the mentoring and supervision of interns, and intern development is documented in a portfolio and evaluated against state or national standards for beginning teachers. All PDS stakeholders are held accountable for the achievement of PreK–16 students as measured by performance assessments.

Organization, Roles and Resources

PDS partners allocate resources to support the continuous improvement of teaching and learning. New roles are created and old roles are modified for PreK–16 students, interns, faculty, and administrators to achieve the mission of the PDS. Effective communication about PDS plans and structures plays a key role in the linkage with school districts, university's, parents, and others. Jointly funded positions are encouraged and supported. Partners provide PDS stakeholders with *Professional Development Schools: An Implementation Manual* and necessary resources to advance PDS work: vision, time, space, incentives, leadership, technology, and access.

Diversity and Equity

The PDS supports equitable involvement of PreK–16 faculty and interns, as well as equitable support of student outcomes. Teacher candidates have equitable access to the PDS internship, and all PreK–16 faculty have opportunities to participate in PDS activities. The PDS is attentive to issues of equity related to student achievement and seeks to address them through research-based program improvements that enable interns to meet the needs of diverse learners.

Professional Development Schools: An Implementation Manual

Standards	Teacher Preparation	Continuing Professional Development	Research & Inquiry	Student Achievement
I. Learning Community *The PDS recognizes and supports the distinct learning needs of faculty/ staff, interns, students, parents, and community members*	a. PDS partners collaboratively integrate PreK–12 instructional content priorities in the teacher education program and field-based experiences b. Interns engage in the full range of teacher activities in the school community c. Interns are placed in cohorts and reflect on learning experiences with their cohort peers and IHE and school faculty	a. PDS partners collaboratively create, conduct, and participate in needs-based professional development to improve instruction and positively impact student achievement b. PDS partners plan and participate in activities where all school staff is encouraged to support and interact with interns c. School and campus-based instructional activities are informed by PDS experiences	a. PDS partners collaboratively engage in inquiry and/or action research b. PDS partners disseminate results of research/inquiry activity	a. IHE and school faculty model the use of state/local learning outcomes and assessments in coursework and field experiences b. Interns demonstrate competency in using specified learning outcomes and assessments to plan, deliver, and assess instruction.
II. Collaboration *PDS partners work together to carry out the collaboratively defined mission of the PDS*	a. IHE and school faculty collaboratively plan and implement curricula for interns to provide authentic learning experiences b. PDS partners share responsibility for evaluating interns c. PDS partners collaboratively meet the needs of preservice mentors d. IHE teacher education, arts and science, and school faculty collaborate in planning and implementing content-based learning experiences for PDS partners	a. PDS stakeholders collaborate to develop, implement, and monitor teacher education across institutions b. IHE and school faculty engage in cross-institutional staffing c. PDS partners identify and address professional development needs of faculty and interns d. PDS partners provide ongoing support for all educators, including nontenured and provisionally certified teachers	a. PDS partners collaboratively examine the action research/ inquiry process b. PDS partners identify the research/inquiry agenda based on the data-driven needs of the PDS	a. PDS partners use demographic and performance data to modify instruction to improve student achievement b. Representatives of PDS stakeholder groups participate on the school improvement teach c. PDS partners collaborate to plan and implement PreK–12 performance assessments and use outcomes to guide instructional decisions

Standards	Teacher Preparation	Continuing Professional Development	Research & Inquiry	Student Achievement
III. Accountability *The PDS accepts the responsibility of and is accountable for upholding professional standards for preparing and renewing teachers in accordance with the redesign of teacher education*	a. IHE and school faculty collaborate on the development of intern performance assessments b. The teacher education program requires that interns be assessed through a standards-based portfolio c. PDS partners develop and implement a collaborative agreement regarding exit standards for interns d. IHE and school faculty solicit and use feedback from interns to modify the teacher education program	a. PDS partners assess the collaborative professional development provided in the PDS b. IHE and school faculty collaboratively prepare to mentor and supervise interns c. PDDS partners work together to meet one another's professional development needs d. PDS partners recognize one another's accomplishments	a. PDS partners collect, analyze, and use data for program planning and implementation b. PDS partners use results of research and inquiry to inform future practice within the PDS	a. PDS stakeholders assume responsibility for improving PreK–12 student achievement b. PDS partners collaborate to determine the impact of PDS on student achievement
IV. Organization Roles and Resources *Partner institutions allocate resources to support the continuous improvement of teaching and learning*	a. PDS partners communicate regarding roles, responsibilities, and operating procedures and use continuous feedback to improve the operation of the PDS b. PDS partners share resources to support the learning of PreK–12 students and PDS partners c. PDS partners seek and assess feedback concerning PDS instruction for interns and new faculty, making changes as needed	a. IHEs recognize and reward the PDS work of IHE faculty and staff through organizational structures and incentives that fully integrate PDS work with the mission of the teacher education program b. PDS stakeholders institutionalize recognition and rewards for preservice mentors c. PDS partners use the PDS as a vehicle for the recruitment and retention of teachers d. A memorandum of understanding signed by PDS partners delineates the organization of the PDS and the resources to be provided	a. PDS partners model professional ethics and engage in substantive examination of ethical issues affecting research and practice b. IHE and local school system partners provide joint resources to support collaborative school-based PDS research/inquiry	a. PDS stakeholders examine the impact of PDS on student achievement b. PDS partners use performance data in strategic planning to design, implement, evaluate, and revise PDS policies, roles, and resources c. The IHE and school district institutionalize resources to ensure the continuity of the PDS

V. Diversity and Equality *The PDS supports equitable involvement of Pre K–16 faculty/staff and interns to support equitable outcomes for diverse learners*	a. The IHE provides all interns equitable access to an extensive internship of at least 100 days over two consecutive semesters in a PDS b. Interns demonstrate skill in working with diverse student, parent and staff populations c. Interns demonstrate the ability to work with students with special needs and collaborate with special educators	a. PDS partners provide equitable opportunities for stakeholder participation in PDS activities b. PDS partners participate in, assess, and refine training to support knowledge, skills, and dispositions surrounding equity issues c. PDS partners represent diverse backgrounds	a. PDS partners plan and conduct action research/inquiry with attention to issues of equity b. PDS partners disseminate research findings related to student equity and use these for program improvement	a. PDS partners work with parents and community members in support of learning b. PDS partners collaborate to ensure that all education is multicultural c. PDS partners focus on meeting the needs of diverse learners to eliminate achievement gaps

Adapted from: "Appendix 9.A: Standards for Maryland Professional Development School," by Maryland Department of Education, 2007, Professional Development Schools: Assessment Framework for Maryland, p.16.

APPENDIX 9.B. ARTIFACT BOX TABLE OF CONTENT

Learning Community

Teacher Preparation

1) "I do, We do, You do framework"
2) Reflection Essays and Reflection Journals
3) UNIVERSITY/COUNTY Inservice Documents

Continuing Professional Development

1) Bully Prevention Survey and Action Research
2) Student Motivation Survey
3) COUNTY Inservice Events with Intern Involvement

Research and Inquiry

1) Intervention Projects
2) Action Research and 604 Seminar Documents
3) 4th Grade Action Research

Student Achievement

1) CFIP Process
2) Grade Level SMART Goals
3) Math and Reading Intervention Monitoring
4) SIP Professional Development
5) Lesson Planning
6) Co-Teaching Model

Collaboration

Teacher Preparation

1) Priorities and Plans
2) Orientation for Interns
3) Triad Meeting
4) E-Portfolio
5) UNIVERSITY/SCHOOL Gatherings
6) Classroom Observations
7) Administrator Observation

Continuing Professional Development

1) Co-Teaching
2) Common Core Curriculum
3) Benefits of Becoming a Partner School
4) SCHOOL Teachers who Teach at UNIVERSITY

Research and Inquiry

1) UNIVERSITY/SCHOOL Gathering with SIP Discussion

Student Achievement

1) SCHOOL Students to be Coded GT and Lesson Plans

2) UNIVERSITY Referenced in the SCHOOL SIP

Accountability *Teacher Preparation*

1) Intern Timesheets

2) Level I/II Evaluations, Post-Internship Evaluations and Summative Evaluation Rubrics

3) Interns and Mentors Complete a Survey

4) Intern Survey Indicating a Change in EDU 460

5) Supervisor Training and Handbook

Continuing Professional Development

1) UNIVERSITY Mentor Handbook

2) Coordinating Council Meetings

3) Weekly SCHOOL Newsletter and Recommendation Letters

4) Mentor Thank-You Cards

Research and Inquiry

1) Attendance Data

2) Intervention Project Change

Student Achievement

1) Intern Lesson Plans

2) Math and Reading Intervention Monitoring Spreadsheets

3) Invitation for Interns to Annual Reading Night

4) Young Authors Contest

Organization, Roles and Resources *Teacher Preparation*

1) Liaison & Site Coordinator Handbook

2) Annual Orientation held at UNIVERSITY

3) PDS Handbook

4) UNIVERSITY/SCHOOL Gatherings

5) Inservice Collaboratively planned by UNIVERSITY and COUNTY

6) Workshops and Seminars at UNIVERSITY

7) Inservice planned by COUNTY

Continuing Professional Development

1) Services for PDS Schools

2) COUNTY 411

3) 15% Tuition Reduction

4) COUNTY Student Teacher Expo

5) SCHOOL Hires UNIVERSITY Interns

Research and Inquiry

1) Maryland PDS Conference

2) Professional Ethics Section of the Handbook

Student Achievement

1) Strategic Planning Meetings

Diversity and Equity

Teacher Preparation

1) School Overview

2) Two Distinct Placements

3) Assistive Technology Assignment

4) Differentiated Instruction with "Math Stations"

5) Accommodation Cards

6) Special Education Schedule

7) Mentor Level II Evaluation

Continuing Professional Development

1) Differentiated Instruction Professional Development

2) Demographics of SCHOOL

3) Reading Conference Email

Research and Inquiry

1) PLC Meetings

Student Achievement

1) Cultural Proficiency In-Services

2) Interns Interact with Parents and Community Members

3) Interns Communicate Directly with Parents

CHAPTER 10

THE UNIVERSITY AND ELEMENTARY SCHOOL

A Partnership Focusing on Kindergarten Through Fifth Grade (K–5) Student Learning

Fran Greb, Naomi Kirkman, and Brett Grunau

ABSTRACT

An ever-evolving eight-year school–university partnership provides opportunities for elementary students, university students, and faculty to learn together. Utilizing the expertise of faculty from multiple colleges within the university, the elementary school curriculum is enriched through hands-on experiences both in the elementary school and on the college campus. By providing cross-curricular experiences that focus on student learning, this sustained and committed partnership provides benefits both to the university and the partner elementary school. Data from a questionnaire gauging students' perspectives of the partnership were collected. Students' reactions to learning with and at the university are presented in this narrative.

The four purposes of school–university partnerships are "improved student learning, pre-service teacher education, in-service teacher education, and a shared re-

Creating Visions for University-School Partnerships, pages 167–177.
Copyright © 2014 by Information Age Publishing
All rights of reproduction in any form reserved.

search agenda" (Patrizio & Gajda, 2007, pp. 20–21). The university, in partnership with a local public elementary school, serves all four of these purposes with an emphasis on the enhancement of K–5 student learning. The partnership connects the elementary students to the university on campus and at the elementary school site. For example, fifth-grade students visit the university's science lab to apply the scientific process by extracting deoxyribonucleic acid (DNA) from strawberries. Kindergarten students are visited by the university's undergraduate students who aid in the development of listening comprehension and literacy skills through read-alouds.

The partnership combines the resources of both schools in order to increase student learning through interdisciplinary connections. Additionally, teacher isolation is reduced as faculty from both institutions work together to develop educational opportunities for students (Johnson, 2013). The partnership provides students with hands-on experiences with university faculty (from multiple colleges), staff, and students who engage with the material in a way that neither the elementary school nor university could do alone. As stated by Patrizio and Gajda (2007), the improvement of student learning is "the most important… purpos[e] around which educational partnerships can and should form" (p. 20).

This chapter will examine K–5 student perceptions of their learning experiences with the university as, according to Talboys, "there is a definitive link between understanding something on a deeper level by seeing or touching it and maybe even experiencing it" (as cited by Tuffy, 2011, p. 22). Data on students' perceptions of the partnership were collected.

OUR SCHOOL–UNIVERSITY PARTNERSHIP SETTING

The partnership between the elementary school and university began in 2004. Both the university and the elementary school are located approximately twenty miles west of New York City. The town has a population of nearly 40,000 residents, a majority of whom would be considered of medium to high socioeconomic status. The elementary school enrolls approximately 500 students in its kindergarten through fifth grades. Of these students, approximately 60% are Caucasian, 23% are African American, 10% are Asian, and 6% are Hispanic. According to the school district's website, the elementary school has had a dynamic partnership with the university, its walking-distance neighbor. This unique collaboration affords many opportunities to share resources, facilities, and teaching and learning experiences among the elementary school's 460 students, their teachers, university faculty, and university student teachers (2013). In elementary school, students are beginning to understand that learning is a lifelong process. Children at the elementary school see their own teachers engaged with university-sponsored professional development opportunities.

These educational experiences are facilitated by Dr. F, MSU associate professor in the college of education and human services; an MSU graduate assistant; and the principal of the elementary school. Dr. F is on site at the elementary school once a week where she meets with teachers to discuss ways that the university partnership can enhance their already rich curriculum. Once possible educational needs are identified, Dr. F and her graduate assistant reach out to the members of various colleges within the university to secure and schedule educational experiences for the students of the elementary school.

The following are a representation of educational experiences that have been coordinated through this partnership. The elementary school students visit the university for weekly music recitals, dance and theater performances, health and physical education activities, telescope nights, visits to the forensics lab and other science experiences, and a host of other learning experiences. In addition, each year, the university's physical education faculty and students facilitate an on-campus six-mile walk-a-thon for fourth and fifth graders. There is also a three-mile walk-a-thon for second and third graders to raise money for a local charity. The university faculty and students organize field days for all the elementary school students, which include physical education stations and team building games on the university's campus.

The university faculty members facilitate weekly Philosophy for Children sessions in many classrooms. These philosophy sessions are implemented by the Institute for the Advancement of Philosophy for Children, which is a program that was developed at the university and is recognized by the American Philosophical Association. The program "provides curriculum materials for engaging young people (pre-school through high school) in philosophical inquiry. It also provides teacher preparation in the pedagogy of the classroom community of inquiry" (Montclair State University, 2012).

University faculty also serve as visiting professors to classrooms to enhance instruction. For example, each year a professor from the university's history department visits the elementary school to teach students about the African American history of the local area.

A university professor from the college of education and human services works on-site at the elementary school one day a week to assist both the elementary school teachers and preservice teachers. The elementary school's experienced teachers, in turn, supervise student teachers from the university in the elementary school classrooms. These student teachers help the elementary school maintain a lower student–teacher ratio. They also provide greater opportunities for small group learning and differentiated instruction.

Our school–university partnership is working to meet the goals of what it means to be a professional development school as outlined in by the executive council and board of directors of the National Association for Professional Development Schools in 2008. At that time, professional development schools were designed to accomplish a "four-fold agenda" that included "preparing future educators, providing current educators with ongoing professional development, encouraging joint school–university faculty investigation of education-related issues, and promoting the learning of P–12 students" (NAPDS, 2008). At this point in time, our partnerships' major emphasis has been placed on preparing future educators and promoting the learning of P–12 students. However, we believe our partnership could be strengthened if there was a stronger emphasis on professional development as well as a more developed partnership infrastructure. The latter goal will be aided greatly in the next school year with the addition of a dean of students and operations in the elementary school. One of the responsibilities of the new dean will be to enhance and strengthen the school's magnet theme. Additionally, we are working towards strengthening the partnership by collecting qualitative data regarding the effectiveness of our collaboration.

Student Voices: What They Tell Us

The elementary school's teachers administered anonymous questionnaires to 158 students in first, third, and fifth grade in the spring of 2012. The questionnaires addressed student perceptions of learning experiences that have been generated by the partnership (see Appendix 10.A). All students responded that they had either visited the university or someone from the university had visited their class during the 2011–2012 school year. Analysis of the data collected from these questionnaires revealed four ways this partnership is working to improve student learning: providing interdisciplinary experiences for students, emphasizing the arts, enhancing content knowledge, and encouraging students to look toward college as a tangible and advantageous future. The following responses have been organized by grade level.

First Grade: A Reflection of the Interdisciplinary Nature of the Partnership

Ninety-six percent of the 68 students in first grade stated that they learned from their experiences with the university. These first-grade students responded to the writing prompt: *"Did you learn anything from [the university] people? (example: your student teacher or a visit to campus). If so, draw a picture or write about what you learned."* The following are samples of the students' responses:

"I learned about shatoes" (shadows)
"We did PE senters [centers] and learnd [learned] how to play some games"
        See Appendix 10.B for child's illustration.
"food chane" (chain) See Appendix 10.B for child's illustration.
"I lened [learned] not to lye [lie] from folosofy [philosophy] joe"
"Symitry" (symmetry)
"I am lerning [learning] art from an [university] stooded [student] how to draw
        your face sideways."
"I learned some sort of sience" (science)

These student responses reveal the interdisciplinary nature of the partnership. The learning experiences they reference include the following subjects: mathematics, art, science, Philosophy for Children, and physical education.

Third Grade: An Emphasis on the Arts

One-hundred percent of the 23 third-grade students responded that they had learned something from their experiences with the university. The students stated that they had participated in the following activities facilitated by the partnership: (1) visiting the university's art gallery, (2) taking part in field day, (3) participating in a walk-a-thon on the university's campus, (4) touring the university's theater for a behind-the-scenes look at a student production, and (5) partaking in a field trip to the university's ADP Center for Teacher Preparation and Learning Technologies, an on-campus curriculum resource center, to learn about and practice best research methods. Additionally, students indicated that they learned about the history of their town from a history professor in the university's college of humanities and social sciences.

The following are samples, without spelling or punctuation corrections, of third graders' responses to the question, *"Did you learn anything from your experiences with [the university]? If so, what did you learn?"*:

> "I learned about poetry and it doesn't always have to rhyme. I also learned that artwork says something."
> "Yes. Art Gallery—I learned how they did abstract."
> "Yes, we learned about art, famous artists, and how theaters work."
> "I learned a lot about the theater."
> "Yes. Learned at [the] theater how it works. Learned about 2 artist at art gallery."
> "I learned that animals with backbones are called vertebrate, and animals without backbones are called invertebrates."
> "I learned about the early days when there were no electronic stuff."
> "I learned about science and social studies. We learned about plants-science."

As a note, many of the responses of the third-grade students seemed to be focused on the arts, which is an important part of this school–university partnership. Although nationally, the arts are often one of the first areas cut from public school budgets, the university, as well as the district, ensures that the arts are an integral part of the students' learning.

Fifth grade: Adding to learning; Looking towards college.

Approximately 80% of 67 fifth-grade students said not only did they learn something new from their experiences with the university but also that their experiences added to previous learning. The fifth graders' responses to the questionnaire reflect the engagement-based learning approach. The following are samples, without spelling or punctuation corrections, of fifth-grade student responses to the prompt, *"Do your experiences with [the university] add to your learning? If so, how?"*:

> "It has because I learn something at my school, then go to [the university] to learn about it on a whole new level."
>
> "They add to my learning by explaining deeply into the things we do."
>
> "Yes. It does add more learning to me because…they are breaking it down more for me."
>
> "Yes. The experiences add to learning with math, science, and more."
>
> "They do help me understand more about the lesson and it helps me learn more about [my town and the university]."

These responses highlight the partnership's ability to provide opportunities that deepen student learning. Together, the elementary school teachers and university faculty enhance the curriculum of each grade level. Providing hands-on experiences that engage students in a variety of ways, the partnership is ensuring that we deepen student learning as sometimes "there is a need to look outside the classroom for other resources that can enhance curriculum effectiveness" (Tuffy, 2011, p. 7). The following are examples of looking outside the classroom to enhance the curriculum:

- Dr. E., associate professor in the college of education and human services with a specialization in critical pedagogy and literacy, facilitated a writer's workshop focused on poetry.
- Dr. F., associate professor in the college of education and human services, department of early childhood elementary education and literacy, engaged with students in the interpretation of wordless books.
- Dr. L, professor of history in the college of humanities and social sciences, provided information about African American history in the area through an interactive discussion with the fifth-graders.

By affording elementary school students opportunities to visit a university campus, experience engaging and varied learning activities, and meet and interact with college students and professors, the partnership encourages students to begin thinking about college in a concrete manner. The following are samples, without spelling or punctuation corrections, of student responses to the questions, *"Are you thinking about going to college?"* and *"If you are thinking about college, has having experiences with [the university] had anything to do with it?"*:

> "Yes, because we see college students a lot and get to see what we can do if we go to college."
>
> "Yes, that some colleges partner with schools."

"Yes. I can see what projects we might have to do in college. I can prepare for it."

"I get to preview things I might do in college."

CONCLUDING REMARKS

The students at the elementary school provided feedback on our efforts to address student learning through a school–university partnership. Trends in the responses appear to indicate that the partnership provides numerous educational activities for students that enhance student learning. By utilizing the resources of multiple colleges within the university, including but not limited to the college of education and human services, the college of humanities and social sciences, the college of science and mathematics, and the college of the arts, the elementary school curriculum is enriched. Students' responses indicated that they had experiences with the university that both reinforced and added to their learning. One fifth-grader, when asked if the experiences with the university added to his or her learning, stated, "Yes, they do add to my learning about how much college and the world has to offer."

As we move forward, we continue to coordinate new learning experiences for students in our school–university partnership. Our goals are not regimented but rather fluid. We continually strive to provide relevant curricular connections for students that are generated through communication between the university and public school faculty.

REFERENCES

Johnson, B. (2013, January 15). Deeper learning: Why cross-curricular teaching is essential. *Edutopia*. Retrieved April 6, 2013 from http://www.edutopia.org/blog/cross-curricular-teaching-deeper-learning-ben-johnson

Montclair School District. (2013, March 17). *Mission*. Retrieved April 4, 2013 from http://www.montclair.k12.nj.us/WebPage.aspx?Id=224

Montclair State University. (2012). Institute for the Advancement of Philosophy for Children. Retrieved February http://www.montclair.edu/cehs/academics/institutes-and-centers/iapc/

National Association of Professional Development Schools. (2008). *What it means to be a professional development school.* Columbia, SC: Author. Retrieved from http://www.napds.org/9%20Essentials/statement.pdf

Patrizio, K., & Gajda, R. (2007). Demystifying an imperative: Understanding and applying collaboration theory in the PDS. *School-University Partnerships: The Journal of the National Association for Professional Development Schools, 1*(1), 18–28.

Tuffy, J. (2011). *The learning trip: Using the museum field trip experience as a teaching resource to enhance curriculum and student engagement.* Master's thesis, Dominican University of California, San Rafael, CA. Retrieved from http://www.eric.ed.gov/contentdelivery/servlet/ERICServlet?accno=ED517713

APPENDIX 10.A

Grade: 5th

Boy Girl (Please circle which one you are)

1. Have you visited the university with your class this year? If so, what did you do there?

2. Have students or teachers from the university visited you at school? If so, what did they do with you?

3. Do your experiences with the university add to your learning? If so, how?

4. Are you thinking about going to college?

5. If you are thinking about college, has having experiences with the university had anything to do with it?

Grade: 3rd

Boy Girl (Please circle which one you are)

1. Have you visited the university with your class this year? If so, what did you do there?

2. Have students or teachers from the university visited you at school? If so, what did they do with you?

3. Did you learn anything from your experiences with people from the university? If so, what did you learn?

4. Are you thinking about going to college?

5. If you are thinking about college, has having experiences with the university had anything to do with it?

Grade: 1st

Boy Girl (Please circle which one you are)

1. Have you visited the university with your class this year? Yes No

2. 2. Has anyone from the university visited your class this year? Yes No

3. Did you learn anything from the university people? (example: your student teacher or a visit to campus) If so, draw a picture or write about what you learned.

4. What do you like the most about coming to campus?

5. Do you enjoy having people from the university visit your classroom? Yes No

APPENDIX 10.B

Grade: 1st

Boy (Girl) (Please circle which one you are)

1. Have you visited _____ with your class this year? (Yes) No

2. Has anyone from _____ J visited your class this year? (Yes) No

3. Did you learn anything from MSU people? (example: your student teacher or a visit to campus) If so, draw a picture or write about what you learned

We did PE senters I learn d how to play some games

4. What do you like the most about coming to campus?

Learning how to play alot of games

5. Do you enjoy having people from _____ visit your classroom? (Yes) No

Grade: 1ˢᵗ

Boy (Girl) (Please circle which one you are)

1. Have you visited ⌐J with your class this year? (Yes) No

2. Has anyone from ⌐ visited your class this year? (Yes) No

3. Did you learn anything from ⌐ people? (example: your student teacher or a visit to campus) If so, draw a picture or write about what you learned.

4. What do you like the most about coming to campus?

I Like to watch the plays

5. Do you enjoy having people from ⌐ visit your classroom? (Yes) No

CHAPTER 11

PREPARING PRESERVICE TEACHERS IN A PDS CONTEXT

Insights into Field-Based Methods Courses

Christina Siry, JoAnne Ferrara, and Diane E. Lang

ABSTRACT

The need to integrate theory and practice in preservice teacher education is well documented. A PDS context can respond to this need, and this chapter elaborates the ways in which a series of three one-semester teacher education courses were redesigned to be field-based and co-taught by university faculty and elementary school teachers. Models of the courses and data excerpts from preservice teachers are provided in order to provide a variety of insights into the use of field-based methods courses.

There has been much written over the years about the need to integrate theory and practice in teacher education in order to best prepare preservice teachers for the complexities of classrooms (e.g., Darling-Hammond, 1999; Tobin & Roth, 2006; Zeichner, 2007). In this emphasis on theory and practice, *realistic* (Korthagen, Kessels, Koster, Lagerwerf, & Wubbles, 2001) and *authentic* (Haston & Russell,

Creating Visions for University-School Partnerships, pages 179–191.
Copyright © 2014 by Information Age Publishing
All rights of reproduction in any form reserved.

2012) approaches to teacher education have been a focus, emphasizing those that create opportunities for preservice teachers to engage in real-world experiences. To that end, professional development schools (PDSs) have a valuable role in the possible integration of theory and practice, as they situate preservice teachers in actual classrooms in order to learn about teaching. It is well documented that PDSs can create opportunities to enhance the education of teachers (e.g., Daemen, Laroes, Meijer, & Vermunt, 2013). PDSs are diverse in the opportunities for the education of teachers, preservice teachers, and children, and there are a variety of approaches that have been developed to support effective teacher education within PDSs. This chapter begins with the assumption that PDSs can provide support to the education of preservice teachers and elaborates on three different models that have been developed to facilitate preservice teachers' learning about teaching in a PDS context.

SITUATING TEACHER EDUCATION IN THE FIELD

Above, the need to find ways to emphasize the relationships between theory and practice in teacher education has been introduced, and by that we mean that both inservice and preservice teachers are involved. If the focus is turned directly to the education of *preservice teachers*, then it can be seen that there are a variety of situations in which this (inseparable) relationship between theory and practice can be explored. Preservice teachers can be observers in a classroom, they can participate for an extended amount of time in their practical, or they can engage in field-based courses. Given that methods courses are commonly described as one vehicle for new teachers to learn ways to "bridge theory and practice," it is in methods courses that this intertwined relationship between theory and practice can be manifested and explored. When university coursework is brought into field-based settings through a PDS, there is a potential to also facilitate the development of preservice teachers' identities as new teachers (Haston & Russell, 2012) and to create new relationships built upon solidarity in teaching (Siry, 2009). It has been shown that one of the common features of effective teacher education programs is that "extended clinical experiences are carefully developed to support the ideas and practices presented in simultaneous, closely interwoven coursework" (Darling-Hammond, 2006, p. 41), and this opportunity for extended clinical experiences coupled with interwoven coursework can be worked towards with teacher education courses situated in a field-based, PDS setting.

Extending field-experiences can improve preservice education (Darling-Hammond, 2005). To this end, we have designed field-based courses that enable preservice teachers to learn to teach through supported, shared experiences in elementary PDSs. Field-based courses are taught with a designated K–5 classroom as a lab where the professor and elementary school faculty teach preservice teachers collaboratively. These courses allow all participants to experience life in the classroom together and critically discuss the implications for content area curriculum. This field-based programming situated within a PDS has been developed to ensure that the focus of methods courses remains on a complex understanding of both the theory and the practice of teaching.

The field-based program for undergraduate teacher education candidates described in this chapter is housed at a small liberal arts college located 30 miles north of New York City in the United States. Most graduates of the program become employed in the New York City public school system and the surrounding suburbs and cities. The college has multiple PDSs that are located in small cities in Westchester County where the university is located. In the context of these PDS relationships, the college and the schools partner to improve learning outcomes for K–5 students, preservice teachers, inservice teachers, and college faculty. The field-based courses are held off-campus in two of these PDSs, and course professors and preservice teachers spend part of their course time working together in classrooms with teachers and children.

The classroom teachers of the host classes are deeply involved in all aspects of the PDS and participate in planning and co-teaching the field-based courses. They are considered by their schools to be master teachers and are valuable resources to new teachers developing their pedagogy. Additionally, the professors of all three courses are academics as well as former elementary school teachers, and thus also well prepared to support new teachers as they develop their pedagogical approaches and understandings. In what follows, the underlying assumptions of the program and theoretical underpinnings that support the work we do within the PDSs are described. The key features of each of these courses are described, and the rationales behind early teaching experiences are explored. An exploration of the successes and challenges of reframing a teacher education program (to include supported teaching experiences in PDS classrooms early in preservice teachers' coursework) conclude the chapter.

Framing the Issues

An epistemology of *teaching as praxis*, as proposed by Roth and Tobin (2002), guides this program. The courses have been structured to create shared experiences over time that are related to university course objectives. As preservice teachers teach and interact with children in the classroom, they experience what Roth and Tobin (2002) have described as the temporal nature of praxis. "Teaching is something that is done, rather than being a static set of procedural and declarative knowledge waiting to be called up" (Roth & Tobin, 2002, p. 8). The course content becomes an opportunity for reflection upon PDS classroom occurrences and implications for teaching and learning. Preservice teachers are encouraged to develop a reflexive stance towards teaching and learning in order to examine their own teaching practices as well as themselves as learners. In this model, preservice teachers learn from teaching in an intentional, systematic way (Hiebert, Morris, Berk, & Jansen, 2007). Learning experiences are deliberately sequenced and scaffolded to encourage the acquisition of pedagogical expertise so that preservice teachers develop their skills over time in a variety of settings (Feiman-Nemser, 2001).

Lave and Wenger's (1991) theory of situated learning supports the structure for all three of the courses described below. As these preservice teachers work together in elementary classrooms, they engage in "social practice that entails learning as an integral constituent" (Lave & Wenger, 1991, p. 35). The shared teaching experiences add a transitional layer of pedagogical awareness between observation-based field experiences and the traditional student teaching experience. As they are engaged in the classroom setting, they are learning in practice as well as participating in a community of practice (Wenger, 1998). Through the practice of supported teaching, preservice teachers can construct and develop their identities as teachers (Wenger, 1998). Additionally, ongoing participation in a classroom community of a PDS enables preservice teachers to develop sustained relationships with children and teachers.

Rationale for Early Field Experiences

The nature of teaching is messy; there are things that come up that cannot always be anticipated. As a result, teaching as it is unfolding, as well as the plans for upcoming experiences, may need to be adjusted. Often the "most appropriate course of action will unfold in the enactment and cannot be pre-specified" (Roth & Tobin, 2002, p. 11). The best way to experience this serendipity and unpredictability of teaching, it is believed, is to have long-term experience in the role of a teacher with the support of an extensive network of peers and professors, which can be developed within a PDS context. The opportunity for weekly discussions as a group is important because despite any amount of planning, there can be unexpected moments that can become valuable opportunities for reflection and learning. Teacher preparation is most effective when it occurs in real classroom settings. Preservice teachers must receive rich and varied experiences throughout their preparation programs (Task Force on Field Experience Standards, 2000). These clinical experiences should be carefully constructed so that they are connected with the teacher education curriculum (Darling-Hammond, 2005). A PDS provides the perfect venue for exposing preservice teachers to the classroom challenges and emerging trends by developing innovative ways to prepare them (Ferrara & Siry, 2011). This field-based program creates authentic roles for teachers to enact with clear tasks and responsibilities. As such, field experiences in a PDS that are connected to university course objectives and authentic classroom interactions are central to the approach at this university.

In addition to providing relevance to the preservice teachers, these early field experiences keep the course professors grounded in current practices and keep them aware of changing trends in the classrooms. This contrasts with teaching as a memory; memory can be clouded (both positively and negatively). By being in the classroom as co-teachers, our current vision of schools is challenged, and we develop both as professors and as teachers. Thus there is a reciprocal benefit for preservice teacher, inservice teacher, and course instructor, each of whom can gain new insights into teaching and learning.

In this chapter, we highlight three education courses that have been adapted for teaching and learning in our PDSs. These courses are components of a bachelor's degree program leading to teacher certification in grades 1–6. The rationale for choosing these particular courses was that their sequence in the program enables the field-based courses to occur over several semesters' time. This provides for field-based experience and learning woven throughout two to three years of the program. As each of the three course models is illustrated, a description of the structure of the course is provided, as well as perspectives from preservice teachers who have participated in the course.

Each of the three courses provides a differing level of participation in elementary classrooms within our PDSs. The first field-based course, Educating Children with Diverse Needs, provides an opportunity for preservice teachers to work in inclusionary classrooms in order to develop an understanding of differentiated instruction. This component involves tutoring of individual students and classroom observation. The second course is an intermediate level course, Childhood Science Methods. The field component in this course is more extensive, as small teams of preservice teachers design lessons to collaboratively teach to the elementary school students. The third course, Social Studies Methods, precedes student teaching. Preservice teachers are supported in developing individual lessons that connect in a whole group unit. This course consists of a 15-week tutoring component, with 13 weeks of co-teaching during which preservice teachers develop and teach a lesson of their own design.

THREE MODELS

Until recently, undergraduate preservice teachers enrolled in the program traditionally have had little or no classroom experience, and, in many cases in the past, student teaching was the first opportunity for prospective teachers to practice pedagogical skills. However, interaction with children must begin prior to student teaching in environments that encourage inquiry and reflection (McDermott, Gormely, Rothenberg & Hammer, 1995; Weaver, Stanulis, & Nevins, 1996). A field-based PDS structure to a teacher education program provides preservice teachers with supported field experiences early in their program and provides opportunities for in-depth analysis of learning over time. Each of the three courses highlighted herein presents a different model for structuring a field-based course. The specifics of each are presented in the following descriptions and followed with reflections from preservice teachers after completing each of the courses. In the layering together of theoretical foundations, the differing course frameworks, and preservice teacher reflections, the reader is presented with a variety of points of reflection for developing structures that can be implemented in PDS settings.

Model 1—Educating Children with Diverse Needs

Educating Children with Diverse Needs is the second course in the sequence of eight required education program courses and is taken following a foundations of education course. It exposes preservice teachers to classrooms that reflect a range of learning differences in order to develop an awareness of special needs students. One of the PDSs was specifically chosen as a host site because of its academic success and ability to work effectively with a high-needs student body. Most of the students in the school qualify for free and reduced lunch, and 40% are English language learners.

The course uses a two-hour block format. The first half-hour is devoted to the field component, and the remaining two hours are reserved for lecture, debriefing, group assignments, and role-play. For the first several weeks of the course, preservice teachers participate in focused observations. Checklists and guiding questions are used to build a context for the types of classroom strategies that support special education students. Pairs of preservice teachers are assigned to a classroom for the entire semester, where, under the guidance of the classroom teacher, they work one on one with a student or in a small group. As they become more comfortable in the classrooms, their roles evolve from observer to tutor. In this way, preservice teachers begin to understand that special education placements include a variety of settings and services.

The classroom teacher and the professor meet once a week to discuss the learning activities in which the preservice teachers and elementary students are engaged. The classroom teacher and the preservice teachers discuss and analyze strategies to use with the children. At the end of the semester, the classroom teacher completes an assessment that provides information about the preservice teachers' demonstrated progress in working with students with a range of abilities in an inclusive setting. The preservice teachers conduct a similar self-assessment and reflect upon their ability to work with students in an inclusive setting. The professor reviews the assessments to address the effectiveness of the course.

Preservice Teacher Reflections on Model 1

Preservice teachers have commented that the course has helped them to understand the complexity of diverse student populations and the social dimensions of teaching. One preservice teacher reported, "I have learned that these students are faced with challenges of high poverty struggle in many different ways." Interestingly, many students started becoming aware of the social context of learning in this class. One preservice teacher wrote, "Aside from the educational aspect of this environment, [I have been]…interacting with children extremely different from me. I am capable of appreciating and respecting those differences." Further, the intensity of engagement and guidance of the professor help preservice teachers begin to consider equity issues. For example, a preservice teacher said, "I have learned that every child comes to a classroom with specific needs. It is good to treat everyone as equals but it is crucial to remember that not every child is the same."

Model 2—Childhood Science Methods

The Childhood Science Methods course is structured around co-participation in an elementary classroom. This course meets twice a week, with the first meeting of the week being held on campus and the second meeting held off-campus in a designated elementary classroom. This format provides a weekly workshop session on campus for preservice teachers to work together with the professor to plan activities to co-teach to the children throughout the semester. This format also provides a reflective space on campus for the group (preservice teachers and professor) to debrief previous lessons, discuss successes and challenges, and examine how theories of learning are manifested and illustrated in practice in the classroom.

The second course session of each week takes place in an elementary classroom. The classroom teacher is instrumental in planning the focus of the unit and meets with the preservice teachers weekly to discuss their upcoming lessons. Each of the lessons consists of a direct instruction introduction, which is co-taught by a preservice teacher, the classroom teacher, and the course professor.

Following the lesson introduction, the children move to working on science explorations in small groups at tables. There are generally two preservice teachers assigned to each group of six children to facilitate children's exploration and discovery. Co-teaching as a form of praxis helps preservice teachers to "learn and understand in and through the sharing of being in the classroom" (Tobin & Roth, 2006, p. 2). This situated, shared experience is the key element of the Childhood Science Methods course. The preservice teachers learn to teach by teaching and sharing moments in the classroom that later form the basis of reflective group discussions and analysis. The preservice teachers in this program learn "at the elbow" of experienced teachers (Roth & Tobin, 2002).

Preservice Teacher Reflections on Model 2

Undergraduate students were asked after the semester had ended to reflect upon their experiences in the course. One preservice teacher compared this course to more traditional methods courses she had taken previously. "I learned more than I ever would have if had taken this course entirely on campus. This was not only about teaching the students, but it is also about learning from them, and I learned a lot." The importance of flexibility as a teacher is a theme that has emerged throughout the courses. One student summed up her understanding of the dynamic nature of elementary school teaching:

> In past classes that were not field-based, we made lessons, but they were only used for the professor to grade them. In this class, it was exciting to be able to do the lessons that we came up with. We learned that things can change within the lesson and that even though you completed a lesson, there still is room for improvement and adjustment.

This sentiment was supported by another preservice teacher when she wrote:

Overall, I feel that I am more comfortable with myself as a whole. I am more confident and feel very able to overcome obstacles that are unavoidable as a teacher. I have come to realize that being a teacher means being flexible. When I say flexible I mean flexible in the sense of planning and implementing plans. Before entering this class I was unaware of how often teachers have to alter their schedules in order to make accommodations for everyday occurrences.

Model 3—Childhood Education Methods for Teaching Social Studies

In this model, the course meets once a week for two and a half hours for one semester. Each session begins with a 45-minute teacher education workshop where issues of social studies education are explored. This is followed by a 75-minute social studies block in an elementary school classroom where the classroom teacher and the professor co-teach social studies lessons that revisit the workshop topics. Preservice teachers are assigned tutees that they instruct through the small group work section of the lesson. After week three of the course, preservice teachers start co-teaching and developing lessons during the social studies block. The preservice teachers are responsible for designing the lessons independently and consult with the professor in order to assure that the lesson is well prepared and is a learning experience for all involved. Preservice teachers develop a novice teacher guide focused on the fundamentals of teaching social studies, write a reflective essay about the experience teaching social studies (including their learning as well as the learning they observed in their tutees), and develop a social studies curriculum unit that includes the lesson they taught to the class.

This course attempts to capture the talents developed in the other two courses by combining teaching and tutoring. Additionally, there is an assumption in this course that preservice teachers are novice teachers. They are becoming teachers who understand how to provide challenging, meaningful education for all children (Cochran-Smith, 2005).

Preservice Teacher Feedback on Model 3

Often preservice teachers are very nervous about teaching social studies at the start of the semester. As the semester progresses, students appear more confident about teaching their own lessons. One preservice teacher reported,

At first I thought I'd drop the course. I was overwhelmed. I'd never worked with fifth graders.... As I started reading more, participating in co-teaching and tutoring, watching / asking, watching / asking, and asking more of [the classroom teacher] and [the professor] I started realizing I can do this. My lesson was the best thing I've done in college. I'm so excited about teaching now. I really get it.

On the internet-based course discussion board, preservice teachers engaged in exploration of the challenges in teaching social studies in the field-based course.

One preservice teacher wrote, "[T]alking with the students, I realized how complicated it is to 'understand' historical time. It made me think about revisiting key historical concepts in teaching social studies. Seeing and hearing how students 'understand' helped me develop as a teacher. Really doing it made a huge difference."

Role of the Classroom Teachers

The classroom teachers are instrumental in all aspects of these courses. As PDS stakeholders, they know what it means to be a PDS and embrace their roles and responsibilities. They are close collaborators and participants, serve as active members of the PDS leadership teams, and have invested themselves in the success of the program. The teachers work closely with the college professors to design the course content and learning experiences. As a result of their involvement with the field-based program, these classroom teachers now see their professional role as expanded beyond the classrooms walls to include a broader context for the teaching and learning environment. They include in their views of themselves as teachers also being facilitators of adult learning and as contributors to the field of teacher education.

CHALLENGES AND SUCCESSES

Preservice teacher and faculty informal responses to the childhood education field-based programs have been positive overall. A comprehensive review the program thus far has yielded many successes and some challenges. Documented successes tend to be centered on the opportunity to engage in teaching and the immediate application of theory into practice. Challenges tend to be related to institutional and structural constraints.

Institutional, Structural, and Confidence Constraints

There are several challenges that have arisen in the development of a field-based program. This format has not been fully implemented across all teacher education programs at the college. Many of the other education courses provided by other departments remain campus-based and have not embraced the potentials of field-based instruction. The program, therefore, is the only fully field-based for undergraduate childhood education candidates at this time. Additionally, there are logistical challenges with working with host teachers—even though the courses are held in the PDSs. Scheduling and calendar conflicts need to be considered and overcome.

Finally, the confidence of the professor to be an elementary teacher is an issue. Professors engaging in this pedagogy need to be risk takers and willing to be vulnerable. This can be an unpredictable journey. Many times the learning explored in the teacher education sessions is reinforced by the co-teaching experience; however, sometimes, professors become carried to another place in the curriculum by children's interests, understandings, and misunderstandings. While providing many realistic forums for learning about teaching, this variability is a challenge to the professors and, sometimes, to the preservice teachers as well. This variability is, however, a crucial part of field-based courses because actual teaching is a dynamic experience. In fact, as new teachers are developing their teaching repertoire and style, they often experience great variability in the classroom. It is important for a program to prepare preservice teachers that have "teacher legs." Just as veteran sailors have "sea legs"—the ability to stand on the deck of a ship during a storm and still navigate the seas effectively—teachers, especially preservice teachers and novice teachers, need to develop their "teacher legs," the ability to perform in a range of conditions—twists and turns—and still focus on the educational goals at hand as well as long term.

Successes in the Field

PDSs

First and foremost, the success of this field-based program is attributed to the PDSs with whom we partner. Had the university attempted to host this program in another setting without the PDS framework and structures in place or the mutual commitment of our in-service teachers to support preservice teacher learning, the results would be less positive. A PDS is the critical linchpin for the success of any teacher education program.

Preservice Teachers

Providing an environment for teaching and learning that is flexible and collaborative is the greatest success of the field-based program. Preservice teachers develop their skills and understandings in the context of actual practice in a school. They are able to participate and observe instruction and school climate and begin to understand first-hand the critical necessity of being flexible and innovative. Some of the successes on which the preservice teachers have commented include seeing teachers dealing with testing pressures and daily classroom issues. Additionally, during Social Studies Methods, preservice teachers are able to observe the administration of the required state testing protocol.

Exit interviews with preservice teachers who have participated in the field-based courses lead us to understand the learnings of these courses. While preservice teachers may have reasonable understandings of what children can and cannot do, they often have unrealistic expectations of how long it takes students to do things. Consequently, their lesson plans written prior to the field-based methods courses are unrealistic. After the field-based courses, their written plans demonstrate a much stronger understanding of what students need and how to teach effectively in the time allotted.

Classroom Teachers

The classroom teachers have stated that this experience "keeps them on their toes." As master teachers they are pushed to think about the ways in which they talk about what they are doing—naming the skills and strategies so that others can think about it with them. The teachers often think aloud with the preservice teachers and share their reasons for using specific instructional strategies. This serves to connect theory to practice for the preservice teachers and reviews and renews it for classroom teachers. The field experiences are designed to model the complex ways teachers can contribute to success for students.

All Parties

Another success that is emerging is a level of commitment of all parties. There is buy-in from the teachers because the professor has developed the course with the classroom teachers' input and perspectives. Both parties are invested in and committed to the activities of the preservice teachers. This commitment seems to contribute to the intrigue and learning potential of the course elements for preservice teachers. Through the courses, the ambiguous nature of teaching and how to deal with that successfully are modeled. Preservice teachers who have progressed through the program note this as a major positive feature of the program. Additionally, former preservice teachers are instrumental in the development of the course. Approximately 15 preservice teachers have been interviewed and asked to provide suggestions for the coming semester. This removes the sense of professor as the complete authority and places her in the role of collaborator and lifelong learner. In this way, the professor demonstrates the importance of flexibility in teaching and that teachers must respond to events as they arise (Kennedy, 2006). When all parties understand that teaching is a series of dynamic encounters, they are then able to face the complexities of teaching with a sense of direction. Finally, a continuum of teacher development and learning experience has been established in the context of these courses (Feiman-Nemser, 2001).

FUTURE DIRECTIONS

It is hoped that the undergraduate teacher education program will be expanded to include a practicum in the semester prior to student teaching and to provide more field-based courses for our graduate-level candidates. This would provide yet other opportunities for both undergraduates and graduates to develop as practitioners in a supported environment.

Moving forward, faculty who embrace a field-based philosophy will be encouraged to be included. In the views of Diez (in Darling-Hammond, 2006), it is seen as important to recruit faculty with recent innovative and successful elementary teaching experience. New faculty must be willing to collaborate with K–5 teachers and be interested in researching and improving their own teaching. Most importantly, they must be willing to engage in the spontaneous, exciting, and often unpredictable events that unfold in elementary classrooms daily. It has been three years since the first field-based course was instituted in this program. During that time, input from the PDS classroom and preservice teachers has been used to modify the course elements and improve the program. Teacher education practices continue to develop and be refined through experience and reflection with preservice and classroom teachers.

CONCLUSION

Anderson, Lawson, and Mayer-Smith (2006) write that there is great potential in "re-imagining and re/forming preservice programs that go beyond traditional campus settings" (p. 352). To that end of re/imagining and re/forming, each of the courses described follows a different structure and purpose, but they are united by an underlying assumption that teaching is something that must be learned through teaching opportunities that are supported by reflection, discussion, and shared experiences. It has been observed that preservice teachers discover that when they teach lessons to children, the children often do not respond in the way the preservice teachers anticipated. Prior to a field-based teaching experience in a PDS, preservice teachers seem to believe that if they are successful in their campus-based coursework, they will be able to immediately teach successfully. This field-based program debunks this myth and demystifies the processes of teaching in a supportive PDS environment.

Teacher education programs must provide opportunities for new teachers to explore and develop strategies that will engage their students in meaningful and relevant work. Such field-based experiences can reframe teacher education to be a reflective, comprehensive approach for learning. The power of this model versus the more common practicum or clinical experience model is that the preservice teachers and the professors experience shared triumphs and struggles with young students and then have a shared repertoire of experiences to deconstruct in order to develop "teacher-legs." The ability to have the content knowledge and simultaneously be able to translate this knowledge into a productive learning environment is developed. Field-based teacher preparation, a critical component of PDSs, provides the opportunity for preservice teachers to learn to teach by teaching, as their development is grounded in real classrooms. It is contended that this model is a valuable approach to new teacher education and that, as preservice teachers' learning is generated through their practice, there emerges a coherent integration between theory and practice.

REFERENCES

Anderson, D., Lawson, B., & Mayer-Smith, J. (2006). Investigating the impact of a practicum experience in an aquarium on pre-service teachers. *Teaching Education, 17*(4), 341–353.

Cochran-Smith, M. (2005). The new teacher education: For better or worse. *Educational-Researcher, 34*(7), 3–17.

Daemen, J., Laroes, E., Meijer, P., & Vermunt, J. (2013). Learning in professional development schools. In M.A. Flores et al. (Eds.), *Back to the future: Legacies, continuities, and changes in educational policy, practices, and research* (pp. 165–187). Rotterdam, The Netherlands: Sense Publishers.

Darling-Hammond, L. (1999).Educating teachers for the next century: Rethinking practice and policy. In G. Griffin (Ed.), *The education of teachers: 98th NSSE Yearbook, Part I* (pp. 221–255). Chicago, IL: NSSE.

Darling-Hammond, L. (2005). Teaching as a profession: Lessons in teacher preparation and professional development. *Phi Delta Kappan, 87*(3), 237–240.

Darling-Hammond, L. (2006). *Powerful teacher education: Lessons from exemplary programs.* San Francisco: Jossey-Bass.

Feiman-Nemser, S. (2001). From preparation to practice: Designing a continuum to strengthen and sustain teaching. *Teacher's College Record, 103*(6), 1013–1055.

Ferrara, J., & Siry, C. (2011). Preparing childhood teachers for changing suburbs: The power of a partnership. *Teacher Education and Practice, 23*(3), 359–369.

Haston, W., & Russell, J. (2012). Turning into teachers: Influences of authentic context learning experiences on occupational identity development of pre-service music teachers. *Journal of Research in Music Education, 59*(4), 369–392.

Hiebert, J., Morris, A. K., Berk, D., & Jansen, A. (2007). Preparing teachers to learn from teaching. *Journal of Teacher Education, 9*(5), 471–505.

Kennedy, M. (2006). Knowledge and vision in teaching. *Journal of Teacher Education, 57*(3), 205–211.

Korthagen, F. A., Kessels, J., Koster, B., Lagerwerf, B., & Wubbels, T. (2001). *Linking practice and theory: The pedagogy of realistic teacher education.* Mahwah, NJ: Lawrence Erlbaum.

Lave, J., & Wenger, E. (1991). *Situated learning: Legitimate peripheral participation.* New York, NY: Cambridge University Press.

McDermott, P., Gormely, K., Rothenberg, J., & Hammer, J. (1995). The influence of classroom practica experience on student teachers' thoughts about teaching. *Journal of Teacher Education, 46*(3), 184–192.

Roth, W-M., & Tobin, K. (2002). *At the elbow of another: Learning to teach by coteaching.* New York, NY: Peter Lang.

Siry, C. (2009). *Fostering solidarity and transforming identities: A collaborative approach to elementary science teacher education.* Unpublished doctoral dissertation. The Graduate Center; City University of New York.

Task Force on Field Experience Standards. (2000). *Standards for field experiences in teacher education.* Reston, VA: Association of Teacher Educators.

Tobin, K. & Roth, W-M. (2006). *Teaching to learn: A view from the field.* Rotterdam, The Netherlands: Sense Publishers.

Weaver, D., Stanulis, R. N., & Nevins, R. (1996). Negotiating preparation and practice: Student teaching in the middle. *Journal of Teacher Education, 7*(1), 27–38.

Wenger, E. (1998). *Communities of practice: Learning, meaning, and identity.* New York, NY: Cambridge University Press.

Zeichner, K. (2007). Professional development schools in a culture of evidence and accountability. *The Journal of the National Association of Professional Development Schools. 1*(1), 9–17.

PART III

ENRICHING CONTENT AREA INSTRUCTION

CHAPTER 12

TUTORING IN MATHEMATICS

Affect on Professional Development School (PDS) Preservice Teachers' Perception of Teaching Mathematics and Effect on Student Achievement

Jeanne Tunks and Caroline O'Brien

ABSTRACT

A professional development school (PDS) partnership in Northeast Texas collaborated to create a project whereby their preservice teachers learned to tutor elementary and middle school students in mathematics. Both the university and schools in the PDS collaborative adjusted instruction, space, time, and general support for preservice teachers to tutor students. One result was an affective change in preservice teachers' perceptions of themselves as teachers of mathematics. A second result was significant differences in student achievement at the $p < .05$ level across all six years. The case study demonstrated the value of using the PDS as a mechanism for bringing about the gains observed.

Creating Visions for University-School Partnerships, pages 195–215.
Copyright © 2014 by Information Age Publishing
All rights of reproduction in any form reserved.

A professional development school (PDS) partnership in Northeast Texas created a project whereby their pre-service teachers learned to tutor elementary and middle school students in mathematics. Both the university and schools in the PDS adjusted instruction, space, time, and general support for preservice teachers to tutor students. One result was an affective change in preservice teachers' perceptions of themselves as teachers of mathematics. A second result was significant differences in student achievement ($p < .05$) level across all six years. The case study demonstrated the value of using the PDS as a mechanism for bringing about the gains observed.

Preparation of preservice elementary teachers as teachers of mathematics requires an understanding of factors influencing candidate success. Various factors influence elementary education preservice teachers' success as teachers of mathematics. Findings on four such factors are discussed: anxiety about learning and teaching mathematics, the methods course, fieldwork, and partnerships. By design, professional development schools (PDSs) create collaborations among university and school personnel, parents, and communities. PDS programs that follow the Holmes model (Holmes Partnership, 1995) foster the collaboration through preservice teacher preparation, inservice teacher development, student achievement, and inquiry. This study is an example of a PDS that incorporated three of the four principles of the Holmes model: student achievement, preservice teacher preparation, and inquiry.

One influential factor, anxiety about performing mathematics skills mathematically and teaching mathematics, inhibits preservice teachers' preparation (Al-Salouli, 2004; Bruce, 2004; Utley & Showalter, 2007; Zacharos, Koliopoulos, Dokimaki, & Kassoumi, 2007). Swars (2005) noted that preservice teachers' anxiety related inversely to their efficacy toward teaching mathematics. Preservice teachers with lower anxiety demonstrated a higher level of confidence in their ability to teach mathematics. Likewise, preservice teachers with high anxiety reflected lower confidence. According to a study by Rule and Harrell (2006), 63% of teacher candidates in a pretest expressed negativity toward their mathematics experiences, and 60% expressed negative emotions toward mathematics learning. These findings suggest that preparation of preservice elementary teachers as teachers of mathematics raises concerns about successful candidate preparation. As a whole, these studies provide weighted evidence for the understanding that a confident PDS candidate who exhibits low lowered levels of anxiety toward mathematics will better deliver mathematics instruction.

Mathematics methods courses, a second influential factor in preservice teachers' success as teachers of mathematics, provide a variety of class experiences that engage and lead to epistemological shifts (Cady & Rearden, 2007; McCormick, Kapusuz, & Al-Salouli, 2004; Wilkins & Brand, 2004). Gill, Ashton, and Algina (2004) randomly assigned preservice teachers to experimental and control groups, where in the former, preservice teachers encountered challenging texts of refutation. The control group preservice teachers read traditional text. Findings showed a greater change in epistemological beliefs about teaching and learning in mathematics among preservice teachers in the experimental group. Vinson (2001) reported that the use of Bruner's framework of concept development, coupled with the use of manipulatives, resulted in significant (p<.05) reduction in anxiety about mathematics.

Fieldwork, as a component of methods courses, contributes to changes in beliefs and anxiety (Downey & Cobbs, 2007). Charalambos, Philippou, and Kyriakides (2007) found that when preservice teachers were able to experiment with teaching mathematics in the field and interact with mentors, their beliefs in their ability to teach mathematics were heightened. Walker (2007) established that when preservice teachers mentored groups of peer tutors of mathematics, that their understanding of both mathematics teaching and urban settings increased. Hedrick, McGee, and Mittag (2000) also found, in an analysis of emails of teacher preservice teachers regarding their tutoring experience in the field, that preservice teachers established their understanding of student learning, why students failed, and personal learning about teaching mathematics. Liljedahl, Rösken, and Rolka (2006) examined journal entries by preservice teachers, finding that their reflections suggested a shift in beliefs toward a positive perception of themselves as teachers of mathematics as a result of their field experiences.

Partnerships, a third influential factor in candidate success, provide a venue for collaborative support between the universities and schools, where mentor teachers in schools, in concert with university personnel, are key to the success of PDS preservice teachers, particularly when mentor teachers and university instructors work together to provide timely, consistent, immediate, and connected feedback that helps preservice teachers tie theories presented in the university to practice in the field. Moyer and Husman (2006) found that when preservice teachers completed coursework in field-based PDS schools, they tended to focus on skill development essential to success as teachers of mathematics, when compared to preservice teachers whose courses were delivered on campus. These teacher candidates often maintained a "college student perspective" rather than developing a view of themselves as teachers.

Mewborn (2000) examined the ecological factors that influenced pre-service teachers' perspective of mathematics teaching. In this study, Mewborn, as a university instructor, worked closely with a fourth-grade mathematics teacher and four preservice teachers, all of whom spent ten weeks in one classroom. The group of six observed, taught, and reflected on the experience and process of teaching mathematics to children. Mewborn points out that as a result of this experience, even preservice teachers who were reluctant to teach mathematics (based on prior learning experiences) found common ground with those who felt comfortable with it from the start. Through reflection, and along with the partnership between the university and the mentor teacher, four students from the cohort group were able to change their perspective of mathematics teaching from seeking activities to seeking understanding of how children learn mathematics. Although this is a small sample size, the results are meaningful.

The PDS model of teacher preparation finds basis in partnerships that are designed to support learning among all constituents and includes: children, teachers, preservice teachers, university personnel, district personnel, and university administrators (Scheetz, Waters, Smeaton, & Lare, 2005; Shulman & Armitage, 2005). PDS programs connect universities to schools in a collaborative manner that fosters shared responsibility for educating both university preservice teachers and school students (Marlow, Kyed, & Connors, 2005; Snow-Gerono, Yendol-Silva, & Nolan, 2002). University and school personnel engage in projects that generate from either source, creating a symbiotic relationship of mutual support and trust. For example, McBee and Moss (2002) described a PDS in which preservice teachers, teachers, and university personnel initiated projects independent of each other, yet created interdependence in their implementation. Preservice teachers created reading projects that were then supported by the university and schools. Likewise, teachers created mathematics mates partnerships that engaged preservice teachers and were supported by university personnel. Finally, university personnel created staff development and master-level courses to assist teachers in their desire to know more about cooperative learning that was used in undergraduate courses. This example demonstrates the intent of the PDS movement, interdependence, and collaboration.

THE SETTING

The project from which this current study was generated involved an interdependent collaborative between a school district and a university were inextricably tied together in a PDS program. In the spring of 2005, at the third-year mark of this reconstructed PDS, two seemingly cataclysmic events occurred. First, the district showed marked drops in mathematics scores on state-mandated tests, putting the district in jeopardy of failing to meet adequate yearly progress, an expectation of No Child Left Behind (NCLB) (Ascher, 2006). Second, due to a burgeoning enrollment in the PDS program, a requirement for all initial certification preservice teachers in the college of education, the PDS cadre increased from 25 preservice teachers assigned to the district in 2004–2005, to 52 assigned in 2005–2006.

Teacher preparation programs at the university, particularly those employing the PDS model, have a unique opportunity to prepare preservice teachers as mathematics tutors who are aware and can apply the principles of the No Child Left Behind (NCLB) supplemental education services (SES) initiatives. PDS programs operate through collaborative partnerships between universities and schools that share governance, agreements, and parity. They also promote the development of teachers while, at the same time, supporting student achievement (Kinsey, 2012). PDS programs that share leadership and responsibility for the success of all constituents adjust instructional programs at universities, accommodate research in schools, and work toward an academic common goal of achievement and learning for all.

To accommodate both the needs of the university for more placements and the schools' needs for more assistance in mathematics supplemental educational services (SES) (tutoring), a collaborative moment was seized. The PDS site coordinator, also the instructor of the mathematics methods course, agreed to change the methods course to prepare preservice teachers to meet NCLB SES expectations—diagnosis, intervention, and post-diagnosis. The principals agreed to find six more schools that would be willing to provide mentorship for the additional preservice teachers; thus, two additional agreements were forged. First, the PDS site coordinator agreed to limit the number of preservice teachers placed in the schools to no more than five. The principals also agreed to allow the coordinator to conduct an experimental study of the tutoring intervention, such that students who were identified for tutoring were all pretested, and then six identified students per preservice teacher were randomly selected for tutoring. In the first year of the study, there were 50 preservice teachers assigned to 12 schools. With agreements in place, the Mathematics Tutoring Project began, and this model continued for seven consecutive years. During this time period, the influences of preservice teachers' anxiety about teaching mathematics, course work, fieldwork, and partnerships were studied. In addition, student achievement, marked during the project each year, was used to measure the effectiveness of the methods presented in the university mathematics pedagogy course. These were studied within the context of a mixed methods study of the preservice teachers' development of themselves as teachers of mathematics and an experimental study of student achievement in mathematics.

Studying both the effect on PDS preservice teachers and effect of candidate interventions on student achievement aligns with the expectations of mixed methods principles (Onwuegbuzie, Frels, Collins, & Leech, 2013). The data in this study combine qualitative data collection in the form of PDS candidate reflective writings about the tutoring project with analyses of variance and t-tests of student pre- and posttest data garnered from the tutoring project requirements. The findings from the two data sources, when combined, provide a broader perspective of both the affect and effect of the project on candidate growth as teachers of mathematics and student achievement in schools as a result of teacher candidate investment and growth. These elements provide a comprehensive view of the phenomenon of tutoring children in mathematics. When both data sets are combined into one, a stronger perspective of the tutoring project emerges.

PURPOSE

The purposes of this study were (1) to examine the affect of the tutoring project on PDS preservice teachers' perception of themselves as tutors/teachers of mathematics to K–8 children, and (2) to determine the effect of tutoring by PDS preservice teachers on student achievement in mathematics.

Research Questions

What is the affect of tutoring in mathematics on preservice teachers' perception of themselves as tutors/teachers of mathematics?

What is the effect of tutoring on student achievement in mathematics?

Assumption

The process of tutoring in mathematics will have a positive effect on candidate perception of themselves as tutors/, as observed in their reflective writing on the tutoring experience.

Hypothesis

Students tutored in mathematics will score significantly higher on posttests at the $p<.05$ level than students who did not receive tutoring. Students will show significant gains at the $p<.05$ level when comparing pre- and posttest scores.

RELATED LITERATURE

Implementation reports of SES (tutoring) reveal a mixed review. Availability and access, two issues confronting parents, resulted in a lawsuit in New Jersey that dismissed parents' position that they were not informed of available SES, leaving needy children unserved (Walsh, 2008). Reports by the Center for Educational Policy disclosed that measuring progress marked by SES remains unknown due to lack of funding and personnel to study progress ("States Lack Funds and Staff to Monitor Supplemental Ed Services," 2007; "Supplemental Education Services Shortchanged by Funds and Staff," 2007). In contrast, providers of SES show marked increases in revenue since the inception of required SES services (Belfield & D'Entremont, 2005). The Department of Education targeted six states for intense monitoring of SES delivery and were chosen on the basis of "a risk analysis" that examined factors such as (1) the percentage of a state's schools in need of improvement, (2) corrective action, or restructuring, (3) the proportion of students eligible for the services compared with their participation rate, and (4) the findings of past departmental monitoring reports (Klein, 2007). In some situations, the Department of Education has reversed the implementation of SES and allowed districts to provide services for students prior to changing schools from a school that has not met AYP for two years (Robelen, 2007).

Evaluation of SES (tutoring) programs call for more rigorous research to study the effects of SES on achievement (Ascher, 2006; Ash, 2007; Taylor, Waters, Nielsen, & Martin, 2008). A number of studies provide some insight into the research currently conducted on the success of SES delivery. For example, Muñoz, Potter, and Ross (2008) found, in a study of tutoring services provided by private tutoring companies and local volunteers, that there were no differences noted on the Kentucky state mathematics examination among children tutored when compared to those who did not receive tutoring. The SES sessions lasted several weeks and consisted of two one-hour sessions weekly, but there was limited knowledge of services provided by either group. In two reports, Pascopella (2004) and Nilles (2005) indicate that gains were made in programs in Philadelphia, Pennsylvania and Muncie, Indiana, respectively, but they provide no research to suggest how these gains were determined. This supports the position for more rigorous research on the success of SES interventions.

SES (tutoring) finds basis in previous research on the positive effects of tutoring. A meta-analysis of 65 tutoring studies were conducted by Cohen, Kulik, and Kulik (1982). The analysis studied the effectiveness of tutoring in mathematics on achievement, attitude, and self-concept. The authors concluded that tutoring, under certain conditions, resulted in improved performance. Among the studies examined, experimental studies focused on achievement in and attitude toward mathematics resulting in significant gains in both. In these studies, tutoring experiences were structured, targeted, and successful when measuring differences in gains in achievement.

The Duolog method (Topping, Kearney, McGee, & Pugh, 2004) requires multiple steps when tutoring students through mathematics problems. These include having students listen, read, question, pause or think aloud, "make it real," check, praise, and summarize and generalize. In an experimental study of the Duolog method, Topping et al. (2004) noted significant differences between experimental and control groups. Parents of 9–10-year-old children in an experimental group applied the method when tutoring children on mathematics homework problems. Parents and children reported that the method provided opportunities to consider mathematics as a shared experience rather than a singular problem resolution moment.

In contrast, Zuelke and Nelson (2001) reported no differences across multiple years in an after-school tutoring program for at-risk students. Tutoring variables (hours, type of tutoring, type of tutor, cost of tutoring, and absence from tutoring) were observed and studied across approximately 300 students, from 1995–1999 with the same results: that is, no improvement observed. The authors concluded that the partnership produced no meaningful results due to several factors: decentralization, lack of commitment by the tutors, no one-to-one tutoring, and low pay.

SES (tutoring) delivery, by law, remains bound to providers sanctioned by teacher education agencies (TEAs) and local education agencies (LEAs) and remains outside the aegis of schools and teachers. However, as noted in studies cited previously, teachers, parents, and preservice teachers as tutors made differences in student success by employing the tenets of well-developed tutoring programs: organization, limited tutor/tutee relationships, targeted practice, and well-prepared and supported tutors. Among the qualifiers for success, preparation of tutors signals a need to consider the multiple aspects of assisting students toward achievement, positive attitudes toward mathematics, and high self-concept as mathematics learners.

The need for well-prepared teacher/tutors indicates action for teacher preparation programs. The distinction between preparing teachers to teach large classes differs considerably from preparation of the roles of teachers as tutors. The former entails knowledge, skills, and disposition toward large group success, while the latter concerns the individual understanding of the needs of one child at a time. Both roles are important for teachers. Targeted diagnosis, intervention, response to intervention, and post-diagnosis become the essence of instruction in a tutoring setting. The principles of a good NCLB/SES program (high quality, research-based, curricular-targeted, and monitored) can be introduced in teacher preparation programs and delivered in mathematics methods courses. Teacher preparation programs, generally oriented toward preparation for large group instruction, would require adjustments to systematically accommodate preparing preservice teachers as SES-ready tutors and/or would provide the candidate with more focused attention on the individual learner.

PDSs provide the structure within which systematic preparation of preservice teachers as mathematics tutors is viable. First, PDS programs operate through collaborative partnerships between universities and schools with the stated goal to strengthen teacher preparation and student achievement through shared governance (Levine, 2001). PDS partners also recognize needs, develop collaborative plans, enact developed plans, and measure progress and success. Third, university personnel, as partners, more readily adjust course objectives to accommodate needs of the collaborative. Finally, through inquiry/research, a component of the PDS standards, constituents develop and learn from modeling the most effective means by which to enhance overall achievement.

METHOD

Design

Setting

The PDS, set in a rural/urban school district in Texas and affiliated with a large university, has coalesced as a collaborative since 1994. An equal balance of Title I and regular schools (six each) set the tone for subsequent years during the study. The balance remained the same across years two and three, when the schools included in the PDS numbered thirteen and nine, respectively. The school district, originally rural, grew rapidly across the years of the study, increasing by one elementary school each year. The school district and university have enjoyed a long history of teacher preparation, partly due to the land grant/teacher college status of the university at its inception.

Subjects

Preservice teachers were university students in their first semester of work in a PDS, a two-semester program. The preservice teachers (total 96: 50 in 2006, 25 in 2007, 30 in 2008) ranged in age from 21–60, and 95% were women. The ethnicity of the preservice teachers was 80% Caucasian, 10% Latino, 8% African American, and 2% Asian. These ethnic groups aligned somewhat with the population of children in the schools, except that several of the schools were 74% Hispanic, and 73% were economically disadvantaged. Of the preservice teachers, 80% were enrolled in the university as early childhood–fourth grade certification seekers, and the other 20% were enrolled as grade 4–8 certification seekers. An initial course survey of the preservice teachers revealed that over 63% exhibited fear of mathematics and fear of teaching mathematics to children. However, two of the 4–8 preservice teachers expressed an interest in teaching mathematics in middle schools.

Structure

Collaboration

Stakeholders in the PDS worked together to create the tutoring project. School principals developed the structure of selection, timing, place, and coordination between preservice teachers and mentor teachers. Mentor teachers received training from the teacher leadership team on the use of the GoToLearn® diagnostic process, the value of tutoring for the students, and the interfacing between preservice teachers tutoring and mathematics instruction in the classroom. Mathematics methods teachers met with mentor team leaders to discuss changes in the mathematics methods course to prepare preservice teachers for tutoring. Preservice teachers worked with university instructors and mentor teachers to coordinate the instruction.

University Instruction

For six weeks prior to the tutoring experience, the mathematics methods course focused on preparing the preservice teachers for the tutoring experience. The concept of number and operation, which was the content focus of the tutoring project and was based on the district scope and sequence, was introduced, applying reform principles of the National Council of Teachers of Mathematics. Preservice teachers studied hands-on techniques, models of instruction, and assessment tools. The course used both in-class experiences with manipulatives, weekly electronic discussions about the readiness and progress of tutoring, and observations in the field to prepare preservice teachers for tutoring. During the process of preparation, preservice teachers examined results of mock diagnostics and recommended a hierarchy of intervention, considering the development of mathematical learning in numbers and operation: number, place value, addition, subtraction, multiplication, division, fractions, decimals, money, ratio, percentage, and proportion. The dialogue between the preservice teachers and instructor led preservice teachers to review and recognize the need to change and/or adjust instructional decisions.

Tutoring Project

Diagnostic Instrument

As mentioned, the diagnostic instrument used to pre- and posttest the students was developed by a company called GoToLearn. This Texas-based company used the state of Texas' curriculum (Texas Assessment of Knowledge and Skills [TAKS]) and released tests (Texas Essential Knowledge and Skills [TEKS]) to craft test items that aligned. The items were designed to resemble those administered on the TAKS tests. The test bank of approximately 200 items per strand of mathematics allowed flexibility and openness for PDS preservice teachers to create grade-level, content-specific diagnostics. The almost identical nature of the items assured the validity of the instrument for measuring the same constructs present in the TAKS and benchmark tests (which were also constructed using the released TEKS tests).

Data from students' TAKS tests, district benchmarks, and teacher-made tests indicated that students selected for tutoring were below the 50th percentile on all tests. The GoToLearn diagnostics, as a parallel form of the TAKS and benchmark tests, resulted in the same—students performing below the 50th percentile. The GoToLearn diagnostic met the expectation of the parallel forms method of attaining reliability. The instrument has multiple questions for the same construct that mirrored the TAKS and benchmark tests and resulted in the same outcomes for the same students.

Selection

All students (1125 total: 391 in 2006, 318 in 2007, and 416 in 2008) identified by school personnel for tutoring were administered the GoToLearn diagnostic in the first week of the project. This diagnostic consisted of 20 items within the construct of number and operations. The diagnostic created by each candidate for the students they tested chose items from the test banks that represented one grade lower than the current enrollment of the students (i.e., third graders were given second-grade items, eighth graders received seventh-grade items, etc.). The reasoning was that the diagnostic was done early enough in the fall that to test at grade level would be detrimental to the tutoring process. In the second, third, and fourth years of the project, following the completion of the diagnostic, six students per candidate are randomly selected from those pretested and assigned to a candidate for weekly tutoring. In the first, fifth, sixth, and seventh years of the project, students were purposefully selected by teachers, and six were assigned to each candidate. All students assigned to each candidate were administered the diagnostic one week prior to the start of tutoring interventions.

Weekly Intervention

Each teacher candidate/tutor worked collaboratively with mentor teachers and principals to arrange space, time, equipment, and availability of students for tutoring. During the interventions, preservice teachers engaged students for 30–45 minutes in groups of two to three students for either once or twice a week. The variance in amount of time and number of days tutored each week varied by school. Preservice teachers used techniques and tools developed at the university, lessons from the electronic resource bank in the course syllabus, and strategies noted from mentor teachers to conduct their tutoring. Preservice teachers used games, technology, hands-on materials, songs, art, and all forms of real-world data with samples of number and operation noted from the lives of the students.

Weekly Running Records

Preservice teachers used a project format to create an electronic running record for the tutoring project. The template for the project included the following components: (1) diagnostic, (2) discussion of students diagnosed, (3) Intervention #1 (based on diagnostic scores), (4) recap of Intervention #1, (5) continuing through six weeks of interventions, (6) post-diagnosis, (7) analysis of findings, and (8) a paper reflecting on themselves as tutors. The preservice teachers electronically submitted the tutoring project weekly and received feedback from the mathematics methods instructor each week regarding their choices for interventions, cohesion from week to week, and the importance of keeping the hierarchical needs of the students as priority. Preservice teachers responded with adjustments, discussions, and questions. The purpose of the running record served to keep the preservice teachers on target with their tutees' mathematical learning needs in mind first—rather than the students' success on the posttest. In essence, teaching to the test was discouraged.

Posttest

At the conclusion of the six weeks of tutoring, preservice teachers posttested all students who had been pretested. The posttest instrument was the same pretest used prior to the start of the tutoring phase of the project. Scores for pretest, posttest, and gains were posted on the GoToLearn site. For each student, success on each of the TEKS in number and operations was shown in the data provided to teacher preservice teachers at the end of tutoring and the posttest. Preservice teachers constructed a spreadsheet that included: (1) pretest scores, (2) posttest scores, (3) number of tutoring sessions attended, (4) TEKS addressed during tutoring, (5) changes in test scores as related to the number of sessions spent on the concept tested, and (6) number of weeks communicated with the mathematics methods instructor.

Post Project Reflective Perspective

Each candidate wrote a 5–10 page reflective paper on the process of tutoring. The paper required preservice teachers to extend beyond a description of the interventions, requiring introspection into themselves as tutors, teachers of mathematics, and critical analysts.

The paper included details of:

- challenges and methods for overcoming challenges
- personal growth of the candidate
- suggestions for personal improvement as a tutor
- professional recommendations for improving the tutoring assignment

Preservice teachers were also encouraged to make recommendations as to how to improve the tutoring process and the assignment in general.

DATA ANALYSES/RESULTS

Qualitative Analysis: Candidate Perceptions of Teaching Mathematics

Reflections from the first five years of the project, approximately 250 candidate papers, were combined as a corpus of data. This was read and analyzed for emergent categories that related to the research question. A constant comparison analysis was conducted to interrogate the data, resulting in emergent themes. *Grounded theory*, as developed by Corbin and Strauss (2007), was used to inductively develop theory from the corpus of the reflection papers. The data were read to develop themes, and categories emerged within the themes and interrelationships among the categories. Using grounded theory, themes were added throughout the reading of the corpus. Open coding was used to identify, name, categorize, and describe phenomena found in the corpus. Words, phrases, and sentences evolved into codes, which were then placed into themes and categories. Initially the themes were general categories. The categories were read for descriptive properties within themes.

The software program QSR nvivo8 ("N8") was selected because of its open format of sharing coding and versatility with a large document. N8 held the reflection papers by year in separate files as well as the entire corpus of text. Key words, phrases, and ideas ("coding") were open for additions of comments throughout the readings of all five years. The themes became "tree nodes" which were then broken into more specific categories, or "branches" within the main ideas.

Results

Based on the parameters of the reflective writing assignment, preservice teachers' reflection papers addressed the following topics:

- challenges and methods for overcoming challenges
- personal growth of the candidate
- suggestions for personal improvement as a tutor
- professional recommendations for improving the tutoring assignment

Four direct themes (tree nodes) emerged: (1) preservice teachers' actions, (2) preservice teachers' challenges, (3) preservice teachers' emotions, and (4) preservice teachers' future recommendations. While the preservice teachers experienced many specific and unique situations, the grounded approach for analysis showed that preservice teachers shared similar actions, challenges, emotions, and recommendations regarding their experiences. In addition, preservice teachers noted that the PDS support system in the university and schools contributed to their success as tutors of mathematics.

A. Preservice Teachers' Actions

The preservice teachers' actions evolved by what they did; that is, the action of tutoring made a difference in how they saw themselves as teachers of mathematics. Preservice teachers also noted awareness for the need of differentiated instruction. They noted that by evaluating their lessons each week, based on the success of the students, they were able to adjust and make learning meaningful and real for the students, which resulted in higher levels of achievement for the students and greater teaching capacity for themselves.

B. Preservice Teachers' Challenges

The theme of preservice teachers' challenges consisted of several categories. One of these included "overcoming challenges" and included those areas of writing lesson plans, deciphering a tutee's needs, differential instruction for a multileveled group, and dealing with time and location constraints. Yet another category was the "candidates' concern of their effectiveness" instructing their tutees. Within this category, discipline within small-group instruction provided challenges. Some preservice teachers attempted to make friends with the tutees while others struggled with their role as teacher. An additional aspect of challenges that evolved was the preservice teachers' emotional challenges of frustration, fear, and their own insecurities.

Seventy quotes were captured dealing with frustration. Preservice teachers were predominantly frustrated with students resisting the intervention. Preservice teachers found that their tutees were reluctant to receive tutoring, did not want to be pulled out, and were embarrassed to be singled out for help in mathematics. In addition, the problems of communication that occurred within a school caused the preservice teachers' frustration.

C. Preservice Teachers' Emotions

1. Negative emotions. One-hundred fifty-four quotes dealt with negative emotions such as fear, frustration, and insecurity. These categories emerged as emotions in preservice teachers' reflection papers. Fear materialized predominately due to previous experiences with mathematics. One noted, "This project most definitely calmed my number one fear in teaching and made me much more comfortable with teaching math."

2. Positive emotions. Preservice teachers reflected for a collective 352 quotes of positive emotions included: (a) a gain in confidence, (b) seeing the assignments as rewarding, (c) feeling successful in tutoring, (d) tutoring as fun, and (e) feeling like a team.

"I feel much more confident now in my management abilities after this project."

"I feel more confident in my ability to reach out to them and teach them in new and different ways that they will understand."

"As I continued to teach the concepts over the five weeks, I became more confident in my abilities to successfully teach math concepts. I was not only able to develop my teaching skills, but also my evaluation skills."

D. PDS support.

Although preservice teachers were not asked directly to comment on the support they received from the teachers and university mathematics methods instructor, this theme was noted in the responses. The following quotes elucidate the preservice teachers' perception of the contribution of the PDS toward their success in the project.

> The PDS program experience as a whole has made me very aware of my attitude. I never saw how set in my ways I was until this last semester when my own plan for student teaching didn't happen.

> The teachers helped out a lot as far as me finding math material to use during the sessions. The school had their own tutoring packet called T.I.P.S. This was a program that the teachers used to identify the level that they felt each student was on due to the pretesting that they had given in the classrooms. I was glad to use the information and it actually worked well with what I needed to do for tutoring.

> From PDS I, I have received a lot of additional knowledge and experience. We usually learn and hear from someone else's teaching experiences, but this time we gained so much hands-on knowledge and practiced from the field. Class observation, tutoring sessions, and substituting gave me an entirely different impression of teaching. Until I had real experience, all the myths and stories felt very distant and vague.

> I loved how my math methods course was there for me to use as a resource. The comments from my teacher every week helped extend my realizations and helped me think in a different way. This opportunity was truly a blessing in disguise and great learning experience.

> Throughout the semester, I could tell that my abilities as an instructor had improved greatly. Thanks in large part to the experience I garnered from observing, tutoring the students, and participating in the PDS classes, I felt that I had grown.

In summary, the analysis of preservice teachers' responses to the challenges of tutoring revealed a group that aligns with those described by researchers (AlSalouli, 2004; Bruce, 2004; Bursal & Paznokas, 2006; Swars, 2005; Utley & Showalter, 2007; Zacharos et al., 2007) who all noted that fear of teaching mathematics is prevalent among preservice teachers eager to teach in the elementary grades. The data analysis also reveals a group that faced and overcame those fears. The mathematics tutoring differed from standard mathematics tutoring projects, due in large measure to the PDS setting in which the project took place. Preservice teachers in this setting were nurtured, supported, mentored, and guided by school and university personnel, who created agreements that fostered learning for both preservice teachers and students alike. Continuous communication between the university instructor, mentor teachers, and preservice teachers fostered preservice growth and development as teachers of mathematics. Because of the uniqueness of the PDS setting, preservice teachers were able to actively participate in a project that could only happen when university and school partners work together collaboratively.

Quantitative Analysis: Student Achievement

Data generated across the years of the project varied. During the first, fifth, and sixth years of the study, the data generated consisted of pre- and posttests of students who were purposefully assigned to groups by teachers. The analysis used for these years was a t-test, measuring differences in pre- and posttest scores. The second, third, and fourth years' data were generated in an experimental study, whereby students were identified for tutoring and pretested. Then six students per teacher candidate were assigned to receive tutoring. The data analyzed were: (1) sample size, (2) effect size, and (3) analysis of variance between groups. The data are presented in Tables 12.1–12.4.

Results

Sample Size Calculations

Table 12.1 shows results of sample size calculations for the three experimental years. As noted in the table, in years 2007 and 2008, recommended sample sizes were met and exceeded. However, in 2006, the sample size fell six students short of the recommendation, accounting for 98% of the recommended number of students to represent the population of students requiring tutoring. In spite of this shortfall, it is noted that the samples used in the three experimental years of the study met the expectations of sample size, representing the population of tutor eligible students.

Effect Size, Cohen's d Calculations

Table 12.2 gives the effect sizes for the three experimental years, 2006, 2007, 2008, indicating a small effect size, with 15–28% non-overlapping between the

TABLE 12.1. Sample Size Calculations for the Experimental Years of the Study

Year	Population	Sample size recommended	Sample size used
2006	391	248	242
2007	318	124	166*
2008	416	171	213*

* Met or exceeded sample size recommendation.

TABLE 12.2. Effect size r and Cohen's d for ANOVAs and t-tests

Year	Cohen's d	Effect size r	Percentile ^	Non-overlap +
1 *	.68	.47	78th	45%
2 **	.21	.11	58th	14.7%
3 **	.46	.22	66th	27.4%
4 **	.27	.14	58th	14.7%
5 *	.64	.40	73rd	38%
6 *	.52	.25	70th	33%

Notes: ^ Percentile represents the post-test score positioning within the pretest. + Non-overlap represents the percentage of non-overlap between the two sets of scores. The larger the percentile and non-overlap percentage, the greater the independence of the posttest score, hence the greater the effect of the treatment on producing differences in scores. ** experimental design years, * quasi-experimental design years.

groups' scores. The implication is that the effect of the treatment is only slightly effective in bringing about differences between the pre- and posttests. The experimental groups' posttest scores overlapped with the control group approximately 72–85%. Effect sizes for the three quasi-experimental years, 2005, 2009, 2010, show medium to large effect size, with 45 and 71% non-overlapping between the groups. The posttest scores overlapped between 55 and 29% with the pretest

TABLE 12.3. Paired T tests comparing pre/posttests for quasi-experimental years 1, 5, 6

Year	t	df	η	p
2005	6.21	285	1.1	.0001*
2009	6.13	376	2.06	.0001*
2010	4.25	328	2.08	.0001*

* Significant at the p<.05 level.

TABLE 12.4. ANOVA of pre/posttests for experimental years 2–4

Scores	df	F	η	p
Between groups	1	4.271	1.378	.039*
Within groups	389		.954	
Between groups	1	16.419	.963	.0001*
Within groups	316		1.152	
Between groups	1	7.234	1.246	.007*
Within groups	414		1.159	

* Significant at the p<.05 level.

scores, indicating that the treatment had a stronger effect in bringing about differences in the quasi-experimental studies when compared to the experimental studies.

Paired t-tests Results

Table 12.3 shows results of the paired t-test calculations for years 2005, 2009, and 2010. In all three years of the quasi-experimental studies, significant differences at the p<.05 level were observed. These differences, when related to the effect size calculations, imply that differences most likely resulted from the interventions provided during the tutoring sessions. The effect size calculations show a medium to large effect, with little overlap between the pre- and posttest means.

Anova Results

Table 12.4 results for years 2006, 2007, and 2008 show significant differences at p<.05 level each year of the experimental study. A closer examination of the effect sizes related to these differences indicates that the overlap between the experimental and control groups, approximately 75%, suggests that differences may have occurred only slightly as a result of tutoring. The effect size calculations show a small effect with a large overlap between the pre- and posttest means.

CONCLUSIONS

This mixed methods case study examined the affect and effect of a mathematics tutoring project in a PDS on preservice teachers' perception of themselves as teachers of mathematics, as well as student achievement at the hands of PDS preservice teachers. The questions posed by the study regarding the affect and effect assumed and hypothesized that preservice teachers' perceptions would alter positively, as would the students' increase in achievement in mathematics. The data analyses indicate that both the assumption and hypothesis were supported to various degrees. The factors aligned with success (fear, field work, methods course support, and partnerships such as the PDS) were apparently influential in the outcomes.

Preservice teachers, when working in a supportive, collaborative environment as in the case of the PDS setting in the study, can transform from fearful teachers of mathematics to confident, ready teachers. What distinguishes this tutoring experience from other ad hoc tutoring projects is the underlying support that this PDS partnership provided its preservice teachers. The relationship between the university mathematics instructor, principals, mentor teachers, and preservice teachers provided a structure in which success could occur more readily. The case study approach used as the project progressed across multiple years demonstrated that when the PDS model is applied to a mathematics tutoring project, preservice teachers grow in their capacity to teach mathematics, and, in addition, students show advances in mathematics achievement.

Building and sustaining confidence in preservice teachers, an essential in teaching excellence, emerged from this project, due in part to continuous feedback and support from mentor teachers and the university instructor. This study of the affect of the project on preservice teachers as they noted the effect they were having on students' achievement in mathematics serves as a model for PDS programs seeking to find ways to bolster preservice teachers while, in turn, supporting students' achievement in mathematics.

The strongest implication of the findings from this study is that partnerships make a difference but only when monitored and studied by the partners. In 2002, the partnership under examination in this study underwent a dramatic reconstruction, whereby many partners convened to examine, recommend, and change the PDS partnership. In 2005, this same PDS applied the rubrics of the NCATE PDS Standards (Levine, 2001) to reassess the standing of the partnership. In this theoretical document, it is noted that PDS programs increase the potential for success by examining their progress through a set of five standards: (1) learning community; (2) accountability and quality assurance; (3) collaboration; (4) diversity and equity; and (5) structures, resources, and roles. Each standard, when applied to a PDS setting, serves to guide and enhance the decisions of the stakeholders. The PDS partnership team determined in 2005 that they had progressed from a beginning level PDS and were working toward the developing level.

RECOMMENDATIONS

It is recommended that partnerships preparing to replicate this study should consider the extent to which the partnership is cohesive. The NCATE PDS standards (Levine, 2001) provide a roadmap to partnership development and growth toward higher levels of collaboration. The original Holmes (Holmes Partnership, 1995) goals (high-quality professional preparation, simultaneous renewal, equity, diversity and cultural competence, scholarly inquiry and programs of research, school- and university-based faculty development, and policy initiation) serve as excellent guideposts for decision making for partnerships.

Most important to the success of the study was the calculation of when the partnership reached a readiness point to initiate a quasi- or experimental design of research. To achieve this required two components working simultaneously— patience and trust. Patience to wait three to five years for a relationship between institutions to gel tests the fortitude of most early researchers. However, this study did not occur until the third year of the reconstructed PDS, which was in the sixth year of the university representative's involvement with the partnership schools. Assistant professors and doctoral students who are eager to conduct meaningful, extensive research in and on PDS partnerships will fall short if the time is not taken to build the relationships necessary to bridge the gap between institutions.

Finally, building trust is crucial to replication of this study. Trust is built when three Cs occur: (1) care for the other institution's needs and concerns; (2) consistency of all constituencies; and, finally, (3) communication, which is key. In the world of electronic communication, the ease of an email seems like a short-cut to getting a job completed and keeping the group together. However, the network building that ensued prior to initiating the project involved three years of walking the halls of elementary and middle schools, shaking hands, listening, talking, and learning the culture of each school. The trust-building element stood out as essential to making the tutoring project occur. The fact that these schools trusted that the teacher preservice teachers were being prepared well enough to release their students to preservice teachers in a high-stakes testing environment is a testament to trust.

REFERENCES

AlSalouli, M. (2004, September). *Pre-service teachers' beliefs and conceptions about mathematics teaching and learning.* Paper presented at the Psychology of Mathematics and Education of North America, Toronto, Canada.

Ascher, C. (2006). NCLB's Supplemental Educational Services: Is this what our students need? *Phi Delta Kappan, 88*(2), 136–141.

Ash, K. (2007). NCLB-related tutoring inadequately studied. *Education Week, 26*(36), 8–8.

Belfield, C. R., & D'Entremont, C. (2005). Privatization after school. *American School Board Journal, 192*(5), 28–31.

Bruce, C. (2004, September). *Building confidence in teaching mathematics: Experiences of pre-service teachers that hinder and enable confidence.* Paper presented at the Psychology of Mathematics & Education of North America, Toronto, Canada.

Bursal, M., & Paznokas, L. (2006). Mathematics anxiety and elementary teachers' confidence to teach mathematics and science. *School Science & Mathematics, 106*(4), 173–180.

Cady, J. A., & Rearden, K. (2007). Pre-service teachers' beliefs about knowledge, mathematics, and science. *School Science and Mathematics, 107*(6), 237–248.

Charalambos, C., Philippou, G., & Kyriakides, L. (2007). Tracing the development of pre-service teachers' efficacy beliefs in teaching mathematics during fieldwork. *Educational Studies in Mathematics, 67*, 125–142.

Cohen, P., Kulik, J., & Kulik, C.-L. (1982). Educational outcomes of tutoring: A meta-analysis. *American Educational Research Journal, 19*(2), 237–248.

Corbin, J., & Strauss, A. (2007). *Basics of qualitative research: Techniques and procedures for developing grounded theory* (3rd ed.). Thousand Oaks, CA: Sage.

Downey, J. A., & Cobbs, G. A. (2007). "I actually learned a lot from this": A field assignment to prepare future math teachers for culturally diverse classrooms. *School Science & Mathematics, 107*(1), 391–403.

Gill, M. G., Ashton, P. T., & Algina, J. (2004). Changing teachers' epistemological beliefs about teaching and learning in mathematics: An intervention study. *Contemporary Educational Psychology, 29*(2), 164–186.

Hedrick, W., McGee, P., & Mittag, K. (2000). Pre-service teacher learning through one-on-one tutoring: Reporting perceptions through e-mail. *Teaching and Teacher Education, 16*(1), 47–63.

Holmes Partnership. (1995). *Tomorrow's schools of education: A report of the Holmes group.* East Lansing, MI: Author.

Kinsey, J. (2012). *National association for professional development schools.* Retrieved from http://www.napds.org" www.napds.org.

Klein, A. (2007). States face federal review on NCLB choice, tutoring. *Education Week, 26*(25), 24–24.

Levine, M. (2001). Standards for professional development schools. *NCATE PDS Standards.* Retrieved from *http://www.ncate.org/public/standards.asp*

Liljedahl, P., Rösken, B., & Rolka, K. (2006, November). *Documenting changes in elementary school teachers' beliefs: Attending to different aspects.* Paper presented at the Psychology of Mathematics & Education of North America Annual Meeting, Toronto, Canada.

Marlow, M. P., Kyed, S., & Connors, S. (2005). Collegiality, collaboration and kuleana: Complexity in a professional development school. *Education, 125*(4), 557–560.

McBee, R. H., & Moss, J. (2002). PDS partnerships come of age. *Educational Leadership, 59*(6), 61–65.

McCormick, K., Kapusuz, A., & Al-Salouli, M. (2004, September). *The beliefs and conceptions of elementary teachers.* Paper presented at the Psychology of Mathematics & Education of North America Annual Meeting. Toronto, Canada. .

Mewborn, D. (2000). Learning to teach elementary mathematics: Ecological elements of a field experience. *Journal of Mathematics Teacher Education, 3*(1), 27–46.

Moyer, P., & Husman, J. (2006). Integrating coursework and field placements: The impact of pre-service elementary mathematics teachers' connections to teaching. *Teacher Education Quarterly, 33(1)*, 37–56.

Muñoz, M., Potter, A., & Ross, S. (2008). Supplemental education services as a consequence of NCLB legislation: Evaluating its impact on student achievement in a large urban district. *Journal of Education for Students Placed at Risk, 13*, 1–25.

Nilles, G. (2005). Helping schools help kids. *School Library Journal, 51*(9), 33.

Onwuegbuzie, A., Frels, R., Collins, K., & Leech, N. (2013). Conclusion: A four-phase model for teaching and learning mixed-methods. *International Journal of Multiple Research Approaches, 7*(1), 133–156.

Pascopella, A. (2004). Signs of improvement with SES. *District Administration, 40*(6), 21–21.

Robelen, E. W. (2007). Department to expand pilot that reverses vhoice, tutoring. *Education Week, 26*(39), 19.

Rule, A. C., & Harrell, M. H. (2006). Symbolic drawings reveal changes in teacher mathematics attitudes after a mathematics methods course. *School Science & Mathematics, 106*(6), 241–258.

Scheetz, J., Waters, F. H., Smeaton, P., & Lare, D. (2005). Mentoring in a PDS program: What's in it for me? *Kappa Delta Pi Record, 42*(1), 33–37.

Shulman, V., & Armitage, D. (2005). Project discovery: An urban middle school reform effort. *Education and Urban Society, 37*(4), 371–397.

Snow-Gerono, J. L., Yendol-Silva, D., & Nolan, J. F. (2002). Reconceptualizing curriculum for the PDS: University faculty negotiate tensions in collaborative design of methods courses. *Action in Teacher Education, 24*(3), 63–72.

States Lack Funds and Staff to Monitor Supplemental Ed Services. (2007). *Electronic Education Report, 14*(6), 6–7.

Supplemental education services shortchanged by funds and staff. (2007). *American School Board Journal, 194*(5), 12–12.

Swars, S. (2005). Examining perceptions of mathematics teaching effectiveness among elementary pre-service teachers with differing levels of mathematics teacher efficacy. *Journal of Instructional Psychology, 32*(2), 139–147.

Taylor, P., Waters, R., Nielsen, C., & Martin, D. (2008). YOU SAY. *American School Board Journal, 195*(4), 18–20.

Topping, K., Kearney, M., McGee, E., & Pugh, J. (2004). Tutoring in mathematics: A generic method. [technical]. *Mentoring and Tutoring, 12*(3), 15.

Utley, J., & Showalter, B. (2007). Elementary teachers' visual images of themselves as mathematics teachers. *Focus on Learning Problems in Mathematics 29*(3), 1–14.

Vinson, B. (2001). A comparison of pre-service teachers' mathematics anxiety before and after a methods class emphasizing manipulatives. *Early Childhood Education Journal, 29*(2), 89–94.

Walker, E. (2007). Teachers' perceptions of mathematics education in urban schools. *Urban Review 39*(5), 519–540.

Walsh, M. (2008). N.J. Parents Lose Suit Over NCLB. *Education Week, 28*(14), 5.

Wilkins, J. L., & Brand, B. R. (2004). Change in teachers' beliefs: An evaluation of a mathematics methods course. *School Science & Mathematics, 104*(5), 226–232.

Zacharos, K., Koliopoulos, D., Dokimaki, M., & Kassoumi, H. (2007). Views of prospective early childhood education teachers, towards mathematics and its instruction. *European Journal of Teacher Education 30*(3), 305–318.

Zuelke, D., & Nelson, J. G. (2001). The effect of a community agency's after-school tutoring program on reading and math gpa gains for at-risk tutored students. *Education, 121*(4), 799–809.

CHAPTER 13

EARLY FIELD EXPERIENCES IN MATHEMATICS

What a Professional Development School Model Allows Future Teachers to Do

Paula Guerra, Stacy DeLaCruz, and Maggie Phillips

ABSTRACT

Field experiences within professional development schools (PDSs) and universities are seen as vital in teacher education programs (Berry, 2001; Oh, Ankers, Llamas & Tomoy, 2005). This study describes research conducted with teacher candidates who taught a mathematics lesson to third graders in front of the collaborating teacher and peers. The peers provided feedback on the lessons. Data revealed that preparing to teach and teaching children as part of field experiences push candidates to critically consider three areas: (1) student thinking, (2) mathematics content, and (3) their own practice. The results of our study were highly positive for all parties involved.

Field experiences should be seen as tools that professors use to show teacher candidates how the theories they study at the university work in the elementary classroom (Mewborn, 2000; Philipp et al., 2007; Wilson, Floden, & Ferrini-Mun-

Creating Visions for University-School Partnerships, pages 217–230.
Copyright © 2014 by Information Age Publishing
All rights of reproduction in any form reserved.

dy, 2001; Zeichner, 2010). Field experiences that challenge the views of teaching and learning that teacher candidates have are the ideal (McDiarmid, 1990). If the content area in which they intend to teach is mathematics, the gains of early field experiences within a program are crucial.

Candidates not only have to confront their prior ideas and experiences about mathematics (positive and negative), but they also have to confront their perceptions of becoming a good teacher of mathematics and the feelings they had and will have towards this content area in the future. Uusimaki and Nason (2004) pointed out that those experiences and beliefs are largely negative and that can be linked to anxiety preservice teachers feel when it comes to the time of learning and teaching mathematics. These results are similar to those of Cornell (1999), who claimed that those experiences can impair the learning of mathematics or contribute to build negative attitudes towards the content area. These past experiences with mathematics and their influences, according to Swars (2005), were associated with mathematics teacher efficacy—hence the reason why they need to be revisited in positive and negative cases the same, to make sure preservice teachers reach their full potential.

Teacher candidates should have plenty of supervised opportunities to teach mathematics to children before they start their own practice, even before student teaching. By interacting with children, candidates can compare and prove the ideas they are discussing during their methods courses for mathematics. Early field experience can work as a tool for the method instructor, who can use them to prove the veracity of the research and methods studied in the course. Field experiences play a major role in the completion of a methods course that targets the comprehension of children's thinking in mathematics.

In order to serve as an effective tool, the design of those field experiences has to include connections with the methods course but also provide opportunities for the candidates to discuss what they are seeing and make sense of it. The field experiences must provide opportunities for candidates to share those experiences (Mewborn, 2000) and build a common ground so they can discuss children's thinking using consistent "language" through the same or very similar observations.

Lastly, it is not only important that they have common experiences to talk about, but candidates are directed to talk about them as being critical in what they observe in their own work. The field experience does not end with the elementary classroom. It continues when the candidates talk about it and think about changing aspects of it based on those observations and class discussions.

In this chapter the authors describe such an integrated field experience. Thanks to the collaboration between the university (where the candidates were completing their teaching certification) and a PDS, the instructors for the mathematics methods course were able to create the conditions for a beneficial field experience. The instructors designed an assignment where candidates taught mathematics to third grade children, then were observed by their peers. Peers had to provide feedback based on those observations. The last piece of the assignment was a reflection where the students shared their thoughts and ideas regarding this experience once they taught their lesson. As time went by, their thoughts not only reflected their experience teaching, but also their experience observing peers.

The authors analyzed the notes they took during teaching demonstrations and feedback sessions where they were observers and leaders, respectively, as well as the reflections the students wrote. They concluded that this experience was vastly beneficial for teacher candidates, and that more opportunities like this should be offered to teacher candidates. They also found that the particular collaboration between a university and an elementary school with a professional development model was the perfect context for this type of project to flourish.

In the following sections, the authors review pertinent literature, describe the methods (including context and design of the project and assignment), and share and discuss the findings.

LITERATURE REVIEW

In this section the authors review the pertinent literature on field experiences in teaching preparation programs. The literature agrees on the importance of an integrated design to these field experiences where all the actors work together to provide students with an experience that coordinates theory and practice. There are also warnings about some weaknesses, such as not moving the teacher candidates from procedural concerns (like classroom management) to reconsider their more complex views of teaching and learning.

Field experiences are crucial for teacher candidates (Berry, 2001; Oh et al., 2005). They expect to test their theories as well as everything they learned during their education courses. Adams and Krockover (1997) state that field experiences are one of the most important concerns candidates have. Yet McDiarmid (1990) and Mewborn (2000) express that these are rarely challenging experiences and that there is a negative body of literature. Zeichner (2010) goes as far as claiming that the disconnect between field experiences and courses is like a plague. Wilson et al. (2001) also express concerns about this disconnect. Field experiences work to reinforce the "folkways of teaching" (McDiarmid, 1990). At times, they reinforce traditional ways of teaching as well as preconceptions of what it means to teach. This is not what methods courses hoped the candidates would implement in their classrooms. In sum, field experiences do not serve the candidates to confront their thinking and feelings about traditional practice.

Another dilemma with field experiences is the inconsistency within the placements. The experiences can be different from one institution to another and, often, even within the same institution (Wilson et al., 2001). Wilson and colleagues point out more flaws such as the lack of coordination with coursework. Candidates could benefit more from both coursework and field experience if both point them in the same direction. If the ideas behind teaching mathematics are different from one to the other, the candidates are faced with the problem of making them fit together, even though sometimes that is not possible.

Candidates have issues applying what they learn in the university classroom to their field experiences (Wilson et al., 2001). Mewborn (2000) also noted the importance of the coordination with coursework. She also highlighted the importance of methods courses being interwoven with the field experiences and notes that the methods instructor should work with the collaborative teachers and establish a common ground where method instructor and collaborative teachers meet. This coordination is important to make the best out of the field experience to improve candidates' content and pedagogical content knowledge.

Learning mathematics as teacher candidates have the opportunity to observe and work with children improved the candidates' mathematical content knowledge (Philipp et al., 2007). Studying how children think when they do mathematics appears to help candidates think about the mathematics itself. On the same, note Zeichner (2010) observes the need of "hybrid spaces" where "academic and practitioner knowledge and the knowledge that exists in communities come together" (p. 480). In order to help preservice teachers grow, what they do in their university classrooms and what they do in the field should be parallel.

These "hybrid spaces" may be the reason why the McDiarmid (1990) project had certain levels of success. McDiarmid was able to have her candidates observe Dr. Deborath Ball (a referent in the mathematics education field, currently dean of the school of education at University of Michigan) teaching mathematics to a group of children, and her methods course was aligned with the teaching philosophy of Ball. The success McDiarmid reached enabled students to actually reconsider their views of learning and what it meant "to teach," in this case, mathematics. The candidates not only realized that teaching is more than just "telling," but they also appreciated the level of sophistication children showed while doing mathematics. Ironically, these were candidates who (in some cases) had first stated they avoided mathematics as students and found it useless. Then the changes go further than content and pedagogical content knowledge. They extend to perceptions and feelings about mathematics in general.

These "hybrid spaces" have to provide candidates with efficient field experiences. For example, being a part of a small cohort group seems to have been a positive aspect in the Mewborn (2000) study. A supportive environment where preservice teachers can establish not only trust but also a common ground with other preservice teachers sharing very similar experiences was a highlight for this author. Developing a sense of community where one is able to dissent and experience conflict helped the teacher candidates not to feel so isolated and to have more in-depth conversations about the field experience. The author expressed: "Teaching is often described as an isolating profession, but the use of cohorts can allow pre-service teachers to experience teaching as a collaborative profession where peers and more experienced others can highlight the depths and complexities of mathematics teaching" (Mewborn, 2000, p. 43). Candidates who can participate in these kinds of experiences early on learn to develop a sense of community where teachers and candidates help each other and share a common ground. Mewborn (2000) is not the only author who found the small cohort idea productive. Wilson (1996) agrees and asserts, "Field experiences that allowed pre-service teachers to participate in small teams (of two or three) were found to be more beneficial to the professional development of pre-service teachers" (p. 56).

Another positive characteristic found in the literature was examining theoretical constructs. According to Moore (2003), field experiences provide the opportunity for candidates to examine theoretical constructs behind pedagogical decisions, instead of just focusing on procedural concerns. This author found that candidates (and also mentor teachers) are often concerned with what they will teach as well as how they will manage the classroom instead of thinking about *how* they will teach meaningfully. This is in alignment with Mewborn (2000), who said good field experiences must be inquiry-based. Teaching mathematics conceptually instead of procedurally aligns with what the National Council of Teachers of Mathematics (NCTM) calls "doing mathematics" (Stein, Smith, Henningsen, & Silver, 2009). This way, candidates would be focusing right from the beginning on higher-level cognitive demand tasks (Stein et al., 2009), while at the same time getting feedback from their instructor, collaborating teacher, and students.

In the following sections the authors describe their study in which teacher candidates experience a particular field experience in the context of a professional development school (PDS), focusing on the teaching of mathematics. This field experience was designed in conjunction with a third grade teacher in the PDS who was also part of the candidates' instructors group. First, the authors will describe the design and context of the field experience; then they talk about the findings, and finally discuss the implications for future practice.

METHODS

Overview

The study took place as part of the coursework teacher candidates experienced in their mathematics methods course. This cohort was part of a bigger research project, and their methods courses block (as well as most of their coursework) took place at Glendale Elementary in the southeastern part of the United States. As an assignment for the course, the teacher candidates were asked to teach a mathematics lesson to third graders, in collaboration with a partner. The rest of the teacher candidates would observe the lesson and meet to discuss it and provide feedback to the "teachers." The design of the assignment as well as details for these lessons will be given in the design section. The candidates taught this class to a group of third-grade children who were students of one of the instructors of the course. The role of this co-instructor/teacher is explained in the setting section.

Background to the Study

The U.S. Department of Education awarded close to a $9 million dollar, five year grant, in 2009 to a state university in Georgia. The funds were used to support a Teacher Quality Partnership (TQP) initiative, which was designed to increase the achievement for all K–12 students within an urban school system near the university. The college of education collaborated with seven schools in this nearby district. The partnership consisted of five elementary schools, one middle school, and one high school. An intention of the grant was to participate in a research agenda that allowed for contributions to link teacher preparation and effectiveness to K–12 student learning.

This urban education (UE) option was offered onsite at the seven schools to undergraduate teacher candidates. For instance, if an undergraduate teacher candidate was involved in the UE option, he or she would have the first five classes during the fall semester, onsite at one elementary school. The next semester he or she would have the next group of classes at another elementary school. Each class was co-taught by a university professor and an elementary school teacher.

Participants in this study conducted mathematics lessons at one of the elementary schools within the TQP. The elementary school housed students in PreK–3 and had a total enrollment of about 743 students. Eighty-two percent of the students were eligible for free or reduced lunch. The student population consisted of: 47% African American, 36% Hispanic, 10% White, 4% two or more races, 2% Asian, and 1% American Indian. The school had an average reading score of 85% while mathematics scores were 77.7% on average.

Within the third-grade classroom in this study, there were 20 students. Thirteen students were girls and seven were boys. Six of the students were English language learners.

Participants

The participants in this project were 20 elementary teacher candidates, in their senior year, who were just one semester away from student teaching. The group consisted of three males and 17 females, ages ranging from 21 to 48. Because of their academic success, they were accepted into the urban education program inside the teacher education program at the state university.

Design

The assignment that the candidates were asked to complete had two phases: (1) planning and teaching a class, and (2) observing lessons to discuss and provide feedback to peers. For Phase 1, the candidates had to plan and teach a class in a group of two. Candidates were free to choose whom they wanted to work with. They were provided with a sign-up sheet of appropriate topics for their lessons through a Google document that also served to schedule the lessons. The groups who signed up first had more options to choose from. The instructors of the mathematics methods course (the university professor and the Glendale teacher) chose the topics for the lessons.

Except in one case, the groups of candidates taught ten children. The candidates not only experienced co-teaching as part of their instruction (for example, the university instructor and the school teacher, a model that was repeated for each of their methods courses that semester), but they also had a seminar in co-teaching. Two groups of candidates taught at the same time: one group in the third grade room, and the other in the room that the elementary school loaned to the university to teach the candidates. The rest of the candidates were separated into two groups, and functioned as observers to each of the lessons. The university professor and the elementary school teacher were also observers in different rooms.

The groups had 45 minutes to teach their lessons, which accounted for the allotted mathematics time during the day for the third-grade group. Candidates were in charge of providing everyone in the audience with a copy of their lesson plan, and they brought any material they needed for their class.

One of the candidates was already placed in the third-grade classroom as part of the field experiences in the program, so she was more familiar with the children. The children were used to seeing the candidates at the school and were somewhat familiar with them.

For Phase 2, the candidates had to observe lessons, take notes, and prepare to meet with the rest of the class and assess its pros and cons as well as give possible feedback. Those who taught the lessons were not present at these meetings to ensure candid feedback (Lim & Guerra, 2012).

Given that some of the observers saw one lesson and the rest saw the other lesson taught that day, the candidates started by describing the lessons so that everyone would have an idea of what the lesson was about. Next they commented on things that they liked about the lessons, and things they thought the teachers should reconsider. They were prompted to also provide alternatives for those situations they thought needed to be addressed.

Two of the candidates in this meeting took notes to be given to the candidates who taught the lesson. These notes also included the comments of the instructors and served to help candidates write a final reflection for the whole experience in this assignment.

Data Analysis

This experiment was a practitioner-research qualitative case study (Merriam, 1998; Yin, 2009). The collection of notes taken by the instructors as well as the reflections written by the teacher candidates were carefully reviewed by the authors. All the data collected were examined for emerging themes, and pieces of information were chosen as examples of those themes (Erickson, 1986). The authors reached consensus about what the main findings were and discussed them accordingly in alignment with the literature.

Limitations

Even though the authors believe they have provided candidates with a positive opportunity to test their skills in teaching mathematics as well as a taste of the real world of teaching, there are some issues that they wished could have been addressed in a second experience. For example, ideally, students would have been able to teach a whole group of children instead of just half of the third graders. The authors also believe that it would have been beneficial for the candidates to teach this lesson individually instead of in pairs. Both of these issues arose as a result of timing. The class was only ten weeks long, and some sacrifices had to be made in order to have all the candidates teaching.

Making those changes mentioned above would have also affected how the feedback sessions would work, as candidates would be discussing only one lesson and providing feedback to only one other person. The instructors would also be able to see all of the lessons taught, instead of only half.

FINDINGS AND DISCUSSION

The group of authors of this chapter, which include the instructors for the mathematics methods course, found this experience to be beneficial for the candidates. The design of the assignment and the close monitoring from the instructors each step of the way created an environment well disposed for the learning of the candidates. The candidates also celebrated this opportunity, which ended up being considered as more than just an assignment, but a real chance to learn. The third grade teacher also found advantages that her students could enjoy. All parties involved in the project had gains, as is meant to occur in a PDS model, and the experiment was more than just enjoyable. In the coming paragraphs the authors will focus on the observations made by the candidates and inspect the benefits they observed during the semester as a result of this experience.

The Candidates' Point of View

The teacher candidates who participated in the experience were anxious about different aspects of the project, as they expressed in their reflections. One concern to the candidates was their lack of experience in teaching children. This may appear a bit strange at first, given the profession they had chosen, but a number of preservice teachers had never been "on the other side of the desk," and the lack of experience of teaching children, in general, was added to their anxiety about mathematics. With regards to teaching mathematics, one of the candidates observed in her reflection:

> Mathematical lessons, on the other hand, are potentially very different and unique especially in the way that the activities and various strategies are chosen to be taught. Overall, teaching this lesson provided me with very helpful insights as to what I need to improve on and what I do relatively well as a future educator.

This opportunity to teach mathematics to children allowed the candidates to know what in particular they need to improve in this area from the content and the pedagogical content point of view without it being the professor who pointed it out.

The candidates posited that there need to be more opportunities for them to try their skills teaching mathematics before they go out in the field to student teach. This was their first time teaching mathematics to children, and they expressed that mini-lessons they had done in the past, where candidates teach each other, do not compare with this experience. About this, one of the female students in the class said: "I very much enjoyed the opportunity to teach my own mathematics lesson to a group of students currently in third grade. This allowed for my reflections to be real, effective and beneficial to my development as a professional as I was not teaching to my own peers." Another one reflected, "I believe that this lesson was a positive experience and that we should have more opportunities like it." This experience made the teaching real in the sense that once graduated they will be working with a similar population of children, not another group of adults. What they experienced during this assignment provided them with information that they can directly connect with their future practice.

The candidates expressed that this was an eye-opening experience demonstrating what children can do in mathematics, and even though student thinking had been discussed in the course, it caused a much bigger impression to actually see it in action. The candidates realized that sometimes they had to change plans "on their feet" and adjust questions and problems they were asking the children. These adjustments were always made to reach the level of sophistication of mathematical thinking displayed by the children, which in the earlier cases was underestimated. While at first doing this appeared as a problem to the candidates, soon they claimed to have adjusted by having a Plan B ready and different levels of questioning planned and rehearsed.

Another reason the candidates were concerned at first was the fact that they were going to be observed by their peers, and those peers were going to be discussing their lessons. Soon after the first lessons were taught and discussed and feedback was provided to the candidates, this fear disappeared, giving space to consider this feedback as a tool for their professional development improvement. For example, one of the candidates observed in his reflection: "I have learned a lot from this experience. I intend to use the feedback from my peers to make me a better teacher." Another candidate commented in her reflection: "After teaching my lesson and reviewing the notes and comments from my peers I realized how important it is to be observed as a preservice teacher." This realization is not a small one as it can only be beneficial for candidates and teachers to open up their classrooms to peers and colleagues and grow based on the discussions that should follow an observation.

Participating in the feedback sessions helped candidates start to think about their class, and taking notes of the things they wanted to replicate and those they wanted to avoid. Candidates claimed that these sessions helped them plan their classes in advance and be better prepared.

The Teacher's Point of View

The teacher in this study is one of the authors of this chapter who had worked for the project in which this collaboration took place. This provided a particularly advantageous point of view for action research. Not only she was working with the candidates, but also with the children the candidates were teaching. At the same time, she is also part of the system into which the candidates aspire to enter soon. She saw some highlights worth reviewing.

All of the third-grade children that the candidates taught were in an early intervention program. The classroom also had seven English language learners (ELLs), and several students with special needs. The class was so diverse that the candidates differentiated instruction and varied instructional styles from the very beginning to meet the needs of the classroom.

The teacher thought that this experience was not only valuable for the candidates, but also for the children in her classroom. The children received instruction in a smaller group setting (as only half the class was in each group). The candidates used a variety of different approaches that maybe she would have not thought of. The teacher claimed that the participation of adults in her classroom would have been beneficial on its own, but these were not just any adults. These were teacher candidates who were almost ready to begin student teaching.

The teacher noted that the excitement of the candidates was clear in the classroom, and the children enjoyed that. The third graders kept referring back to what the candidates did long after the classes were taught, and they were thrilled about participating in this study.

The teacher also found that the experience of teaching a group such as hers helped the candidates adjust and differentiate instruction. Groups as diverse as this one are not that rare, and candidates should be ready to encounter classrooms like this in the future.

The feedback piece was also interesting to the teacher, who gained information about the class and how to proceed with the course. Just like the other instructor, knowing on what the candidates were focusing, as well as what they were overseeing, helped her know what to do in the coming sessions and plan on future discussions and questions for the candidates.

The Professors' Point of View

The results of the study were highly positive. The instructors were pleased to see the candidates engaged in the activity and surprised to even be thanked for creating this type of assignment. The sophistication of the classes being taught grew as the semester went by, as did the level of critical feedback provided to those teaching. The candidates were better prepared to teach, and also better prepared to discuss and provide alternatives.

As the lessons went by, candidates moved from tasks that required lower levels of cognitive demand (Bloom, Engelhart, Furst, Hill, & Krathwohl, 1956; Krathwohl, 2002; Stein et al., 2009), like memorization or procedural tasks, to problems where the student had to "do mathematics" in the terms preferred by the National Council of Teachers of Mathematics (NCTM). The questions they asked to the students during their lessons suffered a similar change. Candidates went from planning too many things to do superficially to slowly planning less, but with more depth.

The feedback sessions were productive as the preservice teachers provided feedback without holding back. Candidates did not have to worry about classmates being hurt by their criticism because those who taught were not in the room. This arrangement, which was discussed in Lim and Guerra's presentation (2012), was particularly beneficial for this study.

Not only did those teaching benefit from the feedback, but the discussions were highly regarded by the class. Teacher candidates not only participated during these sessions, but also took notes of key points they did not want to forget at the time of planning their classes; it was clear those notes helped because the lessons improved over time.

In the feedback sessions, it was not necessary for the instructor to point out the differences between lower- and higher-level cognitive demand tasks, because candidates brought it up themselves. Additionally, comments that the instructor had had to make repeatedly in the past to students in other sessions of this course, regarding the choice of tasks and questioning, were voiced naturally by the preservice teachers in the discussions. The voice was transferred from the instructor to the students. It was the preservice teachers' knowledge and their comments and critical review of their own work that took the center of the class. The theory that was discussed in class had a clear application and did not appear as separate from the practice. It was the students who could refer back to readings and conversations that had occurred before.

Students were surprised of the level of understanding of the children. Even though student thinking had been discussed and the candidates had seen children's work (as well as clips of students doing mathematics), it was not until now that they could really understand the reach of those discussions and clips. However, it was not always the case that the classroom theory had a clear application in the elementary classroom.

Candidates found that the lesson plans they were planning were, in their own words, unrealistic. The candidates claimed during the last meeting, after they had all taught a lesson, observed others, reflected on their own work, and tried to complete every section of the lesson plan template, that they forgot about the reality of the classroom and children. They also realized that their planning was trying to cover too much, doing more things than they could possibly be done in the time allotted. Most important of all, they realized that none of those things were done in depth. Not only did the pedagogical content knowledge improve, but there was also betterment in the content knowledge of the candidates.

Mathematics is sometimes a challenging content area for future teachers, and during mock lessons where candidates teach candidates, those teaching hide behind the assumption that everyone in the room should know the mathematics. When these candidates worked with children they realized the big responsibility it was to teach mathematics themselves. They made sure they knew the content well, and when mistakes happened, those observing were fast to note and helped the ones teaching so children would not leave with the wrong idea. This was particularly clear during the discussions, when students brought up different issues, from vocabulary to conceptual understanding.

DISCUSSION

In a PDS model, the backbone idea is that all of those involved benefit from the collaboration. In this experiment, all of those involved did benefit. From the candidates to the children in the classroom to both instructors, all of the participants ended the project having experienced some growth in various areas.

Candidates need more opportunities to teach mathematics to children. Field experiences of this kind are a necessity. The authors of this paper, as well as others before (McDiarmid, 1990; Mewborn, 2000; Moore, 2003; Phillip et al., 2007; Wilson, 1996), found that the growth of the candidates from the experience of teaching was noticeable. These experiences can change candidates' beliefs about learning and teaching mathematics.

Strong stereotypes that future teachers have about mathematics and how it is taught, as well as feelings they have sometimes of anxiety and dislike, can be modified by allowing candidates to teach mathematics to children before they go into fulltime teaching experiences. In order for that to happen, they need experiences where they can still get feedback from more knowledgeable instructors.

Methods instructors and knowledgeable collaborating teachers should monitor these experiences, as in McDiarmid's study (1990). These events should be designed to help candidates think critically about their practice. Having candidates observe each other was crucial for the success of this experiment. Not only did those teaching feel accountable to the children, but they were also accountable to their classmates.

In summary, field experiences need to be integrated in methods courses, making the theory discussed in the class connect with the practice. The professor and the collaborating teacher need to work together in planning every move. They both need to be mentors in the first steps candidates take in teaching mathematics. The PDS offers a perfect setting for such collaboration.

Another feature of the design that helped this assignment to be meaningful was the feedback piece. Having students talk about the class and help each other by providing ideas to modify that which they thought did not go well was a practice that helped everyone grow as was observed by Lim and Guerra (2012). They also started to create a community where they could share their teaching ideas and exchange comments. If they move into the field keeping such a community and continue to build one at the school where they will teach, this will help them study their practice and improve it with others.

The authors believe that field experiences in mathematics benefitting from a PDS model, like this one, can still improve. For example, given that candidates will rarely find opportunities to co-teach in the future, it would be beneficial for them to do the teaching individually instead of in groups of two. Time and availability of the children dictated this characteristic of the experiment, and these features also dictated that the candidates taught half of the whole grade group. Ideally, a group of at least 20 students will provide candidates with a much better idea of classroom management while teaching mathematics. Not only classroom management, but also deciding how to group children, managing centers, and choosing problems will be slightly different with a bigger group of children. These limitations of the study are nothing but opportunities for further research.

NOTES

1. All names have been changed to ensure anonymity.
2. For the one particular case, three groups of candidates taught at the same time, and the group of 20 third graders was also divided into 3 groups.

REFERENCES

Adams, P. E., & Krockover, G. H. (1997). Concerns and perceptions of beginning secondary science and mathematics teachers. *Science Education, 81*(1), 29–50.

Berry, B. (2001). No shortcuts to preparing good teachers. *Educational Leadership, 58*(8), 32–36.

Bloom, B. S., Engelhart, M. D., Furst, E. J., Hill, W. H., &Krathwohl, D. R. (1956). *Taxonomy of educational objectives: Handbook I: Cognitive domain.* New York, NY: David McKay.

Cornell, C. (1999). I hate math! I couldn't learn it, and I can't teach it! *Childhood education, 75*(4), 225–230.

Erickson, F. (1986). Qualitative methods in research on teaching. In M. Wittrock (Ed.), *Handbook of research on teaching* (3rd ed.) (pp. 119–161).

Krathwohl, D. R. (2002). A revision of Bloom's Taxonomy: An overview. *Theory into Practice, 41*(4), 212–218.

Lim, W., & Guerra, P. (2012, October). *Improving teaching through effective feedback.* Paper presented at the annual meeting of the Georgia Educational Research Association, Savannah, GA

McDiarmid, G. W. (1990). Challenging prospective teachers' beliefs during early field experience: A Quixotic undertaking? *Journal of Teacher Education, 41*(3), 12–20.

Merriam, S. B. (1998). *Qualitative research and case study applications in education. Revised and expanded from "Case study research in education."* San Francisco, CA: Jossey-Bass.

Mewborn, D. S. (2000). Learning to teach elementary mathematics: Ecological elements of a field experience. *Journal of Mathematics Teacher Education, 3*(1), 27–46.

Moore, R. (2003). Reexamining the field experiences of pre-service teachers. *Journal of Teacher Education, 54*(1), 31–42.

Oh, D. M., Ankers, A. M., Llamas, J. M., &Tomyoy, C. (2005). Impact of pre-service student teaching experience on urban school teachers. *Journal of Instructional Psychology, 32*(1), 82–98.

Philipp, R. A., Ambrose, R., Lamb, L. L. C., Sowder, J. T., Schappelle, B. P., Sowder, L., … Chauvot, J. (2007). Effects of early field experiences on the mathematical content knowledge and beliefs of prospective elementary school teachers: An experimental study. *Journal for Research in Mathematics Education, 38*(5), 438–476.

Stein, M. K., Smith, M. S., Henningsen, M. A., & Silver, E. A. (2009). *Implementing standards-based mathematics instruction: A casebook for professional development* (2nd ed.). New York, NY: Teachers College Press.

Swars, S. L. (2005). Examining perceptions of mathematics teaching effectiveness among elementary pre-service teachers with differing levels of mathematics teacher efficacy. *Journal of instructional Psychology, 32*(2), 139–147.

Uusimaki, L., & Nason, R. (2004). Causes underlying pre-service teachers' negative beliefs and anxieties about mathematics. In D. E. McDougall, J. A. Ross (Eds.), *Proceedings of the 28th Conference of the International Group for the Psychology of Mathematics Education* (Vol. 4, pp. 369–376). Ontario Institute for Studies in Education of the University of Ontario.

Wilson, J. D. (1996). An evaluation of the field experiences of the innovative model for the preparation of elementary teachers for science, mathematics, and technology. *Journal of Teacher Education, 47*(1), 53–59.

Wilson, S. M., Floden, R. E., &Ferrini-Mundy, J. (2001). *Teacher preparation research: Current knowledge, gaps, and recommendations: A research report prepared for the U.S. Department of Education and the Office for Educational Research and Improvement, February 2001.* Washington: Center for the Study of Teaching and Policy.

Yin, R. K. (2009).*Case study research: Design and methods* (4th ed.). Thousand Oaks, CA: Sage.

Zeichner, K. (2010). Rethinking the connections between campus courses and field experiences in college- and university-based teacher education. *Journal of Teacher Education, 61*(1-2), 89–99.

CHAPTER 14

UTILIZING A UNIVERSITY– SCHOOL PARTNERSHIP TO IMPROVE THE ACADEMIC ACHIEVEMENT OF MIDDLE SCHOOL STUDENTS (INCLUDING THOSE WITH SPECIAL NEEDS) BY INSTITUTING SCHOOL-WIDE CO-TEACHING

Debra Leach, Lisa Johnson, Felix Blumhardt, and Cindy Bush

ABSTRACT

One of the purposes of professional development schools is to work collaboratively to conduct research on effective teaching practices. This study describes a collaborative inquiry among university faculty and educators from a rural middle

Creating Visions for University-School Partnerships, pages 231–244.
Copyright © 2014 by Information Age Publishing
All rights of reproduction in any form reserved.

school in the southeastern United States. Adams Middle School (AMS) is a partner school in a network associated with a midsized, southeastern land grant university. AMS is one of thirty schools across nine school districts engaging in a dynamic, diverse, and growing collaboration with multiple departments within the university. Goodlad (1984), in his book *A Place Called School*, suggested that in order to improve schools and the work of teachers, a relationship had to exist between institutes of public education and teacher preparation programs. Initiatives at AMS and throughout the network stem from Goodlad's vision of shared responsibility for student achievement through clinically based teacher preparation and sustained collaborative professional learning (along with inquiry and research-based practice). Specifically, the network maintains a shared purpose in the simultaneous renewal of schools and educator preparation with a focus on P–12 student learning. This happens through the engagement of collaborative learning communities involving district and university students and faculty. Using this mission as our foundational cornerstone, partners collaborate to meet four specific goals: (1) improve P–12 student learning, (2) improve professional learning for district and university faculty and teacher candidates, (3) improve quality of teacher preparation, and (4) increase support for new teachers.

The collaboration for this study began when the AMS school principal set up a meeting with two faculty members from the university during the summer of 2011 to address an identified problem: Statewide standardized assessment data had shown that students with learning disabilities were not making adequate yearly progress (AYP) in language arts and math. As a result of the collaborative problem-solving meeting, the school administration decided to implement a full inclusion co-teaching model as opposed to a resource model that had been used during the previous years. This decision was made because the team believed students with learning disabilities would make greater academic gains if they received specialized instruction within general education classrooms alongside their typically developing peers than they had been when placed in resource settings. The team also believed that typically developing students would make greater gains in co-taught classrooms versus traditional classrooms as a result of reduced teacher–student ratios. In order to systematically evaluate the effects of the initiation of school-wide co-teaching, the university faculty members and school administrators designed a study to addresses the question: Will students with learning disabilities and their peers served in co-taught language arts and mathematics classrooms make greater gains on a standardized test of academic achievement than their counterparts served in non-co-taught classrooms? In addition to examining the academic achievement gains, the researchers also examined the co-teachers' perspectives on the co-teaching practices implemented throughout the school year. The university faculty members and school administrators worked collaboratively throughout the year to collect data, train and support teachers and student interns teaching in co-taught classrooms, and evaluate student learning outcomes.

THEORETICAL BACKGROUND/REVIEW OF LITERATURE

Students with disabilities are increasingly being included in general education settings to meet the least restrictive environment (LRE) mandate of the Individuals with Disabilities Education Improvement Act (2004) and to provide adequate access to the general education curriculum (No Child Left Behind [NCLB], 2002). However, the level of special education services and support resources delivered within general education settings often varies among schools, school districts, and states due to varying interpretations of the LRE mandate (Taylor, 2004). In some cases, general education teachers supporting students with disabilities in their classrooms receive minimal consultation from special education teachers (Damore & Murray, 2009). Often, students with disabilities receive their special education services in resource settings ("pull-out services") (Swanson & Vaughn, 2010). Consensus exists among special educators that the most productive way to deliver special education services and support resources to students with disabilities in general education settings is through a co-teaching model (Saloviita & Takala, 2010). Cook and Friend (1995) define co-teaching as "two or more professionals delivering substantive instruction to a diverse or blended group of students in a single physical space" (p. 2). Teachers can use a variety of co-teaching models to support students with disabilities in general education classrooms, including teaming, parallel teaching, station teaching, one teach–one assist, alternative teaching, and one teach–one observe (Friend & Bursuck, 2009).

To increase the use of co-teaching service delivery models, a stronger evidence base for doing so was needed. There is limited research on student learning outcomes to support the use of co-teaching. For example, the most recent meta-analysis of the research on co-teaching and student learning outcomes was done in 2001 (Murawski & Swanson, 2001), and the results of that study indicated that co-teaching is a moderately effective procedure for influencing student outcomes. However, of the 89 articles reviewed by the researchers on the topic of co-teaching, only six met the criteria set for selection in the meta-analysis. Although the researchers were able to discuss positive outcomes on academic achievement for students with disabilities served in co-taught classrooms, cautious interpretation is necessary due to the limited number of studies included in the analysis.

Since the 2001 meta-analysis, other studies published the impact of co-teaching on student learning outcomes. Rea, McLaughlin, and Walther-Thomas (2002) found that students with learning disabilities in co-taught classes performed better according to grades on report cards than students in non-co-taught classes. However, there was no significant difference in student performance on high-stakes tests when comparing scores from students in co-taught classrooms to students served in classrooms with one teacher. Another study on student learning outcomes showed that co-teaching had little effect on scores on high-stakes tests for students with and without disabilities (Idol, 2006). Murawski (2006) studied student learning outcomes by comparing the achievement of students with disabilities served in resource settings (pull-out services), co-taught classrooms (general education and special education teacher working collaboratively in the general education classroom), and general education classes without co-teaching (consultative special education services only). The researcher found no significant differences across settings. The failure to find increased achievement in co-taught classrooms versus other settings can be due to the challenges associated with inconsistencies in co-teaching definitions and fidelity of implementation (Friend, Cook, Hurley-Chamberlain, & Shamberger, 2010; Weiss & Brigham, 2000). The purpose of the current study was to utilize the partnership between the university and school to design a school-wide co-teaching intervention to determine if students receiving instruction in co-taught classrooms will make greater academic gains than those who are taught in traditional classrooms.

The partnership allowed the school to receive training and ongoing consultation by a faculty member to ensure fidelity of implementation of co-teaching models of instruction. Additionally, student interns were placed with the teachers working in co-taught classrooms to further support the co-teaching efforts. This was a great advantage to the university because very few student interns were having opportunities to conduct their internship in inclusive settings. The university faculty assisted with setting up pre- and post-measures to analyze the effects of co-teaching on the academic achievement of the students receiving instruction in co-taught classrooms versus those taught in traditional classrooms. Specifically, gains in mathematics and language arts scores using pre- and post-MAPS (measures of academic progress) scores were measured to determine if students served in co-taught classrooms made greater gains than students served in traditional settings (non-co-taught classrooms).

METHOD

Context and Participants

AMS is a rural middle school located in the southeast United States. It has a population of 615 students: 331 male and 284 female. Twenty-three students are of limited English proficiency, and 28.6% of the students are enrolled in the subsidized meals program. Ethnicity is 74.5 % Caucasian, 14.8% African American, 1.6 % Asian, 7.3 % Hispanic, and .33% American Indian. The mobility rate is 6.4%. Seventy-nine of the students (12.9%) have disabilities. The vast majority of the students with disabilities are categorized as learning disabled.

The university faculty and school administration worked collaboratively to set up language arts and mathematics co-teaching teams across sixth, seventh, and eighth grade. In total, six general education teachers, three special education teachers, one special education student intern, and three middle level student interns were involved in the co-teaching teams. For each of the three grade levels, there was one co-taught mathematics class and one co-taught language arts class. The classes selected for implementation of co-teaching were on grade level and were non-advanced classes utilizing core curriculum. The pilot classes were populated with a heterogeneous mix of students in regards to ethnicity, gender, socioeconomic status, and disabilities. Each pilot class consisted of a general education teacher and a special education teacher working together. In some cases, student interns were also part of the co-teaching teams. Each general education teacher involved in the research also had a matching class of similar demographics that did not involve co-teaching. Teachers utilized the same curriculum across both classes.

The entire faculty and staff engaged in a day-long training during the initial week of school conducted by a faculty member from the partner university who specializes in inclusion and co-teaching. Ongoing support was provided via a professional learning community that met bimonthly. Teachers reviewed co-teaching techniques, viewed videos, read articles, and engaged in discussions. Quarterly workshops were also held for the pilot teachers and their interns to advance co-teaching knowledge in terms of co-planning, co-teaching, and co-assessment. Accountability was monitored through daily feedback forms in which co-teachers and their interns listed the co-teaching model(s) used daily in the classroom. There were, in addition, informal observations by the instructional coach and the professor from the partner university, videotapes of lessons, goal sheets, and feedback forms.

Due to schedule constraints, a limited amount of weekly planning time (maximum 45 minutes scheduled per subject) was available for the special education and general education co-teachers to meet and plan together. The school modified planning days to accommodate the co-teaching initiative with one day per week designated for each content area. On the designated content planning day, the co-teachers for each language arts and mathematics class worked together to plan lessons for the upcoming week. Lessons were planned in tandem for both the co-taught and non-co-taught classes, along with common lessons and assessments for the content partner that was not involved in the study. The pilot teachers utilized a lesson plan template during planning that guided the differentiation component for the co-taught classes.

Data Sources

Data sources for this study included standardized assessments and a co-teaching survey. The measures of academic progress (MAP) system from the Northwest Evaluation Association (NWEA, 2013) measured student growth over time. The MAP assessment provides teachers normative data on individual learners in relation to multiple goal performance areas through RIT (Rasch unIT) scales. The RIT scale is an accurate, equal interval, curriculum scale that uses individual item difficulty values to estimate student achievement and measure growth over time (NWEA, 2013). MAP tests were given in both the fall and spring. Students were selected from the co-taught classes and the matching non-co-taught classes. The selection was made by a third party evaluation group that matched participant demographical characteristics. Students were tested in the areas of language arts and mathematics via computer administration. In addition to the MAP testing, all nine co-teachers completed a co-teaching survey. The 17-item survey allowed teachers to provide feedback about their perceptions of their co-teaching experience.

Design

Using a quasi-experimental design, student achievement scores from students co-taught in mathematics and/or language arts were compared to student achievement scores from students who were not co-taught in mathematics or language arts. To control for teacher effects, the same general education teachers were part of the treatment and comparison groups. In other words, each general education teacher involved in the research also had a matching class of similar demographics that did not involve co-teaching that was used as the comparison. Teachers utilized the same curriculum across both classes. Previous standardized student achievement scores and student sociodemographics were compared to ensure that the students in the co-taught classes were comparable to the students in the classes that were not co-taught (e.g., the teacher who co-taught sixth-grade mathematics also taught traditional sixth-grade mathematics without a co-teacher). All student achievement scores in those classes were analyzed for students who completed a pre- and posttest. Paired sample t-tests were conducted and included only those students with both pre- and posttest data available. The *effect size* (using Cohen's *d*) was calculated to gauge the magnitude of change from pre- to posttest.

In addition to achievement scores, a survey administered to teachers measured perceptions of and experiences in co-teaching upon completion of the academic year. The survey, based on materials from *Creating Inclusive Classrooms: Effective and Reflective Practices* (Salend, 2010), consisted of 17 items and asked teachers to indicate their choice using a 5-point Likert scale with strongly disagree, disagree, neutral, agree, and strongly agree as the five choices. Similar instruments have been used in previous studies to solicit feedback from teachers concerning their co-teaching efforts (Austin, 2001; Phillips, Sapona, & Lubic, 1995).

RESULTS/DATA ANALYSIS

Student Achievement Data

MAP data analysis for 156 students in sixth, seventh, and eighth grades used the mathematics and reading RIT growth scores from fall to spring. Table 14.1 demonstrates the co-teaching designation by grade and subject. Tables 14.2 and 14.3 provide a breakdown of the student participation rates by grade and subject.

The number and percentage of students and co-teaching designation by grade were first cross-tabulated. Across all students, more co-taught students in both mathematics and ELA classes showed growth from the fall to spring. When the grade level is examined, the biggest disparities exist for eighth-grade mathematics and sixth-grade language arts (see Table 14.4).

TABLE 14.1. Co-Teaching Designation by Grade and Subject (numbers/percentage)

Grade	Co-Taught Mathematics	Not Co-Taught Mathematics	Co-Taught Language Arts	Not Co-Taught Language Arts
Sixth	40/57.1%	30/42.9%	19/27.1%	51/72.9%
Seventh	16/41%	23/59.0%	14/35.9%	25/64.1%
Eighth	21/44.7%	26/55.3%	21/44.7%	26/55.3%
Total	77/49.4%	79/50.6%	54/34.6%	102/65.4%

TABLE 14.2. Mathematics MAP Student Participation Rates

Grade	Mathematics Fall	Mathematics Spring	Mathematics Participation Rate
Sixth	56	54	96%
Seventh	30	24	80%
Eighth	41	39	95%
Total	127	117	92%

TABLE 14.3. Reading MAP Student Participation Rates

Grade	Reading Fall	Reading Spring	Reading Participation Rate
Sixth	36	36	100%
Seventh	32	28	88%
Eighth	42	41	98%
Total	110	105	95%

TABLE 14.4. Students Demonstrating RIT Growth (number/percentage)

Grade	Co-Taught Mathematics	Not Co-Taught Mathematics	Co-Taught English	Not Co-Taught English
Sixth	28/77.8%	12/70.6%	11/73.3%	6/33.3%
Seventh	5/38.5%	5/45.5%	9/64.3%	6/42.9%
Eighth	13/72.2%	9/45.0%	12/70.6%	15/65.2%
Total	46/68.7%	26/54.2%	32/69.6%	27/49.1%

TABLE 14.5. Average Mathematics RIT Scores and Standard Deviations by Grade, Fall 2011 and Spring 2012

Grade	Co-Taught Fall 2011	Co-Taught Sp. 2012	Gain	Pre/post Effect Size (d)	Not Co-Taught Fall 2011	Not Co-Taught Sp. 2012	Gain	Pre/post Effect Size (d)
Sixth	213.5	219.8	6.3**	0.6	212.3	221.2	8.9*	0.77
	11.1	10.0			13.7	9.8		
Seventh	218.1	217.9	– 0.3	0.03	217.6	219.6	2.0	0.2
	10.1	17.9			9.5	11.9		
Eighth	216.2	221.2	5.0	0.27	225.9	225.2	– 0.7	0.06
	17.9	19.8			10.5	13.1		
Total	215.1	219.8	4.7*	0.34	219.2	222.5	3.3*	0.28
	13.1	14.6			12.8	11.7		

Notes: * significant at p<.05; **significant at p<.001

Table 14.5 illustrates *standard deviations*, *gains*, and *effect sizes*. The standard deviation (SD) is a measure of dispersion, or variability, within a given variable. A small standard deviation suggests that the data points are all close to the same value (the average or mean), while a large standard deviation suggests larger variability in the data points. Because our focus is on program impacts and not generalization, significance testing can be misleading (it cannot tell us the degree of impact or how meaningful a significant difference is). Therefore, the *effect size* (using Cohen's *d*) as a calculation gauges the magnitude of change from pre- to posttest. Measurement of the strength of the effect sizes occurs through the following scale:

- $\geq$ -0.15 and <.15 = negligible effect
- $\geq$ .15 and <.40 = small effect
- $\geq$ .40 and <.75 = medium effect
- $\geq$ .75 and <1.10 = large effect
- $\geq$ 1.10 and <1.45 = very large effect
- >1.45 = huge effect

As seen in Table 14.5, paired sample t-tests conducted include only those students with both pre- and posttest data available. Overall, students in co-taught mathematics classes had larger gains than their peers in mathematics classes that were not co-taught. While both groups showed significant gains, the effect size was larger for those in co-taught classes.

Table 14.6 presents the average language arts scores at pre- (fall 2011) and posttest (spring 2012) by grade, for students in co-taught language arts classes and for those in non-co-taught mathematics classes, along with standard deviations, the corresponding gain, and effect size. Paired sample t-tests were conducted and

TABLE 14.6. Average ELA RIT Scores and Standard Deviations by Grade, Fall 2011 and Spring 2012

Grade	Co-Taught Fall 2011	Co-Taught Sp.2012	Gain	Pre/post Effect Size (d)	Not Co-Taught Fall 2011	Not Co-Taught Sp. 2012	Gain	Pre/post Effect Size (d)
Sixth	201.6	204.7	3.1	0.24	210.9	206.8	− 4.1	0.33
	12.9	14.1			7.9	16.0		
Seventh	212.4	217.3	4.9*	0.37	218.1	217.4	− 0.7	0.08
	14.5	12.9			7.4	9.9		
Eighth	212.3	217.9	5.6	0.43	217.3	220.7	3.4	0.33
	12.4	14.4			10.7	2.2		
Total	208.8	213.4	4.6*	0.32	215.4	215.3	− 0.1	0.001
	13.9	17.9			9.5	13.7		

Note: * significant at p<.05

include only those students with both pre- and posttest data available. Overall, significant gains were made for language arts students in co-taught classes only (with a small effect size [$d = 0.32$]). In fact, a decrease in the average score occurred for non-co-taught students in language arts classes, although this decrease is not statistically or practically significant. The largest gains were seen in seventh-grade co-taught language arts classes with a small to moderate effect size ($d = 0.37$).

Teacher Survey Data

At the end of the academic year, all nine teachers responded to a 17-item survey that asked them for feedback about their experiences and perceptions of co-teaching. For the most part, the responses were positive ("Agree" and "Strongly Agree") as indicated by the shaded cells. Time appeared to be the most significant issue as reflected in Items c and l of Table 14.7 below. While Item p is marked strongly disagree, it is shaded since it is a positive indicator of integration (in terms of students with disabilities and those without) of the co-taught classrooms.

Only a few teachers chose to add additional comments on the items in the survey. Again, time appears to be the most common concern.

- Item—I have had input in the development of an inclusive program at my school. Comment—"Implementation not development."
- Item—I have sufficient resources to implement inclusion effectively. Comment—"Planning time would be helpful."
- Item—I have enough time to communicate and collaborate with my co-teacher. Comment—"We make time in between classes."

TABLE 14.7.   Co-Teaching Teacher Survey Results

Question	Strongly Disagree	Disagree	Neutral	Agree	Strongly Agree
a. I have had input in the development of an inclusive program at my school.	11.11	22.22	11.11	55.56	0
b. I have sufficient resources to implement inclusion effectively	11.11	22.22	22.22	44.44	
c. I have enough time to communicate and collaborate with my co-teacher.	33.33	44.44	11.11	11.11	
d. I have the necessary cooperation and assistance from colleagues to implement inclusion successfully.	0	22.22	22.22	55.56	
e. I have the necessary cooperation and assistance from educational support personnel (paraprofessionals) to implement inclusion successfully.	0	0	22.22	77.78	
f. I have received the training I need to successfully use co-teaching strategies and implement inclusion.	22.22	0	22.22	44.44	11.11
g. I believe students with disabilities can receive an appropriate education in an inclusive regular education classroom.	0	0	0	44.44	55.56
h. I believe students without disabilities can receive an appropriately challenging education in an inclusive regular education classroom.	0	0	11.11	22.22	66.67
i. I believe that special educators working in inclusion generally take a subordinate role in the classroom.	11.11	22.22	22.22	44.44	0
j. I have seen evidence of improved academic outcomes for students with disabilities in inclusion classrooms.	0	0	11.11	88.89	0
k. It is easy to modify my instructional strategies and my teaching style to meet the needs of students with disabilities.	0	0	0	100	0
l. I have the time to individualize instruction for students with disabilities.	11.11	44.44	33.33	11.11	0
m. I have found that inclusion has encouraged me to experiment with new teaching methodologies.	0	0	22.22	77.78	0
n. I have tried at least five or six different models of co-teaching.	11.11	22.22	0	66.67	0
o. In the inclusion classroom, my co-teacher and I consistently work with all students including those with disabilities and those without disabilities.	0	0	0	33.33	66.67
p. The students with disabilities in my inclusion classroom(s) work separately from their classmates without disabilities a majority of the time.	88.89	11.11	0	0	0
q. In my inclusion classroom(s), students with disabilities and students without disabilities receive equal access to the same general curriculum.	0	0	0	33.33	66.67

- Item—I believe students with disabilities can receive an appropriate education in an inclusive regular education classroom. Comment— "Accommodations are still necessary."
- Item—I have the time to individualize instruction for students with disabilities. Comment—"More time would be helpful."

DISCUSSION

Significant gains were made for students in co-taught language arts classes only (with a small effect size [$d = 0.32$]). Students in co-taught mathematics classes had larger gains than their peers in mathematics classes that were not co-taught. While both mathematics groups showed significant gains, the effect size was larger for those in co-taught classes. Overall, students in co-taught classes performed better on MAP student achievement tests than students who were not in co-taught classes. One factor that may have negatively influenced results in seventh-grade mathematics was that a first-year teacher served as the special education co-teacher for that team. This first-year teacher struggled with effective communication and collaboration skills and also reported that she did not feel extremely comfortable teaching the mathematics content at the seventh-grade level.

The MAP data showed that of the students with learning disabilities served in the co-taught classrooms, 61.5% showed growth in mathematics, and 76% showed growth in language arts. It is also worthwhile to discuss the data from the state standardized achievement test used to calculate AYP. Results of that assessment show significant improvements during the initiation of the co-teaching model compared to the previous academic year. Students with disabilities showed an increase in both language arts and mathematics. As was stated earlier, the lack of growth in AYP in language arts and mathematics for students with learning disabilities in previous years was the primary motivation for the initiation of the school-wide co-teaching efforts. The percentage of students with disabilities meeting AYP the year prior to the initiation of co-teaching was 40.4% in language arts and 40.4 % in mathematics. Data for the co-teaching year climbed to 50% of students with disabilities meeting AYP in language arts and 47.6% meeting AYP in mathematics. The percentage of students with disabilities in the exemplary category in mathematics or language arts rose from less than 8% to 21.4%.

These results indicate that co-teaching was more effective than traditional teaching (without a co-teacher) in mathematics and language arts at Adams Middle School (AMS). Although the external validity of these results is limited, they align with previous reports on the effectiveness of co-teaching. In order to increase the generalizability of the study in the future, the scope should be expanded to include other levels (elementary and high), additional subjects, and increased student achievement data in terms of numbers.

Teachers responded positively about their perceptions of and experiences with co-teaching. Time appeared to be the most prevalent concern. As with the student data, these results provide limited external validity. Increasing the scope of the study in the future will provide increased insight into the perceptions and experiences of teachers who teach different levels (elementary and high), as well as other subjects such as social studies and science.

Other positive outcomes from the study were obtained by interviewing the teachers. The teachers were asked the following broad question:

> In addition to the increase in academic achievement scores, what other positive outcomes did you observe in the students placed in co-taught classrooms?

The teachers reported improved grades among the majority of students in the study and improved morale for both the teachers and the students. The school received positive parent feedback, and there were requests to have students placed in co-taught classrooms due to the extra support available. Teachers in the pilot study self-reported an increased focus on planning and differentiation. As a result of the data from the study, AMS decided to expand co-teaching from one team per grade level to two teams per grade level for the following academic year. The school–university partnership expanded as well with more interns placed with the co-teaching teams, and the university faculty member who provided training and consultation increased her time supporting co-teaching teams to an average of one day per week.

This study demonstrated how a professional development school could promote the effective use of co-teaching to improve student learning outcomes. Much of the literature on co-teaching shows limited positive effects, which are likely due to problems with definitions of co-teaching and fidelity of implementation. Because of the partnership between the university and school, co-teachers received consistent training and support to ensure fidelity of the use of co-teaching models. The special education teachers took the lead role in planning for the varied use of the different co-teaching models during planning meetings and supported the interns and general education teachers throughout the planning and implementation phases. Having student interns on the co-teaching teams enhanced the feasibility of implementing models such as station teaching, parallel teaching, and alternative teaching. In some instances there were four teachers in the classroom (the general education teacher, the intern placed with the general education teacher, the special education teacher, and the intern placed with the special education teacher). The opportunity for special education and general education preservice teachers to collaborate strengthens preservice teacher education programs (Leko, Brownell, Sindelar, & Murphy, 2012). The student interns gained valuable experiences with effectively including students with learning disabilities in general education classrooms and had opportunities to learn the communication and collaboration skills needed to make co-teaching situations work.

Future studies are needed to examine the extent to which beginning teachers with the co-teaching experience during their internship demonstrate more effective collaboration and interpersonal communication skills than those who did not have the co-teaching experience. The AMS co-teaching study is a good starting point for the partnership to begin to explore the effectiveness of the co-teaching modality. Based on the positive results, the partnership may want to consider expanding this practice and conducting an evaluation that is larger in scope, possibly district- or partnership-wide. AMS can serve as a demonstration site for effective use of co-teaching to improve student learning outcomes if other schools in the network decide to initiate similar models. Although the PDS literature includes some excellent innovations that positively impact students, it often lacks hard evidence that an increase is made in student achievement as a result of the innovations. This study provides a clear link between the use of co-teaching and improved student academic achievement.

REFERENCES

Austin, V. L. (2001). Teachers' beliefs about co-teaching. *Remedial and Special Education, 22*(4), 245–255.

Cook, L., & Friend, M. (1995). Co-teaching: Guidelines for creating effective practices. *Focus on Exceptional Children, 35,* 5–22.

Damore, S. J., & Murray, C. (2009). Urban elementary school teachers' perspectives regarding collaborative teaching practices. *Remedial & Special Education, 30*(4), 234–244.

Friend, M., & Bursuck, W. D. (2009). *Including students with special needs: A practical guide for classroom teachers* (5th ed.). Columbus, OH: Merrill.

Friend, M., Cook, L., Hurley-Chamberlain, D., & Shamberger, C. (2010). Co-teaching: An illustration of the complexity of collaboration in special education. *Journal of Educational and Psychological Consultation, 20*(1), 9–27.

Goodlad, J. (1984). *A place called school: Promise for the future.* New York, NY: McGraw-Hill.

Idol, L. (2006). Toward inclusion of special education students in general education: A program evaluation of eight schools. *Remedial and Special Education, 27*(2), 77–94.

Individuals With Disabilities Education Improvement Act, 20 U.S.C. § 1400 (2004).

Leko, M. M., Brownell, M. T., Sindelar, P. T., & Murphy, K. (2012). Promoting special education pre-service teacher expertise. *Focus On Exceptional Children, 44*(7), 1–16.

Murawski, W. (2006). Student outcomes in co-taught secondary English classes: How can we improve? *Reading & Writing Quarterly, 22,* 227–247.

Murawski, W., & Swanson, H. (2001). A meta-analysis of co-teaching research: Where are the data? *Remedial and Special Education, 22,* 258–267.

No Child Left Behind (NCLB) Act of 2001, Pub. L. No. 107-110, § 115, Stat. 1425 (2002).

Northwest Evaluation Association (NWEA). (2013). The RIT scale. Retrieved from http://www.nwea.org/support/article/532

Phillips, L., Sapona, R. H., & Lubic, B. L. (1995). Developing partnerships in inclusive education: One school's approach. *Intervention in School and Clinic, 30*(5), 262–272.

Rea, P., McLaughlin, V. L., & Walther-Thomas, C. S. (2002). Outcomes for students with learning disabilities in inclusive and pullout programs. *Exceptional Children, 68,* 203–222.

Salend, S. J. (2010). *Creating inclusive classrooms: Effective and reflective practices.* Upper Saddle River, NJ: Pearson.

Saloviita, T., & Takala, M. (2010). Frequency of co-teaching in different teacher categories. *European Journal Of Special Needs Education, 25*(4), 389–396.

Swanson, E. A., & Vaughn, S. (2010). An observation study of reading instruction provided to elementary students with learning disabilities in the resource room. *Psychology in the Schools, 47*(5), 481–492.

Taylor, S. J. (2004). Caught in the continuum: A critical analysis of the principle of the least restrictive environment. *Research & Practice For Persons With Severe Disabilities, 29*(4), 218–230.

Weiss, M. P., & Brigham, F. J. (2000). Co-teaching and the model of shared responsibility: What does the research support? In T. E. Scruggs & M. A. Mastropieri (Eds.), *Educational interventions: Advances in learning and behavioral disabilities* (Vol. 14, pp. 218–245). Stamford, CT: JAI.

CHAPTER 15

A SCHOOL–UNIVERSITY PARTNERSHIP'S USE OF ACTION RESEARCH AS AN INSERVICE CLINICAL RESPONSE INITIATIVE TO DEVELOP THE LITERACY-BASED INSTRUCTIONAL PRACTICES OF TEACHERS

David A. Walker and Portia M. Downey

ABSTRACT

A school-university partnership addressed the problem of inadequate student literacy skills by creating an action research-based professional development program to assist high school teachers. Results indicated that teachers used their action research findings to inform their practice, theory, and/or research (based in literacy skills) to assist students, colleagues, and preservice educators. Concepts such as modeling best practices, multiple methods of measurement for assessment, the use of higher-order thinking skills, transition time to a new or revisited literacy-based

Creating Visions for University-School Partnerships, pages 245–258.
Copyright © 2014 by Information Age Publishing
All rights of reproduction in any form reserved.

task or theory, and the pertinence of engagement all emerged as important elements for inservice practice as well as enhancement of student learning.

High school students in a large, urban public school district located in the Midwest have not met adequate yearly progress (AYP) goals for many years. Inadequate literacy skills have been identified as a major cause of low student achievement in all subject areas at the four high schools that comprise the urban district. Literacy skills include areas such as reading and writing, information, visual, and digital technologies. Contextually, the district: (1) has a high rate of low-income students at 78.70%; (2) has reasonably equal percentages across the major ethnic groups (i.e., Caucasian = 34.30%, African-American = 29.70%, Latino/a = 25.80%); (3) is, again, currently not meeting AYP; and yet, (4) 62.40% of the students in all subjects meet or exceed defined achievement standards. At the high school level, the average enrollment for the four schools is 1,858 students. On average, 73.55% of high school students are low income, and the high schools have roughly equal percentages across the major ethnic groups (i.e., Caucasian = 35.18%, African American = 29.03%, Latino/a = 24.03%). None of the high schools meet AYP, and only 35.05% of the high school students in all subjects meet or exceed standards (Interactive Illinois Report Card, 2013).

A large public research university located in the Midwest has a long-established, active school-university partnership with the district. This partnership includes professional development schools (PDS), though not all of the four high schools involved in the project are practicing PDSs models; that is, some are in the development phase where, for example, the candidates' teacher education courses are not yet onsite at a particular school. Typically, per semester, the partnership has about 10 teacher candidates evenly dispersed at the four high schools teaching and interacting with students and personnel (Walker, Downey, & Cox-Henderson, 2010), although the number of candidates varies by semester based on the content area in which the students are specializing for their degrees. Given this backdrop and to attempt to address the problem of inadequate student literacy skills, the partnership established a professional development program using Promoting Achievement through Literacy Skills (PALS). The aim of this professional development program was to assist district high school teachers across subject areas to enhance student achievement by improving teacher-based content knowledge and the ability to integrate literacy instruction into their teaching methods.

PDS PARTNERSHIPS

Teitel (2003) noted that partnerships between schools and universities often are realized via PDS initiatives, where student learning and teacher development are paramount outcomes. According to Teitel, PDSs have a four-part mission: (1) new teacher preparation, (2) faculty development, (3) improvement of teacher practice, and (4) improved student achievement. Additionally, the National Council for Accreditation of Teacher Education's (NCATE) (2001) PDS standards focus on: (1) creating a positive learning environment that supports both professional's and children's learning, (2) upholding professional standards for teaching, (3) developing a university-school community with shared responsibility, (4) ensuring professionals are prepared to meet the needs of diverse learners, and (5) providing resources and structures that support the partnership work. Finally, suggestions provided by the National Association for Professional Development Schools (2008) were used as an overarching framework of guidance for the school–university partnerships, in general, as well as the particular schools involved in the PALS program.

Coupled with these practical, organizational criteria, there is consensus within the scholarly literature that the presence of a PDS model versus a traditional school-university format, tends to have a positive relationship with heightened student achievement although the evidence is still emerging and not quite prodigious as found in other, more established areas of educational research. Nonetheless, Corcoran, McVay, and Riordan (2003) found that sustained professional development, particularly with inservice teachers and in the area of instructional practices, had a positive relationship with student achievement. In a longitudinal study, Pine (2003) found a positive relationship between the presence of a PDS model in a school and increased student standardized test scores in subjects such as mathematics and reading (see Guadarrama, Ramsey, & Nath, 2005, 2008, for a vast collection of related literature in this general area of PDS inquiry).

PROFESSIONAL DEVELOPMENT FRAMEWORK

The underlying theory of change for PALS drew upon the work of Desimone (2009) that established a conceptual framework showing that professional development of quality could lead to an increase in educators' knowledge and skills that, in turn, would lead to changes in instruction, and ultimately improve student learning. To ensure that professional development would be of high quality, the National Staff Development Council's (NSDC, 2001) context, process, and content standards were used in the design of the professional development plan. The focus was on improving student achievement and addressing contextual standards by including learning communities (i.e., within the schools, especially in regards to action research projects), the involvement of principals and academic leaders guiding instructional improvement, and the provision of resources to support professional development and collaboration. With regard to process standards, PALS (1) uses data to determine professional development priorities, monitors progress, and informs continuous improvement; (2) uses a data analysis approach to assess implementation; (3) engages educators in applying research to decision making; (4) focuses on instructional strategies aimed at improving student learning; and (5) develops the collaboration skills of the participants. Under content standards, PALS focuses on the concept that all students can achieve academically and educators can be prepared to use differentiated instruction (i.e., providing students with numerous modes of developing, learning, and assessing content) to meet the needs of individual students.

To be effective, professional development should offer meaningful information and duration of time for a program or an intervention to change practice or correlate with enhanced student learning (Timperley, Wilson, Barrar, & Fung, 2007). In PALS, summer professional development was continued into the school year with mentoring, coaching, co-teaching, and one-on-one interactions with university instructional and curriculum specialists. NSDC (2001) found that this type of approach to professional development was highly effective when comprised of participant engagement in learning new content, applying it in a mentored environment, and testing the new content via the use of action research.

The content of the professional development sessions for the teachers and academic leaders focus on: (1) literacy and technology skills across the curriculum, (2) differentiated instruction, and (3) formative and summative data-driven decision-making. The professional development and continuing activities present research-based best practices for each of the three aforementioned components (Timperley et al., 2007; Wade, 1985).

The selection of the key PALS strategies, emphasizing improvement of ability to teach reading, writing, and other literacies, was based on research by Kamil, Borman, Dole, Kral, Salinger, and Torgesen (2008). This research depicted a link between successful student learning and students' ability to read within content areas. Informed by this and other subsequent research, enhancement activities could assist district teachers in adding a reading endorsement to their current certifications, thus increasing the number of reading specialists in the district, providing professional development for high school teachers to incorporate literacy instruction into their subject areas, and supporting greater proficiency in teaching literacy (American College Testing, 2006; Heller & Greenleaf, 2007; National Reading Panel, 2000; Snow, Burns, & Griffin, 1998). The instructional materials used in professional development included research-based approaches such as those provided and advanced by the National Institute for Literacy (2007).

Langer (2002) found that developing effective individual teachers is not enough to improve student achievement in an urban high school setting, but that successful schools collaborated and developed strong, coherent literacy programs. By focusing on integrating literacy and technology across the curriculum, the district aimed to build learning communities within the schools and robust literacy and technology programs. Using the emphasis on literacy as the basic context, the project assisted teachers who were not highly qualified in meeting content standards by integrating three key skill sets (e.g., data analysis and applications, differentiation of instruction, and engagement with school specialists) into all professional development activities and support and to evaluate the impact of all activities. PALS used the work of Tomlinson (2008) and Tomlinson and Strickland (2005) as the theoretical, empirical, and practical basis for professional development related to differentiated instruction. Lastly, the PALS program's professional development elements were guided, overall, by Guskey's (2002) five-level framework. This framework originally was used with professional development evaluation of teachers, but now is employed widely with the omnibus construct of *professional development*, which in this study's context was with schools: (1) participant reaction, (2) participant learning, (3) organizational support and learning, (4) participant use of new knowledge and skills, and (5) student learning outcomes.

ACTION RESEARCH

The data-driven, decision-making component of professional development was built on differentiated learning and response to intervention research (Fuchs & Fuchs, 2007; Fuchs, Vaughn, & Fuchs, 2008), which has correlates with action research. For the PALS project, the action research component's working definition was multidimensional and, therefore, founded in three areas. First, an aspect of the project's action research was based in the work of Hollingsworth (1994), which was predicated on studies related specifically to urban literacy education. Secondly, action research ideas imparted from Mills (2010) and Stringer (2007), such as the action research spiral and the action research interacting spiral, respectively, were utilized as part of our working delineation with participants to conceptualize context-based teacher/educator-initiated research processes. Lastly, the work of Pelton (2010) was employed as an overall guiding framework and source for participant action research project development and realization. Inclusively, the model proposed in PALS was a synergistic combination of an expanded definition of literacy and technology integrated across the curriculum. Further, the model was supported by differentiated instruction based on formative and summative data in a professional development environment, combining extended learning experiences, and the monitoring of changes in educator practice. The action research projects and project evaluation were used to analyze the effectiveness of this approach related to increasing student learning.

PURPOSE AND QUESTION

The purpose of this clinical professional development project was (1) to help high school teachers in a partnership district where university-based student teachers are placed, and (2) to better understand how to use an action research model to enhance instruction in their classroom as a strategy to connect to an improvement in literacy-based skills and changes affiliated with inservice practice. It was anticipated that the participating high school teachers would be able to model action research back to undergraduate preservice teacher candidates and also make connections to the assessment, methods, and theory courses at the participating partnership university. In particular, the action research component addressed the following question: To what extent does an action research-based professional development school initiative help to enhance inservice educators' instructional knowledge and skills and, ultimately, relate to growth in student learning in the area of literacy?

METHOD

Action research was used to engage inservice teachers and partnership university faculty in activities related to instructional knowledge and skills enhancement. These activities were essential to the research-based model's framework since the action research component supported and displayed the various instructional and learning-based elements that teachers gained via professional development.

RESULTS AND DISCUSSION

Thirty-seven high school teachers participated in a series of action research professional development workshops over a period of two years. The teachers had little to no experience with action research. The initial professional development workshop meetings introduced teachers to the concepts affiliated with and steps involved in implementing an action research project in one's classroom and/or outside of the classroom (i.e., after-school co-curricular activities). Numerous skills were developed. These included (1) research question formation, (2) literature searches, (3) quantitative and qualitative data analyses, (4) reflection, (5) action steps, and (6) the review of practical, successful examples of action research

Title of Research
Researchers: (Names)

INTRODUCTION: CONCLUSIONS:

VISUAL GOES HERE (image, photo etc)

RESEARCH QUESTION:

RESULTS:

LIMITATIONS:

HYPOTHESIS:

METHODS:

IMPLICATIONS:

FUTURE RESEARCH:

FIGURE 15.1. Action research template (Berson, 2012).

TABLE 15.1.   Example Titles from Action Research Projects

1. How do students respond to visual representations to support written information?

2. What are the effects on student engagement and performance with literature circles when the strategy is introduced using conventional English literature or introduced using nonfiction articles?

3. What is the effect of teaching question-answer relationships on students' ability to comprehend and solve mathematics story problems?

4. World history and U.S. history: Student comprehension?

5. How do Quickwrites impact students' DBQ essay scores?

6. What is the effect of using Cornell Notes during teacher direct instruction?

7. When taking Cornell Notes while reading academic texts, what effects will occur related to students' abilities to accurately answer questions?

8. How do students respond to script interpretation with and without directional cues?

9. What is the effect of using graphic classic novels on students' comprehension?

10. Is there a measurable difference between a class of students without access to internet technology and another class with access when taking a quiz on unfamiliar material?

11. What is the effect of using vocabulary strategies with frequent repetition on students' usage in a foreign language?

12. How is student comprehension affected by the use of prereading strategies?

13. What is the effect of infusing social studies instruction with reading and writing strategies on students' Lexile scores?

projects carried out in K–12 settings. Figure 15.1 shows the template followed during the initial primer workshops.

During a second set of more advanced professional development workshops, teachers were asked to bring with them some of their curricula that they wanted to adapt using the action research strategies presented and discussed previously. Participants went in-depth with their action research projects and begin developing these with assistance from the partnership's university instructors.

For the final workshop meetings, participants presented their completed action research projects to the rest of the group for discussion and reflection related to their successfully completed approaches as well as their still developing approaches (i.e., not all of the participants' projects were completed with results and actions; that is, a small number of participants, due to delays and unforeseen circumstances, had projects that were still in a developmental phase). Table 15.1 provides examples of the literacy-based content and instruction related to the projects presented and reflected upon during the final professional development workshops. Further, the subsequent examples are vignettes that highlight four completed action research project results and reflections from two single projects; a duo project; and a large, cooperative, group project.

Action Research Project Vignette # 1

The first action research project vignette highlights the use of graphic novels and traditional text novels in an English classroom. This project was entitled "What is the effect of using graphic classic novels on students' comprehension?" The same novel, *Mark Twain*, was used in two different formats: Two class periods were engaged with traditional text and two class periods were engaged with graphic novels. For both research scenarios, the same set of reading comprehension questions were asked of students at the end of the novel. Results indicated that the use of graphic novels (1) increased the overall level of engagement, albeit slightly; (2) derived more complete inferences from students; and (3) yielded enhanced student comprehension of dialect and themes.

Upon analysis and reflection, the teacher learned from this clinically based research experience that (1) too many variables were left uncontrolled in the study; (2) graphic novels did engage students, but appeared to be above some of their reading levels; (3) the idea of student "improvement," via enhanced test scores, will take time and, possibly, a repeat of the study using other novels is a future next step; and (4) consideration of teaching practices and sharing with other colleagues was extremely valuable.

Action Research Project Vignette # 2

The second action research vignette concentrated on literacy, but from the perspective of literature circles. This project was entitled "Is there a differing effect on student engagement and strategic comprehension behavior with literature circles when the strategy is introduced using conventional literature or using nonfiction articles?" The project introduced the idea of literature circles using different materials for various student groups. Literacy-engaged students were noted as actively using annotated text, preparing a detailed role sheet, and enthusiastically participating in group roles and discussion. Thus, results indicated that the average engagement when using literature circles with narrative text was 84%, when using literature circles with informational text was 91%, and, overall, was 88%.

Upon consideration, lessons learned from the project were: (1) using literature circles augmented the overall engagement of students, (2) the project's teacher had increased requests from other educators to model literacy strategies in their classrooms, and (3) reflection on teaching and sharing with other colleagues was found to be beneficial.

Action Research Project Vignette # 3

The third action research vignette depicts a collaborative effort between two social studies teachers intended to help ninth-grade students gain a better understanding of the current events material discussed in class through enhanced reading and note-taking strategies. The project was entitled "What is the effect of infusing social studies instruction with reading and writing strategies on students' Lexile scores?" Using the same general lesson plan, instructional methods, and classroom activities, all four classes read and engaged in a discussion about a current events article from the course text that was deemed "difficult" in terms of comprehension level. Then, students took a scholastic reading inventory pretest to measure their baseline levels of reading comprehension. During the ensuing month of instruction, two of the ninth-grade classes were chosen as the experimental group. This group learned about the method of Cornell Notes and how the use of this strategy may assist in bolstering note taking and text comprehension and, ultimately, reading-based test scores. The other two ninth-grade classes served as the control group. This group continued on with the status quo of the curriculum and did not learn about the use of Cornell Notes. Four weeks after the baseline scholastic reading inventory measure was collected, all of the students read another difficult article, which was very similar to the former article. After reading the second current events article, a companion scholastic reading inventory posttest was taken by all of the students.

The data in Figure 15.2 indicated that the pretest average Lexile score for all four of the classes was 100 (i.e., the line on the figure indicates the average baseline). However, after a month of study and practice pertaining to the use of Cornell Notes, there were noticeable gains on the posttest scores (i.e., growth extending above the average line) garnered by the experimental group, while the scores from the control group remained stagnant. Additionally, when looking at the improvement by the students from the baseline measure (pre-intervention) to

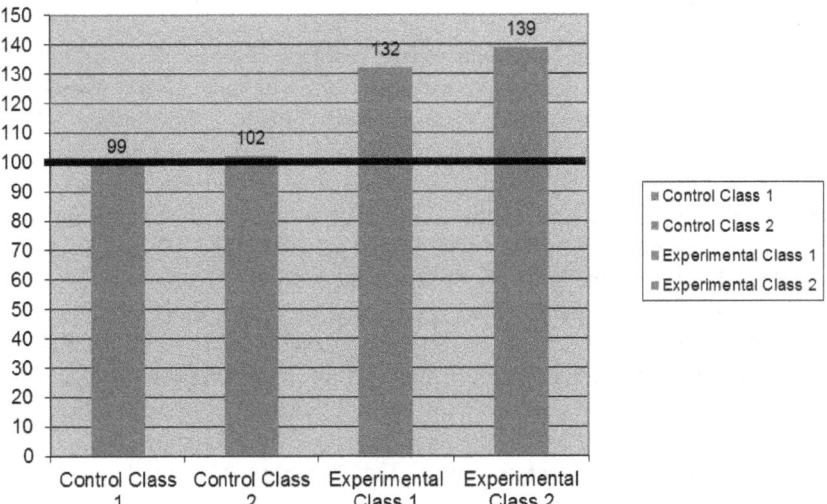

FIGURE 15.2.   Social studies students' reading Lexile scores.

the final measure (post-intervention), both experimental groups' scores were statistically significantly different ($z = 2.10$ and 2.52, $p < .05$, respectively). Given these positive preliminary results, the teachers engaged in this action research project thought that Cornell Notes may be an ideal technique to use with all current and future students to increase their reading comprehension not only with class-based texts but potentially with standardized tests.

Action Research Project Vignette # 4

The fourth action research project vignette, "Thinking Maps," was an instructional strategy where eight different graphic organizers were taught to students and connected to thinking processes by a collective of 14 teachers. The same book, *The Odyssey*, was used in numerous classes, where half of the classes engaged in traditional note-taking strategies and the other half of the classes engaged in the use of thinking maps. The same writing prompt was used to measure reading comprehension among students in all of the classes. First, descriptively, by the end of the academic year, 86% of teachers indicated that they were using thinking maps with their students as compared to 29% at the time of the pretest or the beginning of the school year.

Second, the empirical results of the "Thinking Maps" action research project were measured via pre- and posttests and analyzed by dependent samples t-tests and effect sizes. Data indicated that (1) knowledge of thinking maps increased ($t = 7.274$, $p < .001$, Cohen's d effect size = 1.05); (2) the use of thinking maps with students improved ($t = 7.211$, $p < .001$, $d = 1.02$); and (3) the usefulness of thinking maps in the classroom increased ($t = 2.110$, $p < .05$, $d = 0.58$). Thus, this aspect of the current professional development project had an average effect size of $d = .88$. This result is comparable to what Hattie (2009) found with the effects of professional development in educational research, regardless of a specific intervention, where he reviewed five meta-analyses with over 47,000 participants and found an average d effect size = .62. More specifically, Timperley et al. (2007) determined that the effect of the professional development of teachers on overall student learning outcomes, irrespective of academic subject, was $d = .66$. Given that Hattie (2009), through a synthesis of over 800 meta-analyses (predominately from the international field of educational research) determined that $d = .40$ should be considered the hinge, or tipping point, between the minimum expected, positive effect of a program or intervention and what he deemed a "zone of desired effects," then the fourth action research vignette's $d = .88$ reached a high, desired effect. In fact, per Hattie (2009) and McGraw and Wong (1992), an average $d = .88$ would produce a common language effect size = .73 or probability = .73. Given the present study's focal points of teacher instructional development and student literacy enhancement, this means that 73 times out of 100 the use of professional development with inservice teachers (i.e., the intervention group) would make a positive difference when compared to inservice teachers not involved with professional development (i.e., the control group), which in this instance were high school teachers in the district who did not participate in the PALS project and its intervention.

SUMMARY

The three major, intertwined themes of this study—professional development schools, action research, and teacher professional development—are summarized below with an emphasis on what was learned and advanced for potential best practices.

Professional Development Schools

Results derived from this project pertained to how individual and groups of teachers connected their action research results to inform practice, theory, and/ or research based in literacy skills for high school students, colleagues, and also approximately 10 university-based future teacher educators of which nearly all were involved in the process. Concepts advocated within the PDS, such as modeling best practices, multiple methods of measurement for assessment, the use of higher-order thinking skills, transition time to a new or revisited literacy-based task and/or theory, and the pertinence of engagement all emerged as important elements for inservice practice as well as enhancement of student learning.

Also, participants elaborated on the potential that the action research projects may have had for changing, to some extent, the instructional culture in their PDS (holistically) and also their own in-class practices (individualistically), but also with preservice teacher candidates with whom they may engage and supervise. For example, many of the action research teachers have become more open to reflection pertaining to their own teaching strategies, and also ask for input from their colleagues and teacher candidates. Thus, this is a salient step for the action research teachers to work with fellow teachers and teacher candidates instead of instructing and managing a classroom in isolation and diminishing the ongoing teaching and learning cycle of engagement with preservice and inservice colleagues.

Action Research

From the previously highlighted four action research exemplars, and others presented at the final series of workshops, the following themes emerged as potential predictors of "successful" action research projects based in the domain of literacy:

- Engagement with students
- Higher-order thinking skills of students
- Motivating students
- Predictability with class activities
- Distractions within a learning environment

- Thinking, writing, researching, sharing, and action about teacher instructional practices and student learning

Teacher Professional Development

The action research component of the project addressed the question: To what extent does an action research-based professional development school initiative help to enhance inservice educators' instructional knowledge and skills and, ultimately, relate to growth in student learning in the area of literacy? The following results related to teacher-based professional development contribute to answering this question and are indicators of importance gleaned from the action research projects:

- The action research projects assisted in developing the knowledge and skills of inservice teachers as a strategy to improve students' literacy skills as well as support their own instructional development.
- It is necessary to become familiar with the use of multiple data sources (both quantitative and qualitative) to assess instructional needs and potential instructional solutions as well as the effectiveness of implementing an intervention and/or an action.
- Using data-based results derived from action research projects in collaboration with established best practices, can assist individual teachers, as well as groups of teachers, in mindful engagement with educator preparation programs and school–university partnerships and their connections to practice, research, and theory.

REFERENCES

American College Testing. (2006). *Reading between the lines: What the ACT reveals about college readiness in reading.* Iowa City, IA: Author.

Berson, E. (2012, April). *Developing a researchable question: Open-inquiry in a school garden.* Paper presented at the annual meeting of the American Educational Research Association, Vancouver, British Columbia, Canada.

Corcoran, T., McVay, S., & Riordan, K. (2003). *Getting it right: The MISE approach to professional development.* Philadelphia, PA: Consortium for Policy Research in Education.

Desimone, L. J. (2009). Improving impact studies of teachers' professional development: Toward better conceptualization and measures. *Educational Researcher 38,* 181–199.

Fuchs, L. S., & Fuchs, D. (2007). The role of assessment in the three-tier approach to reading instruction. In D. Haager, S. Vaughn, & J. Klingner (Eds.), *Evidence-based practices for response to intervention* (pp. 29–44). Baltimore, MD: Brookes.

Fuchs, D., Vaughn, S. R., & Fuchs, L. S. (2008). *Responsiveness to intervention.* Newark, DE: International Reading Association.

Guadarrama, I. N., Ramsey, J., & Nath, J. L. (Eds.). (2005). *Professional development schools: Advances in community thought and research.* Charlotte, NC: Information Age Publishing.

Guadarrama, I. N., Ramsey, J., & Nath, J. L. (Eds.). (2008). *University and school connections: Research studies in professional development schools.* Charlotte, NC: Information Age Publishing.

Guskey, T. R. (2002). Does it make a difference? Evaluating professional development. *Educational Leadership, 59,* 45–51.

Hattie, J. A. C. (2009). *Visible learning: A synthesis of over 800 meta-analyses relating to achievement.* London, UK: Routledge.

Heller, R., & Greenleaf, C. L. (2007). *Literacy instruction in the content areas: Getting to the core of middle and high school improvement.* Washington, DC: Alliance for Excellent Education.

Hollingsworth, S. (1994). *Teacher research and urban literacy education.* New York, NY: Teachers College Press.

Interactive Illinois Report Card. (2013). *Rockford SD 205.* Retrieved from http://iirc.niu.edu/ListDistricts.aspx

Kamil, M. L., Borman, G. D., Dole, J., Kral, C. C., Salinger, T., & Torgesen, J. (2008). *Improving adolescent literacy: Effective classroom and intervention practices: A practice guide* (NCEE #2008-4027). Washington, DC: National Center for Education Evaluation and Regional Assistance, Institute of Education Sciences, U.S. Department of Education. Retrieved from http://ies.ed.gov/ncee/wwc

Langer, J. A. (2002). *Effective literacy instruction: Building successful reading and writing programs.* Urbana, IL: National Council of Teachers of English.

McGraw, K. O., & Wong, S. P. (1992). A common language effect size statistic. *Psychological Bulletin, 111,* 361–365.

Mills, G. (2010). *Action research: A guide for the teacher researcher* (4th ed.). Upper Saddle River, NJ: Pearson.

National Association for Professional Development Schools. (2008). What it means to be a professional development school: A statement by the executive council and board of directors of the National Association of Professional Development Schools. *School–University Partnerships, 2,* 10–16.

National Council for Accreditation of Teacher Education. (2001). Standards for professional development schools. Retrieved from http://www.ncate.org/documents/pdsStandards.pdf

National Institute for Literacy. (2007). *What content-area teachers should know about adolescent literacy.* Washington, DC: Author.

National Reading Panel. (2000). *Teaching children to read: An evidence-based assessment of the scientific research literature on reading and its implications for reading instruction* (NIH Publication No. 00-4769). Washington, DC: U.S. Department of Health and Human Services, National Institute of Child Health and Human Development.

National Staff Development Council. (2001). *Standards for professional learning.* Retrieved from http://www.nsdc.org/standards/index.cfm

Pelton, R. (2010). *Making classroom inquiry work: Techniques for effective action research.* Lanham, MD: Rowman & Littlefield Education.

Pine, G. J. (2003). Making a difference: A professional development school's impact on student learning. In D. L. Wiseman & S. L. Knight (Eds.), *LINKING: School–university collaboration and K–12 student outcomes* (pp. 31–47). Washington, DC: American Association of Colleges for Teacher Education.

Snow, C. E., Burns, S., & Griffin, P. (1998). *Preventing reading difficulties in young children*. Washington, DC: National Academy Press.

Stringer, E. T. (2007). *Action research* (3rd ed.). Thousand Oaks, CA: Sage Publications.

Teitel, L. (2003). *The professional development schools handbook: Starting, sustaining, and assessing partnerships that improve student learning*. Thousand Oaks, CA: Corwin Press.

Timperley, H., Wilson, A., Barrar, H., & Fung, I. (2007). *Teacher professional learning and development: Best evidence synthesis iteration*. Wellington, New Zealand: Ministry of Education.

Tomlinson, C. (2008). *The differentiated school: Making revolutionary changes in teaching and learning*. Alexandria, VA: Association for Supervision and Curriculum Development.

Tomlinson, C., & Strickland, C. (2005). *Differentiation in practice: A resource guide for differentiated curriculum*. Alexandria, VA: Association for Supervision and Curriculum Development.

Wade, R. K. (1985). What makes a difference in inservice teacher education? A meta-analysis of research. *Educational Leadership, 42*, 48–54.

Walker, D. A., Downey, P. M., & Cox-Henderson, J. (2010). REAL camp: A school–university collaboration to promote post-secondary educational opportunities among high school students. *The Educational Forum, 74*, 297–304.

CHAPTER 16

PARTNERING TO STRENGTHEN THE TEACHING OF FOUNDATIONAL LITERACY SKILLS

Katherine Egan Cunningham

ABSTRACT

This chapter describes a three-year research study on a foundational literacy skills professional development initiative at a PDS and its outcomes for teachers, student teachers, and students. Based on criteria outlined by the Common Core State Standards, foundational literacy skills include print concepts, phonological awareness, phonics and word recognition, and fluency. While these foundational skills are not an end in themselves, they are an essential component of an effective, comprehensive literacy program designed to support students in becoming independent and proficient readers with increasingly complex texts. The author discusses how the teaching of foundational literacy skills remains one of the greatest needs for teachers at the kindergarten through second-grade levels, particularly for teachers working with culturally, linguistically, and economically diverse student populations. The PDS partnership's focus on building and sustaining intellectual capital

Creating Visions for University-School Partnerships, pages 259–279.
Copyright © 2014 by Information Age Publishing
All rights of reproduction in any form reserved.
259

became the central catalyst for the foundational skills initiative. The PDS liaison was instrumental in (1) lending support to both teachers and administrators, and (2) directing teachers to navigate through dilemmas as they learned about new methodologies and how these and their beliefs about literacy impact student learning. The author concludes that by partnering to strengthen the knowledge and skills of teachers within classrooms, the knowledge and skills of teacher candidates can also be strengthened through observation and guided practice.

RECONSIDERING PROFESSIONAL DEVELOPMENT WITHIN THE PROFESSIONAL DEVELOPMENT SCHOOL (PDS) THROUGH AN EARLY LITERACY FOCUS

Collaboration between schools and institutions of higher education (IHEs) in the preparation of future teachers and in the growth of current teachers requires openness, flexibility, and innovation. As partnerships change to meet the demands of today's educational climate, four goals found across the literature on PDS partnerships remain: (1) the improvement of student learning, (2) the preparation of educators, (3) the professional development of educators, and (4) research and inquiry into improving practice (Teitel, 1998). As the educational landscape shifts to meet the demands of an increasingly global, competitive world with college and career readiness on the forefront of partners' minds, the need for ongoing, job-embedded professional development is of increasing importance. It is through an emphasis on professional development that teachers and teacher candidates can gain access to methods—not only to meet new state mandates and new state testing measures but, ultimately, to better support the learning of K–12 students.

With the introduction and implementation of the Common Core State Standards (CCSS), there has been a critical eye towards the teaching and learning of foundational literacy skills as a necessary and important component of an effective, comprehensive literacy program. Foundational literacy skills include print concepts, phonological awareness, phonics and word recognition, and fluency. However, research has shown that teachers typically do not receive adequate preparation at the preservice level in the reading process or how to teach foundational literacy skills (Bos, Mather, Dickson, Podhajski, & Chard, 2001; Moats, 2010). With the onset of the CCSS, many school leaders have been left wondering if they are prepared to support their teachers and students, particularly in the foundational skills that are fundamental to preventing reading difficulties across the grade levels. At the same time, IHEs have been assessing and refining their courses to better prepare teacher candidates to understand and implement these new standards with methods that are research-based.

This chapter details a research study conducted over three years by the faculty member who was the PDS liaison to assess the implementation of a new foundational literacy skills initiative at Benjamin Franklin Elementary School (pseudonym), a school with a high population of culturally, linguistically, and economically diverse students. The context for this study came out of a growing need in the school to support teachers as they reconsidered what was working in their literacy curriculum and what was missing to support their students, especially their English language learners, as growing readers and writers. Increasingly, the concern returned to foundational literacy skills and the need for greater teacher knowledge on methods of instruction at the kindergarten through second-grade levels. These concerns were addressed in the PDS leadership committee, which recommended the Reading Reform Foundation of New York (RRF) (Rose & Nelson, 2012) to provide training and ongoing consulting twice a week, focusing on how to implement multisensory methods for foundational literacy skill development. Multisensory teaching is simultaneously visual, auditory, and kinesthetic-tactile to enhance memory and learning. With this professional development model, RRF consultants train teachers in a structured, sequential approach of multisensory instruction. The educational philosophy of the RRF is one that: (1) is child-centered; (2) sets high expectations; (3) aligns purpose and meaning; (4) emphasizes higher-level thinking skills; (5) is a direct, sequential form of instruction; (6) requires active participation by all students; (7) stems from diagnostic approaches; and (8) integrates reading, writing, speaking, and listening.

Through the PDS partnership, a professional development model was created whereby a RRF consultant supported two classroom teachers each year through one-on-one mentoring, in-class modeling, and one-on-one debriefing twice a week for a full school year. Research shows that in-depth, continuing professional development for teachers that helps them learn and apply scientific, research-supported methods is critical to improving reading achievement and preventing reading difficulties in students (Foorman & Moats, 2004; Snow, Burns, & Griffin, 2005). The goals of the training were that the teachers learned how to explicitly teach (1) accurate speech; (2) conventional spelling; (3) analysis of vocabulary as to sounds, spelling rules, syllabication and meaning; (4) sentence structure; (5) oral reading with expression; (6) comprehension; and (7) automaticity with letter formation.

Research was conducted to investigate how this specialized model of professional development impacted the teachers' instructional methods and beliefs about student literacy learning, as well as student teachers' understandings of foundational skills within literacy learning. The research process offered a vehicle for reflection and the opportunity to engage in collaborative conversations about their experiences with other teachers and the researcher. By opening up spaces to reflect on their experiences, the teachers in this study had the opportunity to consider ways in which they could advance their literacy teaching practices. Following the study, the teachers continued to open up dialogue about their experiences to inform future pedagogy and, ultimately, to further the comprehensive literacy instruction they strive for at the school as a PDS. Data were collected, organized, and analyzed to assess the benefits of the training and how the results could impact teacher preparation in the college's courses for literacy methods, literacy specialism, and early childhood.

Reconsidering curriculum, methods, and assessment is not a seamless process; however, as the teachers in this study considered what skills that they and their students were missing, the school needed support from the PDS partnership to navigate the dilemmas that surfaced from this type of focused, highly specialized professional development. This chapter details the process of reconsidering curriculum and instruction and of challenging beliefs systems about teaching and learning that come from a professional development model that required ongoing commitment and inquiry on the part of classroom teachers particularly with respect to supporting their culturally, linguistically, and particularly economically diverse students.

BUILDING AND SUSTAINING INTELLECTUAL CAPITAL WITHIN THE PDS

Used as a term primarily in business (but also in psychology and sociology), *intellectual capital* is the collective knowledge of the individuals in an organization that enhances its value to others (Stewart, 1999). Basile (2009) states, "In professional development schools, managing intellectual capital is even more imperative, as there are more resources, systems, and knowledge to manage" (p. 2). Based on Basile's model, Figure 16.1 represents the intellectual capital that was generated as a result of the PDS decision to invest in the foundational literacy skills of its K–2 learners. With guidance and commitment from the school principal and the PDS liaison, the PDS leadership committee launched the initial interest in focusing PDS energy on foundational literacy skills based on low test scores from standardized tests and internal literacy measures.

The PDS liaison became instrumental in creating *internal capital* conceptualizing how the partnership with RRF program would be managed and facilitated within its first year of implementation and then throughout the multiyear model of training for all of the early childhood classroom teachers. The training was limited to two teachers per year, strategically giving the school time to adjust to new methods of foundational literacy skills instruction and an opportunity to create structural and cultural change. As Basile (2009) states, "The more you build intellectual capital, the more you increase growth and competence and create cultural change" (p. 2).

The RRF program provided the *external capital* through the resources it provided for the success of the initiative. Resources included the teacher trainers who were knowledgeable in early literacy acquisition and morphology, the sequential curriculum they provided, and the methods they modeled and guided teachers to master. In addition, the RRF program provided two weeks of training over the summer prior to the onsite coaching that focused on language and literacy acquisition in reading, writing, and spelling.

Human capital was seen through the teachers' investment in learning new instructional strategies, curricula, and methods so that they could develop their skills and knowledge through professional learning. Basile (2009) proposes that the primary themes in building human capital include "relationships, collaboration, and professional learning—all integral to the success of the foundational literacy skills initiative" (p. 75). Without the relationships between the PDS leadership committee, the PDS liaison, the school principal, and the RRF leadership team and coaches, the model would not have been successful. Once strong relationships were established, collaboration became key for questions to be posed and answered, for doubts to surface and be relieved, and for sustained learning for

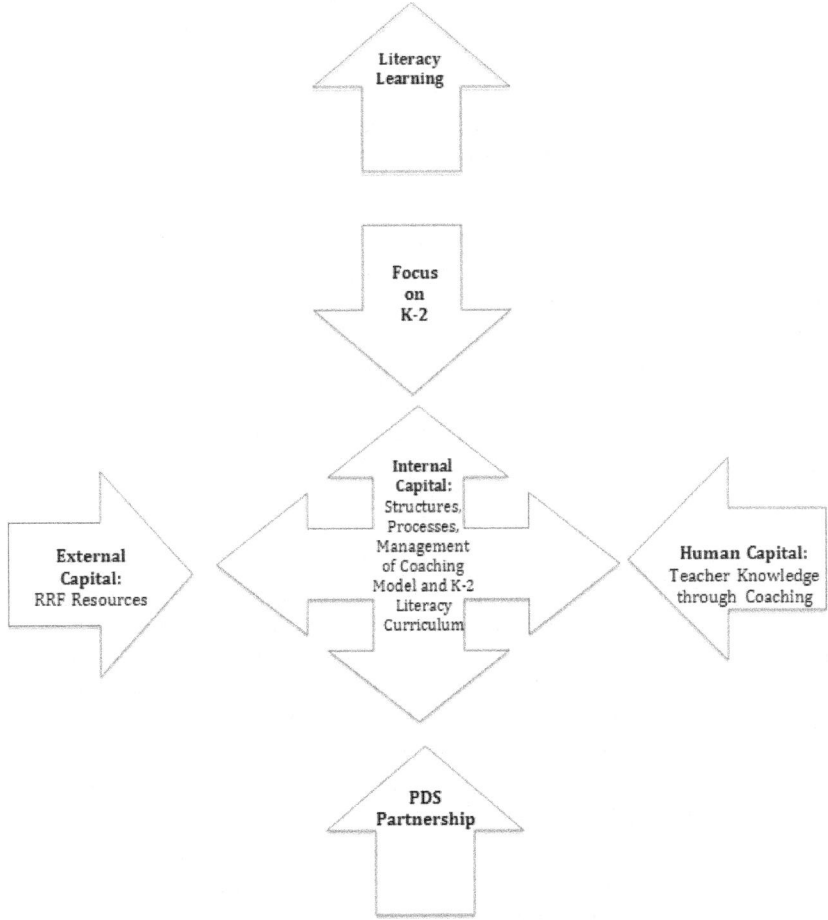

FIGURE 16.1. Intellectual capital through the foundational literacy skills initiative.

the teachers. The collaborative spirit created was crucial to the success of the initiative and its ability to impact school culture and curricular change. Professional learning came from a variety of sources to build human capital. It came from RRF trainers, but it also came through conversations with the PDS liaison as a vested member of the PDS leadership team and as a researcher investigating the process and outcomes of the initiative. Most importantly, perhaps, was the professional learning that came out of teacher–teacher connections as they engaged as learners together.

Building intellectual capital is a community-wide opportunity. As Basile (2009) explained, external capital can provide the resources; internal capital can provide the systems and processes to ensure that partnership activities are organized and understood. However, ultimately it is the human capital that will make the greatest impact. It was the teachers' willingness to grow and change to support student learning that was critical to the success of this focus on foundational literacy skills at the early grade levels.

THE BUILDING BLOCKS OF LITERACY
LEARNING TO OPEN DOORS

The teaching of reading and writing has been a politicized topic for decades with some teachers who advocate for an emphasis on the mastery of discrete sets of skills while others advocate for literacy as a social practice. This research is informed by arguments made by Delpit (2006), who defined "literacy skills" as: "useful and usable knowledge which contributes to a student's ability to communicate effectively in standard, generally acceptable forms" (p. 18). Delpit further explained that "skills are a necessary but insufficient aspect of Black and minority students' education. Students need technical skills to open doors, but they need to be able to think critically and creatively to participate in meaningful and potentially liberating work inside those doors" (p. 19). The teachers in this study were negotiating these tensions and worked to consider the methods they used in the past, how effective they were, and what was missing from their literacy curriculum and instruction to best support their students. The PDS partnership was committed to supporting students to think critically and creatively across subject areas through various partnership activities. However, through the PDS leadership committee, questions began to surface about whether the students had the foundational skills necessary to read and write at high levels and what the PDS relationship could do to support a new initiative.

The PDS leadership committee was committed to renewed attention on the literacy learning of its youngest learners and giving teachers the support they needed, but there was also a concern for the knowledge and skills teacher candidates could gain through their experiences in the school. Research on teacher education programs executed by the National Council on Teacher Quality (2006) found that teachers must incorporate particular research-based practices to prevent reading failure:

- Early identification of children at risk of reading failure
- Daily training in linguistic and oral skills to build awareness of speech sounds, or phonemes
- Explicit instruction in letter sounds, syllables, and words accompanied by explicit instruction in spelling
- Teaching phonics in the sequence that research has found leads to the least amount of confusion
- Practicing skills to the point of "automaticity" so that children do not have to think about sounding out a word when they need to focus on meaning

The PDS saw the opportunity this initiative had to support its students, teachers, and teacher candidates with research-based practices and to build greater consistency with the teaching of foundational literacy skills.

The teachers who participated in this study were seeking professional learning opportunities to provide their students with a more consistent, systematic approach to foundational literacy skills, and they themselves wanted to better understand the roots of the English language—something in which they did not have a strong foundation from their teacher preparation coursework or previous forms of professional development. The teachers all recognized, however, that their students' mastery of skills was not the end goal, but that it was a necessary foundation that would open doors for their students to engage creatively and critically with words and the world. In this way, the PDS partnership could continue to simultaneously spearhead initiatives that fostered critical and creative engagement across subject areas strengthened with a new investment in what structures and resources were needed to provide a more systematic approach to the teaching of foundational literacy skills.

TEACHING READING TO ENGLISH LANGUAGE LEARNERS

The teachers in this study were seeking to create an interactive reading process model in their classrooms and recognized the need for an integrated approach to phonics instruction rather than a scripted, commercial program so that they could tailor instruction to the developmental and linguistic needs of their students and honor the literacies students had in their native languages (Herrera, Perez, & Escamilla, 2010; Reutzel & Cooter, 2005; Vacca, Vacca, & Grove, 2012). In this way, the methods they were implementing included reading, writing, speaking, and listening with an understanding that phonics knowledge is developmental, requires teacher decision making, is important not for itself but in its application, and should not overshadow or supplant other facets of reading instruction (Dahl, Scharer, Lawson, & Grogan, 2001). Consistent with research on English language learners, the foundational literacy skills lessons the teachers implemented during their word study block were then integrated into their guided reading groups, one-on-one reading and writing conferences, shared reading, and interactive writing lessons to support students to build on their existing background knowledge and expedite the process of learning to read and write in English (Vaughn & Linan-Thompson, 2004).

Supported by research, the teachers in this study continued to engage their culturally and linguistically diverse students in rich literacy experiences with authentic texts, providing a contextual frame of reference that meaningfully connects foundational literacy skills activities to the reading and writing process.

The PDS partnership provided a series of collaborative meetings between teachers engaged in RRF training. As such, they were able to form a network to pose questions and consider possibilities about how to integrate the multisensory approaches they were learning into an already existing balanced literacy program to best support English language learners. With support of the PDS liaison, the teachers in this study considered how the multisensory methods they were learning could be utilized throughout the day. The teachers supported one another with collaboration with liaison; as lessons were developed they considered how particular phonograms in English were connected to knowledge students already had from their first language.

PURPOSE

The purpose of this research study was threefold. First, the goal was to open dialogue and keep record of the possible benefits as well as the possible challenges the teachers encountered as they underwent professional development that emphasized multisensory methods for the teaching of foundational literacy skills. In addition, the teachers were supported through the PDS to consider how to embed foundational literacy skills across the curriculum through an integrated approach. This research was to identify and give voice to their views and ideas. In addition, another purpose was to identify how the professional development model in which they were engaged was impacting students' foundational literacy skills acquisition. Finally, the results of the study were analyzed to inform the further development of the literacy courses at the college and whether or not to incorporate greater emphasis on the teaching of foundational skills to better support teacher candidates in becoming highly skilled language arts teachers and literacy leaders in K–12 schools, particularly in schools with culturally and linguistically diverse students.

RESEARCH DESIGN

Context for the Study

Kindergarten, first-, and second-grade teachers at Benjamin Franklin Elementary School participated in the training on how to teach foundational literacy skills through multisensory methods. Although the teachers all had master's degrees and were veterans of the field, they discovered that they were implementing literacy methods that were not addressing the needs of the students in their classrooms. Benjamin Franklin Elementary is a school in a changing suburb outside a major metropolitan area. According to district sources, the school's student population is 93% Latino heritage with 39% limited English proficiency, and 85% of the children are eligible for reduced or free lunch. District-mandated reading assessments conducted by the teachers showed that across grade levels, only 40% of students were at grade level in reading. At Benjamin Franklin Elementary there was a need for the PDS to provide support that could increase the teachers' understanding of the reading process and the structure of language and that could simultaneously strengthen their classroom methods of instruction to better meet the needs of students. The PDS provided a pathway for specialized coaching to become a reality. Funding for the initiative came out of the PDS budget and provided a sustainable way for the school to commit to a coaching model rather than prepackaged curriculum that the teachers would need to understand and implement with limited support. This training not only benefitted the teachers and students at Benjamin Franklin Elementary, but it also benefitted student teachers implementing the literacy methods they learned through classroom observations and guided practice along with teacher candidates engaged in field-based literacy methods courses.

The literacy instruction at Benjamin Franklin Elementary School was undergoing significant curricular revision at the time of the study. While the school was working to become more streamlined in its approach to its language arts curriculum, it was looking for ways to best support its students as growing readers. The school had a commitment, led by the principal, to balanced literacy methods. Throughout the year, the teachers engaged students in the following components of the workshop model:

- Reader's workshop
  - Mini-lesson
  - Student practice/strategy groups/individual conferencing
  - Wrap Up
- Guided reading groups/literacy workstations
- Read-alouds
- Shared reading
- Writer's workshop
  - Mini-lesson
  - Student practice/strategy groups/individual conferencing
  - Wrap up
- Interactive writing
- Shared writing

While a workshop approach remained the heart of the literacy learning, there was a strong need for a more systematic approach to the foundations skills required for students to become successful readers and writers. The word study component of the day varied throughout the school and included multisensory methods in some classrooms and packaged programs in others, with teachers relying on past experiences and personal workshops attended rather than a consistent and unified approach to the teaching of foundational literacy skills. In addition, the teachers were not accustomed to integrating the teaching of foundational literacy skills throughout the literacy block and saw word study as an isolated time of the day.

The school was seeking a stronger approach to the teaching of foundational literacy skills, supporting teachers with methods that could be integrated through meaningful literacy engagements throughout the day to support their culturally and linguistically diverse students. The strategic plan for the school is to incorporate sheltered instruction observation protocol (SIOP) methods for English language learners across all classrooms over the next five years to support the teachers and students with literacy and language research-based practices. The school is also committed to incorporating more multicultural and culturally responsive authentic children's literature into classroom libraries, with an emphasis on Latino-centered selections for read-alouds as well as bilingual leveled books for independent reading and small group instruction to foster literacy and biliteracy development for second language learners. Further, workshops for families on how to support children as readers, writers, speakers, and listeners at home are routinely conducted each year in partnership with PDS constituents to foster the home–school connection. Incorporating multisensory methods for the teaching of foundational literacy skills was one component of the overall strategic plan for literacy teaching and learning.

Participants

Classroom Teachers

Each year two teachers were chosen within a grade level to participate in the training and coaching of multisensory foundational skills methods with the RRF program. In the first year of this study, two first-grade teachers were trained. Both teachers were veterans of the school with eight or more years of experience at their grade level and in the school, and both were members of the PDS leadership team. They took an active role every year of the study and provided feedback during their initial year of coaching and then in their second year of independently carrying out the instructional strategies they learned. In the second year of this study, two second-grade teachers were trained. Again, both teachers were veterans of the school with at least five years of experience at their grade level and in the school. One of the teachers was on the PDS leadership team and the other was routinely a cooperating teacher for teacher candidates. The third year of this study, two kindergarten teachers were trained. One teacher had returned to the kindergarten level after many years in upper elementary grades, and the second teacher had been a kindergarten teacher for two years.

The author of the study met with the teachers at the start of each school year to discuss the research goals and expectations and to identify their initial beliefs about literacy learning and their interest in the foundational literacy skills training. In addition, the author met with each team of teachers throughout the year to provide a philosophical bridge between the school and the professional development team. In the second and third year of the study, the author was the PDS liaison and served dual roles in the implementation of the RRF work as both coordinator and researcher.

Student Teachers

Four student teachers who were placed with kindergarten and first-grade classroom teachers undergoing RRF training were included in surveys and collaborative conversations about the methods.

Data Sources

As coaching in explicit multisensory approaches to the teaching of foundational literacy skills took place, data were collected to understand the impact the training had on the teachers' instructional methods, assessment, and beliefs about literacy learning. Data were collected to analyze how the teachers saw the impact the training had on their students' literacy learning documented through periodic assessments.

The following research methods were used to collect data:

- Pre- and post-training survey questions
- Reflective journaling conducted by the teachers every month (calendar agreed upon by researcher and participants) submitted electronically
- Collaborative conversations between teachers and grade-level teams facilitated by researcher
- Teachers' anecdotal notes from small group instruction and one-on-one conferences with students
- Student reading assessment data

As the data were analyzed, results were shared with the classroom teachers to better understand the teachers' reactions to the multisensory training, to better support future cohorts of teachers trained, and to consider the impact of the results on the literacy courses conducted at the college. In addition, data were shared at the end of each school year with the RRF team leaders, the PDS leadership committee, and the Benjamin Franklin Elementary School administration as they continued to work collaboratively alongside the college to further enhance the literacy vision for the school.

FINDINGS

Openness to Learn

The heart of the literacy initiative through the PDS was the investment in the human capital of the teachers. The implementation of the initiative required an ongoing commitment from the teachers to consider new instructional strategies, professionally engage with a specialized coach, and share their thoughts within a professional learning community. Through the roles the researcher played as a literacy specialist and PDS liaison, questions were asked, issues of implementation were discussed, and the teachers remained open to learn. With the PDS relationship established, the researcher provided a go-between for the teachers, the principal, and the RRF coaches.

At the start of this study, the kindergarten and first-grade teachers (Teachers A,B, C, and D) reflected in their pre-training surveys that their strengths as literacy educators were that they created a community of learners in their classrooms, had strong classroom management techniques, and were engaging teachers. The second-grade teachers (Teachers E and F) felt that their strengths as literacy educators were that they were engaging teachers who were growing in their understanding of assessing and using data to inform instruction. While the teachers recognized their strengths, they also responded in the pre-training surveys that they were all hoping to gain more techniques for how to help struggling readers who were not succeeding with the school's current interventions from this experience. Teachers specifically cited in their pre-training surveys "phonics, phonemic awareness, and writing" as the areas of instruction they most wanted to improve upon at the start of the coaching process.

As training began, the teachers reflected in their monthly journal entries that working with a foundational skills coach helped them to value the importance of baseline data to inform instruction—a critical component of what it means to be a highly skilled teacher according to their district evaluation system. Better understanding assessments on students' knowledge of phonograms became essential as they started the sequence of explicit instruction. In addition to providing planning support, the foundational skills coach modeled lessons, particularly in the first few weeks of the coaching relationship. One of the primary purposes of the modeling was to demonstrate when to incorporate fluent oral reading of extended text into the lesson. Fluency instruction improved oral reading fluency itself, especially in the first- and second-grade students, but it also had a positive impact on children's decoding, word recognition, silent-reading comprehension, and overall reading achievement in kindergarten through second grade according to internal literacy measures. The teachers all reflected on the supportive role the modeling played in their willingness to learn, to make mistakes, and to support their students in new ways.

Overall, throughout the reflective journal process, the consistency of the instructional routine was welcomed by all of the teachers, and they found the coach's modeling of techniques beneficial prior to their own delivery of this method of instruction. In post-training surveys, the teachers indicated that such a supportive coaching method was highly regarded as a highlight of the program and a signature aspect to their training in the RRF methods of instruction as compared to other methods of professional development that they had experienced in past years on a monthly or bimonthly basis.

An openness to learn about their own teaching became a catalyst for the two kindergarten teachers to engage in new ways with the PDS. One became a co-teacher of the literacy methods course held at the school. The other became a cooperating teacher after several years removed from that role. With an openness to learn, these two teachers sought ways to engage with other learners within the PDS.

Refining Beliefs

Collaborative conversations between the PDS liaison, classroom teachers undergoing training, and student teachers in classrooms where training was taking place were an essential component of the research. During the collaborative meetings, the teachers shared that having an onsite liaison and literacy specialist through the PDS relationship provided support for the teachers undergoing intensive coaching to question their own beliefs and assumptions about their teaching practices. During the collaborative conversations, the teachers discussed how the coaching in which the teachers were engaged reinforced their beliefs that English has particular rules that need to be explicitly taught for mastery and for the accumulation of knowledge that leads to deeper understanding of the reading process. The teachers found that by watching the methods impact student learning and hearing the impact in other classrooms, it confirmed their beliefs that phonemic awareness and phonics are critical foundations to a successful literacy program. Teacher F stated, "I know that literacy skills don't just happen all at once, and there is a dynamic flow to literacy development. Often one area develops faster than another (e.g., fluency versus comprehension), and we need to keep our eye on all elements to make each child's literacy profile as strong as possible." Teacher E found that the biggest impact on student learning was the "consistency of this approach and the common language that applied to every lesson." She found that phonics methods in the past touched upon skills but without a consistent approach. To set her students up for success, Teacher E decided to "embrace the method. I wanted to be the canvas. Do it their way. Trust it. I had to dedicate a lot of time but it was doable. This is concrete."

While some teachers embraced the process, others were initially critical of such an explicit approach to teaching and used the collaborative meetings with the PDS liaison and other grade level teachers to question the systematic methods to phonics instruction they were asked to implement. By the spring semester, across all three grade levels, the teachers came to recognize the importance of consistent, predictable routines during phonics instruction and the need for a sequential approach to introducing new lessons that were a result of the training. Teacher C, in particular, shared how the professional development process had a significant impact on her beliefs. She stated, "I'm a very creative teacher but when teaching how language works, I came to realize you can't be creative." This statement shows that her beliefs about when and how to be a creative teacher had to be readjusted as she realized that the systematic approach to delivering foundational skills to her students required a different approach than she was accustomed to using. The collaborative meetings provided an open forum for the sharing of ideas, particularly with regard to how to integrate multisensory methods across the balanced literacy structures, the opportunity to challenge, and a means to engage in dialogue about the foundational literacy skills methods they were being coached in. The PDS network was critical in supporting the teachers to question their own beliefs and practices to benefit student learning.

As teachers moved from the first year of implementation with onsite coaching into independent instruction, confidence with the methods became more apparent. Both first-grade teachers stated that they felt confident about implementing the multisensory methods in their second year and that delivering this type of instruction was now a strength of theirs. As Teacher D stated, "Reading reform has given me an in-depth understanding of spelling, phonics, and word study. It has given me concrete tools with which to teach my students and the knowledge of when and how to use them." In addition, Teacher D stated that reading reform methods continued to influence her beliefs about literacy learning: "I believe that classrooms need a balance of direct instruction and exploration. Reading reform has given me that direct instruction model that most of my students can access." Teacher D found that she was more purposeful in this second year of implementation at reinforcing the skills learned through the methods learned throughout the day.

Teachers also found that they needed to adjust their methods based on the skills and backgrounds of each set of students. Teacher A found that in her first year with multisensory methods, her students soared and could be found reenacting lessons in their free time. The next year's class had significantly greater academic needs, but she found the exposure to language through this method of instruction was "critical for all of her students." Teacher C found that her students needed more support beyond multisensory methods, and she created a chart that she posted in the classroom to help students acquire multiple sounds represented by one phonogram. She saw the benefits it afforded her English language learners and shared this approach with other grade-level teams during collaborative team meetings with the researcher.

It is expected that as the teams of teachers continue to come together to plan and implement multisensory methods within their integrated and balanced literacy program that their beliefs will continue to shift and be strengthened as they gain experience and confidence with a new set of tools for supporting their students.

Student Learning and Motivation

The investment in the intellectual capital through the PDS initiative was ultimately about sustained student learning. The direct, explicit instructional methods that the coaching model provided gave students the opportunity to practice and over practice with reteaching. This highly structured method gave students routines that were predictable and a curriculum with a sequenced plan that helped them develop literacy skills in reading and writing. The students were able to show what they understood not only during the word study segment of each day but also during small group and one-on-one conferences and in other components of the literacy block. Based on the shared reading of records from small group literacy instruction, one-on-one reading conference notes, and reading assessment data, the liaison alongside the classroom teachers found that students were more confident and that they were able to apply more print and comprehension strategies more consistently.

In Teacher D's classroom, students asked to practice the phonogram review and "play teacher" each Thursday afternoon during their afterschool program. The students' initiative to use the time to instruct each other using specific methods the teachers had learned and implemented in their classrooms showed the students' motivation to review and reteach each other using a structure they could synthesize and then apply themselves.

Teacher C reported in post-survey data that her students' strengths were now in their receptive and expressive identification of phonograms and rules as evidenced in isolated lessons and in informal reading assessments. In addition, Teacher E reported in post-survey data that her students were more confident and that they were able to apply more strategies consistently across genres. She explained,

> The application of these skills was seen throughout the day. Their spelling greatly improved. They each showed confidence in trying to spell words in a way that I never saw before. This helped their writing fluency and stamina. They knew to use phonograms when spelling words. You also see how the second graders have succeeded with writing and spelling through this approach when you view their student work in the hallways.

Teacher E further discussed gains in explicit language. "When you tell students 'say it as you write it' versus 'read the word' when they are attempting to spell something, you are providing more concrete specific language that they can understand, remember, and apply." She found that this method moved beyond word families, which was the greatest gain her second graders previously understood about phonics. As she said, "There is so much that doesn't make sense in English. The methods we learned provide firm guidelines for students to understand what makes sense and what doesn't."

In addition to print and comprehension-strategy acquisition, the teachers turned their focus to oral language development, which is particularly critical for linguistically diverse students. The teachers indicated across grade levels in post-training surveys that oral language improved as they looked back at informal teacher anecdotal notes. This was largely attributed to the focus on speaking in complete sentences and greater consideration of vocabulary instruction that was emphasized during the foundational literacy skills coaching sessions.

The teachers all found that students were able to demonstrate on informal reading assessments and in daily practice greater skills as readers, writers, and speakers. Overall, students made greater strides more quickly and retained what they had learned. During initial collaborative meetings, teachers in grades one and two at the start of each school year found that the students needed less review of phonics lessons, and they were able to pick up with more advanced foundational reading skills consistent with the CCSS.

As analysis was conducted of reading, spelling, and writing assessment data across the three years of the study it was found that:

- First-grade classrooms that have had teachers trained show greater student growth in reading and comprehension than classrooms that did not receive training—first grade being a critical year for early reading development and one of the targeted grades this coming school year.
- First-grade classrooms that were trained had an overall average of 88% for oral reading fluency accuracy (the accuracy of how children read individual letters and words aloud words).
- Kindergarten classrooms that had teachers trained showed greater class percentages reaching benchmark status for early reading skills.
- In kindergarten, 54 out of 76 children received benchmark status for their early reading skill development (letter naming/words read correctly).
- The kindergarten classroom that had a teacher who had been trained in RRF methods had 21 out of 25 children reach benchmark status for their early reading skill development.
- Students across kindergarten through second grade are showing progress as readers, spellers, speakers, and listeners.
- Improved spelling was seen in weekly spelling assessments as well as in student writing in first and second grade.
- Students were able to write for longer periods of time and with greater independence as they applied letters and sounds they had learned.
- Students spoke in complete sentences with greater regularity.

As students continue into grades that incorporate standardized testing measures, research through the PDS partnership will be conducted to analyze whether the attention given to K–2 foundational literacy skills seems to be impacting student success on statewide measures. In addition, as teachers switch grades and schools, the PDS partnership is supporting the continued training of teachers at the K–2 levels to ensure continued success with the multisensory methods being implemented in the classrooms.

Moving Towards an Integrated Approach for English Language Learners

As the teachers gained skills in multisensory methods for teaching foundational reading skills, the teachers were able to incorporate foundational skill building into other blocks of the day using literature and content material. Across the grades, the teachers reported that they introduced and reinforced letter recognition, beginning and ending sounds, blends, rhyming words, silent letters, and homonyms. Learning multisensory methods that incorporate reading, writing, speaking, and listening provided the teachers with the tools and routines to ask students during small group instruction and during writing conferences to listen carefully and write what they hear using the phonograms they had been taught previously.

In addition, the teachers also supported one another during planning sessions to critically consider the words they were using during their word study block to demonstrate phonograms. They became more conscious of the need for words to be part of their students' oral vocabulary prior to reading instruction. Particularly in grades one and two, the teachers were more purposeful in their methods for vocabulary instruction as it related to foundational literacy skill development and they became more planned in which words to preteach prior to word study lessons. Teachers C, D, E, and F discussed providing students with opportunities to recognize when and how to use new words, their multiple meanings, and how to use words accurately in different contexts prior to instruction on how to decode and spell the word. Part of the coaching process was designed to give the teachers an awareness of morphology and the roots of the English language. All of the teachers reported both in collaborative meetings and in survey responses that as their understandings of morphology grew, they were better able to integrate foundational skills development across the day as well as better support their English language learners.

Supporting Student Teachers with a Specialized Skill

The PDS foundational literacy skills initiative was primarily focused on classroom teachers at the K–2 levels. However, teacher candidates placed in classrooms with teachers undergoing coaching or previously trained in the methods of RRF benefitted from the methods they observed and were able to actively implement through guided practice. All four student teachers undergoing teacher training at Benjamin Franklin indicated in their final surveys that the RRF methods were beneficial to student learning in the Benjamin Franklin setting. One student teacher felt it had had an "immense impact" and another found "dramatically improved" results during guided reading over the course of the semester in the classroom. All of the student teachers found that RRF methods improved classroom management, impacting reading, writing, and handwriting.

Of all of the methods they experienced in the K–2 setting, all of the student teachers surveyed found that the greatest impact on their development as language arts teachers was learning how to teach phonogram sounds. They all reflected in their surveys on the intense, direct instruction and found application especially useful for students with language-based learning disabilities as well as English language learners. Two candidates had some introduction to instruction of language essentials and phonics through their initial literacy methods course.

Two candidates had no previous exposure to multisensory methods of instruction. All of the student teachers found that as a result of their placements, they had an in-depth understanding of the structures of English and multisensory methods of instruction. Since the start of the RRF training, two student teachers have been hired in the school as a full-time classroom teacher and as a leave replacement. Their knowledge of the multisensory methods being used at the K–2 levels has helped with their transition to supporting students in their own classrooms.

INTERPRETATIONS

The coaching model in which the teachers engaged required PDS support, particularly as dilemmas surfaced tied to the teachers' recognition of their needs. The following steps outline these dilemmas and the steps taken for other PDS partnerships to consider as they support each other's initiatives to improve student achievement as well as teacher preparation through innovative professional development initiatives.

Step 1 was recognizing a need. Previous data from both reading assessments conducted by the teachers and standardized test results showed that decoding and comprehension remained areas of need across grade levels in the school. Professional development in the past had been isolated and district-mandated rather than school-generated. The teachers in this study had previously been exposed to many different programs and philosophies and had to blend these approaches for the benefit of their students. The PDS leadership team was able to come together to analyze data, recognize areas where their students needed support, and consider recent research on early literacy skills.

Step 2 was being open to change. As a PDS, the partners came together to discuss whether or not the students were not demonstrating decoding and comprehension skills because the teachers were not trained in how to deliver sequential lessons in the code-breaking required for fluent, accurate reading. Both the building leaders and the classroom teachers were open to learning and open to the curricular change that went along with it. As some of the teachers underwent the professional development process, they discussed struggles to let go of past methods and hold on to certain practices. Other teachers let go of past practices and fully embraced the methods they were being taught and felt that they needed to follow their coach's modeling without deviation. In every case, however, the teachers needed to be open and willing to add new practices in a consistent way for the initiative to provide a common foundation across classrooms and grade level. The PDS support team, principal, liaison, consisting of the leadership team, principal, and liaison were there to support teachers throughout the process.

Step 3 was recognizing vulnerability. As coaching began, the classroom teachers at Benjamin Franklin Elementary voiced that they did not have the practices to best support their students as growing readers working to decode, comprehend, and fluently read in a second language. The ongoing professional development the teachers received through this new coaching was designed help them recognize that reading is a multifaceted skill gradually acquired over years of instruction and practice and that foundational literacy skills must be taught alongside rich literacy experiences with authentic text. As teachers face changes in meeting new standards, as well as changes to their evaluation systems, it is, perhaps, becoming increasingly more difficult for teachers to voice what areas they need support as professionals who are often in the position of defending their practices. This initiative and research process fostered a growth model of what it means to be a teacher—that teachers are lead learners. This requires considerable recognition for the vulnerability in which teachers and school leaders are placed, and higher education PDS partners can be there to offer support and guidance during the potential curricular and methodological changes schools are facing.

Step 4 was supporting teachers and teacher candidates to reflect on their core beliefs. Supporting teacher candidates to establish their core beliefs as teachers remains one of the college's primary goals, particularly during the student teaching process. As many schools navigate new terrain with new standards, new teacher evaluation systems, new state testing measures, and changing student demographics, the incorporation of new instructional practices is likely to occur across subject domains. As the partnership continues to prepare teacher candidates to take over their own classrooms, it is increasingly clear that a strong sense of one's beliefs amidst change is essential, along with a willingness to challenge one's own beliefs, particularly when one's practices need to be reconsidered. The PDS often provides a safety net for teachers and teacher candidates to question their beliefs and assumptions and consider research-based practices to best support K–12 students that "traditional" professional development does not.

DISCUSSION

In gathering the teachers' reflections, it became increasingly clear that the methods that teachers were implementing in their classrooms supported a critical need in the school to better understand the foundational skills required for early readers. Establishing a comprehensive literacy program that provides multisensory pathways for foundational literacy skills, in addition to the strong reading and writing workshop methods the teachers already used, created a more balanced program where students could become fluent readers *and* strong meaning-makers. After all, reading is about more than decoding—it's about understanding (Allington, 2011; Harvey & Goudvis, 2007; Neuman & Gambrell, 2013). One reads and writes to participate in the world and to engage in the ideas of others (Freire & Macedo, 1987). As the study was completed, the teachers continued to report that to support their students as readers and writers, it will require continued explicit, systematic instruction of foundational skills *coupled* with integrated learning opportunities that expose students to close reading of complex texts and reading and writing in meaningful contexts.

As a PDS team, the partners continue to look at how the literacy program connects to goals the school, district, and state have for 21ˢᵗ-century students. As the

CCSS begins to take a greater foothold, the question of how to teach foundational literacy skills will continue to be considered, particularly for schools that have not had systematic approaches in the past. However, the standards themselves make it clear that the mastery of foundational skills is not an end in itself. Having a strong base in foundational reading and writing skills enables students to engage more easily with complex texts and to participate as readers and writers in the world.

As colleges and universities continue to support PDS schools in unpacking the standards, the PDS network can continue to consider how to support teachers and administrators in what it means to be a literate person in the 21st century, beginning in kindergarten and spiraling up through the grades, and particularly addressing the development language and literacy needs of culturally, linguistically, and economically diverse students. Researchers in PDS schools can support schools to continue to consider what is working within their existing curriculum and instructional methods to increase student achievement (Abdal-Haqq, 1998; Knight, Wiseman, & Cooner, 2000), where the gaps lie, and how to create partnership opportunities that benefit teachers, teacher candidates, and students. Future research is needed to document how the PDS is impacting not only teachers beliefs and instructional practices but how PDS initiatives are impacting students' perceptions of themselves as learners as well as their achievement on internal and standardized measures.

REFERENCES

Abdal-Haqq, I. (1998). *Professional development schools: Weighing the evidence*. Thousand Oaks, CA: Sage.

Allington, R. (2011). *What really matters for struggling readers: Designing research-based programs*. New York, NY: Pearson.

Basile, C. (Ed.). (2009). *Intellectual capital: The intangible assets of professional development schools*. Albany, NY: State University of New York Press.

Bos, C., Mather, N., Dickson, S., Podhajski, B., & Chard, D. (2001). Perceptions and knowledge of preservice and inservice educators about early reading instruction. *Annals of Dyslexia, 51*, 98–120.

Dahl, K. L., Scharer, P. L., Lawson, L. L., & Grogan, P. R. (2001). *Rethinking phonics: Making the best teaching decisions*. Portsmouth, NH: Heinemann.

Delpit, L. (2006). *Other people's children: Cultural conflict in the classroom* (2nd ed.). New York: The New Press.

Foorman, B. R., & Moats, L. C. (2004). Conditions for sustaining research-based practices in early reading instruction. *Remedial and Special Education, 25*(1), 51–60.

Freire, P., & Macedo, D. (1987). *Literacy: Reading the word and the world*. Westport, CT: Bergin & Harvey.

Harvey, S., & Goudvis, A. (2007). *Strategies that work: Teaching comprehension for understanding and engagement*. Portland, ME: Stenhouse.

Herrera, S. G., Perez, D. R., & Escamilla, K. (2010). *Teaching reading to English language learners: Differentiated literacies.* New York, NY: Allyn & Bacon.

Knight, S. L., Wiseman, D. L., & Cooner, D. (2000). Using collaborative teacher research to determine the impact of professional development school activities on elementary students' math and writing outcomes. *Journal of Teacher Education, 51*(1), 26–38.

Moats, L. (2010). *Speech to print: Language essentials for teachers* (2nd ed.). Baltimore, MD: Paul H. Brookes Publishing.

National Council on Teacher Quality. (2006). *What education schools aren't teaching about reading and what elementary teachers aren't learning.* Washington, DC: National Council on Teacher Quality.

Neuman, S., & Gambrell, L. (Eds.). (2013). *Quality reading instruction in the age of Common Core Standards.* Newark, DE: International Reading Association.

Reutzel, D. R., & Cooter, R. B., Jr. (2000). *Teaching children to read: Putting the pieces together.* Upper Saddle River, NJ: Prentice-Hall.

Rose, S. P., & Nelson, G. (2012). *Sunday is for the sun, Monday is for the moon: Teaching reading, one teacher and thirty children at a time.* New York, NY: CreateSpace Independent Publishing Platform.

Snow, C. E., Burns, M. S., & Griffin, P. (Eds.). (2005). *Knowledge to support the teaching of reading: Preparing teachers for a changing world.* San Francisco, CA: Jossey-Bass Education Series.

Stewart, T. A. (1999). *Intellectual capital.* New York, NY: Currency.

Teitel, L. (1998). Professional development schools: A literature review. In M. Levine (Ed.), *Designing standards that work for professional development schools* (pp. 33–80). Washington, DC: PDS Standards Project, NCATE.

Vacca, J. L, Vacca, R. T., Gove, M. K., Burkey, L. C., Lenhart, L. C., & McKeon, C. A. (2012). *Reading and learning to read.* New York, NY: Pearson.

Vaughn, S., & Linan-Thompson, S. (2004). *Research-based methods of reading instruction.* Alexandria, VA: Association for Supervision and Curriculum Development.

PART IV

FAMILY ENGAGEMENT

CHAPTER 17

SUPPORTING MATHEMATICS LEARNING IN A PDS NETWORK

The Parents' Perspective

Jeanne Tunks and Julie Williams

ABSTRACT

A PDS network that includes a university college of education and a single school district recognized a need to engage Latino parents and children in community mathematics learning events. From this need, Fiesta Math Night / Fiesta de Noche de Matematicas was formed through the collaborative efforts of teachers, PDS interns, and university personnel. This event, held for the past six years, served approximately 7,000 parents and children. In the final year of the project, 2012, parents who attended were observed, completed surveys, and were interviewed. Results of the data analysis indicated that parents' perspectives of the events were positive, primarily because the parents were engaged in a fun, inclusive, and culturally relevant mathematics learning environment with their children.

Creating Visions for University-School Partnerships, pages 283–298.
Copyright © 2014 by Information Age Publishing
All rights of reproduction in any form reserved.

The professional development school (PDS), initiated by the Holmes Partner-ship (1986), grew out of a need to connect teachers in preparation to the field of teaching and learning in a more meaningful way. The Holmes Group produced three seminal works (*Tomorrow's Teachers*, 1986; *Tomorrow's Schools*, 1990; and *Tomorrow's Schools of Education*, 1995) following years of deliberation among university and school leaders. The three documents recommended reform in each area by establishing partnerships between schools and universities to create bet-ter teachers who could better serve the P–12 learners. Initial research on PDS in the formative years of development shows a group of professors working to understand how the recommended reforms affected their teaching and research practices (Tunks & Neapolitan, 2007). However, over time, adjustments to the Holmes proposal, based on studies of universities and schools in the reform pro-cess, resulted in systematic accounting for change in the PDS (Tietel, 2000).

In 2001, the NCATE PDS standards (NCATE, 2001) were introduced to the PDS community. These articulated the original PDS position in a set of standards that expanded the perspective of PDS. These included developmental guidelines for PDS partners to determine their current developmental status within the stan-dard areas of learning communities; accountability; collaboration; diversity and equity; and structures, resources, and roles. The NCATE PDS standards, when used as developmental guidelines, assist PDS partners in addressing an element at what level they are performing ("beginning," "developing," "at standard," and/ or "leading") in any category. In their book, *A Framework for Research on Pro-fessional Development Schools* (Tunks & Neapolitan, 2007), the NCATE PDS standards are discussed from the perspective of knowing the developmental levels of the PDS across various elements and for the purposes of determining the most appropriate research to conduct in a given PDS. The principles of the book were applied to this current study.

The researchers, in concert with teachers, principals, PDS interns, school ad-ministrators, university instructors, and district leaders, used the Database of PDS Self-Assessment (Gendernalik-Cooper, 2004) to determine developmental levels of performance of the PDS across standards and elements. Results of the internal study conducted in 2008 indicated that the PDS partnership had begun to consider ways to engage in the expectations of the Diversity and Equity Standard but had not systematically approached the development of formalized practices—with the exception of one project initiated in 2007—the Fiesta Math Night. Applying the principles of the framework, it was noted that the PDS partnership had conducted years of various research, including experimental work; hence, they were poised to conduct community research on the success of programs conducted in the PDS program. The Fiesta Math Night project has been studied for six years (Ander-son, Olstowski, & Tunks, 2008; Montejano & Tunks, 2010; Ortez, 2013; Tunks, 2013; Walker, 2012) with an emphasis on understanding the changed perspective of PDS interns toward the valuing of Latino students and their parents. Because of the strength of the PDS and the willingness to engage in continuous research, a final level of research was approached—the study of parents' perspectives of Fiesta Math Night.

OBJECTIVES OR PURPOSES

The purpose of the study was to examine Latino parents' perspectives of their participation with their children in a mathematics learning environment (Fiesta Math Night) within the context of a PDS partnership.

RESEARCH QUESTION

What are Latino parents' perceptions of their participation with their children at Fiesta Math Night?

THEORETICAL FRAMEWORK

The NCATE PDS Standards were used as the theoretical framework. Standard IV: Diversity and Equity states: "PDS partners include diverse participants and diverse learning communities for PDS work. PDS partners engage increasing numbers of families and community members in support of P-12 student learning. The PDS partnership includes PDSs or affiliated schools in diverse communities" (NCATE, 2001, p. 14).

The PDS Partnership Network used the NCATE PDS standards as the basis for managing the PDS program for 10 years. During that time, Standard IV was supported in various ways, but most strongly through the implementation of the Fiesta Math Night Initiative. The initiative was brought to the network's attention by a classroom mentor teacher who had attempted to conduct a Family Math Night for parents and children, which had previously garnered only five participants out of a school of 600 predominately Latino students. This dilemma caused the network to consider alternatives that would more actively involve the university through the engagement of PDS interns with the schools and parents in the community. The solution was the initiation of Fiesta Math Night/Noche Fiesta de Matematicas.

This initiative prepared PDS interns enrolled in both social studies and mathematics methods cluster courses during the PDS intern placement, to develop a deeper understanding and valuing of the Latino culture. This, in turn, led to the construction of culturally relevant mathematics games centered on Latino themes. Three recent years of themes included: Maya 2012, the 100th and 200th anniversaries of the Mexican Revolution and Mexican Independence (2010), and Free Trade Agreements (2011). In the courses, PDS interns learned how to create and test mathematics games using the Latino culturally relevant themes.

The games were designed, presented, and tested at Fiesta Math Night events in elementary and middle schools, by PDS interns, most of whom were white, middle-class women, whose experience with Latino families was limited prior to the Fiesta Math Night events. Teachers and administrators in the PDS Title I schools created an atmosphere of welcome and learning in which PDS interns, parents, children, and inservice teachers engaged in evenings of mathematics exploration and enjoyment. This was all within the context of dual-language, culturally relevant mathematics games that were specifically designed for elementary-age students.

Studies of PDS interns' perception shifted from gathering information about Latino parents (Input), as in course requirements, to valuing parents as contributors to their students' mathematics learning. The shift was based on PDS interns' multiple experiences participating in Fiesta Math Night events. Interns reported their perceptions prior to the presentation of FMN in addition to their perspectives following each FMN event where they presented their games. Data from the pre-FMN reveals a group that perceives a group (Latino) that does not acknowledge the importance of education and work too many hours to support their students' learning. However, these data shifted considerably following each of the first, second, and third nights of FMN game presentations.

Following the FMN I interns reported that the "night was a great way to connect with students as well as parents." "Children see that their parents are supportive of their education and parents realize that the schools know they are an important part of the process." These statements suggest interns who are shifting from rejecting Latino parent support, to a perspective that the Latino parent sees the school as an important resource. Following FMN II, interns noted that parents and their children were working together to solve the math problems, that parents were more involved, and that parents were big supporters of their students' success in completing the games.

Finally, following FMN III, interns expressed thoughts regarding how much they had learned from the multiple experiences of presenting the games, particularly in the area of the importance of including cultural relevance in instruction, so that parents are comfortable and want to participate with their students. The interns began to think of themselves as teachers later, with the intent to include parents in every aspect of their students' learning. The most important outcome was the report from interns that they recognized now much Latino parents care about their children's learning, because they witnessed parents and children playing math games together and enjoying the time learning in a nonthreatening learning environment. They took ownership of these nights and resolved to take this practice with them as they went forward into teaching in the future.

During a six-year period, this event was staged at 46 schools and engaged over 7,000 parents and students. Although the numbers told the story of a successful program, the reasoning behind parental involvement remained unknown. This study sought to clarify why 7,000 parents and children attended these events, where only five parents and children attended in the year prior to the introduction of Fiesta Math Night.

LITERATURE REVIEW

A goal of holding Fiesta Math Nights was to increase Latino parent participation in various school events. According to Lee and Bowen (2006), European American parents reported more frequent involvement in schools and less frequent efforts to manage children's time at home than do Hispanic and African American parents. In another study, immigrant parents were less likely to participate in events at their child's elementary school than do native-born parents (Turney & Kao, 2009). European American parents reported more frequent discussions with their child regarding education than Hispanic parents (Lee & Bowen, 2006). These researchers (2006) found parent involvement in school activities occurred more frequently among parents whose culture was most similar to the culture of the school. European American parents, parents not living in poverty, and parents with similar or higher levels of education than school staff were more likely to participate in their children's school activities.

Minority and immigrant parents face many barriers to school participation (Carreón, Drake, & Barton, 2005; Peña, 2000; Turney & Kao, 2009). One of the most common barriers is language (Carreón et al., 2005; Peña, 2000; Turney & Kao, 2009). Pena found that some parents felt uncomfortable at events that were conducted predominantly in English. The language barrier contributed to parents feeling disrespected (Carreón et al., 2005) and unwelcome (Turney & Kao, 2009) in their children's schools. Turney and Kao found Latino immigrant parents were 2.5 times more likely than Caucasian, native-born parents to report they did not feel welcome in their child's school. One Latino immigrant mother described the school staff and atmosphere as disrespectful because of the lack of bilingual office staff (Carreón et al., 2005). However, some Mexican American parents found the attitudes of school staff a barrier to participation in their children's schools, regardless of whether staff members were bilingual (Peña, 2000). In parent interviews, Carreón et al. (2005) found parents' lack of personal relationships with teachers posed as a challenge to school participation.

In a qualitative study conducted by Peña (2000), several Mexican American parents who had children enrolled in the same elementary school felt their limited formal education was a barrier to participation. Some parents did not feel comfortable communicating this with teachers, but their limited education prevented them from participating in certain capacities. Even though the school provided all written communication in English and Spanish, some parents could not read either language well.

Several other barriers and challenges to school participation were mentioned, including cultural differences, childcare, meeting times, and transportation. Several subcultures exist within the Mexican American culture, and families wish to participate in different ways (Peña, 2000). Native-born Hispanic parents were most likely to face problems like transportation and inconvenient meeting times. Hispanic immigrants were more likely than native-born Caucasian parents to face childcare barriers (Turney & Kao, 2009).

There is a paucity of articles on parental contact and the examination of equity and diversity in the PDS; however, two articles articulate the need to engage in the process of examining and enacting the principles outlined in the NCATE PDS standards. In one study, interns who were enrolled in a PDS program participated in a semester-long social studies project that culminated in contact with parents and children in a Global Literacy Night, where 87 parents and children engaged in culturally relevant events (Chicola, & Ceprano, 2009). The evening focused on a three-pronged approach that included realms (physical, human), arts, and literacy. Parents and children took materials home and extended the evening of literacy exploration into the home. Candidates' reflections indicated that they were more open to international explorations. Konopak (2006) examined the implication for the inclusion of the NCATE PDS standards on diversity and equity when examining a PDS program in Colorado. The chapter explored the potential for programs that seek to encourage and support social justice in PDS settings.

METHOD

The method used to study the current phenomenon was case study. Case studies emphasize detailed contextual analysis of a limited number of events or conditions and their relationships (Flyvbjerg, 2011). This case study was limited to one PDS network, a limited number of events, and the relationship of the events to the phenomenon of parental support for student mathematics learning. In this case study, observations of Latino parents during the Fiesta Math Night events, surveys about participation in the Fiesta Math Night events, and interviews with parents about their perceptions of the Fiesta Math Night events were collected to create an understanding of the perception of parents of the Fiesta Math Night events.

Setting

The PDS network that was used as the setting for the study has functioned as a network since 1994. The network of nine schools is set in a single district in northeast Texas and was classified as a rural district until 2000, when it changed classification to rural–urban. The district has transformed over the years from one that was predominantly Caucasian. However, during the life of the PDS network, the demographics have grown from 11% Latino to 31%. This shift created a need for more careful attention from the PDS network, particularly in how to prepare teachers who are culturally aware and who value and organize their teaching to align with the needs of Latino students.

Oral history interviews with faculty, school administrators, and teachers, conducted between 2000 and 2002, revealed a PDS network that performed partially in keeping with the precepts of the Holmes Group. The alignment of precepts to the PDS network was observed in the instructional practices of teaching the university courses in schools, use of school faculty as instructors, and shared governance in managing the PDS relationship between interns, school personnel, and university personnel. However, when the PDS program shifted to a university campus instruction-only model, the partnership component of the PDS network was diminished.

However, in 2002, the NCATE PDS standards were applied, transforming the PDS network into one of shared governance and learning community centeredness with a focus on inquiry, parent involvement, and student achievement. All constituents (teachers, PDS interns, school administrators, university instructors, and supervisors) worked collaboratively in the network, applying the principles of parity and equity.

Fiesta Math Night required a commitment to change by the university mathematics and social studies methods instructors. These changes resulted in PDS interns' creations of mathematics games that were relevant to the Latino culture. Fiesta Math Night began in the initial school in 2007, resulting in an attendance of 250 parents and children. Across the six years of the project, over 7,000 parents attended Fiesta Math Night events in 46 schools. Although the attendance numbers alone would signal success, there was an interest in the parents' reasoning for attending this event when, in previous years, they had not attended family math nights.

The games used at Fiesta Math Night combined Latino cultural components with mathematics content. PDS interns enrolled in the professional development school (PDS) at the local university developed the games in their mathematics and social studies methods courses and facilitated the games at each Fiesta Math Night. In the final three years of the project, themes were applied in the social studies methods class, from which students drew out mathematical content for the games. All games were presented in Spanish and English and were physically presented by the PDS interns who created the games. Each PDS intern presented the game he or she had created each month during the fall semester at three different Title I schools. Parents, children, teachers, and administrators attended Fiesta Math Nights, playing games with PDS interns. The observations of parents playing the games with their children in large numbers and with zeal led to the study of parents' involvement and perceptions. This study was conducted in the final year of the project (2012).

DATA SOURCES

Data sources included observations of parental involvement in Fiesta Math Night events and surveys of and interviews with parents regarding their participation in Fiesta Math Night. One hundred twenty-one parents completed the Fiesta Math Night parent survey at three of the participating schools. Fourteen parents who attended Fiesta Math Night at Roosevelt Elementary participated in semi-structured phone interviews. Participants were asked questions regarding their reason(s) for attending Fiesta Math Night, their impressions of the event and games, attendance of other school functions, if and what types of mathematics games are played in the home, and if they would be willing to play more games if they were provided.

All interviews conducted in Spanish were translated to English and analyzed in English.

Participants

One hundred twenty-one parents completed the Fiesta Math Night parent survey at three of the participating schools. Forty-six of the 126 completed the survey in Spanish, and the remaining parents completed the survey in English. Parents were asked to provide contact information if they were willing to answer more questions. Fourteen parents who attended Fiesta Math Night participated in phone interviews. Ten of the interviews were conducted in Spanish, and four were conducted in English. No demographic data were gathered from the participants.

Observations, Survey, and Interviews

Observations were conducted at two Fiesta Math Night events, noting the type of parent participation, actions, and reactions. The parent survey was given to parents when they entered the event. The survey was provided in both English and Spanish and contained four questions. Parents were asked to provide the grade level(s) of child(ren) who came with them to Fiesta Math Night, reasons for coming to the event, how they heard about Fiesta Math Night, and their impression of the event. Parents could choose as many responses as related to their perceptions of the evening.

Fourteen parents participated in semi-structured phone interviews. The interviews were conducted by several researchers. Some interviewers asked follow-up questions for clarification. Interviews were conducted in the language in which the participant completed the survey. Some of the interview questions paralleled the survey questions for the purposes of confirming parents' perspective. During the interviews, participants were asked questions regarding their reason(s) for attending Fiesta Math Night, their impressions of the event and games, attendance of other school functions, if and what types of mathematics games are played in the home, and if they would be willing to play more games at home, if they were provided with math games.

Data Analysis

All interviews conducted in Spanish were translated into English and analyzed in English. The constant comparison method (Glaser & Strauss, 1967) was used to analysis the observation notes and interview transcripts. NVivo software was used as an aid during data analysis. It should be noted that the software was only used as a tool for organization, much like note cards; it did not code or analyze the data. After an initial reading of all transcriptions, data were unitized (Lincoln & Guba, 1985). Due to the way in which the interviews were structured, entire answers from one question often resulted in one unit. The analysis process also led to clear themes based on the questions asked. Each unit was compared to previously coded units to determine if it should be placed in the same category or if a new category had emerged (Glaser & Strauss, 1967). If a unit did not seem necessary to the research questions, it was placed in the miscellaneous category. After all transcriptions had been coded into themes, all units in each theme were reviewed to identify subthemes. Subthemes emerged in most of the categories. Frequency of responses was used to analyze the survey data.

RESULTS AND DISCUSSION

The results from the survey and the emerging themes from the interview and observation transcriptions are discussed in this section of the paper. First, a description of Fiesta Math Night is shared.

Observations

Fiesta Math Nights occurred on school nights at school cafeterias. PDS interns had arrived earlier to set up games around the cafeteria and were ready for students and their families when the event began. At one school, the smell of popcorn contributed to the festive feeling of the event. The voices of teachers, children, and families filled the room, making it necessary to speak louder to be heard. The cafeteria was not overcrowded, and families easily moved from game to game. Children and adults attended this event together. Parents tended to follow their children as they played each game. All interactions between parents and children appeared to be positive. Most of the parents were smiling, laughing, and seemingly interested in the games that their children were playing. Most parents stood near the games and appeared to listen and watch as their children played. A few parents, more often women than men, chose to sit down at the table, but would stand if more children came to play. Occasionally, parents would engage in conversations with the PDS interns while their child was playing.

TABLE 17.1. Parents' Reasons for Attending Fiesta Math Night

Reason	n	%
My child asked me to come.	90	73.8
I come every year.	28	23.0
I just heard about it and thought it would be fun.	32	26.2
I like playing math games with my child(ren).	36	29.5
I always come to events at the school.	33	27.0
I wanted to visit with my child(ren)'s teacher(s).	13	10.7

Notes. Participants (121) could choose multiple reasons for attending Fiesta Math Night.

TABLE 17.2. Learning about Fiesta Math Night

Means	n	%
School sign outside the building	12	9.8
Note sent home with child(ren)	92	75.4
Phone call from school	30	24.6
Child(ren) told me	59	48.4
Friend whose child(ren) attend this school	5	4.1
Child(ren)'s teacher	13	10.7

Notes. Participants (121) could choose multiple means of learning about Fiesta Math Night.

Survey

As shown in Table 17.1, almost 75% of parents reported attending Fiesta Math Night because their children asked them to attend. Parents could report multiple reasons for attending. Only a few parents (10.7 %) reported attending Fiesta Math Night to visit with their children's teachers.

As shown in Table 17.2, most parents reported hearing about Fiesta Math Night via a school note sent home (75%) and/or from their children telling them about the event (48%).

Over two-thirds of parents reported Fiesta Math Night as "fun" (Table 17.3). More than half of the parents described the event as "interesting," and half reported the event as a "great time to be with child(ren) at school." Only 31% of parents reported Fiesta Math Night as "challenging."

Interviews and Field Notes

Six major themes were identified using the constant comparison method when analyzing the transcriptions of interviews and observation narratives. The themes were: (1) reasons for attending, (2) impressions of event, (3) mathematics games, (4) mathematics at home, (5) participation in other school events, and (6) suggestions.

TABLE 17.3. Parents' Beliefs about Fiesta Math Night

Beliefs	n	%
Fun	83	68.6
Interesting	64	52.9
Challenging	38	31.4
A great time to be with my child(ren) at the school	61	50.4

Notes. Participants (121) could choose multiple beliefs about Fiesta Math Night.

Reasons for Attending

Parents were directly asked for the reasons of their attendance during the interview. Reasons for parent participation included child interest in Fiesta Math Night and mathematics, parent involvement, and learning. Parents reported attending Fiesta Math Night because they wanted to support and promote their children's interest in mathematics. Several parents said they attended Fiesta Math Night because their children wanted to attend the event. The majority of parents who completed the survey also reported attending Fiesta Math Night because of their children's interest.

Parents also attended because they wished to be involved in school events. Some parents believed attending school events would demonstrate to their children that they valued their education. One participant stated, "I want to be involved in school, and, if I show my daughter early that I am involved in school, hopefully, she would know how important school is." Another parent reported going because she wanted to know how teachers were helping her daughter in school. An additional reason for attendance among parents was parent and student learning. One parent shared, "I like to take the kids because they learn new information, and I learn something too."

Impression of Events

When discussing impression of Fiesta Math Night, parents described parent and student learning. A few parents reflected on their own mathematics learning at Fiesta Math Night. Two parents commented that they learned something new at the event. Another participant expressed that the games and event "show us different ways to teach them [students]." However, one parent wished there were more games she could understand.

Most of the parents commented on student learning when discussing their impressions of the event. Several parents described Fiesta Math Night as a great and fun way to learn and understand mathematics. One mother said, "It was good to see my kid get excited about math," and another mother discovered "that my daughter is highly interested in math." Two parents expressed surprise at how capable their children were of learning mathematics. Other impressions about the Fiesta Math Night included satisfaction with the event.

Math Games

In several interviews, parents described their impressions of the games played and how they participated in Fiesta Math Night. Several parents described the games as impressive, fun, and interactive. One mother mentioned the relevance of a game her daughter played, "I really enjoyed this game because it is something they can use throughout their lives." When asked about playing the games, three parents responded that they did not play, but rather they watched their children play. Another parent stated that she tried to participate, but had difficulties because she did not understand. In the interviews, not many parents described how they did or did not participate. Based on observations, parents were more likely to watch their children play the math games than play with them.

Math at Home

Parents discussed current mathematics activities played in the home, as well as their interest in learning about new mathematics games. When asked if parents and children play mathematics games in the home, some of the parents responded "no." Other parents responded "yes" and mentioned cards, flash cards, dominoes, Monopoly, Candy Land, or bingo as mathematics games played at home. However, several parents seemed unsure if these constituted mathematics games. One parent responded, "I mean, I don't know if they are games, but…we do flash cards. If we just see an opportunity, we will be like, 'what is this plus this?' You know, we are just trying to throw it in there some way." Another mother replied, "Ummm…we do like Legos and that kind of thing, but not math specific ones."

All parents interviewed welcomed the idea of extending Fiesta Math Night in their homes in the form of mathematics games. One parent mentioned an interest in games in Spanish, similar to those at Fiesta Math Night. The parent stated, "Most games at the stores come in English, and I noticed that many of the games at the school had Spanish components. I would also be open to the opportunity because it would help me practice my English skills and my son's math skills." One mother expressed an interest in learning how to create math games for her family.

Other School Events

In the interviews, parents mentioned school events they had attended this year, how they differed from Fiesta Math Night, volunteering at school, and the affect Fiesta Math Night had on their future attendance of school events. Most of the parents interviewed had attended some other school event this year. Participants reported attending science night, PTA meetings, parent meetings, Fall Carnival, and a fundraiser dance. Only three had not attended any other events. Their reasons for nonattendance included conflicting work schedules and that Fiesta Math Night was the only event that "captures my son's attention."

When comparing Fiesta Math Night to other school events, participants referred to Fiesta Math Night as educational and fun. Fundraiser events and the carnival were also referred to as fun—but not academic. One parent mentioned science night as being similar to Fiesta Math Night. One of the participants described Fiesta Math Night as more interactive for children but wished parents were more involved. A few of the parents reported volunteering at school. However, two participants mentioned they could not volunteer because of their jobs. One mother completed the background check and would not mind volunteering but stated the school has not asked her to volunteer.

Most of the parents reported Fiesta Math Night as affecting their future attendance of school events. Participants expressed that now they understood the importance of these types of events for their children. After attending Fiesta Math

Night, parents felt more open and welcome to attend future school events. Some parents mentioned an interest in becoming more involved in school activities. Other participants said they would attend events regardless of their experience at Fiesta Math Night because they always attend school events.

Suggestions

Overall, parents were happy with the event, but they offered several suggestions for future events. The most common suggestion among the participants was extending the time of Fiesta Math Night and having it more frequently. The participants mentioned that some parents could not attend because of their schedules and thought if the game night were offered on multiple nights, more parents would attend. A participant also suggested opening Fiesta Math Night to the community, not just the school, and advertising the uniqueness of the event to promote more parent participation. A participant suggested asking parents to help create games and volunteer at the event to increase parent involvement in the school. It was also suggested that bilingual volunteers help at the event to explain games to Spanish-speaking parents.

LIMITATIONS

This study investigated the experiences of only some parents who attended Fiesta Math Night at selected campuses. The study did not include participants who did not attend Fiesta Math Night. The results of this study should not be generalized to all culturally relevant events or to the larger population. Demographic information was not collected, and so the data gathered are not transferable to particular subgroups.

CONCLUSION

The participants in this study attended Fiesta Math Night because of their children's interest in the event, a desire to support student learning, and to be more involved in their children's school. Parents described Fiesta Math Night as a place that promoted parent and student learning. During the event, parents tended to watch their children play the math games rather than play the games with them. When asked about mathematics games in the home, parents seemed unsure if the games they played promoted mathematics learning. All participants interviewed welcomed the idea of new mathematics games in the home. Most parents expressed that Fiesta Math Night positively affected their future attendance of school events.

The findings in the study were made possible due to the strength of the PDS network. The PDS network's adherence to the NCATE PDS standards of diversity and equity guided the personnel to examine their performance in this area, prompting action—the creation of Fiesta Math Night. As a result of this action, Latino parents and children were given a forum to connect to the school in a positive way through the exploration of mathematics in a culturally relevant environment. The parity of mentor teacher initiation, supported by university changes in curriculum and embellished by the PDS interns' creativity, led to connections in learning that may or may not have been able to exist without the synergy of the constituents in the network. The findings in this study suggest that parents were comfortable in attending the events, some for many years—all of which was possible because the network provided the safety net of parental involvement in their students' learning.

RECOMMENDATIONS

A number of recommendations surfaced from the interviews. The participants suggested that Fiesta Math Night be offered several times a year. They also suggested promoting parent participation by asking parents to help create games and volunteer at Fiesta Math Night. It may be helpful in future studies to gather demographic information and investigate parents' school participation among all subpopulations in the schools served. This study prompted several questions for future research including:

How do parents promote mathematics learning in the home?
How do parents define mathematics?
What role do parents want to have in their children's mathematics learning?
What role do parents believe they play in their children's mathematics learning?
What role do parents believe they play in their children's mathematics achievement, as measured by state standardized tests?

It is always recommended that PDS networks employ the NCATE PDS standards as a way to examine developmental performance in working towards excellence in PDS work. To best use the standards, it is imperative that all constituents have parity, shared governance, and an open forum for expressing ideas for improving the performance of all constituents. In an ever-shifting demographic in public education, the PDS serves as an ideal model for program building that engages the community in the process of children's learning. This study demonstrates that engagement with parents is not only possible but ideal in advancing the purposes of PDS.

REFERENCES

Anderson, A., Olstowski, A., & Tunks, J. (2008, April). *Noche de fiesta matematica: Transforming PDS candidates*. Paper presented at the National Association of Professional Development Schools, Orlando, Florida.

Carreón, G. P., Drake, C., & Barton, A. C. (2005). The importance of presence: Immigrant parents' school engagement experiences. *American Educational Research Journal,*

42(3), 465–498. Retrieved from http://search.ebscohost.com/login.aspx?direct=true &db=ehh&AN=18504466&scope=site

Chicola, N. A., & Ceprano, M. (2009). Pre-service teachers collaborating with families to foster global literacy connections. *International Journal of Learning, 16*(8), 221–233. Retrieved from *http://search.ebscohost.com/login.aspx?direct=true&db=ehh &AN=18504466&scope=site*

Flyvbjerg, B. (2011). Case study. In N. K. Denzin, & Y. S. Lincoln (Eds.), *The Sage handbook of qualitative research* (4th ed., pp. 301). Thousand Oaks, CA: Sage.

Gendernalik-Cooper, M. (2004). *Documenting and disseminating the effectiveness of professional development schools in improving teacher quality and retention and student learning and achievement.* Washington, DC: Department of Education.

Glaser, B. G., & Strauss, A. L. (1967). *The discovery of grounded theory: Strategies for qualitative research.* Chicago, IL: Aldine.

The Holmes Group. (1986). *Tomorrow's teachers: A report of the Holmes group.* East Lansing, MI: Author.

The Holmes Group. (1990). *Tomorrow's schools: Principles for the design of professional development schools.* East Lansing, MI: Author.

The Holmes Group. (1995). *Tomorrow's schools of education: A report of the Holmes group.* East Lansing, MI: Author.

Konopak, B. (2006). Response on future directions: Community, diversity, and social justice. In J. E. Neapolitan & T. R. Berkeley (Eds.), *Where do we go from here? Issues in the sustainability of professional development school partnerships* (pp. 223–230). New York, NY: Peter Lang.

Lee, J., & Bowen, N. K. (2006). Parent involvement, cultural capital, and the achievement gap among elementary school children. *American Educational Research Journal, 43*(2), 193–218. doi: 10.3102/00028312043002193

Lincoln, Y. S., & Guba, E. G. (1985). *Naturalistic inquiry.* Thousand Oaks, CA: Sage.

Montejano, S., & Tunks, J. (2010). Make a move: Creating a culturally aware community of masters and scholars. *The Eagle Feather, 7,* 1–15. Retrieved from https://eagle-feather.honors.unt.edu/2010/article/149#.Uk5A6yQd5uI.

NCATE. (2001). *Standards for professional development schools.* NCATE PDS Standards. Retrieved from http://www.ncate.org/public/standards.asp

Ortez, E. (2013). Fiesta math night: The parent perspective. *The Eagle Feather, 10,* 20. Retrieved from https://eaglefeather.honors.unt.edu/2013/article/267#.Uk5DQCQd5uI

Peña, D. C. (2000). Parent involvement: Influencing factors and implications. *The Journal of Educational Research, 94*(1), 42–54. doi: 10.1080/00220670009598741

Tietel, L. (2000). *Assessing the impacts of professional development schools.* Washington, DC: American Association of Colleges for Teacher Education.

Tunks, J., & Neapolitan, J. (2007). *A framework for research on professional development schools.* Lanham, MD: University Press of America.

Tunks, J. (2013). Fiesta math night/noche de fiesta de matimática: The initiation of social justice for PDS candidates. In K. Zenkov (Ed.), *Social justice in the PDS* (pp. 215–242). Lanham, MD: Lexington Press.

Turney, K., & Kao, G. (2009). Barriers to school involvement: Are immigrant parents disadvantaged? *Journal of Educational Research, 102*(4), 257–271. Retrieved from http://search.ebscohost.com/login.aspx?direct=true&db=ehh&AN=36419490&scope=site

Walker, W. (2012) Becoming a teacher of mathematics to elementary students. *The Eagle Feather, 9, 10*. Retrieved from https://eaglefeather.honors.unt.edu/2012/article/122#.Uk5BdiQd5uI

CHAPTER 18

ANOTHER LEVEL IN A PDS PARTNERSHIP

Bringing Families and Teacher Candidates Together

Julie Rosenthal, Maika Bonafe, and Mary Lebron

ABSTRACT

Over the past decade, the university-school partnership in this study has evolved into a professional development school (PDS) partnership with several initiatives, including the addition of an onsite initial certification literacy course that is co-taught by school and university faculty. Recently, the school's parent liaison offered to assist in a section of the course to engage teacher candidates in working with families of children in the literacy program. The results of this collaborative effort that are reported herein include impacting teacher candidates' attitudes about family involvement at this large, urban PDS, as well as developing their strategy use and efficacy for engaging families.

It is generally accepted that parents' involvement in their children's school has a positive effect on students' academic development (Epstein, 2001; Fan & Chen,

Creating Visions for University-School Partnerships, pages 299–315.
Copyright © 2014 by Information Age Publishing
All rights of reproduction in any form reserved.

299

2001; Henderson & Mapp, 2002; Yaden & Paratore, 2003). If families are involved, students tend to demonstrate higher levels of engagement in various factors of school life, as well as having better grades, higher test scores, and higher graduation rates, and a greater likelihood of enrolling in post-secondary schools (Henderson & Mapp, 2002). Research supports the notion that the majority of parents, across racial, ethnic, and socioeconomic lines, are extremely interested in their children's academic success (Mapp, 2002). When parents and teachers have a mutually respectful relationship, and when they have a shared vision for how to support children's academic growth, they co-produce a balanced working relationship which can lead to students' achievement (Yaden & Paratore, 2003). However, too often, parents and teachers do not connect, despite good intentions on the part of teachers, schools, and families. This is particularly true when there is a disconnect between teachers' expectations of the ways in which families should be involved in their children's schooling and families' knowledge about, attitude towards, and ability to become involved (Henderson & Mapp, 2002). For example, Lawson (2003) provides some evidence that parents and teachers define "involvement" differently, with parents taking a "community-centric" view, which includes protecting children from being labeled and keeping children safe and "out of the system." Teachers appear to take a "school-centric" view of parental involvement, defining it primarily as parents' physical presence in the school and their reinforcement of the teachers' work with children (Lawson, 2003).

Also predictive of parents' involvement are teachers' attitudes and beliefs about parental involvement. Parents' school-related academic engagement behaviors with their children, at home and within the school building, are largely predicted by teachers' use of effective parent involvement practices (Anderson & Minke, 2007). For example, Mapp (2002) found that parents were more likely to become involved in school-based activities when the school, particularly teachers, welcomed their presence, honored their contributions, and connected with them about their children's learning. Yet teachers' behaviors, so integral to parents choices about how to engage, are linked to their attitudes about parental involvement. Teachers who have cultural differences with parents, negative attitudes towards low-income parents, and narrow visions of parent involvement are less likely to be inviting, welcoming, and honoring of parents' contributions (Christianakis, 2011; DeCastro-Ambrocetti & Cho, 2005).

There are myriad documented factors that can inhibit parents' school-based involvement. This may be specifically true for low-income, urban, Hispanic parents (Smith, Stern, & Shatrova, 2008). Factors include a lack of correspondence from schools written in Spanish, parents' inability to correspond in English, and parents' reluctance to question authority or to advocate for their children (Smith et al., 2008). A Spanish-speaking parent coordinator who is sensitive to parents' cultural needs and focuses on relationship building can play a critical role. One purpose of this chapter is to describe how a parent coordinator at one large urban professional development school (PDS) played a crucial role in dramatically increasing the involvement by parents within an eight-year period.

In its statement *What it Means to Be a Professional Development School*, the National Association for Professional Development Schools provides nine essential characteristics of a PDS (NAPDS, 2008). Included is Essential #2: "A school-university culture committed to the preparation of future educators that embraces their active engagement in the school community" (p. 4). Partnerships that adhere to Essential #2 include "schools whose faculty and staff as a collective whole are committed to working with college/university faculty to offer a meaningful introduction to the teaching profession" (p. 4). In this PDS–university partnership, the school faculty, staff, and administration and the university faculty and staff work together to encourage teacher candidate development as well as to engage the broader school community.

The university has supported the parent program at the school, including offering, at the school's request, campus-based parent education events and professional development for teachers on engaging families. This is evidence that the PDS adheres to NAPDS Essential #3: "Ongoing and reciprocal professional development for all participants guided by need" (p. 4). The PDS's parent liaison serves as a speaker at these events, which currently include an annual event for all of the university's PDS partners. The parent liaison, along with PDS and university faculty, have co-presented at national conferences on family engagement in schools. Another goal of the present study was to further this work by involving the parent liaison with teacher candidate development by facilitating their engagement with families.

It has been suggested that teacher education programs could do more to foster future teachers' understanding of the needs and perspectives of parents who differ culturally from themselves (Patte, 2011). Although communicating with parents and fostering relationships with families is a central role for teachers, not many certification programs help teacher candidates develop their knowledge, skills, and dispositions for family–school partnerships (Walker & Dotger, 2012). The study described in this chapter was an attempt to give teacher candidates first-hand experience working and communicating with parents while receiving assistance in doing so from a successful school parent liaison and classroom teacher.

PURPOSE OF THE STUDY

The PDS partnership has worked for many years on a literacy course in which teacher candidates work one on one with a primary grades reader on reading and writing tasks as part of the coursework. Faculty from the PDS and university co-teach the course. During one semester, with guidance from the parent liaison, the teacher candidates (N=12) were asked to foster communication between parents and themselves by sharing with families information about children's literacy development and by planning activities for families to conduct with children. Teacher candidates met and interacted with children and families on literacy activities during afterschool tutoring sessions and at an end-of-year "publishing party," and additionally, they accompanied families on a trip to the local library.

The study had five primary purposes. The first purpose was to describe how the parent liaison at the PDS dramatically increased parent presence at the school during her eight-year tenure. A second purpose was to describe how she fostered teacher candidates' interest in and ability to work with families. Third, teacher candidates' attitudes and beliefs prior to engaging with parents were examined. A fourth purpose was to describe the sessions during which teacher candidates worked with families and to examine their growing understanding about engagement as a result of their interactions with parents at this PDS. Finally, of interest was how families perceived the teacher candidates in their efforts to engage them in school activities.

METHOD

Context

The PDS in which this study took place is an urban school with over 1,300 students in grades 1–6. The student population is primarily Hispanic, with over 90% of students speaking Spanish in their homes. Also, 90% of children qualified for free or reduced lunch at the time of this study.

The school has partnered with State University (pseudonym), a suburban campus of approximately 12,000 undergraduate and graduate students, for 14 years. The college of education plays a large role in certifying teachers for the state, with over 1,200 teacher candidates recommended for licensure or additional endorsements each year. Several partnership initiatives have evolved, including: (1) a university faculty member serving as a "professor in residence" at the school, (2) research collaborations involving school faculty and staff and university faculty, (3) the placement of many student interns in the school, and (4) campus-based events requested by the school, including family education events. Several years ago, the school began hosting an onsite literacy course that is co-taught by a classroom teacher and a university faculty member, in which teacher candidates tutor children in an afterschool program as part of the course requirements (Rosenthal, Donnantuono, Feola, Lebron, Flynn, & Wasserman, 2008).

The current study was the result of conversations between the school's parent liaison, the classroom teacher, and the university faculty member. It had been noted anecdotally that many of the teacher candidates in the university's teacher certification programs had exhibited negative stereotypical views about low-income families' lack of concern for their children's education. On the other hand, the parent liaison was reporting increased parent involvement at the PDS in various family engagement functions such as classroom events, parenting workshops, English classes, and monthly "family nights" as well as family events at the university. The liaison felt the increased involvement was a result of her efforts to build relationships with family members. At the same time, the certification program's recent NCATE review had indicated that programmatically, not enough was being done to have teacher candidates collaborate with families. It was decided that a "family engagement" piece would be added to all sections of the onsite literacy course, including those at the PDS and at other partner schools. This requires that teacher candidates provide written communication to families about the activities in which children are engaged during tutoring sessions. During the final session of each semester, parents are invited to attend a "publishing party" during which children share their written work and teacher candidates have the opportunity to meet families.

In one section of the course, held at the PDS, the parent liaison worked with teacher candidates to support their growing comfort level with and ability to engage families. Before bringing parents in, she gave teacher candidates an overview of her work at the school and the types of family outreach she had found successful, and she helped them brainstorm ways to have families participate in reading and writing activities with their children. Families were invited to join in three of the afterschool tutoring sessions where they played literacy "games" devised by the tutors, shared books with their children, and created instructional materials to bring home. During one of these sessions, families, children, teacher candidates, the parent liaison, and the co-teachers went on a walking trip to the nearby local library where all children applied for and received their first library cards. Finally, at the end-of-semester "publishing party," children shared their work, and several families brought in food representative of their native cultures to share with teacher candidates. Following the program, the parent liaison met with parents to obtain their feedback and feelings about the experience.

Participants

Participants included the school's full-time parent liaison, who had been at the school for eight years at the time of this study. The parent liaison is from the community where the school is located, has a child in the school system, and speaks Spanish and English. Also included was a second-grade teacher, co-instructor of the literacy course, who had been teaching for 18 years. She teaches a transitional bilingual class and is fluent in Spanish. The university faculty member is a European American female with an advanced degree in education who had been teaching in the education program for 8 years. The 12 participating teacher candidates included 10 European Americans, one Latin American, and one African American. There were 11 females and one male. The 12 second-grade students are all Hispanic and spoke Spanish in their homes. The 12 participating parents are Hispanic and speak Spanish as their first language, with one of the 12 also speaking fluent English.

Data Sources and Analysis

Data sources for this study included: (1) an interview of the parent liaison; (2) teacher candidates' responses to a written questionnaire administered before interactions with the parent liaison and parents; (3) teacher candidates' reflective journals; (4) observations of the parent liaison and teacher candidates discussing approaches to engage families; (5) course co-instructors' written observations of children, teacher candidates, and parents as they worked together on literacy activities; and (6) parents' responses to an open-ended interview conducted and transcribed by the parent liaison. These written documents were perused for common themes or summarized where appropriate. Statements from and observations of participants provide insight and help to reveal the impact of this experience on perspectives.

RESULTS AND DISCUSSION

The Parent Liaison Significantly Increased the Presence of Families at the School

The parent liaison program had been initiated in the district within the past decade. Prior to that, there was a single district parent–teacher coordinator who handled communication with families and organized any family events there may have been. The parent liaison shared that prior to her arrival at the school eight years earlier, there was basically no parent involvement beyond common events such as parent–teacher conferences. Parents tended to stay out of the school, frequently dropping children off at the corner rather than at the front door and rarely entering the building.

A primary charge for her in her role as parent liaison was to set up events such as English language classes, family literacy nights, and parenting workshops. She arranged these events but was dismayed by low turnout. She realized a different approach was necessary and began trying to get to know families so that she could let them know that she was at the school to serve as a link between them and school staff. Starting with children, she began to build relationships, and students helped to begin building bridges. Children introduced her to their adults, and, one by one, she got to know several families. As more and more families came to know her as not only a resource for them but also as a fellow member of the community, word spread, and more and more parents interacted with her. She intentionally made an effort to get to know as much as she could about each family, thereby building personal connections. Subsequently, when running events at the school, she made sure to invite families individually, on the phone, or face to face. This additional effort to get families to attend school events is congruent with recommendations made by Lawson (2003) for additional family outreach, beyond simply sending home flyers in children's backpacks. Within her first year, numbers of attendees at school functions soared. This success with engaging families was based on shared interest in children's welfare through fostering respectful relationships between school staff and families and making families feel welcome in the school. This mirrors what Mapp (2002) found to be important ingredients in helping parents stay engaged in their children's school lives.

Holiday-themed evening events at the school are now often "standing room only," and monthly workshops are also well attended. The school has weekly English language classes for families for which there is a waiting list. Families no longer drop children off on the corner but, instead, can often be found in the school building speaking to the parent liaison, consulting the "family events" bulletin board, helping in lower grade classrooms, or giving their children final hugs goodbye. The parent liaison credits her ongoing outreach efforts and interpersonal ability for the huge increase in several types of family engagement at the school and strongly feels that with effort, most families can be engaged.

The parent liaison has since collaborated with teachers to set up a range of events, including classroom-based events, which allow parents to get a better idea about what goes on in the classroom. Teachers come to her for help, either with contacting families because there is a problem with a student or to assist them in getting parents to attend classroom events. She also works with teachers to consider how to build relationships with families or to offer help in contacting Spanish-speaking families for teachers who do not speak Spanish. She has presented to families and to teachers about various aspects of family support for children's learning at events held on the university campus.

The accomplishments the parent liaison has experienced are attributable to the PDS context. Teachers and administration are likely more open to innovation, aligning with PDS Essential #4, "A shared commitment to innovative and reflective practice by all participants" in which all stakeholders are "professionally developed via their work in the PDS" (NAPDS, 2008). Teachers in the school are accustomed to trying new and different approaches to enhance their students' learning. They regularly collaborate with colleagues and are therefore open to the liaison's recommendations for engaging families. In addition, the university partner supports her efforts by hiring her to work with school faculty and families at campus-based events and by sending her to national conferences to present on her successful efforts at engaging families at the PDS.

Teacher Candidates' Initial Ideas about Engaging and Communicating with Parents

At the beginning of the course, teacher candidates were given a brief written questionnaire about their expectations for parent involvement in: (1) high-poverty schools in general, (2) this school specifically, (3) their self-efficacy for engaging parents, and (4) hopes and fears they had about meeting families during the course.

Responses to questions about their expectations for family involvement revealed that some candidates had low expectations about parent involvement in high-poverty schools, attributing anticipated low levels of family engagement to parents' ambivalence about their children's educations.

> Unfortunately, in some communities parents don't realize the importance of communication with their children and don't think it's important to be involved in their schooling. Maybe parents are too stressed or too busy but these children are too often simply ignored.

> Parents who did not have a great education themselves might not realize how to help their children with school or realize how important it is to be involved.

> I don't know what parent involvement is like at this school. I do kind of feel like maybe C's parents won't come because I don't think she gets much attention at home. Her hair is always dirty and she said she has no books at home.

Other responses indicated that teacher candidates expected low levels of family involvement but assumed this was because parents had jobs that were demanding of their time. As one said, "I don't know if parents would be able to come to the school even if they want to. Parents probably have to work a lot just to make ends meet."

In response to questions about their hopes and fears about meeting families and about their self-efficacy for engaging parents, some teacher candidates indicated that they were anxious about the family sessions. Much of that anxiety related to the perception that they would have difficulty communicating with Hispanic parents when they themselves spoke no Spanish. Their initial anxiety is not surprising, since a language barrier between Spanish-speaking family members and non-Spanish-speaking school personnel is a major inhibiting factor for Latino families' school involvement according to Smith et al. (2008). Several responses follow.

> I obviously can't speak Spanish at all and it will be a bit difficult to communicate with the parents since they are not fluent in English.

> The language barrier is a little nerve-wracking, but this is something that is going to have to be tackled sooner or later (sooner is always better).

> I know my student's parents have 2 baby girls and don't speak English at all really, so this is where my problem lies mostly.

> The only problem that I have is the language barrier. I don't know how to have a conversation in Spanish, even after taking two classes of Spanish. I would like to be able to communicate with the parent.

> It's up to the parents. I know that most foreigners try to not be put in these types of situations because of language barriers.

Overall, responses on the questionnaire administered to teacher candidates revealed that their perceived barriers to parent involvement mirrored those identified in previous studies. Similar to those surveyed by Patte (2011), the teacher candidates in the present study identified language differences between parents and teachers, parents' socioeconomic status, parents' educational level, and parents' negative personal experiences with education as primary impediments to their ability to engage families.

The Parent Liaison Encouraged Teacher Candidates to Consider Approaches to Engaging Families

During one regular class session, the parent liaison came to speak to teacher candidates about her work and about the importance of involving families. She shared the evolution of family involvement at the school, explaining that parent turn-out at the school's events was very high, but that this was because she made contact in multiple ways, including sending notes home with children and following up with individual phone calls. If teachers and future teachers want to engage families, they can be successful if they put forth effort. Her clear message was one that many of the teacher candidates might not have considered previously: Parents love their children. Parents want their children to do well, and they care about what goes on in school. Parents in this community work hard and may have a scarcity of time available, but if teachers and school staff plan curricular events and want them to attend, they can be encouraged to do so.

When teacher candidates expressed their concern about language barriers between themselves and families, she helped them brainstorm possible ways to overcome those barriers. Teacher candidates noted that they could call on her or the classroom teacher if they needed help communicating with parents. Others realized that the children could likely serve as translators, since they were native Spanish speakers. They also talked about the possibility of nonverbal communication, such as conducting a "picture walk" in the books they would read with the children.

Candidates' journal entries following the session with the parent liaison indicated increased confidence in their ability to communicate with parents. Several included ideas that had come up during their conversation with the parent liaison, demonstrating a sense of ownership and internalization of these ideas.

> I'm sure the student can translate to and from with information and we have Mrs. L. [classroom teacher] who speaks Spanish to help us out.

> Meeting the parents will help us work with parents who speak other languages and make us comfortable with the idea of parent involvement. We also have the students to translate along with Mrs. L. if communication is difficult at first.

The parent liaison stressed that the parents in the community tended to look up to teachers and respected their authority and knowledge. She emphasized that parents would perceive candidates as teachers and that they would be eager to learn strategies to support their children's literacy development. Candidates' journal entries following the session imply a sense of wanting to appear competent and knowledgeable as teachers, with several teacher candidates hoping to share instructional ideas and encourage parents to "do more." While some comments might give the feeling that teacher candidates assumed parents did not do enough to help their children with literacy, there does appear to be an increased sense that the relationship between teachers, families, and children should be a partnership.

> I think meeting the parents is a good approach to collaborate the student's school life with their home environment. This way, the parents can get involved with their child's academics. My student tells me that her parents do not read to her, so I hope this can be a learning experience for them as well and encourage family reading.

> I think that this would be very informative for the parents, we can show them how to read to their children, and we as tutors can see how our student interacts with their parents.

> I think it is a great opportunity for all parties involved. It gives us a chance to get comfortable working with and speaking to parents. As Ms. B. [liaison] said, parents are always excited to see what their children are doing in school. Even if the parents don't understand a word we are saying, they will understand the joy their children feel as we read to them. Most importantly, it gives the students a chance to showcase what they know in the classroom...the students can interact by partner or echo reading, and they can translate for their parents if needed.

Candidates' comments underscore their developing sense of being "participants of the school community" (NAPDS, 2008, p. 4) and can be attributed in part to the parent liaison's use of the PDS "as a learning laboratory for the development of teacher candidates" (NAPDS, p. 5). Apparently, the parent liaison's words of encouragement, modeling of perseverance, and facilitation of candidates' sense of their own competence positively affected their attitudes about engaging with families.

Teacher Candidate and Parent Interactions during Tutoring Sessions and Resulting Teacher Candidate Development

Family turn-out for the first session where families joined children and teacher candidates was very high, with ten out of twelve children having at least one adult family member attending. Fathers and grandfathers were well represented, with five of the eleven adults being men. Teacher candidates were prepared with simple literacy games and picture books on their students' independent reading level. Several also organized children's prior work so that it could be shared with families easily. As teacher candidates had expected, several children (or their older siblings in some cases) served as translators for parents and tutors, although teacher candidates were also observed to communicate nonverbally, by demonstrating how to play games and facilitating play between children and adults. Several tutors had their student's work organized so that the children could easily share with their families what they had been doing during the sessions. The classroom teacher circulated and provided language support as needed, while one mother spoke English with her child's tutor. One tutor was herself Spanish speaking and was able to communicate with the mother in Spanish. Children appeared to be very proud to bring together their tutors, of whom they were clearly fond, and their families. One boy smiled the entire time, leading his father by the hand as he showed him the classroom; another read aloud to his parents from the book his tutor had supplied.

One tutor had devised a literacy game in which printed words were matched to pictures in a "concentration/memory match" format. She cleverly had included several pictures for which the word was an English–Spanish cognate, such as "lion," "banana," and "family/familia." The words were printed in English but spellings were the same or close, allowing a Spanish speaker some success. With the child's assistance, the participating grandfather successfully played the game with the tutor and child, and language barriers were alleviated.

Teacher candidates' reflective journals following this session revealed ways in which their ideas about engaging parents (and, specifically, about working with parents in linguistically diverse schools) were beginning to evolve. Their journals point to a growing sense of themselves as "the experts," able to share with families their knowledge about literacy instruction and their understanding of individual children's strengths and needs. Those potential barriers to engaging with parents, which candidates expressed prior to the session, appear to have been replaced by a developing awareness of strategies with which they could work and communicate with families.

> In my opinion, playing the picture-word match game with A's family was the best part of the parent's session. We all got to interact, and A's grandpa got to see how well A does. Even though A's grandfather did not understand all of the words, since he could not read all of the words on the cards, A was able to tell him whether he had a match. We made sure to read the words out loud, so her grandfather could understand what the card said, and maybe begin to understand more words he was familiar with. A won both times that we played. When counting the number of matches, A counted them in English, while her grandpa counted them in Spanish. It was great that they were able to work together like that.

> Even though her mother did not speak English, she saw how I was stopping while reading and asking her questions. Her older sister, who does speak English, understood that I was asking prediction questions. Now she can do this when she reads with J…. We were able to communicate about J's improvement through her sister. Her sister would ask me questions that the mother had for me about the tutoring program, and she would translate my answers back to her mother in Spanish.

It was great to get everyone involved and learning together. Everyone seemed to enjoy the project. D and her sisters, who speak fluent English, would translate words from English to Spanish and Spanish to English. This enabled her mother to be fully involved in the project. If there are words that D's mother does not know in English, she will usually ask D to translate it. I have found that the use of gestures also helps D's mother and me to communicate.

I learned that visual representations are the best thing to use. I also learned that next time, I definitely want to find a book that is written in both English and Spanish, so that parents understand the book and realize that they can read to him at home using those books. I have also learned that even with a language barrier, the main focus is the child and knowing whether they are succeeding.

Examination of these reflections reveals that teacher candidates are truly becoming participants of the school community, and are developing professionally through their work in the PDS (NAPDS, 2008). Further, they are considering ways to engage and communicate with parents despite language differences, which was found to be a major obstacle to school involvement for Latino parents (Smith et al., 2008).

One candidate indicated that the experience made her question her own assumptions. "I had no reason to be so worried. Y's mom spoke perfect English. I have learned that you cannot assume what languages someone speaks just based on their last name!" This comment sheds light on the value of providing candidates opportunities to interact with students and families who are culturally and linguistically different from themselves, as recommended by DeCastro-Ambrosetti and Cho (2005). This type of field experience is more likely to be available in a PDS where faculty and staff are committed to offering teacher candidates a meaningful introduction to the profession of teaching (NAPDS, 2008).

Families, Children, Teacher Candidates, Parent Liaison, and Course Co-Instructors Visit Library

For one of the sessions, all participants went on a walking trip to the nearby public library. For all but one of the families, this had been their first time to the local library, which was less than a quarter of a mile from the school. Most of the participating families had not known where it was or that it was so close. Utilizing public resources, such as a library, aligns with NAPDS Essential #1, in which community agencies become participants in the work of a PDS (NAPDS, 2008).

At the library, the librarian spoke about the history of that branch, which was one of the oldest in this post-industrial city. She gave an overview of library rules and regulations and described the process of obtaining a library card and borrowing books and materials. After each section of her talk, the classroom teacher translated what she had said into Spanish for the participating parents who spoke no English.

Children were then given time to explore books with the help of their tutors, while families filled out library card applications for their children. When applications had been completed and children had found books, the families, children, and tutors spent some time reading together until the session ended.

Comments from teacher candidates' reflective journals showed that they saw great benefit to the incorporation of a trip to the library for fostering family literacy.

> Another important fact about our visit to public library was the parents' contribution to their children's learning process regarding literacy. Parents were involved throughout the entire experience and read together with their children and tutors. Parents not fluent in the English language read bilingual books with their child. Parents read the parts in Spanish and the child read the English parts to the parent. I not only noticed mothers participating in this event, but also observed some fathers who were engaging in the readings as well. This shows us that the "macho" figure in the Spanish culture has been degrading and now both mothers and fathers are committed to be part of their children's academic life.

> Indeed, I was really glad, pleased, and amazed to see almost all the parents attending this important event, which was meant to expose children to library, the biggest source of literature in their neighborhood and develop their reading skills. This definitely achieved instructional goals not only for the second graders and their parents, but also for the university students who appreciated the chance to help these families.

> He has never been to the library. When I asked his mom and his sister, his sister said she was there once but his mother never was. None of them had a library card. I thought the library was a great start to the family to start reading to each other more often. Now that his mother knows there is a local place they can rent books for free, I think they will start reading to and with A more.

Candidates' reflections point to a developing understanding of the importance of facilitating opportunities for families to work with children and support their learning outside of school. Their recognition that they can serve as sources of information about public resources is evident, as is their awareness that parents are eager to embrace such opportunities. Lawson (2003) similarly found that parents desire access to public resources and educational opportunities, although they might not know how to access them.

The Final Session: A Publishing Party and Cultural Feast

For the final session of the course, teacher candidates and course co-instructors planned a publishing party during which time students would have the chance to share a piece of writing on which they had their tutor over the semester. The parent liaison invited families to participate, and parents expressed a desire to prepare food for the party. On the day of the party, parents brought in trays of food typical to their native cultures, including *arroz con gandules*, tamales, and flan. The parent liaison indicated that parents were grateful for the work teacher candidates had done with their children and wanted to "give back."

Children and tutors waited expectantly to share with families final drafts of texts children had written and illustrated. The course co-instructors prepared a "comment sheet" to allow participants to give feedback on children's work. When families came to the class, they put food on a table (which became piled high) and joined their children who were brimming with pride and eager to present their work. Parents were asked to write comments on the feedback sheets, which most did in Spanish. Children were told they had to comment on at least two class-mates' books before being allowed to eat. Teacher candidates, too, commented on their own students' work as well as work of other students. This experience was intended to give teacher candidates a sense of how publishing parties could be run on an ongoing basis in their future classrooms.

Following reading classmates' books, children, families, and teacher candi-dates shared a meal and some informal time to relax together before saying good-bye. Teacher candidates' responses on their final journal indicate that most found the experience of working with families over the semester was a positive one, and they gained insights that they expect will spill over into their future work. Several comments are noted below:

> I was glad to have the opportunity to work with parents in this course. To be honest, I was worried about the whole thing because I did not know if I was going to be able to communicate with them or if they would ask what I was doing with their son when I myself was so new to teaching reading. As it turns out, we communicated just fine between my little bit of Spanish, his mom's little bit of English, him doing some translating, Ms. L helping.... And I really feel like I helped her see how easy it is to just read with him more. I am absolutely going to ask to be a part of parent conferences in my practicum and I know I will make an effort to include parents in my future classroom.

> This whole experience has made me much more keen on parental involvement. I no longer fear parental involvement in the classroom. This class has given me much insight of how to deal with the students' parents and communicate with those who speak another language. I know that the children themselves can help with transla-tion, or I can look to a colleague, or there are nonverbal ways to communicate. The library trip impacted me greatly. I realized how easy it is to plan a class trip to some-where local. The students were so excited for the trip to the library and I believe they learned a great deal from the trip.

> I thought it was great and I was so glad to see how excited J was to have his dad there. I think it is a great motivation for the students to have their families involved and I plan to have family events when I am a teacher.

Not all teacher candidates, however, seem to have experienced a change in their attitudes about school-family partnerships, with at least one maintaining her view that poor parents may simply not care about their child's school life. It should be noted that this teacher candidate's student was the only child whose parent, a single mother who works long hours, was unable to attend any sessions. The child was visibly sad that her mother was unable to attend, and the candidate may have felt defensive on the child's behalf, although it is surprising that she clung to the idea that parents don't care as expressed in her reflection.

> In a town like P. [the city in which the PDS is located], some parents may be involved in their child's life and other parents can care less if their child is in school or not. It is the teacher and school's job to be there for the child. If the parents aren't giving the child the love and support they deserve then who else will. Being a teacher and a role model for these children is the greatest reward anyone can ask for.

Parents' Views on Interacting with Teacher Candidates

Following the literacy tutoring sessions, library visit, and end-of-term publishing party, the parent liaison asked parents to respond to a written questionnaire to share their thoughts and feelings about the program. They were asked what, if anything, they felt they learned from participation in the sessions, what they liked most and least about the program, and if they felt their child's tutor effectively communicated with them. Responses were very positive, with parents expressing that they got great ideas from working with the teacher candidates who were assigned to their children, such as having their child read to them, reading books with their child written in English and Spanish, and playing word-card games. Most parents indicated that they had done some of these activities with their children at home following the sessions. Of the ten families who accompanied children to the library and applied for library cards, eight had returned to withdraw books and read with their child. Parents also expressed appreciation for what they perceived as effort on the parts of their child's tutor to make them feel welcome, to communicate with them, and to share with them ideas for working with their children on literacy tasks.

The parent liaison asked parents about their thoughts about the trip to the library, and responses were positive across the board. Many expressed pleasure at learning that this resource was so close to their homes. All had received library cards, and more than half reported having returned to the library to borrow books since that initial visit.

CONCLUSION

This chapter described a study intended to facilitate teacher candidates' interaction and communication with parents, specifically parents who differed from them socioeconomically, culturally, and linguistically. The course in which this experience was embedded had been meeting onsite at the PDS for years; teacher candidates tutor primary grades children in reading and writing as a way to learn about teaching literacy. This study allowed for additional collaboration with colleagues, family, and the community by bringing families and teacher candidates together to support children's literacy development.

The work of the experienced and successful parent liaison at the PDS where the study took place was described, including how her work adheres to *NAPDS Essentials for Professional Development Schools* (NAPDS, 2008). The parent liaison met with teacher candidates to give them an overview on her work and possible reasons for her success and brainstormed with them various methods to improve communication with families. Her work with the teacher candidates positively influenced their feelings of self-efficacy to work with parents, as well as their desire to do so, as evidenced by their ensuing reflections.

Family members attended tutoring sessions and engaged with children and teacher candidates on literacy activities that teacher candidates carefully planned. Teacher candidates appear to have grown in their sense of themselves as professionals and benefited from experiencing communication firsthand with those who are culturally and linguistically different from themselves (Patte, 2011). The PDS in this study served as a learning laboratory for preservice teacher development, and PDS staff and faculty, as well as university faculty, facilitated teacher candidate learning (NAPDS, 2008).

The goals of this pilot program have been met for the most part. These include that (1) teacher candidates seem to have gained ideas and strategies for communicating with Spanish-speaking parents (Smith et al., 2008); (2) they developed in their feelings of competence in their attempts to engage parents in children's literacy development (Patte, 2011); and (c) finally, attitudes and perceptions about parent involvement, particularly for low-income parents, appear to have been impacted by teacher candidates' experiences during this program. Negative ideas about low-income parents' school involvement are well documented (Patte, 2011), and many of the teacher candidates in this study expressed perceived barriers similar to those found in previous literature. However, this initial experience seems to have helped these teacher candidates begin to overcome negative attitudes, with many claiming that they will strive to include parents in their future classrooms.

It must be noted that the study described was rather informal in nature and has yet to be replicated. The sample size was quite small, as it included only one PDS with an individual parent liaison and only 12 teacher candidates. It is the hope, however, of the classroom teacher, university faculty member, and parent liaison that a similar experience can be implemented in all sections of the onsite literacy course in an attempt to find ways that teacher preparation programs, along with their school partners, can begin to do more to prepare future educators to build relationships with parents for the benefit of children.

REFERENCES

Anderson, J., & Minke, K. M. (2007). Parent involvement in education: Toward an understanding of parents' decision making. *The Journal of Educational Research, 100,* 311–323.

Christianakis, M. (2011). Parents as "help labor": Inner city teachers' narratives of parent involvement. *Teacher Education Quarterly, 3,* 157–178.

DeCastro-Ambrosetti, D., & Cho, G. (2005). Do parents value education?: Teachers' perceptions of minority parents. *Multicultural Education 13*(2), 44–46.

Epstein, J. (2001). *School, family, and community partnerships: Preparing educators and improving schools.* Boulder, CO: Westview Press.

Fan, X., & Chen, M. (2001). Parental involvement and students' academic achievement: A meta-analysis. *Educational Psychology Review, 13*(1), 1–22.

Henderson, A. T., & Mapp, K. L. (2002). *A new wave of evidence: The impact of school, family, and community connections on student achievement.* Austin, TX: Southwest Educational Development Laboratory.

Lawson, M. A. (2003). School-family relations in context: Parent and teacher perceptions of parent involvement. *Urban Education, 38,* 77–133.

Mapp, K. L. (2002). Having their say: Parents describe why and how they are engaged in their children's learning. *The School Community Journal, 4,* 35–64.

NAPDS. (2008). *What it means to be a professional development school.* Retrieved from *http://www.napds.org/nine_essen.html*

Patte, M. M. (2011). Examining pre-service teacher knowledge and competencies in establishing family–school partnerships. *The School Community Journal, 21,* 143–159.

Rosenthal, J. L., Donnantuono, M., Feola, D., Lebron, M., Flynn, C., & Wasserman, N. (2008). Learning about best practices literacy instruction in the context of professional development schools. In I. Guadarrama, J. Ramsey, & J. Nath (Eds.), *University and school connections: Research studies in professional development schools* (pp. 79–87). Charlotte, NC: Information Age Publishing

Smith, J., Stern, K., & Shatrova, Z. (2008). Factors inhibiting Hispanic parents' school involvement. *The Rural Educator, 29*(2), 8–13.

Walker, J. M. T., & Dotger, B. H. (2012). Because wisdom can't be told: Using comparison of simulated parent–teacher conferences to assess teacher candidates' readiness for family–school partnership. *Journal of Teacher Education, 63,* 62–75.

Yaden, D. B., & Paratore, J. R. (2003). Family literacy at the turn of the millennium: The costly future of maintaining the status quo. In J. Flood, D. Lapp, J. R. Squire & J. M. Jensen (Eds.), *Handbook of research on teaching the English language arts* (2nd ed., pp. 546–565). Mahwah, NJ: Lawrence Erlbaum.

CHAPTER 19

NEGOTIATING THE EXPANDED ROLES OF PDS LIAISONS IN FULL-SERVICE COMMUNITY SCHOOLS

JoAnne Ferrara and Diane Gómez

ABSTRACT

Professional development school (PDS) liaisons are accustomed to developing relationships between the university and its partner school(s). When the partner school is also full-service community school, the partnerships, and particularly, the role of the university liaison's dynamics change. This chapter describes the expanded roles of two PDS liaisons as they negotiate the new dimensions of working to facilitate collaboration among all the partners in a full-service community school while also fostering a focus on whole child education. Qualitative data sources from the classroom teachers, partners and liaisons demonstrate how three of the nine National Association for Professional Development School's (NAPDS) Essentials (1, 3, and 8) are fundamental to the success of all partners of the full-service PDS community school.

Creating Visions for University-School Partnerships, pages 317–326.
Copyright © 2014 by Information Age Publishing
All rights of reproduction in any form reserved.

Professional development school (PDS) liaisons are the "glue" that sustain the university–school partnerships and serve as the conduit between the two partners. Central to the work of liaisons is the ability to advance the partnership's collective mission by serving in several capacities. While most PDS liaisons find themselves serving as resource finders, problem solvers, and critical friends, liaisons who work in the unique setting of a PDS also designated as a community school (as discussed below) engage in expanded roles. Not only do they serve as links between the school and university but also as the links among the several partners/service agencies that are all located at the school site. The PDS liaison is the common denominator among all partners who work closely with the personnel of the community school's partnerships. In doing so, their roles shift beyond a sole focus on the school–university partnership to include the seamless integration of the PDS, along with the co-partners of the community school. By weaving the PDS into all aspects of the community school, liaisons foster a collective mission to help all constituents successfully negotiate with the wide range of professionals who comprise a community school model.

FULL-SERVICE COMMUNITY SCHOOLS

Full-service community schools are public schools serving as hubs of programs and services for various community-based organizations located within the school building and are often found in high-poverty neighborhoods. Their programs and services are offered before, during, and after regular school hours to ensure that children are physically, intellectually, emotionally, and socially ready to learn when they enter the school building (Children's Aid Society, 2011; Dryfoos, Quinn, & Barkin, 2005). The full-service community school is unique in that it hosts all community agencies on-site in the school. These community agencies provide easy access to programs for children and their families in such areas as health and social services and youth development—all combined at a site that focuses on best educational practices. The community school mission supports children's overall developmental and academic needs while simultaneously strengthening families and neighborhoods (Blank, Melaville, & Shah, 2003; Santiago, Ferrara, & Blank, 2008).

Fundamental to the community schools' mission is educating the whole child. Given that community schools are located in high-poverty areas, which often suffer from limited resources and a multitude of socioeconomic needs, the pooling of resources from community partners forms the perfect collaboration in which to support children and their families (Gómez, Ferrara, Santiago, Fanelli, & Taylor, 2012). With a focus on community partnerships as the building blocks that assist student learning, community schools have the power to transform educational outcomes for the most needy of students and families.

COMMUNITY SCHOOL CONTEXT

The authors of this qualitative project were two full-time tenured college faculty members serving as PDS liaisons in two community schools within the same suburban district. They were required to spend a minimum of two days per week at the public elementary schools overseeing all aspects of PDS work, which includes the supervision and placement of student teachers, teaching onsite graduate and undergraduate courses, and providing professional development to the schools' teachers and staff.

The full-service community schools network consisted of five partnerships that support the whole child philosophy: (1) Open Door, a school-based medical health service provider; (2) The Guidance Center, a school-based social and emotional intervention service of social workers and psychologists; (3) OASIS, an afterschool enrichment program; (4) Board of Cooperative Educational Services (BOCES), a provider of adult education programs; and (5) our PDS school–university partnership.

As the complex setting of a community school was negotiated, what Zeichner (2010) called *boundary spanning,* the shared responsibilities that allow teachers to move fluidly and comfortably across roles, emerged. *Boundary spanning* activities often place a teacher in the role of mentor, collaborator, advocate, expert, and learner which require an expanded set of skills not usually associated with the role of the teacher. Likewise, as liaisons in a community school, the role widened to include collaboration with all the educational, social, medical, and mental health personnel *in boundary spanning.* In doing so, the roles have expanded and stretched beyond those of the traditional PDS liaison. This created a network of several partners, not just a single partnership, between the college and the public school, and the goal was to seamlessly embed the National Association for Professional Development Schools (NAPDS) Essential 1, " a comprehensive mission that is broader in its outreach and scope than the mission of any partner and that furthers the education profession and its responsibility to advance equity within schools and, by potential extension, the broader community" (National Association for Professional Development Schools, 2008a, p. 2), within the school's community school and whole child education context. In this expanded role, liaisons are called upon to ensure that the PDS classroom teachers and preservice teachers have a thorough and thoughtful understanding of the mission and purpose of community schools. Experience has shown that teachers must believe that what happens outside of school constitutes important factors that critically impact children's learning. Therefore, liaisons in this context must have heightened awareness of the complex interconnectedness between a child's home life, community, and school between individual groups and among all groups of the school community.

EXPANDING ROLES

With the increased number of partners in the school, the PDS liaison has evolved into the nucleus of all the partnerships, serving as an ally in the classroom. In this role he or she communicates with and relates directly to teachers and the other service partners and their relationships involving the students. For example, the PDS liaison could bridge the gap between the teacher and the afterschool program (OASIS) by consulting with the classroom teachers about their students' tutoring needs and arranging for communication between the afterschool provider and the teachers. While the afterschool program provider worked directly with the child and interacted with parents (and perhaps the school administrators), he or she had minimal contact with the teacher or the preservice teachers of the children who attend the service program.

Since the community partners generally pulled the students out of the classroom individually or in small groups during instructional times, the teachers often encountered conflicts between completing the curriculum within the allotted time

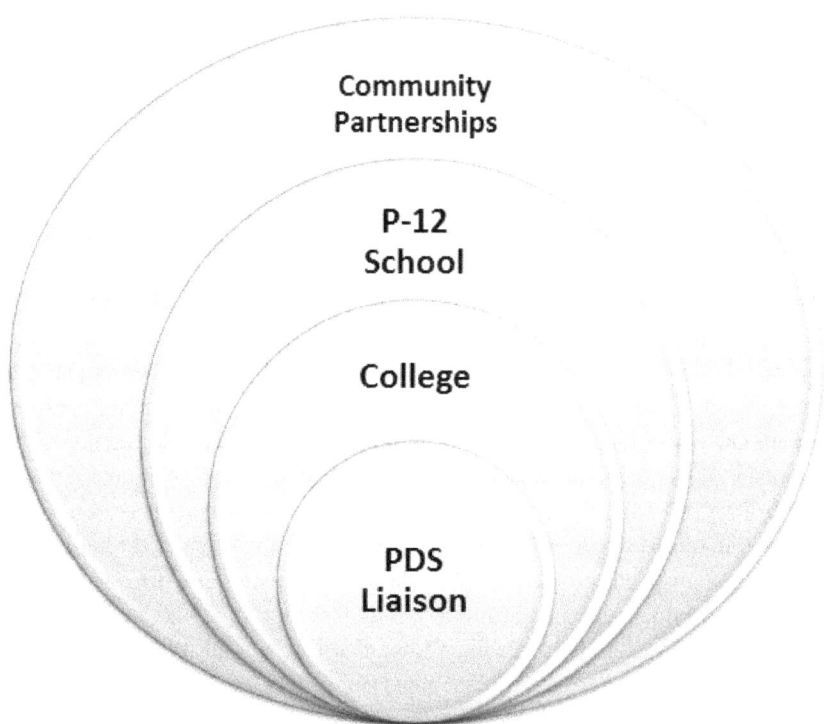

FIGURE 19.1. The PDS liaison becomes the nucleus of collaboration among the many partners in the full-service community school.

available and their commitment to cooperating with the service providers a full-service community school. Therefore, the liaisons frequently acted as advocates for the partner agencies by guiding the classroom teachers and preservice teachers through the realities of working with the other partners in the school. The liaisons also worked with the community partners to help them understand the roles and concerns of the teachers and the students' families, as well as those of all the other service partners and the PDS participants who worked in the school.

These PDS liaisons were accustomed to supporting faculty as they applied educational theory to practice. In going beyond instructional strategies and methodologies, other layers of policy were often encountered and navigated in order to collaborate with additional partners. Developing a sense of collaboration between partnerships in the community school is critical to community school work and exemplifies NAPDS Essential 3: "ongoing and reciprocal professional development for all participants guided by need" (National Association for Professional Development Schools, 2008a, p. 3). PDS liaisons in community school often take on the additional responsibility of ensuring that teachers value the work of school partners, that all partners value each other's work, and that all of us focus what is best for children's education (see Figure 19.1).

EXPLORING THE EXPANDED LIAISON ROLES

Intuitively, it was known that serving as a PDS liaison in a community school was somewhat different and "more than" working with a single university–school partnership. It was anticipated that there would be more demands on time and on more interaction with various personnel in the collaborative process with the other community school partners. Therefore, an overarching question began to be explored: What is the PDS liaison's role in a community school? Using a qualitative research lens, the multitude of roles and the changes that occurred as liaisons in a community school was dissected. Data were collected in the form of field notes, observations, conversations/meetings, personal reflections, and assigned reflective activities from onsite college courses.

Observational Findings

The initial and most visible differences observed were those related to negotiating physical space within the schools and management of time for liaison work at the school. By virtue of the number of partners, the physical space to house several partners and schedule each partner's time and space and avoid conflicts was a recurring challenge. The PDS liaisons were committed to attending additional individual and joint partners' committee meetings and advisory boards. Traditional committee membership in this PDS network included the monthly PDS working committee, bimonthly consortium meeting, and semiannual PDS advisory meetings, as well as the individual PDS's monthly faculty and PDS leadership meetings. In a full-service community PDS, attendance of the liaison is also requested at each partner's monthly meeting, the community school advisory board meetings, and the joint community school advisory board of the two PDS community schools. Usually, these additional meetings overreached the two required liaison days per week at the schools. No longer did the liaisons solely represent and serve the individual partner, the college. They found that they must now incorporate and live the whole child philosophy "through and with" the multiple partners in the PDS.

The liaisons found themselves taking the information gained through meetings with the other partners and "teaching" it to the classroom teachers and preservice teachers, thus serving the role of advocate throughout the PDS for each community partners. This involved working with individual partners and between community partners. As an example, the health service partner, Open Door, reported the need to increase student participation in their asthma program. They reached out to the classroom teachers but found limited support—other than making sure the permission slips were sent home. The PDS liaison discussed the asthma program in student teaching seminar, which moved a student teacher to incorporate the topic into a health lesson. The student teacher sought and received support from the Open Door provider about asthma. Once the lesson was taught, the student teachers themselves became interested in participating in the program. The liaison coordinated with OASIS to extend the topic as a poster project in the afterschool program. School partners began to collaborate with other community partners as well as the classroom teachers, their students, and their families. In this case, the liaison served as the catalyst and conduit between all parties.

REFLECTIVE PARTNERS' FINDINGS

The most revealing data resulted from a reflective assignment given in a graduate class held in one of the full-service community PDS schools. The class was specifically designed to address the needs of the PDS classroom teachers enrolled in a mentoring course that was taught by the PDS liaison of the school. These seasoned teachers were selected by the district to serve as mentors for new hires within the community school. The purpose of the assignment was to reflect upon how teaching in a full-service community school had changed their teaching practice. There were several reflective questions to which they were asked to respond. The most relevant were: (1) What have you learned about educating the whole child? (2) What have you learned about providing services for poor children and families? (3) What were your challenges working in a community school? and (4) how has your practice changed as a result of participating in PDS initiative?

As evidenced through the reflective assignment, the teachers could discuss and value the whole child concept within a community school in theory but might not totally accept their presence in the school. In one example, classroom teacher wrote about the medical service provider, stating, "Open Door has many wonderful aspects to service the child. I do like the fact that the child can receive medication, and be seen (well visits or if they are sick) in the school. I have found that it can impact your teaching." From her statement, it appeared that she values the community school philosophy. Conversely, her following statement suggested that when it is not convenient, she does not honor the partnership: "I will admit that if it is not convenient for the child to go out of the classroom, I will send them later."

Another example of not totally embracing whole child education occurred during a faculty meeting in which all the community school partners provided updates of their programs and events. One classroom teacher remarked, "I don't need to hear an update from every partner every month in faculty meetings. I need to work on my curriculum." The frustration of time constraints and completing curriculum seemed to override the basic commitment of teaching in a community school.

These reflections and comments underscored the important role the PDS liaison can play as a collaborator between the partners of a community school. The reflections demonstrated the need for additional professional development of the teachers in whole child education, particularly in the importance of addressing children's nonacademic needs for successful learning to occur. The liaison also helped the other community service providers to see the point of view of the teachers and coordinated relationships between the community partners and the teacher by developing protocols and schedules for students receiving services outside the classroom.

These liaisons remained steadfast in their belief that teachers must philosophically commit to the tenets of the community school for it to work effectively. Therefore, they sought ways to extend reflection, collaboration, and innovation beyond the university–school partnership to include all stakeholders, which is a vital component of the community school model and the basis of NAPDS Essential 8: "work by college/university faculty and P–12 faculty in formal roles across institutional settings" (National Association for Professional Development Schools, 2008a). This process takes time and nurturing. There was evidence that progress was being made in helping teachers embrace the innovative practices of service partners within a community school. As one teacher reflected,

> The breakfast and lunch programs insure that students are fed and ready to learn. All aspects of the child are taken into account: medical, dental, nutritional, social, economic, and familial issues that may impact learning. Opportunities exist for parents to become educated themselves in parenting, nutrition, citizenship, accessing social programs, and continuing their own education. Working at [our] school has raised my awareness of the cultural countenance of my students.

Another teacher noted,

> The community school setting has helped me recognize that teaching stretches far beyond curriculum and content. With Open Door Clinic [on-site medical provider], students experience a minimal amount of time spent away from the classroom and

instruction. Less interruption in instruction, faster medical attention and recovery, allows for students to increase their learning capabilities.

The community school concept became part of the college's student teaching curriculum so that teacher candidates can "live" the community school mission. In addition to course readings about community schools, student teachers were required to shadow a community school partner for a day. One partner from medical services reflected, "Having student teachers engage in the shadow activity helps them understand partners' roles, but also demonstrates that the PDS values the work of the partners."

The presence and the professional development that liaisons initiated and led at the schools have brought community school partners into the PDS relationship and, in doing so, have fostered a deeper connection to the role of the liaison. Because the liaisons were viewed as advocates, the school partners often relied on them to interface with classroom teachers on their behalf.

RECOMMENDED STRATEGIES

These PDS liaisons naturally fostered the nine essentials of a PDS (National Association for Professional Development School, 2008a). However, when working as a PDS liaison in a community school, they often found it necessary and advantageous to reach out and include other agencies represented in the community school, especially when employing NAPDS Essentials 1, 3, and 8. The mission became very comprehensive as they extended their role to work alongside community service partners housed at the school (NAPDS Essential 1). There are two overarching recommendations for fostering whole-child education philosophy with all partners in a full-service PDS community school: (1) communication and (2) formal and informal professional development.

Communication

Developing a mechanism that allows current and relevant communication between all stakeholders is essential. For a full-service community school to operate smoothly, all partners need to be apprised of critical information. The type of mechanism employed completely depends on the school, its needs, and its resources. Some possible avenues are electronic newsletters, electronic master calendars, a posted master room allotment schedule, bulletin boards, and regular public announcements.

Personal communication (face-to-face and one-on-one) also needs to be fostered. Understanding the rationale for each partner's actions can make the various partner members of a PDS site, especially a full-service one, understand the others' concerns. All partners should be encouraged to communicate with each other. A personal follow-up note, for example, from a service partner who pulled a student out of class to the teacher of that student explaining the outcomes or recognizing the time missed from class can alleviate the resentment and further the whole-child efforts.

Professional Development

Ongoing professional development for both preservice and inservice teachers that embeds the whole child philosophy within in all who work in the PDS and its community partnership endeavors is recommended. Formally requiring preservice teachers to complete assignments related to whole-child education begins to instill the foundation of the philosophy. Such assignments can be scaffolded before the student teaching experience, beginning with the reading of articles about PDSs and full-service community schools and culminating in a video case study of the community to which the school belongs. In addition to the shadowing activity, student teachers were required to complete assignments to promote whole child education. They were present at parent workshops related to their children's education; attended faculty meetings; completed a service project, such as a clothing drive; and left a legacy project (gave something back to the school) before they completed their student teaching.

Hosting a student teacher in a full-service community school indirectly impacts the inservice teachers who are cooperating teachers—as it does their colleagues. Often, inservice teachers receive direct and formal professional development from the university partner. As always, the needs are partnership-specific. Some successful professional development options for this PDS were action research projects, inservice and credit-bearing courses, modeling whole-child philosophy by co-teaching with inservice teachers, and facilitating lunch-and-learn sessions.

A significant part of teachers' and liaisons' daily work in a community school is the ongoing interaction between themselves and the agency partners who service the students and their families. In essence, liaisons were constantly advocating the development of a community of practice (Wenger, 1998). The interagency collaborations of a full-service PDS community school require a unique set of skills best learned through participation in communities of practice. When one interacts with others, an understanding of differing perspectives and practices is gained. Through *boundary spanning* in a community school, PDS liaisons can guide the community partners to build a community of practice. Through a community of practice, the partners can shape how they see themselves and how they view their own practices while striving towards the goal of partnerships of educating the whole child.

REFERENCES

Blank, M., Melaville, A., & Shah, P. (2003). Making the difference: Research and practice in community schools. *Coalition for Community Schools.* Retrieved from *www.communityschools.org/CSSFullReport.pdf*

Children's Aid Society. (2011). *Building community schools: A guide for action.* New York, NY: Author.

Dryfoos, J., Quinn, J., & Barkin, C. (2005). *Community schools in action: Lessons from a decade of practice.* New York, NY: Oxford University Press.

Gómez, D. W., Ferrara, J., Santiago, E., Fanelli, F., & Taylor, R. (2012). Full-service community schools: A district's commitment to educating the whole child. In A. Honigsfeld & A. Cohan (Eds.), *Breaking the mold of education for culturally and linguistically diverse students: Innovative and successful practices for the 21st century* (pp. 65–73). Lanham, MD: Rowman and Littlefield Education.

National Association of Professional Development Schools. (2008a). *NAPDS releases policy statement on professional development schools*. Retrieved from *http://www.napds.org/nine_essen.html*

National Association of Professional Development Schools. (2008b). *What it means to be a professional development school.* Columbia, SC: Author. Retrieved from *http://www.napds.org/9%20Essentials/statement.pdf*

Santiago, E., Ferrara, J., & Blank, M. (2008). A full-service school fulfills its promise. *Educational Leadership, 65*(7), 44–47.

Wenger, E. (1998). *Communities of practice: Learning, meaning, and identity*. Cambridge, UK: Cambridge University Press.

Zeichner, K. (2010). Rethinking the connections between campus courses and field experiences in college-and university-based teacher education. *The Journal of Teacher Education, 61*(1-2), 79–99.

ABOUT THE CONTRIBUTORS

ABOUT THE EDITORS

Dr. JoAnne Ferrara serves as the associate dean for undergraduate advising, PDS coordinator, and a PDS liaison at Manhattanville College in Purchase, NY. She is the author of *Professional Development Schools: Creative Solutions for Educators* and the co-author of *Changing Suburbs, Changing Students: Helping School Leaders Face the Challenges* and *Whole Child, Whole School: Applying Theory to Practice in a Community School.* She is a former urban public school teacher and administrator. She created the college's first professional development school in 2002. Dr. Ferrara serves as section-editor of *PDS Partners.* Her pioneering work with a professional development school nested in a community school transformed her vision for preservice teacher education. Her research interests include whole-child education, community schools, and educator preparation.

Dr. Janice Nath serves as professor at the University of Houston–Downtown in the department of urban education. She has also served as the associate dean of the College of Public Service. *Becoming a Teacher in Texas* was her first co-edited book on professional development teacher certification for elementary and secondary education, followed by *Becoming an EC-4 Teacher in Texas, Becoming a*

Creating Visions for University-School Partnerships, pages 327–333.
Copyright © 2014 by Information Age Publishing
All rights of reproduction in any form reserved.

Middle School or High School Teacher in Texas, and *Becoming an EC-6 Teacher in Texas.* She has also co-edited three books for the TExES Generalist in teaching content areas. Dr. Nath has worked in professional development schools (PDSs) for almost 20 years and has previously co-edited four volumes in research on PDSs. In addition, she edited the *Texas Forum*, a journal on educational research and topics in Texas. Her writing and research was recognized with her university's Scholarship/Creativity Award in 2003–2004. She received the Howsam Award from the Texas Association of Colleges for teacher education in recognition of significant contributions to the educator preparation process in Texas. Dr. Nath has presented to local, state, national, and international organizations numerous times and is a member of the board for an international organization on case study research.

Dr. Irma N. Guadramma recently retired after a 44-year career of teaching and research. She started out as a bilingual teacher and has worked as a professor at various universities, the most recent ones being the University of Houston and the University of Texas Pan American in Edinburg in South Texas. She served as co-editor with Janice Nath and John Ramsey for the PDS Book Series, volumes 1–4. Other research interests include second language learning in border areas in educational and social contexts. She received a bachelor's degree from Texas Christian University in Fort Worth, master's degree from the University of Texas in San Antonio, and a PhD from the University of Texas at Austin. Her area of study was education with an emphasis in reading and language and culture.

ABOUT THE AUTHORS

Dr. Gwendolyn Benson is associate dean of the College of Education at Georgia State University, where she is responsible for establishing and maintaining school partnership initiatives.

Dr. Michael Blocher is a faculty member at Northern Arizona University. Michael strives to bring his elementary classroom teaching experience into to his courses, where his students learn to support learning with technology.

Felix Blumhardt is the regional manager of the Carolinas at the Evaluation Group, an independent evaluation firm with offices in Columbia, South Carolina and Atlanta, Georgia.

Maika Bonafe has been a parent liaison in Passaic, New Jersey for over 10 years. Her passion is facilitating parents' involvement in their children's school lives.

Cindy Bush is an instructional facilitator with experience teaching multiple middle school subjects. She has a BS and MEd from Furman University with an education leadership add-on from Western Carolina University.

Joann Carlino teaches 3rd grade at the Belmont Elementary PDS. She has been a lead teacher, seminar leader, and action researcher in the Dowling College–North Babylon School District PDS Partnership for over 15 years.

Dr. Linda A. Catelli is a professor at Dowling College and has served as the director of the Dowling College–Belmont Elementary PDS /North Babylon School District Partnership since 1998. She was nationally recognized as a pioneer in s/u collaboration by the AAHE and CUNY.

Dr. Carrie Chapman is assistant professor in the department of educational studies, K–12 and secondary programs, at Minnesota State University, Mankato.

Dr. Nancy Chicola is chair and associate professor in the department of elementary education & reading at SUNY Buffalo State.

Dr. Myrna D. Cohen is an associate professor of the department of urban education and serves as the associate dean of the College of Public Service at the University of Houston–Downtown.

Dr. Katherine Egan Cunningham is an assistant professor of literacy at Manhattanville College. Her teaching and research focuses on literacy methods, children's literature, and professional development.

Dr. William Curlette is chairperson and professor in the department of educational policy studies at Georgia State University where he teaches courses on research methodology.

Dr. Anne Dahlman is associate professor and department chair in the department of educational studies, K–12 and secondary programs, at Minnesota State University, Mankato.

Leslie Day is lecturer in the department of elementary education & reading at SUNY Buffalo State and co-director of the Professional Development Schools Consortium.

Dr. Stacy DeLaCruz is an assistant professor of elementary literacy at Kennesaw State University. Her research interests include balanced literacy, digital literacy, and K–5 PDS partnerships.

Dr. Portia M. Downey is the manager of the COE's School–University Partnership Office and is involved in various professional development school partnerships throughout the northern Illinois region.

Dr. Janna Dresden is a clinical associate professor in the early childhood program at the University of Georgia. She coordinates PDS partnerships and studies teacher education and classroom assessment.

Dr. Sarah Anne Eckert served as Notre Dame of Maryland University PDS co-coordinator from 2011 through 2013. Her research interests center around teacher preparation for urban environments and education policy.

Dr. Joanne Ferrara is the associate dean for undergraduate advising at Manhattanville College. In addition to her advising role, she serves as the PDS coordinator and PDS liaison. Her researcher interests include community schools, whole child education, and new teacher induction.

Dr. Diane W. Gómez is Assistant Professor of Second Language Education and Chair of Educational Leadership and Special Subjects at Manhattanville College, Purchase, NY. Her research interests include multicultural education in field-based settings, literacy in the context of dual language and second language programs, and professional development schools.

Dr. Fran Greb is an associate professor at Montclair State University in the College of Education and Human Services. Previously, she was a special educator and learning consultant.

Brett Grunau received her BA in English from New York University. She is currently a graduate student at Montclair State University where she is pursuing her master's in teaching.

Dr. Paula Guerra is an assistant professor of elementary mathematics at Kennesaw State University. Her research focuses on mathematics education for social justice, and English language learners' mathematical schooling.

Dr. Robert Hendrick is a research associate at Georgia State University and is assigned to the evaluation team for the Network for Enhancing Teacher Quality (NET-Q), a large federal grant.

Dr. Prixita del Prado Hill is an associate professor in the department of elementary education & reading at SUNY Buffalo State and co-director of the Professional Development Schools Consortium.

Allen Hoffman is school superintendent in the Comfrey School District in Minnesota and assistant professor in the department of educational studies, K–12 and secondary programs, at Minnesota State University, Mankato.

Dr. Patricia Hoffman is a professor in the department of educational studies, K–12 and secondary programs and the director of Center for Excellence in Teaching and Learning at Minnesota State University, Mankato.

Dr. Lisa Johnson is an associate professor and director of a nine-district school–university network in the Richard W. Riley College of Education at Winthrop University.

Pamely Kennedy is a classroom teacher in Faribault Public Schools in Minnesota and a teacher on special assignment (TOSA) at Minnesota State University, Mankato.

Naomi Kirkman is the principal of Bradford School in Montclair, NJ. She received her BA from New York University and a master's degree in elementary education from Hunter College, CUNY.

Dr. Julie Kittleson is an associate professor of science education at the University of Georgia. Her work focuses on teaching and learning science in the elementary grades.

Dr. Diane E. Lang is director of instructional support at the Orange–Ulster Board of Cooperative Educational Services. She researches and provides support to teachers and administrators in the areas of curriculum, assessment, inquiry, and classroom community

Dr. Debra Leach is an assistant professor of special education at Winthrop University who specializes in effective practices for supporting students with disabilities in inclusive classrooms.

Mary Lebron has taught the primary grades in Passaic, New Jersey for over 20 years. She continually strives to improve her practice and share her knowledge with future teachers.

Dr. Laura A. Mitchell is a professor at the University of Houston–Downtown. She completed a doctorate at Fielding Graduate University and has worked in elementary schools and universities for over 30 years.

Dr. Amanda Morales is an assistant professor and diversity coordinator in the College of Education, Kansas State University. Morales has been actively involved in PDS initiatives to promote social justice for over ten years.

Dr. Janice Nath is a Professor in the Department of Urban Education at the University of Houston-Downtown. She has worked with PDS sites and PDS publications for many years.

Dr. Caroline Clark O'Brien, in 2008, she began study at University of North Texas for a PhD in Curriculum and Instruction with a minor in Applied Neurocognition from the University of Texas at Dallas.

Dr. Susan Ogletree is director of the Educational Research Bureau in the College of Education at Georgia State University. Professional development schools' impact on academic achievement is her primary research interest.

Dr. Scott Page is professor in the department of educational studies, k–12 and secondary programs, at Minnesota State University, Mankato and directs the TeachLiveTM lab in the department.

Gina Marie Petraglia teaches 3rd grade at the Belmont Elementary PDS. She has been a course instructor and supervising teacher in the Dowling College–North Babylon School District PDS Partnership for over seven years.

Maggie Phillips is a 3rd grade teacher at Hollydale Elementary. She is currently pursuing a master's degree in educational technology at Kennesaw State University.

Greg Prater teaches in the College of Education, Northern Arizona University. Greg has been involved in partnerships since 1992. He managed and started partnerships on the Navajo Nation and at other sites in Arizona.

Paul Preimesberger is assistant director of the Center for School–University Partnerships and coordinates the AVID initiatives at Minnesota State University, Mankato and the PDS partner schools.

Dr. Emilie Rodger is a faculty member at the College of Education, Northern Arizona University. Her major areas of research are school–university partnerships and multiage education.

April Rosendale is a classroom teacher in Le-Sueur–Henderson Public Schools in Minnesota and a teacher on special assignment (TOSA) at Minnesota State University, Mankato.

Dr. Julie Rosenthal has been a professor of education at William Paterson University since 2005. Her research focus is on the intersection between schools, community, and teacher preparation.

Dr. Stephanie L. Savick serves as assistant professor of education and PDS cocoordinator at Notre Dame of Maryland University. Her research interests include educational leadership, teacher preparation, and urban education.

Dr. Hibajene Shandomo is an associate professor in the department of elementary education & reading at SUNY Buffalo State.

Dr. M. Gail Shroyer is a professor and chair in the department of curriculum and instruction, College of Education, Kansas State University. Shroyer initiated the PDS Partnership and served as a PDS Coordinator for over 20 years.

Dr. Christina Siry is an associate professor in educational sciences at the University of Luxembourg. Her research focuses on the teaching and learning of science at the elementary school level, and she is particularly interested in the interwoven relationship between teaching, learning, and learning to teach.

Dr. Jeanne Tunks is an associate professor at the University of North Texas where she teaches courses in mathematics and social studies methods, within the context of a professional development school network.

Dr. David A. Walker is a professor of educational research and assessment at Northern Illinois University and is actively involved in the College of Education's (COE) school–university partnership office and professional development school initiatives and projects.

Dr. Julianne Wenner earned her PhD from the University of Georgia and is currently a postdoctoral fellow investigating elementary science achievement and school organization/leadership at the University of Connecticut.

Julie Williams is a graduate assistant at the University of North Texas, seeking a PhD in curriculum and instruction with a minor in family studies. She teaches mathematics methods courses.

Dr. Sally Yahnke is an associate professor and coordinator of the PDS partnership for over 15 years in the College of Education, Kansas State University. Dr. Yahnke initiated the middle school/high school PDS model.

Dr. Ginger Zierdt is an associate professor and department chair in the department of educational studies, elementary and early childhood and the director of the Center for School-University Partnerships at Minnesota State University, Mankato.